Myth and
Literature in
the American
Renaissance

Myth and Literature in the American Renaissance

Robert D. Richardson, Jr.

Indiana University Press
Bloomington and London

This book was brought to publication with the assistance of a grant from the Andrew W. Mellon Foundation.

Manufactured in the United States of America

Library of Congress Cataloging in Publication Data
Richardson, Robert D., 1934–
Myth and literature in the American renaissance.
Bibliography:
Includes index.
1. American literature—19th century—History
and criticism.   2. Myth in literature.   I. Title.
PS217.M93R5   820'.9'37   77-22638
ISBN 0-253-33965-0   1 2 3 4 5 82 81 80 79 78

For my mother
Lucy Marsh Richardson

CONTENTS

Acknowledgments

I am deeply grateful to the Henry E. Huntington Library for a Visiting Fellowship during 1973–74, and to James Thorpe, Claude Simpson, and Paul Zall in particular. Rare book and special collection librarians at the Huntington Library, the Boston Public Library, the Boston Athenaeum, the Houghton Library, the New York Public Library, the Yale University libraries, the University of Chicago libraries, the American Antiquarian Society Library, the Massachusetts Historical Society Library, and the Morgan Library have been unfailingly helpful. Lester Beaurline, Richard Herrnstadt, Herbert Schneider, Allen Mandelbaum, Leo Lemay, Vincent Freimarck, and W. J. Bate have offered help, advice, and encouragement. Deans Edward Lindell and Robert Amme of the University of Denver have been generous with faculty research funds. William Gravely has helped me in matters of American religious history. Gene Patterson-Black has spent many hours on bibliographic matters. Without the knowledgeable skill and helpfulness of Denver's Inter-Library Loan librarians, including Catherine Zuck, Barbara Thiele, and Anna Boklund, this book would have taken much longer. Betty Adamson has faithfully typed (and cleaned up) version after version of the manuscript.

There are two people I will never be able to thank adequately. One is Burton Feldman, with whom I have walked dogs and talked myth for thirteen years without wearing out the subject, the friendship, or the dogs. The other is my wife, Elizabeth, who has never for a single moment allowed me to doubt the value of the work involved in trying to make sense of my subject.

University of Denver   Robert D. Richardson, Jr.

Myth and
Literature in
the American
Renaissance

Introduction

The main purpose of this book is to show how nineteenth-century American writers from Emerson to Melville dealt with the problem of myth. The emphasis throughout is on how these writers themselves understood myth consciously and used it in their writing. My method has therefore been first to analyze each writer's acquaintance with myth, then to appraise the mythic element in his work, as nearly as possible from his own point of view and that of his contemporaries. I have not followed—nor have I intended to refute—those historians and critics beginning with D. H. Lawrence who have sought to delineate and explain "the myth of America," as Lawrence himself called it in his essay on "Fenimore Cooper's Leatherstocking Novels." The present book is entirely different in both method and scope from, say, Richard Slotkin's recent *Regeneration through Violence: The Mythology of the American Frontier 1600–1860*. Slotkin's deservedly well-received study examines a wealth of materials from John Filson's *The Adventures of Colonel Daniel Boon* to Melville's *Moby-Dick* by means of a concept of myth as the "intelligible mask" of the American "national character." Slotkin argues that "true myths are generated on a sub-literary level by the historical experience of a people and thus constitute part of that inner reality which the work of the artist draws on, illuminates, and explains." The focus and scope of Slotkin's book are made clear in this summary of his subject:

In American mythogenesis the founding fathers were not those eighteenth-century gentlemen who composed a nation at Philadelphia. Rather they were those who (to paraphrase Faulkner's *Absalom, Absalom!*) tore violently a nation from the implacable and opulent wilderness—the

3

rogues, adventurers, and land-boomers; the Indian fighters, traders, missionaries, explorers, and hunters who killed and were killed until they had mastered the wilderness; the settlers who came after, suffering hardship and Indian warfare for the sake of a sacred mission or a simple desire for land; and the Indians themselves, both as they were and as they appeared to the settlers, for whom they were the special demonic personification of the American wilderness. Their concerns, their hopes, their terrors, their violence, and their justification of themselves, as expressed in literature, are the foundation stones of the mythology that informs our history. (p. 4)

Slotkin's concept of myth is representative of the current myth and symbol approach in American Studies and is, as he informs us, based on Joseph Campbell's *The Masks of God* and *The Hero with a Thousand Faces,* Richard Chase's *Quest for Myth,* Frazer's *Golden Bough,* Jung's *Psyche and Symbol,* Levi-Strauss's *The Savage Mind* and *Totemism,* Lévy-Bruhl's *How Natives Think,* the various essays in Thomas Sebeok's *Myth: A Symposium,* and J. L. Henderson's *Thresholds of Initiation.* By interpreting early American history, culture, and literature through the lenses of twentieth-century theories of myth, Slotkin has advanced the bold and challenging assertion that "the myth of regeneration through violence became the structuring metaphor of the American experience." Previous attempts to locate central structuring metaphors for the American experience include Lawrence's myth of a white America progressing from Age toward Youth, Henry Nash Smith's *Virgin Land: The American West as Symbol and Myth,*[1] R. W. B. Lewis's argument in *The American Adam* that the figure of Adam before the Fall is the crucial archetype and image for the American hero, Leo Marx's insistence on the centrality of the title image of his *The Machine in the Garden,* and Leslie Fiedler's quaternion of myths in his and Arthur Zeiger's *O Brave New World:* "The Myth of the Runaway Male," "The Myth of Pure Love in the Woods," "The Myth of the Good Companions in the Wilderness," and "The Myth of the Indian Captivity." Most recently, Sacvan Bercovitch's *Puritan Origins of the American Self* argues that the "Myth of America is the creation of the New England Way," the link being a continuing interest from Puritan times down to Emerson in "the celebration of the representative self as America, and of the American self as the embodiment of a prophetic universal design" (p. 136).

The present study has an entirely different aim. It deliberately refrains from the use of twentieth-century myth theory, seeking rather to explore the concepts of myth that were available to mid-nineteenth-century writers, and limiting itself to discussion of the conscious uses of myth in the literature of the American Renaissance. Much modern myth criticism has addressed itself mainly to explicating themes and images unintended by the author, and while no one can ignore the often impressive results of such an approach, it can also be argued that we have paid too little attention to the self-declared purposes of some of our major writers. On this point I agree fully with Michael Colacurcio's comment on the general preference for the "symptomatic" as opposed to the "intentional" meaning of a work: "I personally see no way to avoid the conclusion (of E. D. Hirsch) that before we can know what a work 'reveals,' even in relation to the psyche of an individual writer, we have got to develop some adequately historical sense of what it could possibly have been intended to 'mean,' as a complex of intention designed rationally to communicate between an individual writer in history and an audience, also in history."[2] The following pages, then, are intended to complement and balance existing studies of the subject by offering an essentially historical view of nineteenth-century American conceptions of myth and its use in literature.

F. O. Matthiessen once noted that "where the age of Emerson is most like our own is in its discovery of the value of myth." Much of the masterwork, the literary achievement of the American Renaissance, grows out of an overt interest in myth. Even at first glance, the sheer array of the period's myth-minded undertakings, both minor and major, is simply astonishing. Bronson Alcott tried repeatedly to write a new myth of Psyche; a journal account of the birth and growth of his daughter Anna was mythologized into a story about the growth of the Soul. Margaret Fuller turned to myth for important aspects of her reassessment of the proper role of women in society. Theodore Parker was an important early advocate for the mythical view of the Bible championed in Germany by the higher criticism, culminating in the work of D. F. Strauss. Emerson's *Representative Men* is a bold new application of the Euhemerist idea that the gods are human beings who, because remarkable in their own time, were deified by their posterity. *Walden* is, among other things, an attempt to create American nature myth. Hawthorne set out to de-classicize myth in his *Wonder Book,* while some of his short stories and novels depend on a myth-derived concept of metamorphosis. Even his definition of romance owes something to contemporaneous—mainly German—ideas about myth. Whitman's plan for *Leaves of Grass* led him to an explicit rejection of the language of myth. Melville's work, from *Mardi* to *Clarel,* is deeply involved in myth, and *Moby-Dick* is, in one sense, a book about the actual process by which myths come to have a powerful hold even on the modern imagination.

In trying to show these writers' common assumptions about myth, it must be recognized that no two shared exactly the same view. Alcott, for example, uncritically accepted myth as the highest religious truth, while Parker on the other hand was a resolute rationalist for whom myth meant falsehood and was the opposite of history. Most of the important writers avoided such one-sided stands. Emerson tried to create modern mythic heroes and he argued for a modern mythology for modern times, but his work was tempered by a strong rationalist opposition to myth. Whitman was just the opposite. *Leaves of Grass* rejects myth, but the rejection is mitigated by Whitman's desire to create a modern equivalent for myth. Hawthorne opposed the classical element in myth, but valued myth itself enough to try repeatedly to modernize it. Thoreau used myth in *A Week on the Concord and Merrimack Rivers* for a radical critique of Christianity, and in *Walden* for a lyrical and religious view of nature. Melville was equally well aware of the affirmative and the skeptical views of myth. Indeed, a major conclusion of this study is that an important part of the success of the major literary endeavors of the mid nineteenth century is due to the fact that all the major writers of this time had a dual outlook on myth, and whether they eventually came out for myth or against it (to put the matter in a drastically oversimplified form), they were equally familiar with the case for myth as a form for imaginative philosophical or religious truth and the case against myth as fraud, illusion, and falsehood.

The first chapter of this book describes the development of these two traditions in American literary approaches to myth. The second chapter, on Alcott and Parker, shows the achievement and, more importantly, the limitations of taking one view or the other exclusively. Subsequent chapters show how each of the major writers of the time succeeded in using myth precisely because he was aware of both traditions and because he effected a creative solution between the conflicting claims of skepticism and assent. Whitman's rejection of myth, for example, has all the more force because he was aware—and makes the reader aware—of the claims in favor of myth. And Melville's great strength, to take another example, is that his sharp awareness of both sides of the question led him to look beneath the surface arguments for and against myth to concentrate on the *processes* by which myth arises and by which it comes to be believed.

The existence of two distinct and opposed traditions of myth criticism had the result of making it difficult for a serious writer in America after 1830 to take up a simpleminded or a single-sided attitude toward myth. Yet it is a subject which is still marked by strongly urged one-sided views—often of great brilliance and persuasiveness. Peter Gay, for example, makes the following distinction between critical and mythical thinking in his *A Loss of Mastery: Puritan Historians in Colonial America*.

> Critical thinking is disenchanted thinking; in holding nothing sacred, it moves freely through every subject and asks questions of all; it ranges from the crudest positivism to the most refined intellectual inquiry. Mythical thinking, on the other hand, is incapable of this sort of penetration; at a low level, it is animistic and superstitious; at its highest level, it allegorizes and sublimates but retains at least a shred of the miraculous—of that which must remain untouched by profane hands. . . . I regard critical thinking as essentially superior to mythical thinking, no matter how lovely the myth or elegant the allegory.[3]

There is simply no common ground between that and such a typical utterance of Joseph Campbell's as this: "Mythology, that is to say, resides along the interface of timelessness and time, exactly between the nowhere-nowhen that ever was, and is, and shall be, and is to be recognized in all things, and on the other hand, the passing world of these things in which we all, for a brief time, reside."[4] Gay's articulate opposition to mythical thought leaves little if any room for a reasonable affirmation of myth, while Campbell's enthusiastic affirmation of myth is rarely tempered by any recognition that there exists a strong case against myth. In this regard, we can still learn from the great writers of mid-nineteenth-century America. With remarkable self-consciousness, they explored both approaches. The concept of myth that appears in the best of their writing is thus more complex, more subtle, and more balanced than the myth literature of eras which simply affirm or simply deny the undoubted power of myth.

One

The Two Traditions

There are perhaps as many definitions of myth as of romanticism, but a renewed interest in myth as "authentic tidings of invisible things" is one of the most commonly remarked characteristics of early nineteenth-century literature. It is too simple, however, to say that the Enlightenment rejected myth while the romantics embraced it. That neat shift of emphasis is complicated by the existence of a "preromantic" affirmation of myth and mythical thought that reaches back into the eighteenth century to Vico, Blackwell, Lowth, and Herder, tempering much of the Enlightenment's well-known hostility to myth, while at the other end, the nineteenth-century enthusiasm for myth had constantly to contend with such formidable anti-myth forces as the higher criticism of the Bible as it evolved from Eichhorn to Strauss, the new critical study of history associated with Barthold Neibuhr, and the long-lasting aftereffects of the radical critique of myth and religion evidenced by the continuing popularity of Paine, Volney, and Voltaire. In American literature especially—though not exclusively—both skeptical and affirmative views of myth can be seen, often side by side in the same writer, during the late eighteenth and through at least the middle of the nineteenth century. During this time it was in fact characteristic of American writers to be actively aware of the competing claims of both positions. Between 1835 and 1855 a new American literature was created, a literature of subjective epic, internal discovery, and heroic individualism, all subjects which invited comparison with the same traditional myths they were trying to supersede. No longer content with decorative classicism—with what Emerson called "modern antiques"—the new users of myth were to be literarily successful in direct proportion to their success in working out an approach to myth that gave due recognition to both opposing viewpoints. The characteristic American approach to myth, at least among those usually thought of as major writers in this period, was a creative counterpointing, something more than a dialogue but less than a dialectic, a complex interplay and balancing of ideas about myth derived from two rich, well known and opposed traditions of mythic interpretation. The resulting mythic literature is neither simplistically reductive nor uncritically affirmative. From Emerson's concern with myth as history, his pervasive imagery of metamorphosis, and his modern Euhemerizing to Melville's fictional technique of mythic investiture in *Moby-Dick,* American writers subordinated myth as subject, myth as form, and myth as symbol to their overriding interest in the process of mythical thought and the process of myth formation. From their own vantage point as writers, they were—understandably—not so much interested in myth for its own sake as in the deliberate application of mythic methods and processes to the purposes of modern literature.

The first and in some ways the most important problem myth presented to those American writers who were self-consciously concerned with the meaning of myth arose again and again in the almost embarrassingly blunt question of whether one accepted myth as deeply and importantly true or rejected it as dangerous, delusive, and false. Both attitudes have a long, complex history which one must know, at least in outline, to appreciate the nature, complexity, and, above all, the urgency of the problem of myth for Emerson and his contemporaries.

To begin with, it must be stressed that the word "myth" was not used in English until the nineteenth century. The word does not occur in eighteenth-century dictionaries or encyclopedias. When a single myth was referred to, it was always as a "mythological fiction," a "poetical fiction," a "tradition," a "poetical history," or, most commonly, a "fable." Sometimes this last was further refined to "mythological fiction" in order to prevent confusion with other eighteenth-century uses of "fable" to mean apologue or modern fable (such as Aesop's or La Fontaine's) and plot or story line. Almost everything relating to what we now think of as myth came, for the eighteenth century, under the heading of the word "mythology." This word did not then mean primarily a collection of myths or fables; it meant, first of all, an explanation or interpretation of myths. Johnson's *Dictionary* (1755) defines mythology as a "system of fables; explication of the fabulous history of the gods of the heathen world." This view is echoed as late as 1806 when Noah Webster defined mythology (there being no entry for "myth" in his dictionary either) as "a system or explanation of fables." The first edition of the *Encyclopaedia Britannica* (1771) calls mythology a "science" concerned with "the history of the gods" and "the theology of the pagans," and maintains that "mythology, when properly treated, begins with making learned researches into the real origin of fables, of paganism, and of that idolatry which was its consequence." What these examples suggest—and they could readily be multiplied—is that the most common eighteenth-century meaning of mythology is "pagan theology," and that religious concerns constitute the usual context in which mythology was discussed.

From a Christian point of view, then, mythology is the opposite of true or Christian theology. It is false theology or pagan theology. Many Christians refused even to allow mythology the dignity conferred by the very word "theology," preferring to call it pagan or heathen idolatry. A book such as Joseph Spence's *Polymetis,* which undertakes to illuminate classical fables by means of Roman poetry, and vice versa, is the exception, not the rule. It is far more common to find myth simply dismissed, as it was, for example, by Samuel Shuckford, whose *Connections* (a reconciliation of nonbiblical "traditions" to "sacred," that is biblical, history) begins "Whatever may have been the opinions of philosophers, or the fables of poets, about the origin of mankind, we are sufficiently informed from history, that we are descended from two persons, Adam and Eve." The most popular of all eighteenth-century mythological handbooks, Andrew Tooke's *Pantheon of the Heathen Gods,* defines its subject at the outset by saying "The Fabulous Pantheon, is, as its name imports, the temple of all the gods, which the superstitious folly of men have feigned through a gross ignorance of the true and only God."

It should not be surprising then to find Christian writers in America denying all independent authority to classical mythology. Cotton Mather, for example, subscribes to a standard seventeenth-century view that used etymological arguments to show that classical myths were degenerate or garbled versions of Scripture. Thus, for Mather, Janus is just another name for Noah, and Cadmus was originally one of the Gibeonites overcome by Joshua.[1] Another familiar Christian explanation, that pagan gods belong in the category of demons, with Lucifer, may be seen, among other places, in Elizabeth Rowe's *The History of Joseph* (Philadelphia, 1767), in which a "congress of infernal powers" includes Nefroth, Belus, Osiris, Baal, Mithra, and Astarte. While the explanation might vary, the result was always the same; Christian scholars and writers denied the autonomy and validity of myth, which was by their definition pagan theology and synonymous therefore with falsehood and idolatry. This is the most frequently voiced conception of mythology during the late eighteenth century in America. It is the one articulated at length by such standard-bearers of orthodoxy as Timothy Dwight, who condemned all polytheism as "imperfect and immoral," consisting of gods "limited in their powers and operations, odious by their vices, and contemptible by their follies."[2] This is the basic attitude with which any new view of myth had to contend.

It was not only orthodox Christians who were skeptical about the validity of myth. Their deistic opponents from the late seventeenth century on were themselves skeptical about myth, but for a quite different reason.[3] The deists perceived that orthodox Christians made a great point of denouncing myth. They also perceived—as the Christians did not or would not admit—that many things in the Bible, especially the miracles, bore a very close resemblance to certain elements of classical or pagan myth. By showing the similarity between a Greek myth and a biblical story, the deists could turn the orthodox attack on myth back on orthodoxy itself. One approach, common in countries such as France where laws against blasphemy were enforced, was to insist upon the absurdity of the miraculous element in pagan myth, trusting the alert reader to draw a parallel conclusion about the miraculous element in Scripture. Fontenelle's elegant and influential essay "Of the Origin of Fables" (1724) could deride the credulity of pagans being led "to believe that a god had had an affair with a woman," without openly sneering at the biblical account of the events leading to the birth of Christ.[4] Pierre Bayle, whose *Dictionary* (1697) was, according to David Lundberg and Henry May, as common in American colonial libraries as John Locke's *Two Treatises on Government,* conducted no direct attack on Scripture, but by treating both pagan myth and Scripture with an exactly similar skepticism he paved the way for later systematic comparison of pagan and Christian stories, while his eye for detail and his insistence on discussing any act—even any hint—of outrageous conduct did nothing to ennoble either pagan myth or Scripture.[5] Bayle's account of Jupiter opens by pointing out that "there is no crime, but what he was defiled with; for besides that he dethroned his own father, that he castrated him, and bound him in chains in the deepest hell, he committed incest with his sisters, daughters, and aunts, and even attempted to ravish his mother." His discussion of David, on the other hand, gets off almost at once on a long footnote about whether or not David really was illegitimate, about how his mother tricked his father, à la Helena in *All's Well That Ends Well,* and so on until the dignity of King David is dissolved in a stream of backfence gossip.

Because of the very considerable influence of the entertaining *Dictionary,* Bayle's resolutely literal treatment of both mythical and Scriptural figures as though they were all simply historical figures—a crude but effective comparative approach to myth—was to remain important for a hundred and fifty years. Theodore Parker, Emerson, and Melville were all influenced to varying degrees by Bayle's own work as well as by the eighteenth-century tradition of skeptical deistic attitudes toward myth that stemmed in part from Bayle, in part from Spinoza and Richard Simon. All three of these men agreed on the principle that the Bible should be approached exactly as any other book written by men, exactly as one approached Homer, for example. From this seventeenth-century beginning eventually grew the nineteenth-century higher criticism of the Bible and the "mythical viewpoint"

of D. F. Strauss. The essentially historical criticism of Spinoza,
Bayle, and Simon also descended to English deists such as Collins
and Toland and to the French *philosophes*. By the middle of the
eighteenth century, there was in England and France a wide variety
of skeptical, rationalist, non-Christian or anti-Christian approaches
to myth which were to affect American thought and writing principally in the last two decades of the eighteenth century. Voltaire's
Philosophical Dictionary (1764; trans. 1765; first American edition
1790) has an article on "Fables" describing the "old fable of Venus"
as an allegory of nature but adding that "the majority of other fables
are either corruptions of ancient history or caprices of the imagination." Far from having any respect for the mythmaking imagination, Voltaire mocks the ignorance and gullibility of those early
people who naively mistook a symbol for a thing and thus created
myth. "The Astronomers of all ages," Voltaire wrote in a sketch
called "Ancient Faith and Fable," "have been wont to distinguish
the two points of intersection, upon which every eclipse happens,
and which are called the lunar nodes, by marking them with a
dragon's head and tail. Now the vulgar, who are equally ignorant in
every part of the world, took the symbol or sign for the thing itself.
Thus, when the astronomers said the sun is in the dragon's head, the
common people said the dragon is going to swallow up the sun."[6]
Voltaire thinks some myths are allegorical, some corrupt history,
and some derived from misunderstood astronomical symbolism.
These are the three most influential eighteenth-century rationalist
theories—all three appear prominently, for example, in Diderot's
Encyclopédie—and each of these three theories was championed by a
man whose work was to have a major impact on American attitudes
toward myth. The idea that myth reflects the popular understanding
of symbols originally associated with observation of the heavens
(Sabeism)—that the zodiac, for example, began as an agricultural
calendar and degenerated into animal worship—was worked out by
the Abbé Pluche and came to its culmination in the work of Charles
Dupuis, whose monumental *Origine de tous les cultes* (1795) reduced
all religions, including Christianity, to sun worship.[7] Dupuis's
work lies behind and informs the work of Paine and Volney: ex-

President John Adams made a surprisingly thorough study of Dupuis in the last ten years of his life, while strong traces of Dupuis can be found all the way to Melville and beyond.[8]

The idea that myths were corrupt history—and the corollary idea that mythic figures, including gods, are but magnified human beings—was most ably defended by the Abbé Banier.[9] His Euhemerist view, which treats myth as a special kind of history, was ultimately to prove very important for American literature, and a good deal of the present study will show how Euhemerist ideas, which began as a skeptical tool with which to undermine the authenticity of myth, gradually came to supply enthusiasts of myth with their most effective rationale for affirming myth as primitive truth.

The view that mythology represents an early effort to allegorize or symbolize nature itself—the third of Voltaire's three explanations—was given its most eloquent and most famous exposition in Holbach's *System of Nature* (1770), which drew a crucial distinction in a chapter called "Mythology and Theology." Holbach held that mythology resulted from early man's perfectly intelligent impulse to worship nature. To encourage this, Holbach thought, wise civilizing leaders personified nature through poetry to make figures, images, and eventually stories that would appeal to the popular imagination. Theology begins, according to Holbach, when men go beyond mythology—which personifies only natural forces—to posit some force beyond or behind nature. Thus Holbach, and the materialists and atheists who followed his lead, both tolerated mythology as vastly superior to theology (because mythology dealt with nature while theology dealt with what was beyond nature, i.e., nothing) and condescended to it as something necessary only for the common sort of person who couldn't worship the abstract principles of nature and needed something tangible.[10]

The Euhemerism of Banier, the Sabeism of Pluche, and the nature allegorism of Holbach all fed into the radical mythologizing of the period of the French Revolution, when the skeptical attack on myth was carried to its most outspoken extreme by writers hostile to all institutional religions, including, especially, Christianity. The effect of this skeptical and radical mythologizing on American thought was very considerable, and may best be suggested by briefly considering the works of two men, Thomas Paine and Constantine Volney.

Paine's *Age of Reason: Being an Investigation of True and of Fabulous Theology* (part I, 1794; part II, 1796) was a popular and influential instance of the extreme deist attack on the Christian church and the Bible. Paine's concept of myth is a negative one, which he uses with crude effectiveness as a destructive weapon. Instead of following Holbach's distinction between theology and mythology, Paine's subtitle shows that he preferred to see a distinction between "true" and "fabulous" theology. The true theology was, for Paine, science. In chapter eleven of the first part of *The Age of Reason,* he claimed: "that which is now called natural philosophy, embracing the whole circle of science of which astronomy occupies the chief place, is the study of the works of God, and of the power and wisdom of God and his works, and is the true theology." Fabulous or false theology is, for Paine, mythology, and *The Age of Reason* is an important early example of the open application of the word "mythology" to the sacred writings and traditions of Christianity. In Paine's polemic, mythology now overtly embraces both pagan and Christian stories. "The Christian system," wrote Paine, "was only another species of mythology." It is also perfectly plain that in applying the word freely to pagan and Christian accounts alike he was praising neither. His utter scorn for what he calls mythology is perfectly apparent; the following is merely typical. "The Christian mythologists, calling themselves the Christian Church, have erected their fable, which for absurdity and extravagance is not exceeded by anything that is to be found in the mythology of the ancients."[11] Paine found pagan mythology silly, and by dwelling repeatedly on the connection between it and Christian accounts, he clearly intended to discredit the latter. Over and over, Paine hammers home this thesis. "The mythologists had gods for everything; the Christian mythologists had saints for everything"; "The Christian theory is little else than the idolatry of the ancient mythologists, accommodated to the purposes of power and revenue."[12] Following Dupuis, Paine treats Christianity as a mere modern variant of ancient sun worship. "The fable of Christ and his twelve apostles," Paine wrote, "is a parody on the sun and the twelve signs of the zodiac copied from the ancient religions of the Eastern World." Elsewhere he insisted that the account in the third chapter of Genesis of the Fall of Man "is no other than a fable borrowed from . . . the religious allegory of Zoroaster," and really means "the fall of the year" and not "the moral fall of man."[13]

With Paine, the concept of mythology is extended from false theology to include Christian theology and Scripture. Paine still uses the word in an exclusively religious context. His endorsement of science calls for a rejection of mythology: he says flatly science is the true religion, mythology the false. In the broad sense, Paine's influential posing of the religious problem as the problem of science versus myth is an important step in the evolution of the word "mythology" toward its meaning (for modern skeptics) of false ideals, whether religious, social, or political.

The impact of *The Age of Reason* was enormous. According to Henry May, it was reprinted twenty-one times within ten years and it called out thirty-five replies.[14] Written to appeal to the common man, and widely available in inexpensive reprints, the book enjoyed broad and lasting popularity. Down through the nineteenth century, religious radicals from Thomas Jefferson to Robert Ingersoll and Moncure Conway kept Paine's work alive. Melville's *Clarel* includes an appreciative estimate of the book, and whether one agrees with Paine or not, it must be conceded that *The Age of Reason* did as much as any other single book to fix the terms of the debate between science and myth and to give to the word "mythology" the connotation of ridiculous falsehood it still bears for many American intellectuals who get their bearings habitually from the Enlightenment.

Paine was a deist. *The Age of Reason* begins with his credo "I believe in one God and no more," and the force of his argument was to identify myth with false religion. But in another very influential book of the 1790s, mythology was made synonymous with all religion. Volney's *Ruins* does not try to salvage true religion from its mythological encrustations. With a boldness that foreshadows Marx, he argues that religion itself is the true enemy of civilization. Linking myth with religion and both with history and politics, Volney insists that myth is not just false, but deliberate falsehood consciously encouraged by tyrants as one of the tools of despotism.

The Ruins, or Meditations on the Revolutions of Empires was read, reprinted, translated and retranslated, excerpted and quoted from its appearance in 1791 until the middle of the next century. It has been claimed that Volney got the idea for the book from Franklin, and it has been demonstrated that Thomas Jefferson translated a large part of it, though he took care to conceal the fact and allowed Joel Barlow—who actually only finished Jefferson's translation—to have credit for the whole.[15] John Adams knew the book, Joseph Priestley took it up, and Barlow's own *Columbiad* shows the influence of Volney.[16] In the nineteenth century Lincoln read it, Thoreau, Poe, and Melville may have, and it was an important early influence on Whitman, who described it as one of those books "on which I may be said to have been raised."[17]

The book is cast as a modern dream vision, the subject of which is the destructive part played by religion and myth in the history of great empires. Volney's thesis is that all traditional religion and myth are the enemies of human happiness and freedom, and his highly readable treatment of the subject ends with a vision of the collapse of all the old mythological and institutional religions and the rise of a new secular "religion" of humanity. *The Ruins* is the preeminent example of the radical view of myth during the era of the French Revolution, a view grounded in biblical research, seeing myth as falsehood neatly aligned against history as truth, and insisting on the close connection between myth and politics. The book's long popularity in America further suggests the importance of such a view of myth for the next two generations of American writers. In its insistence on myth and religion as imposture and fraud, *The Ruins* parallels Barlow's *Columbiad* and foreshadows Melville's *The Confidence Man*.

Volney's book begins with a survey of the physical ruins of the great legendary cities of the past—Nineva, Babylon, Persepolis, Balbec, Jerusalem, Tyre, Arad, Sidon. Volney's description of these cities in Jefferson's translation is a classic lament for the past grandeur that still haunts the modern imagination. But Volney gives the subject a new twist by observing that in pagan times, before either Christianity or Mohammedanism arose, these cities were great flourishing places, whereas "now, when a people of saints and believers occupy these fields, all is become sterility and solitude. The earth," Volney goes on, "under these holy hands produces only briars and thorns."[18] While the protagonist is thus led to his first tentative suspicion of the baleful influence of modern religion, a spirit from the past now arrives and begins to lecture on how myth and religion have repeatedly led only to desolation.

In the beginning of human society, Volney says, the unbridled selfishness of the strong led them to subjugate the weak. The weak, prostrated by natural as well as political calamities, reasoned that there must be tyrants in heaven as well as on earth. Having satisfied himself as to the motive for imagining gods and goddesses as beings of superior power, Volney now draws on Dupuis to explain the actual process by which the various myths or stories about the gods came to take the puzzling forms they did. Volney's summary, which loses nothing in Barlow's forceful translation, is that "all the theological dogmas on the origin of the world, the nature of God, the revelation of his laws, the manifestation of his person, are known to be only the recital of astronomical facts, only figurative and emblematical accounts of the motion of the heavenly bodies."[19] Much of *The Ruins* now proceeds to analyze, in appropriate detail, the development of "religious" ideas and their expression via mythology. The conclusion is that "God" begins as "the visible and various action of the meteors and elements" and ends as "a chimerical and abstract being, a scholastic subtlety of substance without form, a body without a figure, a very delirium of the mind, beyond the power of reason to comprehend."[20] In a word, God is a chimera, a mythical being who simply does not exist.

Thus Volney destroys myth, linking it with error and fraud and fear, tying it to political subjugation on one side, and on the other arguing that it leaves man alone and lost in a maze. Volney ends by claiming that

> The whole history of the spirit of religion is only the history of the errors of the human mind, which, placed in a world that it does not comprehend, endeavors nevertheless to solve the enigma; and which, beholding with astonishment this mysterious and visible prodigy, imagines causes, supposes reasons, builds systems; then, finding one defective, destroys it for another not less so; hates the error that it abandons, misconceives the one that it embraces, rejects the truth that it is seeking, composes chimeras of discordant beings, and thus, while always dreaming of wisdom and happiness, wanders blindly in a labyrinth of illusion and doubt.[21]

The case against myth—as the distorting mechanism of the religious spirit—could hardly be put more forcefully. The net effect of Volney's grand sweep through the gods of not only Greece but the Middle East, India, and the Far East was to equate religion with myth and to discredit both by demonstrating their destructive influence upon the political life of nations.

Paine represents the deist and Volney an atheist point of view toward myth. Together they epitomize the rational, skeptical attack on myth, and the influence of this line of attack is evident in American writing from the late eighteenth century on. Thomas Jefferson advised his nephew to "read the bible, then, as you would read Livy or Tacitus," and assembled his own collection of scripture (which purged myth and mystery from the moral teachings of Jesus) in order "to justify the character of Jesus against the fictions of his pseudo-followers, which have exposed him to the inference of being an imposter." Jefferson is only using a standard deist tactic when he asserts, for example, that "the day will come when the mystical generation of Jesus, by the Supreme Being as his Father, in the womb of a virgin, will be classed with the fable of the generation of Minerva in the brain of Jupiter."[22]

John Adams spent a large part of the last ten years of his life, as Frank Manuel has shown, studying the works of Dupuis, Volney, Court de Gebelin, Sir William Jones, and other mythographers, coming to the conclusion, apparently, that Dupuis's conclusions were the most satisfactory. The later career of Joel Barlow is another example of the literary use of the skeptical distrust of myth. Joel Barlow's notebooks and the writings—both published and unpublished—written after his arrival in France in 1789 are filled with skeptical mythologizing. A significant additon to book nine of *The Columbiad* treats the rise of religion in the manner of Paine and Volney. Some of Barlow's best verse describes how fear led men to personify the forces of nature and how then from

> Hence rose his gods, that mystic monstrous lore
> Of blood-stain'd altars and of priestly power,
> Hence blind credulity of all dark things
> False morals hence and hence the yoke of kings.

Barlow's notebooks show his wide reading in mythology and show him speculating, for example, that "had it been known that the earth moved around the sun, the latter would not have been considered as a god."[23] His papers also include an unpublished translation of a French piece tracing the liberty pole back to pagan phallic rituals, and an unfinished poem, "The Canal," about the evolution of science from its primitive beginnings in zodiacal myths down to late eighteenth-century hydraulic mechanics.[24]

The rationalist's position that myth is at bottom false can be traced both through orthodox Christian denunciations of pagan religion and through their opponents, the rationalist denouncers of pagan and Christian religion. There is also a third line of development. A rationalist and skeptical approach to myth was also evolved by those biblical critics who sought to bolster Christianity not by exalting the whole of the Bible over pagan beliefs and traditions, but by purging it of its mythical elements in order to arrive at a pure and trustworthy historical core that could command belief in a rationalist age. This movement, usually called the higher criticism and most marked in Germany, used an historical-critical approach to the Bible and may be traced back to the same roots as the deists and the rationalist French mythographers. From Bayle, Spinoza, and Richard Simon down through Jean Astruc to Lessing, Reimarus,

Eichhorn, and eventually D. F. Strauss, this historical approach to the Bible depended upon the clear opposition of history and myth.[25] The new criticism was textual, critical, and historical and, as Hans Frei has recently shown, it reversed a long tendency in theological studies toward typology, that technique—also called "figural realism" or "phenomenal prophecy"—which, from St. Paul on, interprets the events and figures of the Old Testament as historical prefigurations or prophecies (types) of New Testament events and persons (archetypes).[26] For an orthodox literalist, of course, the Bible was historically true by definition, and other historical accounts were judged true or false as they approached or diverged from the biblical standard. For the higher criticism, the Bible itself was judged by the ordinary standards of secular history, by the same standards one applied to Livy or Tacitus. Anything not rationally acceptable or corroborated by external evidence was relegated to the category of myth. As we have noted, the higher criticism as practiced by Eichhorn, Paulus, Gabler, Semler, G. L. Bauer, Vater, De Wette, and Strauss has its origins in the same rationalism that produced English and French deism. Indeed from 1775 (the year of Eichhorn's *Urgeschichte*) on, rationalist biblical criticism evolved its mythical view of the Bible on two levels at the same time. While the German tradition produced work after work of formidable scholarship, a popular line ran through such late eighteenth-century writers as Voltaire, Volney, and Paine. In late eighteenth-century America, and until about 1810, this popular strain in biblical myth criticism was far more influential than the scholarly German line and included such writers as Priestley, Jefferson, Adams, Ethan Allen and Thomas Young, Elihu Palmer, and George English. The two traditions, the scholarly and the popular, came together most impressively in America with the work of Theodore Parker, and the debate over the extent to which the Bible is basically history or basically myth is still alive as a central issue in Melville's *Clarel*. The critical historical view of the Bible was intended by the higher criticism as a defense of Christianity, by the deists to defend "pure" religion, and by atheists to attack both of these; it was used by no one to defend or affirm the value of myth itself.

Most skeptical rejections of myth in America in the period we are considering were based on three distinct theories about the origin of myth. It is important to insist on the distinction between *attitudes* toward myth (i.e., the acceptance or rejection of myth), and *theories* of myth (i.e., Euhemerism, Sabeism, or Allegorism), because the same three theories, by and large, also underlie the whole movement toward the acceptance and endorsement of myth. The view of Holbach or Spence that myths originate as allegories intended to express primitive conceptions of nature (Zeus as an allegorical representative of the primitive's fear and awe of thunder, for example) can be used negatively as proof that primitives are unable to grasp complex abstract or scientific truths but must personify natural forces and construct stories to convey their rudimentary "science." From the negative or disparaging point of view of the skeptic, this sort of myth is inferior to science, which eventually drives the myth out by providing superior explanations of natural phenomena. But the romantic revolution in taste made it possible, in the late eighteenth century, to exalt primitive wisdom over civilized sophistication, and thus the way lay open for a revaluation of primitive allegorical mythmaking as the earliest, noblest expression of the heroic age. The conversations and writings of Margaret Fuller, for instance, are full of romantic affirmations of myth as sublime allegories of ancient wisdom that the modern age would do well to rediscover.

A similar case could be made for Sabeism, the theory (championed by Pluche, Dupuis, Volney, and Paine) that myths arise as a result of primitive worship of heavenly bodies. Skeptical Sabeists emphasized the idea that early efforts to construct an agricultural calendar produced the zodiac. A given star that appeared above the horizon when the Nile was about to flood was called the "dog star" because it served a watchdog function and put all the farmers on notice. But subsequent ages (this example comes from Pluche and is repeated by Dupuis and others) forgot the original application and, led by crafty priests, began to worship images of dogs set up to warn an illiterate population of the approaching flood, and eventually came to worship actual dogs. Here again, romantic primitivism could turn the same theory into something admirable. By concentrating on sun worship

rather than zodiac worship, primitive mans's solar myths could come
to seem a splendid example of early rational adoration of the source
of all life. Joel Barlow is an example of a transitional figure who, at
different times in his life, supported both these positions. In his
early *Vision of Columbus* he praises primitive sun worship and approves of solar myth, while in his later work he reverts to standard
Enlightenment skepticism. A notebook entry for 1796–97 records
Barlow's question "If man in all ages & countries had understood
astronomy & physics as well as they do now generally in Europe
would the ideas of God and religion have ever come into their
minds?"[27]

Euhemerism is an important theory for American literature,
whether skeptically or affirmatively applied. As elaborated by Banier
and as reflected by the adoption of Banier's work in most important
encyclopedias and handbooks until well into the nineteenth century,
classical Euhemerism explained gods as the result of early man's
credulous tendency to worship his ancestors and to exalt great rulers
and leaders into deities. According to Euhemerists, Zeus was a
Cretan king who was admired first as a man, then as a hero, and at
last as a god by successive generations of his posterity. In Christian
hands (Banier, Shuckford, Fourmont), this view was a tool with
which all pagan myth could be reduced to secular history and thus
be shown to be outside of and inferior to the sacred history of the
Bible. In anti-Christian hands (Bayle, Voltaire, Boulanger),
Euhemerism could be turned against the Bible by insisting on the
historicity of all its characters, from David in the Old Testament to
Jesus in the New. Used skeptically or negatively, whether by Christians or *philosophes,* Euhemerism *reduces* myth to mere history. Thus
Emerson, in a skeptical mood, could say "romance grows out of
ignorance, & so is the curse of its own age & the ornament of those
that follow. . . . Unprincipled bandits are Red Cross Knights, &
Templars & Martyrs even, . . . In Greece, such a person was a hero in
the second generation, a giant in the third & a god in the fourth."[28]
But when history and especially primitive history is revalued, then
myth becomes newly important because it is seen as the earliest
history of man. For the German classical historian K. O. Müller

and his American followers, which included most of the Transcendentalists, myth is treated as the major source of our knowledge of prehistory. Thus Emerson's essay on history rests on the argument that myth embodies all that is essential in history. And with the growth of the idealist tendency to locate the divine in the human, Euhemerism turns into romantic glorification, deification, and mythologizing of American heroes. On a popular level, Parson Weems's Washington and Davy Crockett are mythologized via patriotic and affirmative Euhemerism, while, on another level, Emerson's *Representative Men* creates an intellectual pantheon of modern heroes.

Despite the remarkable expansion of interest in theories about the origin and nature of mythology in the eighteenth century, the dominant attitude of the time toward its worth, its value as truth, was negative and skeptical. The positive or affirmative view of myth that became widespread during the Romantic movement can, it is true, be traced back into the eighteenth century, but it must be emphasized that however important the romantic enthusiasm for mythic truth became, its beginnings were fitful and occasional and made only slow headway against the dominant rationalist position.

Just as the case against myth was made by both Christian and anti-Christian writers, so the eighteenth-century argument in favor of myth had two sides, both having a strong literary element from the start. One affirmation of myth stemmed from an interest in Homer and the other from a literary interest in the Bible. Thomas Blackwell's *Enquiry into the Life and Writings of Homer* (1735) and his *Letters concerning Mythology* (1748) undertake to explain why Homer became a greater poet than anyone after him, and find part of the answer in Homeric mythology. Blackwell is familiar with Banier's Euhemerism and Pluche's Sabeism. He rejects the former because of Banier's evident intention "to render the ancient mythology odious," and he distrusts Pluche because he "reduces the whole Gods of antiquity to certain statues or emblematical figures set up in public places by way of Almanac to warn the people of seed time and harvest."[29] In short, Blackwell rejects these rationalistic and reductive explanations of myth, including, of course, Homeric myth.

Blackwell instead is disposed to find Homeric mythology admirable rather than absurd. His own theory is that Homeric myth is allegorical wisdom. In other words, Blackwell accepts the allegorical view of myth, but unlike such skeptical allegorists as Holbach, he accepts the results as valid. Blackwell argues that Homer arrived at just the right moment in Greece when the "older heroic ways had not yet disappeared and before debilitating decline had set in." Blackwell believes that the earliest age of a civilization is its best, that "a people's felicity clips the wings of its verse," and he also argues that in Greece "the ancient mythology and poetry grew together." Where the skeptics saw myth introduced by crafty priests and leaders to enslave people, Blackwell sees the same myths introduced for benevolent reasons. "In the early ages of the Grecian state, the wild and barbarous inhabitants . . . wanted a mythology to lead them by *Fear* and *Dread* (the only Holds to be taken of a rude Multitude) into a feeling of natural causes, and their influence upon our lives and actions. The Wise and Good among the ancients saw this necessity and supplied it. . . . They had religion for their theme and the Service of Mankind for the End of their song." Beyond insisting on the benevolent social usefulness of myth, Blackwell also affirms it as poetic wisdom of an inherently admirable sort. "The Veil of Fables is of such surprising Virtue," he says, "that it magnifies the Object which it covers: It shows them in a grander light, and invites the Eye to contemplate them more eagerly than if they were open and undisguised." Blackwell thus argues that the superiority of early Homeric poetry rests on its mythology, which is composed of allegorical wisdom (Egyptian doctrines of the origin of things, etc.) literarily enhanced—not enfeebled—by its mythical form, and on the fact that it exerts a civilizing force socially beneficial rather than harmful.

Over the next hundred years, Blackwell's views (akin to but more influential than Vico's until 1827, when Vico was finally "discovered" by Michelet) gradually spread, offering a whole new perspective on the role of myth in heroic poetry. The force of Blackwell's work, as evidenced in American literature from Barlow to Thoreau and Melville, is to make myth attractive by identifying it with the vigorous natural expression of early heroic ages. One important culmination of Blackwell's point of view is Thoreau's essay on "Walking," in which Thoreau identifies the early heroic spirit with his term "wildness" when he says, "It is the uncivilized free and wild thinking in 'Hamlet' and the 'Iliad' in all the scriptures and mythologies not learned in the schools that delights us."

Another main line along which the reappraisal of the value of myth moves begins with Robert Lowth's *Lectures on the Sacred Poetry of the Hebrews,* published in Latin in 1753 and translated into English in 1787. Accepting the argument that the Greeks "considered poetry as something sacred and celestial, not produced by human art or genius, but altogether a Divine gift," and noting that among the Greeks, "poets were accounted sacred, the ambassadors of Heaven, men favoured with an immediate intercourse and familiarity with the gods," he urges that this conception not be limited to Greek poets but be extended to the ancient Hebrew poetry of the Old Testament.[30] Pointing out that Hebrew uses the same word for "poet" and "prophet," Lowth's primary argument is that religious truth naturally finds its fullest expression in poetry. Secondarily he argues that to understand the sacred poetry of the Hebrews we must "be acquainted with the language of this people, their manners, discipline, rites, and ceremonies; we must even investigate their inmost sentiments, the manner and connexion of their thoughts; in one word, we must see all things with their eyes, estimate all things by their opinions; we must endeavour as much as possible to read Hebrew as the Hebrews would have read it." Lowth thus rejects eighteenth-century rationalism in order to urge that we understand the scriptures from inside, on their own terms. "He who would perceive and feel the peculiar and interior elegances of the Hebrew poetry," Lowth says, "must imagine himself exactly situated as the person for whom it was written." Instead of demolishing the Bible by applying a modern rationalist criticism, Lowth urges that we try, through an act of sympathetic historical imagination, to understand the Bible as the writers of the Bible understood it. Lowth thus places the Bible beyond rationalist disintegration and urges a view that could immediately be transferred to any other early sacred scripture or mythology. Lowth's influence was considerable: in Germany his approach influenced Herder and led to an affirmation of mythical thought and experience that claimed, in essence, that religious truth expresses itself in early noble ages as poetry and myth, which cannot be reduced or explained away but which must be accepted as valid. Myth thus becomes the essential expression of religious truth.

In America, Lowth's ideas spread slowly. Timothy Dwight knew Lowth's work by the time he wrote his long poem *Greenfield Hill* (1794), Calvin Stowe (Harriet Beecher Stowe's husband) brought out an extensively revised translation of Lowth in 1829, and the line that goes from Lowth to Herder (whose *Spirit of Hebrew Poetry* was translated by New Englander James Marsh in 1833) leads on directly to Emerson, Thoreau, and Whitman.

Blackwell urged that Homeric myth be taken seriously as Greek wisdom and religion. Lowth urged that the Bible should be approached as poetry. The effect of these two ideas, together with the general climate of preromantic interest in myth, was a tendency, beginning in the late eighteenth century and manifest in most of the romantic poets, to raise mythic truth to the level of religious truth and to regard both as the natural province of the highest poetry. One example of this new attitude toward myth is the work of Thomas Taylor, later to exert such an important influence on some of the American Transcendentalists. Beginning in 1787 with a translation of Plotinus and a book called *The Mystical Initiations; or, Hymns of Orpheus,* Taylor argued tirelessly for his belief that "there formerly lived a person named Orpheus, who was the founder of theology among the Greeks," and that Orphism was a philosophical religion superior to Christianity.[31] Taylor approached Greek mythology as one aspect of this religion, he characterized Greek mythological thought as a complex and wholly admirable species of poetic symbolism, and his conception of symbolism was picked up by Emerson and Alcott in America.

Two other major events contributed to the later eighteenth century's increasing interest in the relationship between myth and literature. The first was the Nordic Renaissance, the rediscovery and subsequent popularization of old North European myth and epic;

the second was the Oriental Renaissance, the European rediscovery of the ancient sacred writings of the East, and of India in particular. The Nordic Renaissance, at least as it affects American literature, has two aspects: the eighteenth-century revival of interest in Norse mythology, and the success of the Ossianic poems of James Macpherson.[32] To understand the initial impact of Nordic myth, it must be remembered that when Paul Henri Mallet published large parts of the texts of the *Eddas* and a discussion of the mythology contained in them in a book on the history of Denmark, published in 1775–76, it was the first time that stories about Odin, Thor, Loki, Heimdall, Freya, the Valkyries, Sigurd (Siegfried), Valhalla, Ygdrasil, Ragnarok, and Niflheim were introduced to a modern European audience. Before 1755, knowledge of Norse myth was rare and usually inaccurate; the whole subject was obscure because the *Eddas* were available only in Latin or in ancient Scandinavian languages in manuscripts few could reach or read. Mallet's French edition quickly became popular, and after Thomas Percy translated it in 1770 as *Northern Antiquities,* Mallet became and remained the standard source of knowledge about Norse myth for English-speaking people. When Thomas Bulfinch expanded his *Age of Fable* to include Norse mythology, he simply went to Mallet.

Much of the excitement over Mallet was due to the fact that he had uncovered a mythology indigenous to northern Europe, a European mythology to rival the Homeric. With the higher criticism investigating Jesus as a human being and Euhemerism insisting that pagan gods were originally human, a new interest in the historical Odin now arose. Even Gibbon, in the early sections of *The Decline and Fall,* accepted the idea of Odin as an historical figure, though he eventually came to doubt it, declaring in a later section that "all beyond Caesar and Tacitus is darkness or fable in the antiquities of Germany."[33] (Not even scholars distinguished between Nordic and Teutonic mythology until the 1830s.) The historicized version of the mythology of Odin appeared in America in the work of a minor Connecticut wit named Richard Alsop. His fragmentary "Conquest of Scandinavia" and his 130-line poem on the Twilight of the Gods were both printed in Elihu Smith's *American Poems* in 1793. Alsop seems to have relished particularly the dark ferocity of the Norse myth of the end of the world.[34] From Alsop on, there is a steady interest in Norse myth in America, which received a new and most important impetus later from Esaias Tegnér's *Frithiof's Saga* (1825), and especially from Carlyle. The opening lecture of Carlyle's *On Heroes, Hero-Worship, and the Heroic in History* is on Odin. Carlyle views Odin as the altogether admirable prototype of the great man, and Carlyle's enthusiasm for the subject was communicated to both Thoreau and Melville.

The early and widespread interest in Mallet's work also helped prepare the way for the very remarkable success enjoyed by the Ossianic poems of James Macpherson, poems which themselves helped create the vogue of myth. When Macpherson's *Fingal* and *Temora* appeared in 1762 and 1763, apparently quite independent of Mallet, the early European heroic poems we now take for granted, *Beowulf*, the *Chanson de Roland*, and the *Nibelungenlied*, were unknown. Ossianic poems appeared to be indigenous European epics, even fitter than the *Eddas* to stand beside Homer. Indeed, not only was Ossian hailed as the Homer of the North, his poems were praised above Homer's. In an age that was remolding itself on new nationalistic bases, Ossian's poems established northern Europe's cultural independence from classical epic and classical myth. A further reason for the wide success of the Ossianic poems (which were admired by Goethe, Chateaubriand, Byron, and Jefferson, to name only a few) is that they presented an ancient heroic world that was neither superstitious nor barbaric, with heroes who were primitive but noble and refined. Ossian's heroes behaved chivalrously, displayed a noble deism, and worshipped the sun as giver of light and life. For a time, the Ossianic poems solved one of the dilemmas of romantic primitivism—how to admire the early ages without admiring savagery. Even when the poems were shown to be largely modern fabrications, the vogue for Ossian continued, because the exposure of Macpherson itself suggested that *modern* poets could still assemble and refashion ancient materials into compelling modern poems. The acceptance of Ossian was an important step toward the acceptance of the idea that a modern poet can transmit, refashion, and even perhaps create myth.

Ossian's influence in America was considerable. Jefferson in 1773 said he thought "the rude bard of the North the greatest poet that has ever existed" and he wrote Macpherson's embarrassed brother asking for a Gaelic grammar and a copy of Ossian in the original.[35] John Trumbull's 1775 satire on the American Revolution was called *M'Fingal,* obviously assuming a general knowledge of Ossian. By 1800, the poet John Blair Linn could write an Ossianic prose poem on the death of Washington ("And is the chief of Vernon fallen?— said he with a rising sigh"), which shows how Ossian was by then furnishing materials of American hero-worship.[36] Emerson was impressed with Ossian, Whitman wondered "Can it be a descendant of the Biblical poetry?" Ossian reminded Thoreau "of the most refined and the rudest eras of Homer, Pindar, Isaiah and the American Indian." For Thoreau, Ossian was one more example of how the old mythologies present "only the simplest and most enduring features of humanity."[37]

At almost the same time as the rediscovery of Nordic myth and epic, another group of scholars, jurists, and poets were uncovering, translating, and reporting to an excited Europe the great sacred writings of India and Persia.[38] Until Anquetil-Duperron's edition of the *Zend-Avesta* in 1771, Eastern religions were known in Europe only through dim, secondhand reports. The *Zend-Avesta* was the first authentic Eastern scripture (excluding the Koran) to reach the West in anything like an adequate version. And as book after book appeared during the last three decades of the eighteenth century, modern Europe became aware, for the first time, that there was a great ancient Eastern culture with a literature, a philosophical tradition, and scriptures that seriously rivaled the Christian tradition. In 1774 Sir William Jones extended Lowth's methods to the sacred poetry of the Persians. In 1785 Charles Wilkins translated and published the *Bhagvat-Geeta* (part of the *Mahabarata*), a book deeply important to Emerson and others in Concord. In 1786 Anquetil-Duperron's edition of four Upanishads in his *Recherches historiques . . . sur l'Inde* brought another admirable scripture into view, and in 1787 appeared Wilkins's edition of the *Hitopadesa,* a book that was important to Thoreau later on. In 1789 Jones's version of Calidasa's *Sacontala or the Fatal Ring* showed Europeans that ancient India had achieved a great dramatic literature. In 1796 Jones brought out an edition of the *Institutes of Hindu Law or, The Ordinances of Menu,* a book at once seen to rival the Pentateuch in antiquity, in philosophical depth, and in religious feeling. Joseph Priestley— then living in Pennsylvania—quickly brought out a detailed *Comparison of the Institutions of Moses with those of the Hindoos and other ancient Nations* (1799), in which he treated Menu and Moses with equal seriousness as lawgivers and founders of civilizations. Priestley's book is extremely interesting because while he concludes in favor of the Mosaic dispensation, he treats its Indic equivalent with respect as an argument for religious lawgivers, and he includes in his volume a sharp attack on such rationalist reductionists as Dupuis and Volney. For Priestley, as for Thoreau later, the ethical wisdom of the laws of Menu was an argument in favor of the essential and enduring truth of the ancient mythological scriptures. A similar impulse came from Jones's famous essay "On the Gods of Greece, Italy and India" (delivered as an address in 1785, printed in *Asiatick Researches* in 1799, reprinted in part by Noah Webster in 1814, and ultimately of interest to Melville), an essay which pioneers the study of comparative mythology by its detailed analysis of the then surprising similarities to be found between the newly discovered Indic deities and the familar gods of Greece and Rome.

Taken together, the Nordic Renaissance, beginning in 1755, and the Oriental or Indic Renaissance, beginning in 1771, vastly and suddenly expanded the mythological materials available to Europe and America and lent plausibility to a serious comparative point of view in religion and mythological research by showing that mythology was an element not only in Homer and in the Bible but in other ancient cultures and literatures as well. All this made it necessary to approach the problem of myth with redoubled energy and seriousness. And from a literary point of view, the new Nordic and Indic mythologies, the *Eddas,* the *Bhagvat-Geeta,* and even Ossian furnished new grounds for testing the ideas of Blackwell and Lowth that the mythological element in early heroic and religious literature was not to be skeptically demolished but enthusiastically understood as an inevitable and valuable aspect of an indigenous early heroic or sacred poetry. With fresh Indic and Nordic materials, with the example of Ossian to show what could still be done in modern times and in an era of new nationalism, modern writers began to wonder if indeed it might be possible for a poet-prophet to write heroic, perhaps even sacred poetry for the modern age. In Germany, Friedrich Schlegel and in America, Emerson put this aim explicitly as a call for a new mythology. In America especially, the spectacle of a new and as yet epicless land led writers from Joel Barlow to Emerson, Thoreau, and Whitman to wonder if there were not mythological materials to be found or perhaps even created fit for heroic poems for the New World. This is what Thoreau, for one, meant when he called for an "American mythology" and claimed that "The West is preparing to add its fables to those of the East."

Two

Parker and Alcott

1. The Higher Criticism: Theodore Parker and the Mythical View of the Bible

The skeptical rejection of myth that had become fully articulate before the end of the eighteenth century continued strongly down into the nineteenth. Conservative Christians continued to call mythology "heathen idolatry" in sermons, essays, and handbooks, while the rationalist, non-Christian attack on myth launched by Voltaire, Paine, and Volney continued in the work of George English, Frances Wright, Abner Kneeland, and Robert Ingersoll (and eventually H. L. Mencken).[1] But for the main body of mid-nineteenth-century American literature, the most important argument against myth was the "mythical" explanation of the Bible propounded by the higher criticism. E. S. Shaffer has recently shown how the concept of myth that emerged from the new biblical criticism was important to English literature from Coleridge to George Eliot, and a similar claim can be made for much of the work of Emerson, Thoreau, and Melville.[2]

The higher criticism of the Bible as it was fully formulated by Eichhorn, and as it descends from him to Gabler, Semler, G. L. Bauer, Vater, De Wette, and D. F. Strauss, was a double-edged tool; both its practitioners and its historians have testified that while it was intended to revitalize Christianity, it frequently had just the opposite effect.[3] The higher critics began by applying secular critical standards to the study of biblical texts. Furthermore, in their effort to deal with miracles—events that plainly contradicted the ordinary laws of nature—they insisted on separating biblical narratives into those that were historical and those that were mythical. First the Old Testament, then the New was gradually and with immense, seemingly unanswerable learning shown to consist largely of myth. This formidable body of work had two opposed effects, corresponding closely to the two traditions I have described as skepticism and affirmation toward myth. Those who believed that history was by definition true while myth was false found the higher criticism essentially destructive, since it set out to find the historical basis for Christianity but found instead that there was little if any history in the Bible able to stand up to critical scrutiny. Instead of history, the Bible was seen to consist largely of myths. But there were others (Herder and Schelling in Germany, Coleridge in England) who saw a different possibility in what Eichhorn and Strauss always insisted, that myth was the *necessary* form of expression for any early people. These writers and critics perceived the affirmative thrust of the higher criticism to be an effort not to destroy the authority of Scripture but to shift it from a reliance upon the historical accuracy of certain events to a reliance upon the mythic truth of the narratives. Coleridge is an early example of a writer who grasped this second, affirmative aspect, and saw that Christianity would be better off if it based its claims on the essentially imaginative, mythic truth of the gospel narratives than if it tried to insist, against mounting evidence to the contrary, on the factual historical accuracy of those same gospels.[4] So for Emerson, and for some American writers after him, the higher criticism forced an opposition between history and myth, obliging the defender of an historical concept of truth to disparage myth and the proponent of a mythic concept of truth to attack the rational, empirical, factual, chronological concept of history.

The higher criticism came to America early in the nineteenth century; it obtained a solid foothold at Harvard, and exerted a considerable influence on the Transcendental generation. As Jerry W. Brown has recently shown, the new biblical studies began at Harvard with Joseph Buckminster, who in 1811 was appointed the first Dexter Lecturer.[5] His charge was to teach "a critical knowledge of Holy Scripture." Buckminster had become interested in the subject by reading John Locke, Anthony Collins, Lowth, and Michaelis; he acquired a spendid three-thousand-volume library in Europe, and though he died before he could really settle into the subject, it is nevertheless true, as Brown says, that "Biblical studies in America may be traced by following those who came into Buckminster's sphere of influence." At the auction in 1812 of Buckminster's library, Edward Everett and Moses Stuart competed hotly for the prize item, a complete edition of Eichhorn's *Einleitung in das Alte Testament* (1780–82). Stuart went on to introduce the higher criticism at Andover Seminary, where it was made to serve Calvinist orthodoxy, while Everett was sent to Germany by President Kirkland of Harvard to take a Ph.D. with Eichhorn himself. Everett returned to Harvard, where, instead of lecturing on biblical studies, he turned the new critical methods on the study of the classics. Among Everett's students was Emerson, who later wrote that "Germany had created criticism in vain for us until 1820, when Edward Everett returned. . . . He made us for the first time acquainted with Wolf's theory of the Homeric writings, and with the criticism of Heyne. . . . the rudest undergraduate found a new morning opened to him in the lecture room of Harvard Hall."[6] Everett never lectured on the Bible after his return. His studies in Germany had led him to see that Christianity could no longer be based on unassailable historical truths. Impressed by the skeptical argument, his faith shaken, he never took the step of abandoning historical truth in favor of "mythical" truth. George Bancroft, who followed Everett to Göttingen as a student of Eichhorn and was supposed to return to Harvard to carry on the higher criticism in America, also suffered a skeptical reaction from the new methods of study. Theology is "reduced," said Bancroft in a letter home to President Kirkland, "to a mere matter of learning. . . . they neither begin with God nor go on with him, and there is a great deal more religion in a few lines of Xenophon, than in a whole course of Eichhorn. . . . The Bible is treated with very little respect, and the narratives are laughed at as an old wife's tale, fit to be believed in the nursery."[7] Bancroft, like Everett, did not lecture on biblical studies when he returned to America. William Ellery Channing held that Dexter chair for a year and was then followed by Andrews Norton, whose massive work on *The Evidences of the Genuineness of the Gospels* (Boston, 1837–44) was intended to answer the Germans on their own ground. Norton was followed by John G. Palfrey, Theodore Parker's teacher. Parker became the most extreme advocate in America of the higher criticism, especially of "the mythical point of view" as developed by D. F. Strauss. But Parker was not so much a pioneer as the culmination in America of a twenty-year period of intense interest in the subject. He is an important figure and a representative one, showing as he does how one side of the higher criticism fostered a new and highly sophisticated rejection of myth.

Theodore Parker (1810–1860) was, as Perry Miller puts it, "the man who next only to Emerson—and in the world of action even above Emerson—was to give shape and meaning to the Transcendental movement in America."[8] Brilliant and studious (he knew perhaps twenty languages and had a library of fifteen thousand volumes at a time when the Harvard College Library had seventy thousand), Parker is remembered chiefly for his turbulent career as a Unitarian minister and an antislavery agitator. He was at or near the center of nearly everything in Boston in the thirties and forties; Brook Farm was in his parish of West Roxbury, his wife attended Margaret Fuller's conversations, and he was a leader in the antislavery movement. Parker wrote for *The Dial* and other periodicals and eventually started his own in 1847, *The Massachusetts Quarterly Review*. His energy was limitless, his learning prodigious; he was especially fond of and versed in German literature, scholarship, theology, and criticism. In an 1841 article on "German literature" for *The Dial,* he showed an astonishing knowledge of contemporary German work. "Where are the English classical scholars in this country who take rank with Wolf, Heyne, Schweighauser, Wyttenbach, Boeckh, Herrmann, Jacobs, Siebelis, Hoffmann, Siebenkis, Müller, Creutzer, Wellauer, and Ast? Nay, where shall we find the rivals of Dindorf, Shafer, Stallbaum, Spitzner, Bothe, and Bekker. . . ?"[9] Whether in the classics, in theology, or in philosophy, Parker was a major American exponent of modern German scholarship.

Octavius Frothingham claimed that the entire Transcendental movement in America could be traced directly to Kant, and while this is no longer considered an adequate account of the origins of, say, Emerson's thought, it is true enough of Parker, who once wrote: "I found most help in the works of Immanuel Kant, . . . if he did not always furnish conclusions I could rest in, he yet gave me the true method, and put me on the right road."[10] What Parker got from Kant, particularly from Kant's method, he summarizes as "the foundation of Religion, laid in human nature itself" and enlarges as follows:

> I found certain great primal Intuitions of Human Nature, which depend on no logical process of demonstration, but are rather facts of consciousness given by the instinctive action of human nature itself . . .
>   1. The Instinctive Intuition of the Divine, the consciousness that there is a God.
>   2. The Instinctive Intuition of the Just and Right, a consciousness that there is a Moral Law, independent of our will, which we ought to keep.
>   3. The Instinctive Intuition of the Immortal, a consciousness that the Essential Element of man, the principle of Individuality, never dies.[11]

Believing then in a religion validated from within the individual rather than from on high, in intuition rather than authority, in the spirit rather than the letter, it was inevitable that the young minister would sooner or later be troubled by the assumption current among even the Unitarians that the Bible is the "Word of God," "His only Word," miraculous and infallible, and that belief in it is indispensable to Christianity. Parker was ready to embrace the ethical teachings of Jesus; he admired what he called the Bible's "free Genius for Religion," but could not accept the entire book as infallible revealed truth and protested vigorously against what he daringly and calculatingly called the "fetishism" of those Protestant ministers who blindly and uncritically adored the Bible. As he wrote to his parishioners in 1859 in a long letter summarizing his career:

I had not been long a minister, before I found this worship of the Bible as a Fetish, hindering me at each progressive step. If I wished to teach the nobleness of man, the Old Testament and New were there with dreadful condemnations of Human Nature; did I speak of God's Love for all men, the Bible was full of ghastly things—Chosen People, Hell, Devil, Damnation—to prove that he loved only a few, and them not overmuch. . . . There was no virtue, but the Scriptures could furnish an argument against it. I could not deny the existence of ghosts and witches, devils and demons, haunting the earth, but revelation could be quoted against me. Nay, if I declared the Constancy of Nature's Laws, and sought therein great argument for the Constancy of God, all the miracles came and held their mythologic finger up. Even Slavery was "of God," for the "divine statutes" in the Old Testament admitted the Principle that man might own a man as well as a garden.[12]

The above is in Parker's best popular style and is calculated to impress a general audience. The argument is perfectly plain; the ironic and exasperated tone reveals the practiced polemicist. But Parker was not a latter-day deist or provincial philosopher; his misgivings about the Bible were undergirded by extensive scholarship. In 1835, just a year after entering the Harvard Divinity School, Parker, with two friends, took over the editing of a magazine called *The Scriptural Interpreter*. Along with translations of Eichhorn, Herder, and Paulus, Parker printed in 1836 a translation, made by himself, of Jean Astruc's famous *Conjectures sur les mémoires originaux dont it paraît que Moyse s'est servi pour composer le livre de la Genèse,* first published anonymously in 1753.[13] Astruc's main finding was that since God was spoken of sometimes as Elohim, sometimes as Jehovah, and that since the same stories appeared in slightly different forms, Moses had compiled his account from at least two different prior documents.

Also in 1836, Parker began to translate W. M. L. De Wette's *Beiträge zur Einleitung in das Alte Testament,* first published in 1806 and meticulously kept up-to-date in successive editions all through the first half of the nineteenth century. Parker completed the actual translation in 1837, but the extensive commentary, which was Parker's own contribution and which doubled the size of the project,

was not completed until 1843. He added references, long critical
dissertations, and essays, some of which were not included in the
final printed version "for want of space." It was a prodigious effort of
learning, and if it had little effect on biblical studies, as Parker
disappointedly told De Wette in a letter, it certainly had a profound
effect on Parker, on his preaching and writing, and thus on American religious liberalism and on American Transcendentalism.[14]

De Wette's approach is made clear early in the book, when he
clearly announces that "the Bible is to be considered as a historical
phenomenon, in a series with other such phenomena, and entirely
subject to the laws of historical inquiry."[15] "The design of criticism," De Wette says, "is to determine what was originally written
by the author, consequently to ascertain facts."[16] The result of these
views systematically applied, in great detail and at great length,
yields what is commonly now called the documentary hypothesis,
which argues, in part, that the Pentateuch was compiled from three
sources: the Elohist as the base, the Jehovist added on, with
Deuteronomy added later still. It follows, of course, that any strict
or literal reliance on the Bible as the seamless web of God's truth or
as historically accurate in all respects is no longer easy. De Wette,
and Parker with him, go farther yet, treating the Old Testament
as Hebrew epic. Instead of history, the Bible is poetry and myth. As
Parker put it, "the Hebrew histories and poems, considered as primitive works of the human mind in Asia, are the most valuable documents for the history of human progress. . . . They contain, then,
not only the history of the Hebrews, and pictures of their civilization
and culture, but, by the collection of legends from the old world,
they serve as contributions to the history of all mankind."[17] De
Wette, using blunter language, refers to these legends, dealing with
revelation and miracle as "theocratical mythology," and Parker adds
a long note to explain exactly what he understands mythology to
mean:

> The application of the term *mythology* to certain narratives and opin-
> ions in the Bible need excite no surprise. The Jews had their mythology
> as well as the Hindoos, the Goths, and the Greeks. Symbols and myths

are necessarily used, by a rude people, to clothe abstract truths. It is evident the ancient Hebrews made use of them as the drapery of religious truth. This appears from the temple ceremonies, the visions and symbolic actions of the prophets; from the figurative expressions relating to the Deity, and the perpetual recurrence of anthropo-morphitic views of him. It is often difficult to determine where the myth begins, and the plain statement ends. But the Hebrew Scriptures have this difficulty in common with all very ancient, and especially Oriental writings. Symbolical language is sometimes used *consciously,* as properly symbolical, and sometimes *unconsciously,* when the writer himself had no clear conception of the subject, but confounded figure and fact.

A dogma is a creation of the Understanding, a symbol, of the Feelings; and a myth, of Fancy. The first expresses itself in ideas, the second, in aesthetic images, the third in history. The first is an object of faith; the second of devout reverence; but the third is, originally, neither the one nor the other; it is a free play of fiction.[18]

One example of how Parker thinks myth uses history to express itself, taken from a section called "Origin and progress of the Mosaic Mythology," will suffice:

In Gen xix, 26, it is said, Lot's wife looked back as she was fleeing, reluctantly, from Sodom, and became a pillar of salt; but from the Wisdom of Solomon, (x, 7,) it seems a pillar of salt was erected on the spot where she turned back. Josephus says such a pillar was standing in his time. . . . In the popular legend, there came an idealo-poetic element, and mingled itself with the real historical elements. By this means the tradition was transformed, gradually, into the miraculous and the ideal. . . .[19]

One must constantly remember that in the hands of men such as De Wette and Parker these arguments were not intended destructively or negatively. The mythical viewpoint, as it came to be called, offered a way to separate the historical kernel of the Bible from fabulous mythic encrustations, thus rendering the Bible acceptable even to a critical age. But the process of strict historical investigation, once started, was not easily stopped, and the more the Bible was examined, the greater the number of problems it presented.

Nor was the inquiry limited to the Old Testament. The critical, rational, historical approach was also applied to the study of the New Testament, one culmination of which was the publication in 1835 of D. F. Strauss's *Das Leben Jesu*. This volume made a great stir, ruined Strauss's life, and was said to have made the year 1835 as memorable in theology as 1848 was in politics.[20] The book was a systematic application of the mythical viewpoint of the four Gospels. Strauss was widely reviewed in America and one of the first was a long review of sixty-five printed pages by Theodore Parker. In this essay-review, which presents Parker's thought with much greater clarity and detail than his more famous sermon on "The Transient and Permanent in Christianity," Parker summarizes the entire modern movement in biblical criticism from the late seventeenth-century work of Richard Simon on down, stressing the modern scholarly recognition of the evolution of the mythical point of view among the writers of the Gospels.

> The progressive study of mythology shed light upon this subject [the problem of biblical interpretation]. Eichhorn had made the reasonable demand, that the Bible should be treated like other ancient books; but Paulus, attempting to treat others as he treated the Bible, could not naturalize the Greek legends and myths. Such scholars as Schelling and Gabler began to find myths in the Bible, and apply to them the maxim of Heyne "a mythis omnis priscorum hominum cum historia, tum philosophia procedit" [from myths proceed all of both the history and the philosophy of earliest men]. Bauer ventured to write a Hebrew mythology of the Old and New Testament. A myth was defined to be a narrative proceeding from an age, when there was no written authentic history, but when facts were preserved and related by oral tradition. It is a myth, if it contains an account of things, related in an historical way,—which *absolutely* could not be the objects of experience, such as events that took place in the supersensual world, or, which could not *relatively* be objects of experience, such, for example, as, from the nature of the case, no man could witness. Or, finally, it is a myth, if the narrative is elaborated into the wonderful, and is related in symbolic language.[21]

Parker calls these critics, including, presumably, himself, "Christian Euhemerists" because their fundamental assumption is that behind the extravagance of the mythic overlay is to be found a solid historical base. As Euhemerus had claimed that Zeus was only a fanciful or imaginative version of a certain historical Cretan king, so the German biblical scholars were claiming that there was an historical Moses behind the mythical Moses, and an historical Jesus behind the miracle-working mythological Jesus of the New Testament. In Euhemerus' hands—or in Voltaire's—this method led to atheism and irreligion. German scholarship apparently believed—even as late as Schweitzer and Bultmann—that this method would at length reveal the true (meaning historical) basis for religion. At any rate, the application of the mythical theory to the Gospels led Strauss to his celebrated conclusion that the Gospels are essentially mythic, a position which is brilliantly recapitulated by Parker:

> Mr. Strauss next inquires, whether it is possible there should be myths in the New Testament, and, judging from outward arguments, he thinks it possible. Most Christians, he says, believe that is false which the Heathen relate of their gods, and the Mahometans of their prophet, while the Scriptures relate only what is true respecting the acts of God, Christ, and the holy men. But this is a prejudice founded on the assumption that Christianity differs from heathen religions in the fact, that it alone is an historical, while they are mythical religions. But this is the result of a partial and confined view; for each of the other religions brings this charge against its rivals, and all derive their own origin from the direct agency of God. It is supposed that the Gospels were written by eye-witnesses, who were not deceived themselves, and were not deceivers, and, therefore, no room is left for the formation, or insertion of myths. But it is only a prejudice, that the Gospels were written by eye-witnesses. The names of Matthew and John, for example, prefixed to these writings, prove nothing; for the Pentateuch bears the name of Moses, though it must have been written long after him; some of the Psalms bear the name of David, though they were written during the exile, and the book of Daniel ascribes itself to that prophet, though it was not written before the times of Antiochus Epiphanes. He [Strauss] finds little reason for believing the genuineness of the authenticity of the Gospels. Indeed, he regards them all as spurious productions of well-meaning men, who collected the traditions that were current in the part of the world, where they respectively lived.[22]

Such an approach, as one may easily imagine, reduces nearly everything in the Gospels to myth. One is left with a Jesus who is not an historical figure, but the mythical embodiment of an idea. "Setting aside, therefore, the notions of the sinlessness and absolute perfection of Jesus, as notions that could not be realized perfectly, by a human being in the flesh, we understand Christ as that person, in whose self-consciousness the unity of the Divine and Human first came forth."[23]

On the other hand, Parker is clearly aware of the extent to which Strauss had ridden his thesis. He chides Strauss, observing "his mythical hypothesis has carried him away," and he goes so far as to satirize Strauss's heavy-handed imposition of the theory. "The story of the Declaration of Independence," Parker writes with mock seriousness,

> is liable to many objections, if we examine it *a la mode* Strauss. The congress was held at a mythical town, whose very name is suspicious,— Philadelphia,—Brotherly Love. The date is suspicious; it was the *fourth* day of the *fourth* month, (reckoning from April, as it is probable the Heraclidae, and Scandinavians; possible that the aboriginal Americans, and certain that the Hebrews did). Now *four* was a sacred number with the Americans; the president was chosen for *four* years, there were *four* departments of affairs, *four* divisions of political powers. . . .[24]

The fun goes on for several pages, but it would be a mistake to think that Parker himself dismissed Strauss's main arguments. Parker might parody excess, but Strauss's fundamental, laborious, chapter by chapter and verse by verse demonstration of the mythical nature of the gospel accounts of Jesus had a deeper effect on Parker than he allowed to appear in the review. Published in *The Christian Examiner* for April 1840, the review was actually written during March of the preceding year, and in that same month Parker wrote to his old friend and teacher Convers Francis in terms that leave no doubt about his own deepest convictions at that time:

> Is this not plain that the New Testament contains numerous myths? Certainly the book of Acts has several,—Paul's Damascus journey, Peter's delivery from prison, Paul's shipwreck: the story of the ascension; of the miraculous gift of tongues. We can explain all these things naturally, but did the compiler of this queer book explain them in this way?

What right have we to use a different system of exegesis from that we apply to the apocryphal gospels and every other writing? Not the smallest. But we cannot believe the literal statements of Luke: so we attempt to save his credit, and invent a system of interpretation for the purpose. But, in the same manner, we could make the story of John Gilpin an allegorical history of the origin, progress and perfection of Christianity.

The Gospels are not without their myths,—the miraculous conception, the temptation, etc. Now, the question is, Where are they to end? Who will tell us where the myth begins, and the history ends? Do not all the miracles belong to the mythical part? The resurrection—is not that also a myth? I know you will not be horror-struck at any doubts an honest lover of truth may suggest; and certainly I see not where to put up the bar between the true and the false. Christianity itself was before Abraham, and is older than the creation, and will stand forever, but I have sometimes thought it would stand better without the New Testament than with it.[25]

It was one thing to come to such conclusions privately, or even in sober scholarly work such as the review of Strauss or the "version" of De Wette. It was quite another matter to put such conclusions in popular form, into lectures, sermons, and pamphlets, but this is what Parker now proceeded to do. Despite the fact that Strauss had brought the wrath of Christian Europe down on his head for similar views, Parker began to put into practice and into plain language the results of his biblical scholarship. He maintained that Christianity had to rest on the truth of its moral and ethical teachings, not on any miraculous or mythological base. In 1840, the same year as the Strauss review, a dispute broke out in Boston between the orthodox Unitarians, led by Andrews Norton, and a radical faction roughly coincidental with the group usually called the Transcendentalists. Emerson's *Divinity School Address* in 1838 had rejected "historical Christianity," which was in turn stoutly defended by Norton, who attacked Emerson's ideas as "the latest form of infidelity." Norton himself believed in the miraculous basis of Christianity. Unitarianism had begun as a rational religion, but in the eyes of Emerson and Parker, Norton's miracle-encumbered version was now mired in the very superstition it had sought to escape. Writing under the pen name Levi Blodgett, Parker rode into the dispute in

1840 with a pamphlet called "The Previous Question between Mr. Andrews Norton and his alumni." Here, finally, and in plain language, is his first clear statement of the ground that was available to rational Christianity after the higher criticism had shown the Bible to be myth, not history.

> . . . it seems to me much easier, more natural, and above all more true, to ground Christianity on the truth of its doctrines, and its sufficiency to satisfy all the moral and religious wants of man in the highest conceivable state, than to rest it on miracles, which, at best, could only be a sign, and not a proof of its excellence. . . . To me, the spiritual elevation of Jesus is a more convincing proof of his divinity, than the story of his miraculous transfiguration; and the words which he uttered, and the life which he lived, are more satisfactory evidence of his divine authority, than all his miracles, from the transformation of water into wine, to the resurrection of Lazarus. I take him to be the perfect religious incarnation of God, without putting his birth on the same level with that of Hercules.[26]

Elsewhere in the same pamphlet Parker put the essence of his position thus: "God has laid the foundation of religion in man, and the religion built up in man must correspond to that foundation, otherwise it can be of no more use to him than St. Anthony's sermon was to the fishes." It may be objected that Parker lacked a sense of the sacred, but his writings suggest rather that he saw the sacred in human nature. At any rate the two key differences between Parker's "natural religion" and that of the seventeenth and eighteenth centuries are that Parker looks for the divine not in nature so much as in human nature and the fact that Parker's position, unlike that of most of the early deists, rests on solid textual scholarship. One has to have some sense of the very considerable labor Parker had expended mastering Astruc, Eichhorn, De Wette, Strauss, as well as their opponents, to appreciate the scholarly learning which Parker possessed but would not parade in his sermons and books during the rest of his life.[27] Perhaps enough has been said in this chapter so that one can see what lies beneath the surface, supporting the visible part of the iceberg in such famous utterances of Parker's as his *A Discourse of the Transient and Permanent in Christiantiy,* delivered on May 19, 1841.

Many years of patient textual scholarship lie behind what seems at first only a commonsense argument:

> But if, as some early Christians began to do, you take a heathen view and make him [Jesus] a God, the Son of God in a peculiar and exclusive sense, much of the significance of his character is gone. His virtue has no merit, his love no feeling, his cross no burden, his agony no pain. His death is an illusion, his resurrection but a show. For if he were not a man, but a god, what are all these things? . . . Then his resignation is no lesson, his life no model, his death no triumph to you or me, who are not gods, but mortal men.[28]

And, in the same sermon, Parker explains the consequences of an uncritical belief in the Bible as the word of God. "On the authority of the written word man was taught to believe impossible legends, conflicting assertions; to take fiction for a fact, a dream for the miraculous revelation of God, an Oriental poem for a grave history of miraculous events, a collection of amatory idyls for a serious discourse 'touching the mutual love of Christ and the Church.'"[29] Whatever the disclaimers, and however subtly it might be put, it came down eventually to this. In Parker's view, the higher criticism denied the historical accuracy, and hence the reliability and indeed the actual authority, of the Bible. It also denied the divinity of Jesus and left Christianity to base itself as well as it could on what remained, namely Christian morals and ethics and a collection of myths.

The mythical view of the Bible, as it came to be focused on the New Testament, contended that the Gospels, filled with miracles and inconsistent with one another on many counts, are collections of stories or myths, the inevitable results of primitive mythmaking by men who were not eyewitnesses or followers of Jesus, but who came later. This view cuts two ways. For those who continued to believe that history is synonymous with factual truth, the mythical view of the Bible undercuts and destroys the authenticity of the Bible because it undercuts its historical basis. In America, Theodore Parker is the leading example of such an historical-minded critic who found the mythical view essentially negative and destructive.

On the other hand, for those writers who treat imaginative writing as closer to the truth of the human heart than mere history, the mythical view of the Bible offered a new way to affirm Scripture as imaginative truth. Coleridge, for one, had perceived this and had argued that by interpreting the myths of the Bible as mere history—however "true"—"the whole Bible had been surrendered to the ridicule of its enemies."[30] In other words, the effort to historicize myth was reductive and led to skepticism. But if one turned the tables and accepted the mythologizing of history as the truer account, then one had a new reason to accept the Bible as true. One also had the groundwork for a revaluation of all imaginative and mythological literature, because mythological literature was now seen to be not distorted history but a genuine branch of imaginative literature, and if one accepted what the imagination conceived as true then one could indeed accept mythology as true.

2. The Affirmation of Myth: Bronson Alcott and the Orphic Mode

Modern acceptance of myth as an authentic form of imaginative truth arose as part of the reaction against the Enlightenment's skeptical rejection of myth as superstition. Indeed, the affirmation of myth is a hallmark of romanticism; the revaluation of myth is just one result of the romantic emphasis on the integrity of what the imagination seizes upon as true. In another way, the resurgence during the early nineteenth century of a new, broader and more philosophical Christianity created a climate favorable to the reassessment of myth as the religious expression of other peoples and times. Though the impulse to accept myth as somehow true is present, at least fitfully in America in a Barlow or a Freneau, it remained for the Transcendentalists to work out a thoroughgoing acceptance of myth and to carry that acceptance over importantly into their writing. Though its roots reach back well into the eighteenth century, it is only from about 1820 on that the various elements making up the characteristic American affirmation of myth begin clearly to emerge and it is only from about 1835 on that these elements creatively coalesce into literary achievement.

Sometime between 1819 and 1824 Emerson read both Lowth and Blackwell, two of the eighteenth-century writers from whom so much of the nineteenth-century revaluation of myth—both skeptical and affirmative—seems to spring. In 1825 appeared a French translation of Friedrich Creuzer's *Symbolik und Mythologie der alten Völker* (1810), an epoch-making work of German classical scholarship which impressively argues that myths were an essentially symbolic—*not* allegorical—mode in which ancient Eastern wisdom had expressed itself.[31] Creuzer's views spread widely in England and America after the French edition (incredibly there never has been an English translation) and may be traced to Emerson through several channels. Edward Everett's lectures, which began in 1820 and which Emerson heard, were laced with references to Creuzer; Degerando's *Histoire comparée des systèmes de philosophie* (2d ed., Paris, 1822–23), which Emerson studied carefully beginning in 1830, is full of Creuzer; and Creuzer's ideas also appear in G. Oegger's *The True Messiah* (published 1842), which had been partially translated earlier (by Elizabeth Peabody), and used in manuscript by Emerson around 1835.[32] Creuzer's views were taken up also by Francis Lieber, and the articles on mythology in the *Encyclopedia Americana* (1829–33) are openly Creuzerian. Finally, Charles Anthon inserted Creuzer's interpretations into the various editions of Lempriere's *Classical Dictionary*, which he (Anthon) began editing in 1825 and finally put his own name to in 1841.

K. O. Müller's *Introduction to a Scientific System of Mythology* also appeared in German in 1825 (English translation, 1844). From this book and from the same author's study of *The Dorians* (translated into English in 1830) came another view of myth, opposed in part to Creuzer but also essentially affirmative to myth itself. Müller, the most eminent classicist of his time, agreed that myths were essentially symbolic representations, but he insisted that Greek myths revealed not transplanted Asian wisdom but the earliest era of Greek history.[33] Müller's ideas strongly marked the writings and conversations of Elizabeth Peabody. Her textbooks on Greek history from

1833 on treat myth seriously as the earliest record of the Greek mind. One of her conversation "classes" went so deeply into the problem that one of the ladies did a translation of another of Müller's books for the occasion. Elizabeth Peabody's own later essay "The Dorian Measure" (1849) links Greek myth to Greek religion and education.[34] For Emerson, who first read Müller's *The Dorians* in 1831, or indeed for anyone in the 1830s, Müller was the preeminent authority on early Greek history. Müller held Greek myths to be imaginative accounts of that history; he considered the myths to be the key to the Greek mind, and rigorous philological analysis the key to myth. From about 1825 on, then, Creuzer's work lent new weight to the effort to understand myth as symbolic form, while Müller's work gave myth research pride of place in investigations into early Greek history.

By 1826 Emerson was reading Thomas Taylor's translation of Plato, with its startling reinterpretation of Greek mythological thought as a symbolic representation of the "perennial philosophy" (which Taylor said originated with Orpheus) that assumes the primacy of mind and sees nature as a system of appearances or images in which a metaphysical order is reflected. In 1829 Coleridge's *Aids to Reflection* was published in New England by James Marsh. The book quickly became important to Emerson and others because of its opposition to Locke and its persuasive call for a philosophy that would be religious and a religion that would be philosophical. Also in 1829, at Andover Theological Seminary, Calvin Stowe reannotated the translation of Lowth's *Lectures on the Sacred Poetry of the Hebrews*. By 1833 Alcott was discovering Taylor's Plato, James Marsh was bringing out his English translation of Herder's *Spirit of Hebrew Poetry* in Vermont, Margaret Fuller was reading and translating some of Goethe's modern poetic reinterpretations of such Greek myths as that of Prometheus, and Elizabeth Peabody was writing textbooks that treat Greek myth sympathetically as Greek religion. It is a far cry from the old charge of "heathen idolatry" and shows how far the new affirmative spirit had penetrated when Miss Peabody could say, in a book intended for children, "The Religion of the Greeks is strikingly different from any other which has been seen on earth. The principle of fear seems hardly recognizable in any of its earlier expressions, whether we consider the festivals and other religious rites, or the earliest records of it in the Homeric poems, which are the most joyous strains that the human mind has ever sent forth toward the Superior Powers."[35]

By the mid thirties, then, the materials for a new view of myth were at hand in New England. The ideas of Lowth, Blackwell, Herder, Taylor, Creuzer, Müller, and Goethe were in the air. Emerson's reading in Oriental myth, going back to Edward Everett's Creuzerian insistence that everything comes from the mysterious East, and becoming especially strong after 1837, together with the impact from 1841 on of Carlyle's brillant interpretation of Nordic myth, added other important bodies of myth to the ferment of mythic ideas. These began to yield literary results as early as 1835, when Alcott began work on his *Psyche,* a modern myth of the Soul, and 1836, when Emerson's lectures on the philosophy of history began to urge that myth is the truest history. It is a great irony that during this same year, 1836, Theodore Parker was beginning work on his translation of De Wette, whose purpose, diametrically opposite to Emerson's, was to dissolve myth by turning the light of history on it. It is one of Emerson's strengths that he saw both sides of the argument. But in order to see clearly the American affirmation of myth at its wholehearted, unalloyed, one-sided fullest, one must turn not to Emerson, but to Alcott.

Amos Bronson Alcott (1799–1888), the gentle mystic who had once been a peddler and who taught school with the passion of a reformer, was known as the American Pestalozzi. He was also known as an impractical dreamer who founded the short-lived model community Fruitlands, an enthusiastic admirer of Thomas Taylor the Platonist, a spreader of Neoplatonism in midwest America, and the "dean" of the Concord School of Philosophy in the 1880s. Alcott was considered by Emerson to have been a great man. Others found him incomprehensible, and part of the problem, no doubt, was Alcott's fondness for the then rather novel terminology of myth. In an essay called "The Garden," which argues that nature is best reflected in the civilized activity of gardening, Alcott presses his argument by claiming "Our human history neither opens in forests nor in cities, but in gardens and orchards whose mythologies are woven into the faith of our race."[36] The mythologies he means are those both of Eden and of Arcadia. Alcott never uses words such as "myth" or "mythology" in pejorative or negative ways. Myth for him is always something fine and creative. Myth is not just the past, either; it is something to which we still have access in these latter days. He points out that "we associate gardens and orchards with the perfect condition of mankind," and he adds, "Gardeners ourselves by birthright, we also mythologize and plant our Edens in the East of us, like our ancestors; the sacredness of earth and heaven still clinging to the tiller of the ground."[37] Even more direct is his praise of Thoreau, whom he calls a modern mythmaker, an assessment Thoreau himself would have been pleased with:

> Like Homer, Hesiod, and the earliest poets, Thoreau saw and treated Nature as a symbolism of the mind, as a physiological theology. His mysticism is alike solid and organic, animal and ideal. He is the mythologist of these last days—reminds more of the ancients in his mode of seeing and saying than any recent naturalist and poet.[38]

Alcott is at home with the terminology of myth, he sees great significance in it, and while he talks about it often in connection with the Greeks or the Bible, he seems usually to be concerned more with the present than with the past. Alcott is always making the case for *modern* myth. Myth is, for Alcott, entitled to serious consideration because it seems to provide a way to reconcile classical and Christian ideas with modern philosophical thought. As the following passage suggests, classical ideas and Christianity can both be dealt with in terms of myth if one thinks of myth as something positive, noble, and compelling—in short, as a high ideal, held with genuine religious conviction.

> The Greek gods had the infirmities of men, and hence stood nearer to men than if they had been conceived as perfect. So the Christian view aids the weakness of man's conception by the humanities of the second person in the Trinity.
> The Greek gods were men ennobled by the attributes of poetry,

exalted by art and religion, never monstrous, as were the Eastern, but shaped in accordance with the ideal of the human figure.

Our gods are partly pagan—composites of Greek, Roman, British; and the process of humanizing them, modifying their forms and attributes from the Puritans, is fast going forward. Ours are not our own. Hebrew largely. Not in accordance with western genius.[39]

At least one reason for Alcott's interest in myth, then, is his sense that new gods, new religions, and new beliefs were in the very process of being formed as he was writing. Indeed, one of the most attractive aspects of New England Transcendentalism is its sense of excitement, adventure, and discovery, its enthusiastic prizing of the momentous present. Myth played an important part in the Transcendental movement, for some of the various thinkers and writers who can be gathered together under that vague label shared a belief that myth was not solely something in the distant past of mankind but was a live force in their modern world.

This is not the place to discuss the Transcendental movement as a whole, but even a treatment of the part played by ideas of myth in the movement necessitates mention of a few general points. As Harold Goddard has put it, Transcendentalism was "the mingling of an old world and a new world element, the blending of an idealistic, Platonistic metaphysics and the Puritan spirit, the fusion—at a high revolutionary temperature—of a philosophy and a character."[40] Leaving aside the complex problems of greater and lesser influence, which differed almost from person to person among the Transcendentalists, it is clear that the movement has an English strain from Coleridge, Carlyle, and Thomas Taylor the Platonist, German strains partly through the above, partly directly through the translated works of Herder, Goethe, and the philosophers of German idealism, Kant, Fichte, and Jacobi, French strains from Constant and Jouffroy and Cousin, and a strong native American strain. The point to be stressed here is the rich profusion, the variety which was scooped up and more or less assimilated by the excited group of New Englanders. Of course the mingling and the fusion were done differently by an Alcott and by a Thoreau, but taken all together, the impressive inpouring of new ideas and the transformations in thought and literature wrought with the new ideas were underlain by a drive to revitalize the religious spirit in the America of the time. As a movement, Transcendentalism was simultaneously religious, philosophical, and literary in emphasis; in its religious aspect it was sufficiently radical to lead a modern scholar to say "Transcendentalism was the French Revolution of American Religion."[41] The description is apt, if we take it to suggest not the destruction but the democratizing and radical transformation of religious ideas. Transcendentalism revitalized Christianity by applying idealist thought to inherited Christian concepts. As spirit manifested itself in matter (or as form evolved through the concrete), so God manifested himself in man. The parallel with the Christian idea of incarnation and with Christ is apparent. Pushed one more step and taken out of history into the present, spirit must manifest itself in all men at all times. All men participate in spirit or—as it could still be called then—divinity. The Christian parallel here is in the implication that all men, not just Christ, are in the incarnated condition of Christ. The second way in which Transcendentalism revitalized the religious spirit of the times follows from and is really only an extension of the above; it was an effort to reconcile classical paganism and Christianity in a modern way which would then enjoy the best aspects of each outlook.

It is with this idea that Bronson Alcott was concerned; his "Orphic Sayings" try to reconcile German philosophy and Christian teachings through Greek forms modified for nineteenth-century America. Myth is the catalyst, the common denominator, and at times the form of Alcott's Orphism. Fifty of his often ridiculed "Orphic Sayings" were printed in The Dial in July 1840, and another fifty the following January. They are not only deliberately mythic, but quite complex and not to be understood apart from Transcendentalism in general and the work of Thomas Taylor the Platonist in particular.

Taylor's five-volume Works of Plato, published in England in 1804, was a major though not always recognized force behind the American Transcendentalist movement. As George Mills Harper says, "In any discussion of the influence of Plato on English and

American literature for the next half century or so [after 1804], we should be mindful of two facts about Taylor's *Plato;* it was the only complete English translation, and it was a book with a mission." That mission, "to convey the idealistic convictions about the nature of man and the universe which he had acquired from a lifetime of reading in the Neoplatonists," was exactly what interested Alcott and Emerson in Taylor.[42] Taylor's numerous books included translations from Proclus, Plotinus, Iamblichus, Porphyry, and it is never forgotten, even in the briefest discussions of Taylor, that he was much more a Neoplatonist of the Alexandrian school than what is now understood as a student of Plato. Alcott and Emerson both read Taylor over and over; they collected his works, inquired after him in England (where he was, it seems, all but forgotten), and spread Taylor's Platonism as far as the middle western states of America, where Plato clubs sprang up in such places as Jacksonville and Quincy, Illinois.[43]

It was Taylor's version of Orphism that had such great mythological significance in Alcott's eyes and which led Alcott to his own attempt to compose Orphic Hymns for his own times. Alcott's own Orphism is not a bizarre aberration or even an unexpected outcropping, but only an extreme expression of the philosophical idealism common at the time, an expression couched in deliberately "mythic" terms.

According to Taylor, the Orphic theology—that is, the idea that can be drawn from the Orphic Hymns—asserts the primacy of mind and regards physical nature as a system of appearances. Taylor's "A Dissertation on the life and theology of Orpheus" contains a characteristic account:

> ... the deity is an immense and perpetually exuberant fountain whose streams originally filled and continually replenish the world with life. Hence the universe contains in its ample bosom all general natures, divinities visible and invisible, the illustrious race of daemons, the noble army of exalted souls, and men rendered happy by wisdom and virtue. According to this theology, the power of universal soul does not alone diffuse itself to the sea, and become bounded by its circumfluent waters, while the wide expanse of air and aether is destitute of life and soul; but

the celestial spaces are filled with souls, supplying life to the stars, and directing their revolutions in everlasting order. So that the celestial orbs in imitation of intellect, which seeks after nothing external, are wisely agitated in perpetual circuit round the central sun. While some things participate of being alone, others of life, and others are endued with sentient powers; some possess the still higher faculty of reason; and lastly others are all life and intelligence.[44]

This is abstruse stuff; high, noble, rarified, and with very little dirt clinging to its roots. Taylor's prose is no doubt a major source of the characteristic vices of the Transcendental style, but if one can look on the above as an effort not only to present the idea of pantheism but to urge us to see it, and to describe the world as the pantheist sees it, not heaving and throbbing with animal life or Dionysian urge but shining and awake with a life of mind or spirit, then one may glimpse the attractiveness of this rather elusive view of the world. Like Plato, Taylor concludes "that there is another certain nature exempt from the passivity and imperfection of bodies, existing not only in the heavens, but in the ever-changing elements, from which the motion of bodies is primarily derived. And this nature is no other than soul, from which animals derive their life and motive power, and which even affords an image of self-motion to the unstable order of bodies."[45]

Here, too, the difficulty of the passage may be forgiven when it is seen that Taylor is questioning the material assumption, common since Hobbes and reasserted by Holbach, that the universe is only matter and motion, both of which have always existed. When he is summarizing, Taylor can be quite straightforward. "Hence we may with reason conclude, that not only the universe, but each of its eternal parts is animated, and endued with intellect, and is, in its capacity similar to the universe."[46] Taylor's argument presents a conception of mind as deity which seems to fit both a pagan and a Christian outlook. The "grand arcanum of the Orphic theology" is finally "that God is all things; which is likewise an Egyptian doctrine, from whence it was derived through Orpheus into Greece; and this sublime truth Plotinus himself proves with his usual sagacity and depth. But here it is necessary to observe, that Orpheus and the

Platonists do not conceive the Deity to be all things, as if he were a divisible, corporeal nature, but that he is all things, because present everywhere, and to every being totally, though more or less intimately present, according to the various gradations and approximations of being."[47] What all this leads to is the perception that the best of pagan philosophy and its mythological expression and the best of Christian theology come to the same point, that God is all things.

Alcott's "Orphic Sayings" do not set out to demonstrate the above: they take it for granted and proceed from there. Alcott is not a chronicler of divinity; he takes the idea of pantheism seriously and thus sets out to record the appearances of deity in his own life and his own times. He bears witness, and the form in which the witness is expressed is half that of Orphic Hymns and half that of biblical Scripture. His "Orphic Sayings" are clearly intended as new scripture, resulting from new revelation. They are filled with a sense of the divine, but it is made quite clear that the divine is a quite common appearance. Alcott deals in the deific, but it is a daily, all-purpose concept, the modern equivalent of which might be expressed as "the sense of the sacred" as opposed to the profane. The third saying shows Alcott's workaday idea of deification as well as his undeniable sincerity.

> Hope deifies man; it is the apotheosis of the soul; the prophecy and fulfillment of her destinies. The nobler her aspirations, the sublimer her conceptions of the Godhead. As the man, so his God; God is his idea of excellence; the complement of his own being.[48]

What looks like merely a standard Unitarian and Humanist earnestness becomes here a fresh way of saying man creates god in his own image. This is not meant satirically of course; the power of creating or becoming godlike is the source of Alcott's sense of the divine. This is strongly expressed in the tenth saying, on "Apotheosis":

> Every soul feels at times her own possibility of becoming a God; she cannot rest in the human, she aspires after the Godlike. This instinctive tendency is an authentic augury of its own fulfillment. Men shall become Gods. Every act of admiration, prayer, praise, worship, desire, hope, implies and predicts the future apotheosis of the soul.

Saying number thirty-nine, called "Embryon," is put more simply, and with an effort at eloquent pithiness. "Man is a rudiment and embryon of God: eternity shall develop in him the divine image."

Like some other Transcendentalists, Alcott found it difficult to express or explain adequately some of his ideas. What he struggled for, often without success, was a way to demonstrate and prove his intuitive convictions about the primacy of mind or spirit. In saying number thirty-one, on "Calculus," he puts his idea of deity or deific energy and at the same time shows his awareness of the need for a better means of expressing the difficult, easily mocked doctrines of his Yankee Platonism.

> We need, what Genius is unconsciously seeking, and, by some daring generalization of the universe, shall assuredly discover, a spiritual calculus, a novum organon, whereby nature shall be divined in the soul, the soul in God, matter in spirit, polarity resolved into unity; and that power which pulsates in all life, animates and builds all organizations, shall manifest itself as one universal deific energy, present alike at the outskirts and center of the universe, whose center and circumference are one. . . .

What Alcott does not quite say, though it is hinted at when he admiringly calls Thoreau or Elizabeth Peabody a mythologist, is that myth is the "spiritual calculus" of "universal deific energy."

Though it is not put so bluntly, this is the idea that animates the last three of the first group of "Orphic Sayings." Number forty-eight, on "Beauty," begins with what the modern reader quickly recognizes as Alcott's standard attempt to fuse Neoplatonism and Christian ideas; here the Christian idea is that of fall or lapse:

> All departures from perfect beauty are degradations of the divine image. God is the one type, which the soul strives to incarnate in all organizations. Varieties are historical. The one form embosoms all form; all having a common likeness at the base of difference. Human heads are images, more or less perfect, of the soul's or God's head. But the divine features do not fix in flesh; in the coarse and brittle clay. Beauty is fluent, art of highest order represents her always in flux, giving fluency and motion to bodies solid and immovable to sense. The line of beauty symbolizes motion.

Something quite remarkable grows out of this seemingly routine fusion of Platonic and Christian versions of lapse. It is as though Alcott had rediscovered the whole idea of metamorphosis. Alcott's language stresses change; "flux," "fluency," "incarnate," and "embosom" all work to create the idea of some essential breath or spirit passing from one form to another. What Alcott would call "Deific energy" is not fixed; it is always becoming, transforming, changing, evolving, or devolving.

The argument of saying forty-eight is carried on in the next. In fact, the last three sayings are a unit, forming a short essay on modern metamorphosis. Forty-nine is called "Transfiguration" and concerns itself directly and explicitly with the process of transformation:

> Never have we beheld a purely human face; as yet, the beast, demon, rather than the man or God, predominate in its expression. The face of the soul is not extant in flesh. Yet she has a face, and virtue and genius shall one day reveal her celestial lineaments: a beauty, a majesty shall then radiate from her that shall transcend the rapt ideal of love and hope. So have I seen glimpses of this spiritual glory, when, inspired by some thought or sentiment, she was transfigured from the image of the earthly to that of the heavenly, the ignoble melting out of her features, lost in the supersensual life.

Alcott's apprehension of change, transformation, or metamorphosis is clearer here, though still put in completely abstract terms. The center of Alcott's conception of metamorphosis, the reason for dwelling on it and using it to conclude the first group of sayings, is the need to search out and distinguish what is divine, what human, and what bestial. Rather than argue that the human contains in it both the divine and the bestial—a rather static conception—Alcott approaches the problem as one of transformation from one state or form to another. And, interestingly, in the final saying Alcott changes his mode and expresses his conception of metamorphosis in mythical and imaginative terms. For once he rescued an idea from the barrenness of neo-Alexandrian abstraction:

Know, O man, that your soul is the Prometheus who, receiving the divine fire, builds up this majestic statue of clay and moulds it in the deific image, the pride of gods, the model and analogon of all forms. He chiselled that godlike brow, arched those mystic temples from whose fanes she herself looks forth, formed that miraculous globe above, and planted that sylvan grove below; graved those massive blades yoked in armed powers; carved that heaven-containing bosom, wreathed those puissant thighs, and hewed those stable columns, diffusing over all the grandeur, the grace of his own divine lineaments, and delighting in this cunning work of his hand. Mar not its beauty, spoil not its symmetry, by the deforming lines of lust and sin; dethroning the divinity incarnated therein, and transforming yourself into the Satyr and the beast.

There is a compelling quality to this baroque, romantic language which is redolent of Victor Hugo.[49] Alcott here combined the mythologist and the reformer; the passage starts with a remarkable vision of metamorphosis—physically imagined—of man into god. Despite the moralistic ending, however, the passage as a whole suggests that Alcott really did rediscover the live idea behind the classical, Ovidian concept of metamorphosis. It would be Hawthorne who would give it a satisfactory modern literary form, but it was Alcott who showed the way, who suggested how the modern reformer or moralist could use the classical myths of transformation to illuminate modern problems of internal, perhaps psychological, metamorphoses. Alcott's weakness is not a lack of ideas, but rather a deficiency of concretizing imagination and a pallid style of writing. He prefers to discuss the idea of metamorphosis in philosophical terms most of the time, rather than try to imagine a story through which the idea could work itself out in concrete human terms. He preferred abstract reasoning to literature, not knowing apparently that the "mythology" he so admired in Thoreau was not possible except when literary expression succeeded in embodying those philosophical ideas. Like his beloved Neoplatonists, he was usually content to write *about* myth, leaving the actual creation of myth to others.

Yet Alcott did try on occasion to do something that looks very much like the deliberate creation of myth. In the manuscript versions of a book that began as observations on the birth and development of his first daughter, Anna, and that grew into the odd narrative called *Psyche,* Alcott blended his reading and his experience in a book about the origins and growth of the soul. It is beyond question that certain books were important to him. He himself laid great stress on the importance of his having read Coleridge's *Aids to Reflections* in 1832 and Thomas Taylor's translations of Plato's *Cratylus, Phaedo, Timaeus,* and *Parmenides* in 1833. He continued to read and reread Coleridge and Taylor's Plato for the rest of his life, but, as Odell Shepard notes, Alcott read mainly to find extension and corroboration of his own ideas. "As a reader, Bronson Alcott had neither talent nor training, so that he was obliged to get on as best he could with a thin streak of genius."[50] This thin streak stamped all his writing and thinking, it fused his reading with his daily life, and it may be observed at work in the successive books or versions of one book which he began to produce in 1831, when Anna was born. The first manuscript was called "A Record of Observations on the Phenomena of Life as Developed in the History of an Infant During the First Year of its Existence," and it is full of detailed comment, much of which bears out a more or less Lockeian view of mind, then generally accepted, that the child is an empty vessel, a blank slate on which experience begins to record impressions taken in through the senses.[51] This manuscript was reworked into one called *Psyche or the Breath of Childhood,* which Alcott wrote from June 24, 1835 to June 24, 1836. In this work, childhood has become an emblem of the spiritual. "The infant is to all an emblem of goodness," Alcott wrote, in language that seeks to modify, but does not openly contradict Locke.[52] Later, in the same manuscript, the child has progressed from being an emblem of revelation to being the Revelation itself. As the following passage shows, Alcott was clearly and consciously aware that he was engaged in penning scripture, or as we might call it, in mythopoesis.

Of the various media of Revelation, the child is, perhaps, the most significant of all. The *history of a child,* including its inner as well as outer movements, with its relations both spiritual and material and the varying phenomena of the sensual and the supersensual—this would be a

Revelation indeed—an Incarnate Word to humanity. We have the history of an adult in the life of Jesus. In the Gospels both his inner and outer experience is given. The supremacy of the spiritual comes forth to our senses. The Word is incarnated, and man looketh on the face of his brother in the flesh, seeing it in the image of the Divine Life that he inheriteth. Yet the revelation of childhood hath not yet been promulgated. The "eyes have not seen nor the hands yet handled the Word of God" as presented in infancy. To the penning of this gospel let me apply myself.[53]

The central point here is that the child is more than a mere emblem of the spiritual, the child is in fact the vehicle of the spiritual, the form through which Spirit manifests itself. Alcott's final version, called *Psyche an Evangele,* finished in 1838, is a narrative working-out of this idea. It is no less than a new myth of the soul. Not content to follow Apuleius' version of the story of Psyche, Alcott took ideas from Coleridge and from Taylor's Plato, and, with his own daughter's growth and development before his eyes, he tried to write a modern myth of Psyche as an inspiration—a scripture— for his own times.

There is no model or parallel for this extraordinary piece of writing that I know of in American literature of this era. But Alcott's fable, when set beside certain productions of German romanticism, such as Klingsohr's Fairy Tale in Novalis's *Henry of Ofterdingen* (1802; tr. by J. Owen and published at Cambridge, Mass. in 1842), would seem to be a perfectly explicable work of romantic idealism. Alcott's *Psyche an Evangele* has never been published. (The opening chapter is printed in an appendix to this volume.) The trouble, as Alcott himself knew, was that he, like Emerson, distrusted the adequacy of language itself. In a letter to Sophia Peabody, Alcott wrote, with his own *Psyche* in mind, that his words "have a significance borrowed from their inmost being; and are to be interpreted, not by ordinary and popular acceptation, but by the genius of the individual that utters them. These [especially gifted minds] have a significance of their own. They commune not with words but in spite of them. Ordinary minds mistake them. For they cannot be revealed through the illusory medium of words."[54] *Psyche* has a sort of late eighteenth-century quality in its diction, its capitalization, and its vague resemblance to William Blake's prophetic works. It is written in an unusual style to be sure, but we can indeed perceive its main lines through his incantatory and unliterate language. No longer is the child a mere emblem of spirit; the child is now the important thing. To give an adequate account of the manifestation of spirit as child requires nothing less than a new myth, a narrative fable of Psyche in Concord, a modern scripture, a gospel of childhood.

It is not quite fair to leave Alcott without emphasizing that myth touched him as it touched a few others of his time, such as Emerson or Margaret Fuller, not just in their ideas and writings, but in their lives. As Alcott understood the story, Orpheus was a bringer of civilization, one who could charm beasts and draw the very rivers out of their courses by the sweetness of his song. As a teacher of the young, as the reformer who founded "Fruitlands," as "dean" of the Concord School of Philosophy, and even or perhaps especially as a gardener, Alcott lived the life of a religious teacher and philosopher. Emerson thought him a sage and a prophet, recognizing in him a man bringing a gospel. Judged by what he tried to be rather than by what he actually wrote or accomplished—and Emerson's judgment here must be respected—Alcott was a kind of minor modern Orpheus. But he was an Orpheus of intention, for he lacked the instrumental imagination. Alcott could say, grandly, that "the world is but the symbol of mind, and speech a mythology woven of both."[55] He himself never published his major effort. Final judgment will have to wait, however, until his *Psyche* has had its critics. That he, along with other Transcendentalists, was trying to make myths is undeniable. Even the enemies of the "movement" saw that much. Noah Porter noted in 1842 that "Transcendentalism was rather unbelief than belief. Subtle, refining, symbolizing all living truths and real facts into inert and powerless mythi."[56] The description fits Alcott and other minor Transcendentalists, and with a few exceptions it characterizes the literary side of Transcendentalism up to 1842. But the main work of Emerson and that of Thoreau and Whitman, not to mention the counter-Transcendental writing of Hawthorne and

Melville, cannot be so dismissed as "inert and powerless" myths. Avoiding Parker's one-sided rejection of myth and Alcott's too-easy acceptance of it, these writers pursued various middle courses, exploring the problem of myth both skeptically and affirmatively at the same time. The result was a powerful, vital literature which deliberately and extensively used myth as subject, as form, and as process.

Three

Emerson

1. The Quality of Mythic Experience

Emerson once noted it would be "a good subject for book or lecture . . . to read the riddle of ancient Mythology." He saw clearly and said quite simply that "we need a theory or interpretation of Mythology." But it was not only ancient mythology and myth theory that interested him. In the middle of one of Margaret Fuller's Conversations when she was defending the ancient myths, Margaret said: "the age of the Greeks was the age of Poetry; ours was the age of Analysis. *We* could not create a Mythology," and Emerson had broken in to ask "Why not? We had still better material."[1] Much of Emerson's best work is just such an attempt to fashion a new mythology out of new materials, a new mythology which would be an important part of that "original relation to the universe" he wanted for his own generation. Though he wrote no essay called "Myth," the subject is thus central to his thought. His conception of history is fundamentally mythic, his understanding of the process of change, especially organic change, is most forcefully expressed in the myth-derived concept of metamorphosis, and his book of modern heroes, *Representative Men,* is in part the result of his efforts to create a worthy mythology for the America of his day.

Emerson was remarkably well read in myth and mythological scholarship, and from his college days on he was thoroughly familiar with both skeptical and affirmative views of myth.[2] The side of Emerson accepting myth as something deeply and importantly true is the side that can be traced back through Taylor, Creuzer, Goethe, K. O. Müller, and Herder to Lowth and Blackwell. Emerson had read all of these writers and many more, but however Emerson's sympathetic interest in myth may have evolved, the form it took was characteristically concerned with the relation of the individual to history. Over and over, Emerson strove to enter imaginatively into the myth-creating mind, to recover for himself the kind of empathic openness to experience that his reading told him had marked the early mythopoeic ages. From the beginning, then, Emerson was interested in mythic thought as an imaginative means of projecting oneself into the past, of participating in the process of history, to understand what was important about the past for any given individual.

In an interesting and unusual early effort to determine whether man can exist in solitude, Emerson tried to recreate, imaginatively, the condition of utter solitude which must have existed at the beginning of things, projecting himself and his reader backward into Adam, prototype of the solitary man.

> We must quit the city, the house, the cleared road, the simplest improvement of civilization, and stand up on the banks of the river which no dams have confined, amid woods which no axe hath felled, in a solitude which none partakes but the invisible Being who hath just now made it. I think that person who stands there alone among the trees with his eye on the waters and his hand upon his lips—is an object of interest. His name is Adam.[3]

Emerson was nineteen when he wrote that; it shows clearly a sympathetic willingness to understand the past by entering into it in imagination and trying to relive it. Emerson is not usually conceded to have had much interest in the past, but his repeated efforts to grasp the presentness of some past event suggest that he was indeed interested in historical process, in how certain religious attitudes had arisen, how gods and myths originated. His imagination ran to both Christian and pagan examples. In the same year as the description of Adam on the riverbank, Emerson also noted that he "who wanders in the woods perceives how natural it was to pagan imagination to find gods in every deep grove & by each fountain head." Such statements are not surprising perhaps in one who believes that myth arose from early perception of nature. What is a little surprising, though, are the turns of phrase and the unmistakable tone of delighted discovery suggesting that such moments of insight were not just academic exercises but intimately meaningful for Emerson in a most personal way. In another early notebook entry he writes, "Joy comes, but is Speedily Supplanted by grief & we tremble at the approach of transient adversities like the mists of the morning fearful indeed & many, but fairies are in them & White Ladies beckoning."[4]

Emerson obviously had precociously grasped the idea that any serious understanding of the past would have to reanimate what seemed dead, regarding as present and unfinished what one had previously thought of as past and done. "It is pleasant when you hear in autumn the song of the reaper which is a spontaneous expression of joy springing directly from the heart, to revert to former ages and to find in the earliest gathering of the harvest the same pleasant music from those whose bones have slept for ages and whose song hath been echoed back at every annual labour for thousands of years and is echoed back today."[5] Only in this way does the past become alive. Only through this imaginative habit of sympathetic participation can myth cease to be old curious folktales and come to be immediate personal experience. Emerson knew this so well that he could both describe and experience the process at the same time. And where some saw mythic religious conceptions springing from fear, Emerson saw something quite different. He could imagine that in primitive times "some fortunate youth bounding over the mountains & enlivened by the splendour of a summer morn, may occasionally feel the expansion of social thoughts within him which for want of other objects will fix upon inanimate objects—upon the mountains or the clouds & endow them with life & thought, or on the Sun & call him God of Day." He could suggest such congenial conditions for the creation of myth, and he himself tried to write a bit of Arthurian legend in which "Arthur wandered in the wood of Cornwall as the day dawned and, by the better vision of his eye, he discerned, as he passed among the trees, the daucing fayries in companies, that had not yet departed before the face of the sun."[6]

He did the same thing also in modern terms: "How does Nature deify us with a few cheap elements. Give me health and a Day & I possess more magnificence than emperors covet. The Morning sky before sunrise is my Assyria; the sunset my Paphos & unimaginable realms of Faerie; the night is my Germany."[7] This is a complex state of mind, one that could easily be interpreted as mystical—or even just misty. But this and other passages reflect experiences which are deliberately put in a context of myth, and are understandable if thought of as a deliberate effort at imaginative or sympathetic participation in the creating of myth. These passages all have an excited sense of being present at the creation. Emerson was also conscious of such moments in the lives of others. Shortly after the death of his brother Charles, Emerson wrote:

> He sympathized wonderfully with all objects & natures, & as by a spiritual ventriloquism threw his mind into them, which appeared in the warm & genial traits by which he again pictured them to the eye. I find him saying to E. H. [Elizabeth Hoar] 3 April 1834 "I do not know but one of the ancient metamorphoses will some day happen to me, & I shall shoot into a tree, or flow in a stream. I do so lose my human nature & join myself to that which is without. Today even Goethe would have been satisfied with the temper in which I became identified with what I saw, a part of what was around me."[8]

The image of a respectable New Englander shooting up into a tree or flowing off in a stream is delightfully silly, but of course the point, as Charles and his brother both saw, is one's sympathetic identification with the world around one. Difficult to express, it is often experienced as a mystical trance, as in Yeats's "Vacillation," for example. Emerson usually turned to myth—or the mythic experience or mood—to record such moments:

> Come out of your warm angular house resounding with few voices into the chill grand instantaneous night, with such a Presence as a full moon in the clouds, & you are struck with poetic wonder. In the instant you leave behind all human relations, wife, mother, & child, & live only with the savages—water, air, light, carbon, lime, & granite. I think of Kuhleborn. I become a moist cold element. "Nature grows over me." Frogs pipe; waters far off tinkle; dry leaves hiss; grass bends & rustles, &

I have died out of the human world & come to feel a strange cold, aqueous, terraqueous, aerial, ethereal sympathy & existence. I sow the sun & moon for seeds.[9]

It is scarcely necessary to know that Kuhleborn is the water spirit uncle of Undine in La Motte-Fouqué's story in order to grasp the experience Emerson is describing. Indeed, the reference to Kuhleborn could be deleted and the passage would lose nothing. At any rate, it is the experience and not the label that matters most. Myth matters because it provides or suggests a form, a language for expressing those remarkable moments when we feel somehow greater or other than our everyday selves. Emerson's personal acquaintance with the internal working, the "feel," of the mythmaking mood helped him to use myth in his writing in a creative way. For Emerson as for Wordsworth, myth was "authentic tidings of invisible things."

Myth was for Emerson an almost direct expression of that great original power or energy that lay behind and created all appearances. As early as 1822, Emerson noted that "the idea of *power* seems to have been every where at the bottom of the theology." The kind of power he had in mind was present in mythology as well as theology, and could be seen, for example, in the terrific disparity between ordinary mortals and gods. Commenting on a drawing by Flaxman, Emerson noted that

Orestes supplicates Apollo whilst the Furies sleep on the threshold in Flaxman's drawing. The face of the God expresses a shade of regret & compassion for the sufferer, but is filled with the calm conviction of disparity & irreconcileableness of the two spheres. He is born into other politics, into the eternal & beautiful; the man at his feet asks for his interest in turmoils of the earth, into which his nature cannot enter. And the Eumenides there lying express pictorially this disparity. The god is surcharged with his divine destiny.[10]

Emerson sees in Apollo a calm superiority of power so great it needn't be demonstrated. It is typical of the way myth affected Emerson's imagination that he should apply the myth to himself.

Accordingly, a short time after the above, we find Emerson trying to encourage the Apollo in himself. "A preoccupied attention is the only answer to the importunate frivolity of other people. An attention, & to an aim which makes their wants frivolous. This is a god's answer, & leaves no appeal & no hard thoughts."[11]

2. The Verdict of Reason

Balancing this natural sympathy for myth in Emerson's mind was a streak of cool skepticism. At various times in his career, Emerson was dubious about the religious origins of myth, disturbed by the misuses of myth, and uncertain as to whether myth really was a vehicle for truth. In a comment probably written around 1820, we find the young Emerson grinding away like a good Christian polemicist at heathen superstition. "Examine the gods of all barbarous nations, and you will find that their characters offend against every article of Moral law; you will find thieves, murderers, adulterers, & liars, enshrined in heaven by the zeal of ignorance; and these motley deities form the best illustration of the religious influence which a savage life promotes." Five or six years later Emerson was debunking a wide range of mythological figures with the supercilious swagger of a Yankee *philosophe*. "If Hercules & Ajax & many a Templar & knight & titled brigand of the middle ages were to be born again it is plain that they must descend from the dignified condition the ignorance & fear of men assigned them & be content to take up the cudgels in a common street with the lowest of mankind for their competitors & the applause of alehouses for their reward."[12] These are cheap shots; the easy sneer gives them away. But such comments at least show that from an early point in his career Emerson was sometimes inclined to dismiss myth, just as he was sometimes moved to try to relive or re-create it. He could also use myth as a tool for social criticism. Assuming that a people's heaven in their mythology represents their idea of perfection, Emerson compares Greek, Teutonic, and Persian heavens for what they reveal about those peoples. Here the negative view of myth is more subtle. It is assumed that each mythology is a limited, culture-bound reflection of the humdrum aspirations of a group of people. After reviewing the Greek and Roman views of heaven, Emerson turns to the Teutonic, about which he remarks:

> They too had a mythology, they had a *war*like heaven; a paradise of the strong, a glorified gymnasium, fresh air, fine horses, robust good health & good game—filled up to the brim all their conceptions of wellbeing; blood & thunder in the background of Valhalla. Then go a little further Southeast, & you shall find the vestiges of the Persian & Turkish idea of perfection. They saw in the clouds all voluptuous forms; they asked for nothing but women; away with the trumpet, away with virtue, enough of that in the earth. They wanted nothing but coffee, tobacco, opium & sensual love. [13]

This is a sociological view of myth, an intellectual tool for discussing a society. It is notable that most of Emerson's appreciative comments on myth concern its effect on the individual, his negative comments generally applying to groups.

Emerson did not use mythic and theological terminology carelessly. For example, he once bluntly wrote: "the words 'I am on the eve of a revelation,' & such like, when applied to the influx of truth in ordinary life, sound sad & insane in my ear." This may have been a comment wrung from him in his exasperation over some of Alcott's writing, but whatever the cause, it shows him to have had a clear critical sense of when one should use such terms and when one should not. Emerson accepted mythology no more uncritically than he did revelation. A good example is his discussion of demonology. The problem is that if the invisible world is accepted as real, as it must be in any thoroughgoing Platonism or idealism, then how can one avoid accepting as real the "underside of theology," which is demonology. Emerson's compact answer to this problem occurs in a journal passage written in 1839 and incorporated into his lecture on "Demonology" later.

> Demonology seems to me to be the intensation of the individual nature, the extension of this beyond its due bounds & into the domain of the infinite & universal. The faith in a Genius; in a family Destiny; in a

ghost; in an amulet; is the projection of that instinctive care which the individual takes of his individuality beyond what is meet & into the region where the individuality is forever bounded by generic, cosmic, & universal laws. . . . The divine will, or, *the eternal tendency to the good of the whole, active in every atom, every moment,* —is the only will that can be supposed predominant a single hairbreadth beyond the lines of individual action & influence as known to experience; by a ghost, a Jupiter, a fairy, a devil, and not less a saint, an angel & the God of popular religion, as of Calvinism, & Romanism is an aggrandized and monstrous individual will. The divine will, such as I describe it, is spiritual. These other things, though called spiritual, are not so, but only demonological; & fictions.[14]

Mythology is here included among those things that are sometimes mistakenly thought to be spiritual. This is, in fact, a sweeping attack on mythology and demonology together as emanating from the individual will though posing as a divine or at least as a non-human will. From this point of view mythology, like demonology, misrepresents the way things really are. Mythology if not a distortion is a veil. In another place Emerson puts it more simply, saying, "the Father is a convenient name & image to the affections; but drop all images if you wish to come to the elements of your thought, & use as mathematical words as you can. . . ." From about 1838 through the mid-1840s there runs through Emerson's thought a persistent streak of this sort of distrust of myth as a falsifying veil over nature, while during these same years Emerson was elaborating, in other notes and essays, a view of myth as the necessary language of nature, as the only means by which to express certain kinds of elusive experiences and complex truths. Much of the skeptical attitude of these years was directed at what Emerson now habitually referred to as "Christian mythology." He would for example note down that "Christianity must quickly take a niche that waits for it in the Pantheon of the Past, and figure as Mythology henceforward." But it goes deeper than mere anti-Christian sentiment. It seems clear from such comments as the following that Emerson had moments when he simply distrusted the adequacy of mythology to express anything important. "Does it not seem imperative that the

Soul should find an articulate utterance in these days on man and religion? All or almost all that I hear at Church is mythological."

But Emerson was far too aware of the many possible ways to look at myth to resort often to such a flat, uncompromising negation. In a mood of less sweeping condemnation, he sometimes considered mythologies as systems that were once but are no longer believed, and he included Christianity as just one example.

> In talking with William Ellery Channing on Greek mythology as it was believed in Athens, I could not help feeling how fast the key to such possibilities is lost, the key to the faith of men perishes with the faith. A thousand years hence it will seem less monstrous that those acute Greeks believed in the fables of Mercury & Pan, than that these learned & practical nations of modern Europe & America, these physicians, metaphysicians, mathematicians, critics, & merchants, believed this Jewish apologue of the poor Jewish boy, & how they contrived to attach that accidental history to the religious idea.[15]

This comment is unusual for Emerson. It sounds very much as though he had been reading D. F. Strauss or Theodore Parker. Whatever the immediate spur, he rarely allowed this sharp edge of rationalist criticism into his published work. It is interesting to see that virtually all the disparaging things he said about myth are embedded in contexts where Emerson affirms the historical school, rather than his own characteristic view of the past as unimportant except as it is still a felt pressure on the individual. In other words, Emerson's disparagement of myth coincides with untypical moments of enthusiasm for the conventional view of history. In 1846 Emerson still entertained such moments, and when he spoke of an essay he was projecting having as one of its merits a "resolute rejection of the faded or regnant superstitions, as of the Christian mythology, of the agricultural, commercial, and social delusions which pass current in men's mouths, but have long lost all reality," he meant it as an exercise in debunking.

But in general, Emerson called popular delusions "superstitions" and reserved the word "mythology" for something more complex. In a list of the "Superstitions of our Age" drawn up in 1847, he included "the fear of Catholicism; the fear of pauperism; the fear of immigration; the fear of manufacturing interests; the fear of radicalism or democracy; And faith in the steam engine." Superstition usually involved fear; mythology was, even to Emerson in his skeptical moods, a phenomenon that involved belief. The most perceptive of Emerson's skeptical estimates of myth is a brilliant prefiguring of Marx and also of the particularly twentieth-century meaning of myth as reigning ideology. "History," he wrote in his journal in 1848,

> . . . is the group of the types or representative men of any age at only the distance of convenient vision. We can see the arrangement of masses, and distinguish the forms of the leaders. Mythology is the same group at another remove, now at a pictorial distance. . . . The forms and faces can no longer be read, but only the direction of the march, and the result; so that the names of the leaders are now mixed with the ends for which they strove. Distance is essential. Therefore we cannot say what is our mythology. We can only see that the industrial, mechanical, the parliamentary, commercial, constitute it, with socialism; and Astor, Watt, Fulton, Arkwright, Peel, Russell, Rothschild, George Stephenson, Fourier are our mythological names.

Emerson is here using myth as a way to frame a critique of the invisible assumptions of his own times. From this viewpoint, myth is not so much a term of praise or disparagement as it is a way of describing pervasive social and cultural ideas and beliefs.[16]

It cannot be too strongly emphasized, as we turn to Emerson's more imaginative uses of myth, that his willingness upon occasion to doubt, to look on the other side of the question, did not prevent him from valuing myth. Far from it. His skeptical and critical analyses helped balance out his frequent enthusiasm for myth, and his acceptance of myth for some purposes and in some contexts deserves more careful attention precisely because it was a tested, not an unthinking, acceptance. In fact, Emerson usually avoided dealing with myth as flatly true or false. There is an obvious sense of the word "myth" which then as now carried unavoidable overtones of "false," and there was a general sense then as now that "myth" along with "fiction" and "poetry" was a word you could not usefully apply to things which were expected to be historically "true"—yet myth, like fiction and poetry, had uses, values, and a reality of its own. Emerson's greatest achievements vis-à-vis myth all stemmed from his persistent efforts to utilize his understanding of mythic processes to lead the individual to fresh ways of thinking about history, about change, and about great men.

3. Myth and History

Emersonian thought is usually understood to have a strong antihistorical bias. This is true only in a limited sense. Emerson did indeed distrust the flat-footed historical literalism that accompanied biblical literalism in such writers as Humphrey Prideaux or Sharon Turner, and he distrusted any view of history that tended to praise the past at the expense of the present or to intimidate living men by magnifying dead ones. In these attitudes Emerson is very close to Alfred North Whitehead's insistence that "no more deadly harm can be done to young minds than by depreciation of the present," or in Whitehead's urging that we try to gain a *sense* of the past rather than an inert knowledge of it. Instead of memorizing the fact that Caesar died in 44 B.C., we should try to imagine that the cry "Caesar is murdered" was once still an unsubstantiated rumor flying the streets of Rome.[17] Sharply aware of what W. J. Bate has called "the burden of the past," Emerson was, for example, oppressed by the 420,000 volumes on the twelve miles of shelves in the British Museum when he visited that library in 1848; he was moved to complain that "it is impossible to read from the glut of books." It was precisely because Emerson had read so much history that he reacted strongly against any approach to history which extolled the golden past while looking down on the present as a degenerate time. For such a point of view he had only scorn, and he borrowed a phrase from Byron to describe these seekers-after "the unreached paradise of our despair." Emerson was against any view of history that did not emphasize its usefulness. As he viewed everything else, so he saw history as valuable only if it helped the individual to self-realization and self-reliance.

Emerson's own notebooks and journals and his early lectures, especially those he delivered under the general heading "Philosophy of History," bear ample witness to his extensive historical reading and to the overriding interest early in his career in establishing a right view of history. In such passages as the following one can see him working toward his characteristic position by studying rather than by rejecting history:

> I think it will be the effect of insight to show nearer relations than are yet known between remote periods of history & the present moment. . . . Homer, Greece, Rome, & Egypt certainly have come nearer to us for Bentley, Wolf, Niebuhr, Müller, Winckelmann & Champollion.[18]

By the time of Emerson's first series of essays (1841), the problem of history had become paramount. His journal notes show that the essay on "History" was planned all along as the crucial first essay. And indeed, the much more famous second essay, "Self Reliance," cannot be properly understood without the first essay's preparation of the ground. The two essays are on the same theme, that of the relation between the individual and society or history. The emphasis is different in each essay, of course, but an understanding of one's relation to history was a necessary first step to self-reliance. The main purpose of the essay on history is to undercut the ordinary, overly respectful, and, Emerson thought, disheartening view of history and to suggest a more useful approach. Emerson was trying to persuade his readers to turn to nature rather than to the past, to ask for historical insight rather than historical details, and to trust myth and biography instead of chronological accounts of battles and leaders.

Emerson's reason for wanting to dislodge the customary deferential view of history is always perfectly apparent. "The Centuries are Conspirators against the sanity & majesty of the soul. The greatness of Greece consists in this, that no Greece preceded it." If we understand the real lesson of Greek history, we will not tell over again the Greek's exploits, but we will seek to re-create for ourselves the conditions which made possible the exploits of the Greeks, so that we can get on with our own exploits.[19]

Emerson argued for nature over history, on grounds of superior antiquity and prior influence, pointing out that "the knowledge of nature is *most permanent,* clouds & grass are older antiquities than pyramids or Athens. . . . Goethe's plant a genuine creation." Emerson prefers the organic principle illustrated in Goethe's concept of the *Urpflanz* to the monumental principle represented by the pyramids. Just as the past needs to be replaced by nature in our thinking, so the dry recital of facts must give way to myth and biography. Thus Emerson could say of Aeschylus' *Prometheus Bound,* "it is a part of the history of Europe. The Mythology thinly veils authentic history & there is the story of the invention of the mechanic Arts."[20]

The great thing was to replace a sense of pastness with a sense of presentness. "All inquiry into antiquity . . . is simply & at last the desire to do away with this wild, savage, preposterous *Then,* & introduce in its place the *Now:* it is to banish the *Not Me* & supply the *Me.*" As he talks about the change, his examples show why he thought either myth or biography was the right medium for such a change. "We say Paradise was; Adam fell; the Golden Age; & the like. We mean man is not as he ought to be; but our way of painting this is on Time, and we say *Was.*"[21]

Just as he insisted that "our admiration of the Antique is not admiration of the Old but of the Natural," so he argued that history properly understood is not chronicle but myth, and he made the point in several different ways. First he argued (and here Emerson's reading of Müller lies back of the argument) that earliest history is known to us chiefly through myth.

Time dissipates to shining ether the solid angularity of facts. No anchor, no cable, no fences avail to keep a fact a fact. Babylon and Troy and Tyre and even early Rome are passing already into fiction. The Garden of Eden, the Sun standing still in Gibeon, is poetry thenceforward to all nations. Who cares what the fact was when we have thus made a constellation of it . . . ?[22]

The facts behind these stories, whatever they were, are now lost, but Emerson's point is that it does not matter. The story and its point are more significant to us than any bit of local history could ever be. Emerson argued a similar case for the story of Prometheus. "Besides its primary value as the first chapter of the history of Europe, (the mythology thinly veiling authentic facts, the invention of the mechanic arts, and the migration of colonies) it gives the history of religion with some closeness to the faith of later ages. Prometheus is the Jesus of the old mythology." Myth provides the meaning of history. "Look then at history as the illustration by facts of all the spiritual elements. Stand before each of its tablets with the faith, Here is one of my coverings: Under this heavy & odious mask did my Proteus nature hide itself."[23] The full force of this is apparent only when it is read in the context of the opening argument of "History." Emerson starts by saying: "There is one mind common to all individual men. . . . Of the works of this mind history is the record." Furthermore, as each man participates in the common mind, so "the whole history is in [each] man," and "it is all to be explained from individual experience." Myth makes history from bare chronicles, and turns lists into story; it renders history in terms of persons and actions, brings out what is human in history, and provides each reader with his "own secret biography" as he finds that "one after another he comes up in his private adventures with every fable of Aesop, of Homer, of Hafiz, of Ariosto, of Chaucer, of Scott." Not chronicle but myth contains the truth we need. "The beautiful fables of the Greeks," says Emerson, "are universal verities," and he then gives a long illustration, starting with Prometheus, working through two pages of examples and ending with an analysis of Proteus in which Emerson epitomizes the art of reading history through the glass of myth.

> The philosophical perception of identity through endless mutations of
> form, makes him [man] know the Proteus. What else am I who laughed
> or wept yesterday, who slept last night like a corpse and this morning

stood and ran? And what see I on any side but the transmigrations of Proteus? I can symbolize my thought by using the name of any creature, of any fact, because every creature is man agent or patient.[24]

Emerson learned from classicists that myth, including religious myth, contained all that was left of prehistory. "First nations were remembered by their religion," he wrote in his journal in the early 1820s.[25] Emerson came to perceive that myth generalized historical data into a comprehensible and, above all, a usable form. Through myth, the individual saw himself in history. Only when he had achieved this viewpoint, which freed him from subservience to the past, could he live his own life, realizing in the present the latent pattern that myth told him was there if only he could see it.

History must thus be reworked and understood as myth, according to Emerson, in order to see the past as an extended present, to understand the "identity of human character in all ages" and myth as the key to that character. We are to admire the Greeks, not because they are old but because they are natural. Above all we are to live in the present without always looking over our shoulder. Why should the kind of man "who looked Apollos into the landscape with every glance he threw" spend his time carving statues of Apollo?[26]

4. Metamorphosis, Metaphor for Organic Process

Myth, then, reveals human character. And therefore myth can be found in literature as well as in history. Emerson was emphatic in his recognition of the creative writer's mythmaking function.

The point of praise of Shakespeare is, the pure poetic power: he is the chosen closest companion, who can, at any moment, by incessant surprises, work the miracle of mythologizing every fact of the common life; as snow, or moonlight, or the level rays of sunrise—lend a momentary glory to every pump and woodpile.

What Emerson means here by "mythologizing" is a process of creative transforming. The idea of creation as a transforming process runs all through Emerson; in one way it is linked to his interest in organic form, and in another it led him, via Ovid, to a lifelong fascination with metamorphosis. Once when he was planning a book or a lecture on mythology, Emerson had noted that "an obscure & slender thread of truth runs through all mythologies & this might lead often to highest regions of philosophy." His interest in metamorphosis is a perfect example of how a single aspect of ancient myth served as the touchstone for one of Emerson's leading ideas.[27]

In 1843 Emerson put "metamorphosis" at the head of a list of "the capital lessons of life." The idea of metamorphosis had appealed to Emerson rather early; in 1829 he noted, apropros of an unnamed person he thought had changed for the worse, "we must beware of the nature of the spiritual world. It has this terrible power of self change, self accommodation to whatsoever we do [and thus] Ovid's Metamorphoses take place continually. The nymph who wept became a fountain; the nymph who pined became an echo. They who do good become angels. They who do deformities become deformed. We are not immoveably moored as we are apt to think to any bottom." Most of Emerson's early comments on metamorphosis are warnings; he is most keenly aware of the degradation that can overtake and transform us for the worse. The passage above continues: "that part of us which we don't use dries up & perishes. Perhaps thus (I shudder whilst I write) a good spirit may become a bad spirit by insensible departures & whilst yet my acquaintance is praised for the former amiableness of his character he is rapidly declining on the road to malignity & lowest sensuality." In 1834 Emerson used the image of Proteus (a favorite with him, found all through his journals and in virtually every essay in *Representative Men*) to suggest much milder transformations, but here, too, the direction of change is unfortunate. "One of the forms the Proteus takes is that of civil self-depreciation. 'You quite mistake, sir; I am not that you took me for. A poor evanescent topic not really worth your consideration.'" And some time later, around 1840, Emerson was concerned with the same general idea, but set now in terms of transmigration; "*Transmigration* of souls: that too is no fable. I would wish it were; but look around you at the men & women, & do you not see that they are already only half human. . . ."

As long as Emerson thought of metamorphosis principally as change for the worse, as a process of deterioration, the idea was of no great consequence to his thought, but when he began to see it as a process that operated in the opposite direction as well, it gathered all sorts of associations around it and took on great importance for him. In the late 1830s, he noted that "Goethe says the mind & the endeavor of the Greeks is to deify man not to humanize the Godhead. Here is a theomorphism not anthropomorphism." From this time forward, metamorphosis, with the stress on morphology, began to have a developmental or even an evolutionary aspect for Emerson. "We fable to conform things better to our higher laws," he had noted in his journal, while in "The Poet" he links the idea of metamorphosis with ascension: "But nature had a higher end, in the production of new individuals, than security, namely *ascension,* or, the passage of the soul into higher forms." From this linking of ideas of change, including metamorphosis, transmigration of souls, evolution, and ascension (with the inevitable overtones, respectively, of Greek, Hindu, scientific, and Christian thought), Emerson soon came to refer simply to "the metamorphosis" as a central aspect of nature itself.[28]

He noted how "the different ages of man, in Hesiod's *Works and Days,* signify the mutations of human lives. . . ." These and other observations were subsumed into a general rule. "The method of advance in nature is perpetually transformation . . . ," he wrote in 1840. "Nature ever flows, stands never still. Motion or change is her mode of existence. The poetic eye sees in Man the Brother of the River, and in Woman the Sister of the River. Their life is always transition." Metamorphosis is the method of nature, but so deeply is that method ingrained that Emerson at times describes metamorphosis as nature itself. "What we call nature," he wrote in "The Poet," "is a certain self-regulated motion, or change; and nature does all things by her own hands, and does not leave another to baptize her, but baptizes herself; and this through the metamorphosis again." Elsewhere, thinking of metamorphosis not just as change but as "the necessity of progression or onwardness in each creature," he proclaims that "Metamorphosis is the law of the Universe." Metamorphosis became Emerson's symbol or shorthand for his version of evolutionary idealism, or the belief that idea or spirit progressively evolves and reveals itself through a series of concrete mutations or morphological changes.[29]

This concept is central to Emerson's view of things, and the language of metamorphosis is part of his effort to domesticate the vague and abstract language that usually went with philosophical discussions of idealism, whether evolutionary, Christian, or transcendental. The problem of adequate expression was very real. Sometimes Emerson fell back on Ovidian stories, and often he invoked the figure of Proteus. Sometimes he borrowed expressions from Hindu or Pythagorean concepts of the transmigration of souls. Sometimes he used Heraclitean or Neoplatonic abstractions, and often he combined several of these. In "History" it is expressed this way:

> Genius watches the monad through all his marks as he performs the metempsychosis of nature. . . . Nature is a mutable cloud, which is always and never the same. She casts the same thought into troops of forms, as a poet makes twenty fables with one moral.[30]

The problem, how to express the metamorphosis that Emerson saw at the heart of nature, leads always to the poet, for it is he that must perform that second metamorphosis, transforming nature into thought and adequate expression. First, of course, the poet must perceive the perpetual change in the nature of things. It was for this reason that Swedenborg struck Emerson as "a right poet. Every thing Protean to his eye." Indeed Swedenborg was, for a time, Emerson's ideal of "the person who of all men in the recent ages stands eminently for the translation of Nature into thought. I do not know a man in history to whom things stood so uniformly for words. Before him the Metamorphosis continually plays." The poet's means for expressing metamorphosis is the symbol. And of course Emerson would claim that this is fitting because nature itself is symbolic.

"The Metamorphosis of nature shows itself in nothing more than this that there is no word in our language that cannot become typical to us of nature by giving it emphasis. The world is a Dancer, it is a Rosary; it is a Torrent...."

The language and the idea of metamorphosis are Emerson's way of talking about organic form. This is clear from a passage in his notebooks for 1847.

> The interest of the gardener and the pomologist has the same foundation as that of the Poet,—namely in the metamorphosis: these also behold the miracle, the guided change, the change conspicuous, the guide invisible; a bare stick studs itself over with green buds, which become again leaves, flowers, and at length, delicious fruit.[31]

The Ovidian concept of metamorphosis as a story or myth in which characters change their outward appearance but retain their inner or essential identity was validated for Emerson and given an exciting new meaning by his reading of Goethe's *Metamorphosis of Plants,* a book Emerson summarized as follows: "Thus Goethe suggests the leading idea of modern botany, that a leaf or the eye of a leaf is the unit of botany, and that every part of a plant is only a transformed leaf to meet a new condition, and by varying the condition, a leaf may be converted into any other organ, and any other organ into a leaf."[32] Emerson's interest in organic form—in literature and in nature—and in the process of change itself found its best expression in his constantly reiterated image of metamorphosis, an image that expressed Emerson's lifelong conviction that changes in external form are directed by inner purposes, needs, and forces.

5. The Heroic Life and the Uses of Myth

Emerson looked at everything as potentially present now or as usable for present purposes. He energized or activated every idea he touched, and his best writing still evokes an answering energetic self-assertion in the reader. What Emerson said of Goethe is equally true of himself. He "teaches courage, and the equivalence of all times; that the disadvantages of any epoch exist only to the faint-hearted." Emerson considered the past as only a version of the present extended backward in time, and he perceived a metamorphosing or transmutation of form at the heart of reality. Mythology not only expressed these things, it showed how such knowledge might be used. Perhaps following Goethe, or perhaps merely reinforced by him, Emerson came to believe that mythmaking, when it was a serious business and not just a matter of superimposed imagery or arbitrary apologue, was theomorphic rather than anthropomorphic. This put a whole new face on the mythmaking process. Where Christianity had started with an idea of God, his revelation to men, and his incarnation as a man, and where Enlightenment skeptics had refused to accept the idea that there was anything at all beyond the human, Emerson (and other romantic writers) sought the meaning of myth and also of religion by starting with man and seeking the spark of divinity in man himself. Emerson's theism sought "the great God far within." By reversing its polarity, so to speak, Emerson made myth vital again, both as explanation of certain appearances in nature and as the expression of genuine religious impulses. It was of course not myth itself that Emerson cared about, but how it could help men lead heroic lives. If Emerson played a part—many would insist it was a founding part—in creating a heroic literature for America, it is mainly because he saw clearly that unless Americans undertook to live heroic lives there would be no heroic literature.[33]

Heroism and greatness had appealed to Emerson's imagination as early as he began to keep journals, and as he said of Napoleon, "whatever appeals to the imagination, by transcending the ordinary limits of human ability, wonderfully encourages and liberates us." In 1822 he was making notes for an essay on "Greatness" which show him aware not only of "the stupendous greatness which men rather believe than behold," but of another, lesser, more useful impulse toward greatness that could warm "each ordinary day of common life." By the mid 1830s he was inclining toward a rather aristocratic view of greatness. "The great man should occupy the whole space between God and the mob." A notebook passage which also shows up in "The American Scholar" (1837) says "Men behold in the hero or the poet their own being ripened and are content to be less so that [other] may attain to its full stature. . . ." This is the principle of aristocracy in history. Ultimately, in *Representative Men,* Emerson was to make a serious effort at reconciling his recognition of greatness with his fervent democratic idealism. Indeed, he saw this as part of the promise of America. He thought that "when all feudal straps & bandages were taken off an unfolding of the Titans had followed & they had laughed & leaped young giants along the continent & ran up the mountains of the West with the errand of Genius & of love." Sometimes he felt himself part of such an adventure. "We early men," he wrote in 1843, "at least have an advantage; we are up at four o'clock in the morning and have the whole market,—We Enniuses and Venerable Bedes of the empty American Parnassus." Here, as elsewhere, he was sure that there would one day be a literature which "will describe the new heroic life of man, the now unbelieved possibility of simple living." Heroism was always associated in Emerson's mind with the grand simplicities of life, with clear perceptions and basic religious feeling. One day in 1838 he wrote "I woke this morning saying or thinking in my dreams that every truth appealed to a heroic character." A year later Emerson commented that the live religious feeling of his day was not finding expression in institutionalized religion. As he put it, "Religion runs now not to cultus, but to heroic life."[34]

More and more, though, Emerson's ideas about greatness and heroism were drawn together over the problem of the uses of great men for the people of a democratic republic. The germ of *Representative Men,* the idea that the greatest men are representative or typical or symbolic of all men, goes back clearly at least to 1841 and the remark in his journal that "the history of Jesus is only the history of every man written large." Emerson came to believe that all men had more in them than they commonly realized; the use of *great* men was, simply, to awaken *all* men to their own possibilities. Emerson's method in *Representative Men* reflects this. The book consists of seven sketches, each sketch beginning with a biographical view of a single great man. This is followed in each sketch by a section on that man's meaning for the present written from a generalized or "mythological" point of view. Emerson clearly expects the reader to be attuned to both approaches. The opening paragraph strikes the mythological tone clearly:

> It is natural to believe in great men. If the companions of our childhood should turn out to be heroes, and their condition regal, it would not surprise us. All mythology opens with demigods, and the circumstance is high and poetic; that is, their genius is paramount. In the legends of the Gautama, the first men ate the earth, and found it deliciously sweet.

By association, Emerson links great men, heroes, kings, and demigods in an explicitly mythological context. He is concerned that we find ourselves mirrored in the great men whose lives he is about to present. He is not interested in the great men as historical specimens, nor as entertainment. Emerson is the American Plutarch, expecting us to take these "lives" seriously as models. *Representative Men* illustrates Emerson's conviction, phrased with a directness rare among writers on myth, that "the gods of fable are the shining moments of great men." This approach amounts to nothing less than a modern Euhemerism; it became Emerson's most frequent and I think his most deeply held conviction on the subject. Emerson's originality turned this theory, often used to debunk, to positive uses. Mythology becomes the best means of expressing the essential—and repeatable—qualities of human character. "Our colossal theologies of Judaism, Christism, Buddhism, Mahometism, are the necessary and structural action of the human mind." Mythology and theology both result from theism, and, Emerson goes on, "theism is the purification of the human mind. Man can paint, or make, or think nothing but man."

Emerson presents the reader with seven great men, each representative or symbolic of some one human quality. Emerson calls them heroes, demigods (he sometimes tries to freshen up this phrase by calling them half-gods), or types. They are epitomes, deliberately drawn archetypes. Plato, the philosopher, is the archetypal thinker who can perceive multiplicity in Unity. Swedenborg, the mystic, stands for the perception of the world as symbol and the primary relation of mind to matter. Montaigne, the skeptic, is the archetype of the reasonable man, the man of cool, witty mental equilibrium. Shakespeare, the poet, stands for "the translation of things into song." Napoleon, the man of the world, is the prophet of commerce, money, and material power, epitome of the common man and worshipped by him. Lastly, Emerson chooses Goethe as the archetypal hero of that group to which Emerson himself belongs, "the class of scholars or writers, who see connection where the multitudes see fragments, and who are impelled to exhibit the facts in order, and so to supply the axis on which the frame of things turns."

Representative Men is part mythology, part theology, and part hagiography. Emerson proposes saints and heroes for the self-reliant. It is remarkable that none of his demigods or types are American, none are biblical, none are Christian. If Emerson is trying to set up a canon of heroes, it is very different indeed from most. First, all but Napoleon are heroes of thought or art. Secondly, the only founder of a religion included is Swedenborg. Third, and most important, Emerson does not intend to work up his audience into a servile adulation or stunned admiration. Each sketch ends with a thorough critique of the figure's weak points and failures. Emerson as much as says that we are not to be intimidated by great men, but encouraged, and if he learned from myth how to magnify man, he had also learned how to approach a magnified figure skeptically. As Emerson treats his seven men, his Seven against Conformity, we are made to see that the great heroes of the past have not exhausted all possibilities, that they all have shortcomings, and that there is plenty of room for us. "Great men exist that there may be greater men."

Emerson thus accomplishes something quite unusual. He simultaneously cuts down the greatest of men to ordinary human size and then builds them up into representative figures, symbolic heroes in whom we recognize ourselves. Emerson makes the reader believe in their representativeness. In theological jargon, he was both mythologizing and demythologizing. He was in fact doing with his seven modern wise men just what he describes Goethe doing in *Faust*. Goethe, says Emerson, was one of those "who found himself master of histories, mythologies, philosophies... ," and he exclaimed "what new mythologies sail through his head!... in the solidest kingdom of routine and the senses, he showed the lurking daemonic power; that, in actions of routine, a thread of mythology and fable spins itself; and this, by tracing the pedigree of every usage and practice, every institution, utensil, and means, home to its origin in the structure of man."[35] Sometimes in his pursuit of the proper form in which to express "the structure of man," Goethe must demythologize. So with the Devil, who "had played an important part in mythology in all times." In order to make him seem real and believable, Emerson says, Goethe "stripped him of mythologic gear, of horns, cloven foot, harpoon tail, brimstone, and blue-fire, and, instead of looking in books and pictures, looked for him in his own mind." So well did Goethe succeed that his new figure becomes a permanent addition to our stock of images. We would call it a new mythological figure. Emerson says simply that Goethe "flung into literature, in his Mephistopheles, the first organic figure that has been added for some ages, and which will remain as long as the Prometheus." The *process* of mythmaking is valid, though sometimes the old results of the process become fixed and dated and have to be replaced or reformed. But just as the process of forming myth is valid, so the process of demythologizing is not just simple debunking, nor is it essentially antimythic in outlook. It is a matter of being able to discard old mythological forms from which the vitality has departed, in order to let the informing idea reemerge in a new and currently believable form. It is here, as always with Emerson, the idea, or the spirit, or the power behind the form and compelling the form that he was most deeply interested in. His philosophical, literary, and religious views all converged on the idea that there was a great informing energy or creating power animating our words, our symbols, and our myths.

Myth was, for Emerson, a medium for important wisdom. It was one of the many ways in which Spirit manifested itself in form—to use the familiar terms of the German idealism which so closely resembles New England Transcendentalism—but (unlike Hegel, for example) there is no indication in Emerson's writing that he assigned myth a place lower than any other mode of expression. If anything, the opposite is true. Mythology comes up, as a subject, a process, a touchstone to some vital emotion or idea, over and over, all through his career. Myth was evidently real enough to him, if by real we mean what is persistently valued. He could write after a walk in the storm, "I love the wood god. I love the mighty PAN." He sought ceaselessly to find and explain what it was in nature that was so well expressed in what he called "mythology and the Undersong of Epics." Myth seemed to have a vitality and a truth of its own, independent of its creator. Emerson called Greek mythology "a wonderful example . . . of profound sense overmastering the finite speakers & writers of the fables."[36] Emerson thought it the office of his age "to annul that adulterous divorce which the superstition of many ages has effected between the intellect & holiness." Myth was one of the things that tended to unite the two, partly because myth was both necessary and useful, and partly because it lay behind both literature and religion as a symbolical form of communication. "There are always a few heads, and out of these come the mythology and the machinery of the world," he remarked. To be useful, myth needed only to be read aright. "The poet writes fable, but I read truth in it."

Throughout Emerson's work myth served well as one of his habitual resources. Often enough myth itself revealed something or was the best possible explanation of a thought or a feeling. Often, his theomorphic humanism found its characteristic expression in mythic rather than in strictly theological (or in Christian) terms. There is some evidence that he believed in the American Adam; there is equally good evidence that he believed in the American Proteus. But he did not rest his case on these external images, which are, after all, no more than what he called "modern antiques." It was only typical, but typically brilliant, that he borrowed an idea from myth to argue that the human soul will never have peace while it seeks an external god, but will when "it sees the Great God far within its own nature."[37] In Emerson's perception of the nature of the divine or sacred, in his view of history as present time, in his understanding of the metamorphosing principle in nature and his urging the possibility of our living lives of intellectual or spiritual heroism, myth was indispensable to his heroic vision.

Four

Thoreau

1. "To link my facts to fable"

Of the New England Transcendentalist writers, Henry Thoreau made the most deliberate, extensive, original, and successful use of myth. Sherman Paul has pointed out that while Thoreau "saw in the myths he was reading many that spoke to his condition—that of Apollo and Admetus, those on the origin of music, and those that related the invention of the practical arts of life—he did not, as so many contemporary authors do, use the myth itself for his structure. Instead, like Whitman and Melville, he created his own by going back to the original conditions of myth."[1] Thoreau did not in any way adapt existing myth to his literary needs. He did not use a single myth as a form (as Joyce did in *Ulysses*), nor did he take a mythical figure as archetype for his own (as Byron took Cain or as Thomas Mann took Faust for Adrian Leverkuhn or as D. H. Lawrence took Christ for the *Man Who Died*), nor did he look to myth for a familiar theme such as Prometheanism, Metamorphosis, Orphism, Pan-ism, or Aenean piety. Instead, and the point is important, he tried to recover for himself the original conditions in which the early creators of the great myths found themselves.

Of almost equal importance was Thoreau's perception that the "original conditions" surrounding the creation of myth were not so much social, cultural, or historical as they were personal or individual. The mythmaking poet was neither helped nor hindered by the times in which he lived; he had only to place himself in a simple and original relation to nature. "Wood, water, earth, air are [now] essentially what they were; only society has degenerated. This la-

ment for a golden age is only a lament for golden men,"[2] Thoreau
wrote in his journal. If conditions were right for the individual—
whatever the condition of society—then myth would arise naturally
from nature to be expressed by the poet.

> He is richest who has most use for nature as raw material of tropes and
> symbols with which to describe his life. If these gates of golden willows
> affect me, they correspond to the beauty and promise of some experience
> on which I am entering. If I am overflowing with life, am rich in
> experience for which I lack expression, then nature will be my language
> full of poetry,—all nature will *fable,* and every natural phenomenon be a
> myth.[3]

Not only did Thoreau see that the usefulness of myth to him depended on his recovering for himself the original and essential individual conditions of myth, but he also developed a technique for
handling myth, which he articulated in a way that throws a good
deal of light on his literary purpose. Since fact and fable stood at
opposite poles in most people's minds, Thoreau hit upon the device
of always leading fables or myths toward facts and always leading his
facts toward fable or myth. In this way he could play on his readers'
stock responses and could press continually forward, in unlooked for
ways, his own conviction that myth was deeply and importantly
true.

> I, too, would fain set down something beside facts. Facts should only be
> as the frame to my pictures; they should be material to the mythology
> which I am writing: not facts to assist men to make money, farmers to
> farm profitably, in any common sense. . . . My facts shall be falsehoods
> to the common sense. I would so state facts that they shall be signifi-
> cant, shall be myths or mythologic.[4]

In *Walden,* too, Thoreau mentions "a faint recollection of a little fish
some five inches long, with silvery sides and a greenish back, somewhat dace-like in its character, which I mention here chiefly to link
my facts to fable."[5] His thoroughly conscious procedure may be seen
anywhere in his journal. Characteristically, he will discuss a phenomenon, such as echoes, then say, "I should think that savages

would have made a god of echo." Apropos of the many ominous signs of approaching winter, such as insects hiding, ice forming, the grass dying, Thoreau would ask, "If the race had never lived through a winter, what would they think was coming?"[6] The opposite and more familiar process of starting with myth and leading it down to a fact is also everywhere apparent in Thoreau's writing. In the following, he connects mythical figures with the idea of evolution:

> The figures of serpents, of griffins, flying dragons, and other embellishments of heraldry, the eastern idea of the world on an elephant, that on a tortoise, and that on a serpent again, etc., usually regarded as mythological in the common sense of that word, are thought by some to "indicate a faint and shadowy knowledge of a previous state of organic existence" such as geology partly reveals.[7]

This technique of juxtaposing the mythical and the factual so that they appear to be two ways of talking about the same thing, two versions of a single reality, is very clearly seen in Thoreau's earliest important extended treatment of myth, the "Sunday" and "Monday" sections of *A Week on the Concord and Merrimack Rivers,* in which he explicitly puts an unusually high value on myth and makes quite clear why mythic thought and writing are very near the heart of his own enterprise.

When Thoreau launches into a full-scale discussion of myth in "Sunday," it does not come entirely by surprise. The short opening section of the book, "Concord River," begins with exaggerated comparisons between the Musketaquid and the Nile and Euphrates, and ends by comparing Concord River to the Xanthus, the Scamander, the Mississippi, and the Ganges. This technique of dignifying the local and parochial by means of epic association—which sets the stage for heroic association—puts the reader on notice that, since Thoreau's river is made out to be the equal of the great and famous rivers, we may expect its hero to be placed in the company of great and famous heroes, while the writer will aspire after, even if he cannot quite claim, equal station with Homer. The second section of the *Week,* "Saturday," is given over to detailed descriptions of nature and bits of local history. By the time the reader reaches "Sunday" it is already plain that an effort is being made to knit together detailed natural observation and local history by means of individual experience but nonetheless to give the result general, not just local, significance. The attempt to wrest general significance from particular events leads Thoreau directly to a discussion of myth, the central subject of both "Sunday" and "Monday."

Thoreau starts by saying that modern knowledge is too detailed and thereby misses the grand truths. He complains that "these modern ingenious sciences and arts do not affect me as those more venerable arts of hunting and fishing, and even of husbandry in its primitive and simple form; as ancient and honorable trades as the sun and moon and winds pursue."[8] For the kind of truth Thoreau is interested in, myth is the surest guide. Taking his illustration from Alexander Ross's *Mystagogus Poeticus,* Thoreau says "we read that Aristeus 'obtained of Jupiter and Neptune, that the pestilential heat of the dog-days, wherein was great mortality, should be mitigated with wind.' This is one of those dateless benefits conferred on man, which have no record in our vulgar day. . . ."[9] Myth has not ceased; according to Thoreau, something approaching myth can still be found in dreams, "in which we have a more liberal and juster apprehension of things, unconstrained by habit, which is then in some measure put off, and divested of memory, which we call history."[10] In other words, myth is the result of a certain way of seeing things, a mode of perception which is not historical-minded and the results of which have some resemblance to dreams. Thoreau now gives another short myth, taken from Ross, which he uses to argue that while myth may not seem historical, in fact it is so, but in a large and special sense.

> According to fable, when the island of Ægina was depopulated by sickness, at the instance of Æacus, Jupiter turned the ants into men, that is, as some think, he made men of the inhabitants who lived meanly like ants. This is perhaps the fullest history of those early days extant.[11]

As if recognizing the obscurity of his two brief examples, Thoreau now turns to an extended and explicit discussion emphasizing the primary appeal of successful myth to the imagination. "The fable, which is naturally and truly composed, so as to satisfy the imagination, ere it addresses the understanding, beautiful though strange as a wild-flower, is to the wise man an apothegm, and admits of his most generous interpretation." Citing the story of Bacchus' making "the Tyrhenian mariners mad, so that they leapt into the sea, mistaking it for a meadow full of flowers, and so became dolphins," Thoreau argues that our interest here is not in biographical or historical accuracy, not in any literal reading, but in what he calls "a higher poetical truth." A successful myth is, he says, "the music of a thought," and appeals to a faculty above the understanding.

He goes on to remark on the "singular unanimity [with which] the farthest sundered nations and generations consent to give completeness and roundness to an ancient fable, of which they indistinctly appreciate the beauty or the truth." In trying to account for the widespread and long-lasting appeal of certain myths, he describes the organic evolution by which successive generations each "add some trait to the mythus." Myths arise by gradual evolution, they "migrate from east to west, and again from west to east." They are changed and shaped by all those who take them up, becoming, eventually, common possessions. At its most impressive, then, the vogue of certain myths seems to be evidence of a common humanity, and the myths themselves "an approach to that universal language which men have sought in vain."[12]

The ideas come thick and fast in this short section, and Thoreau seems to assume a certain familiarity with ideas about myth on the part of the reader. In an effort to separate the positive concept of myth from the negative one in common use, Thoreau takes pains to explain in just what sense myth is to be considered true. "To some extent, mythology is only the most ancient history and biography. So far from being false or fabulous in the common sense, it contains only enduring and essential truth." Myth gives us a compacted and refined version of history, stripped of useless detail. Myth then is partly the result of an historical process of sifting, shaping, and retelling. Thoreau playfully suggests that by this process, Benjamin Franklin will come in time to be an entry in a classical dictionary,

"Son of _____ and _____. He aided the Americans to gain their independence, instructed mankind in economy, and drew down lightning from the clouds."[13]

Behind the playfulness, Thoreau shows himself aware that this particular form of mythic distillation of biography and history is no longer possible in an age of literacy and cheap printing. So, instead of looking to historical process for the creation of myth, Thoreau turns instead to the activity of the poet, described as one who can create myth all at once, without having to wait for the distillation and refinement of his work by later ages. This is what is meant by Thoreau's terse summary comment, "The poet is he who can write some pure mythology today without the aid of posterity."[14] Here, as so often in his mature work, it is in the possibility of creating new myths that Thoreau is most interested. For he goes on to argue that all the different interpretations of myth are interesting not so much because any one of them has "solved" the problem, as for what their very profusion of "meanings" suggests about the complex and end-lessly suggestive nature of myth. "The hidden significance of these fables which is sometimes thought to have been detected, the ethics running parallel to the poetry and history, are not so remarkable as the readiness with which they may be made to express a variety of truths."[15]

The myths, he concludes, seem to be "the skeletons of still older and more universal truths than any whose flesh and blood they are for the time made to wear. It is like striving to make the sun, or the wind, or the sea symbols to signify exclusively the particular thoughts of our day." This remarkable section, amounting indeed to an essay on the value of myth, ends with this definition. "In the mythus a superhuman intelligence uses the unconscious thoughts and dreams of men as its hieroglyphics to address men unborn."[16] Myth appeared to Thoreau to be the product of a magnificent simplicity of perception, which resulted from a certain kind of closeness to nature. Thoreau himself strives for this condition, both for the heroic quality of such a life and because living habitually at a pitch of mythic intensity would undoubtedly help him to write myth.

A heroic life and primal mythmaking vision are easily talked about, but they are in fact difficult to carry out and require that we abandon many of our stock responses and conditioned attitudes. In an effort to jar us into taking a fresh look at the problems, Thoreau's *Week* next insists that we look on Greek myth as religion and on Christianity as myth. His technique and his tone may at times seem paradoxical and exasperating, but he has a perfectly serious point to make. "I am not sure but I should betake myself in extremities to the liberal divinities of Greece, rather than to my country's God," he begins, going on to enumerate the shortcomings of Jehovah, who, for Thoreau, lacks the "intimate and genial influence on nature" which many Greek gods exhibit. He has too great a power, too inflexible a justice, and he is too exclusively masculine. There is "no sister Juno, no Apollo, no Venus, nor Minerva, to intercede for me." Not only does he regard Greek myth seriously as a religious system, but he presents himself as an actual believer in Greek religion, a devout pagan worshipper:

In my Pantheon, Pan still reigns in his pristine glory, with his ruddy face, his flowing beard, and his shaggy body, his pipe and his crook, his nymph Echo, and his chosen daughter Iambe; for the great god Pan is not dead, as was rumored. No god ever dies. Perhaps of all the gods of New England and of ancient Greece, I am most constant at his shrine.[17]

Before one smiles at a passage like this, it is well to remember how it would have shocked the Christian faithful of Concord and Boston, and that its brag and its robust Goethean paganism were designed so to shock. But the real significance of the passage, the point which the confident overstatement is designed to make us recognize, is that it is an argument for Pan-theism, pressed on religious rather than on merely philosphical grounds.

Having asked us to take Greek myth seriously, as religion, Thoreau now reverses the arguments and goes on to talk about Christianity as mere myth in a way that recalls Thomas Paine and Theodore Parker.

One memorable addition to the old mythology is due to this era,—the Christian fable. With what pains, and tears, and blood these centuries have woven this and added it to the mythology of mankind! The new Prometheus. With what miraculous consent, and patience, and persistency, has this mythus been stamped on the memory of the race! It would seem as if it were in the progress of our mythology to dethrone Jehovah and crown Christ in his stead.[18]

The sources of this sort of comment, as well as for such references as the one to "the humble life of a Jewish peasant," are hard to determine exactly, though we may note that Emerson made frequent comments about Prometheus as a version of Christ, that Thoreau himself had translated Aeschylus' *Prometheus Bound,* that he was probably familiar with Shelley's radical poems, that (thanks to Parker and others) the ideas of D. F. Strauss and Charles Hennell were in the air at the time, and that the era which witnessed Abner Kneeland's trial for heresy still found the problem of "infidelity" a live issue. Thoreau was not being obscure or farfetched in his choice of weapons; but the real point, of course, is not where he got his material but what he does with it. His remark about Christ is not satirical, nor does he believe that we would really erect altars to Pan. His point is that we invest our religious heroes with so much intolerance and superstition that we become incapable of seeing that what they really teach us, by their example, is that every man's life can be remarkable and, if written, could resemble a myth.

Thoreau approvingly quotes Sir Thomas Browne's autobiographical observation that "his life has been a miracle of thirty years, which to relate were not history, but a piece of poetry, and would sound like a fable."[19] Later in "Sunday" Thoreau claims that the serious infidelity of his time is that "which prays, and keeps the Sabbath, and rebuilds the churches." His anti-clerical, anti-ecclesiastical, anti-institutional bias is not confined to Christianity, and is indeed deliberately extended. "One is sick at heart of this pagoda-worship. It is like the beating of gongs in a Hindoo subterranean temple." The Sabbath bells of New England awaken other associations too, "as the sound of many catechisms and religious books twanging a canting peal round the earth, seeming to issue from some Egyptian temple and echo along the shore of the Nile, right opposite to Pharoah's palace and Moses in the bulrushes, startling a multitude of storks and alligators basking in the sun."[20]

The point to which all this builds is now put, appropriately enough, in a fable from Saadi whose point is that true religion is a matter of personal conviction—not institutional loyalty. The reader comes away feeling that a careful attention to mythology, whether Greek or Christian, may in the end be of more religious benefit than attendance at church, temple, or pagoda. Furthermore, the proper expression of true religious feeling is through scripture, poetry, and myth, not through buildings and sects and intermediary priests. Thus Thoreau now turns to discuss first scripture and then poetry in "Sunday." The "loftiest written wisdom is, in form as well as substance, poetry." Thoreau describes poetry in much the same terms that both he and Emerson use to describe mythology. "It is as if nature spoke." It is "a natural fruit. As naturally as the oak bears an acorn, and the vine a gourd, man bears a poem, either spoken or done. It is the chief and most memorable success, for history is but a prose narrative of poetic deeds. What else have the Hindoos, the Persians, the Babylonians, the Egyptians done, that can be told?"[21]

Poetry and mythology are often bracketed by Thoreau. Homer's poetry, including of course his poetic treatment of inherited mythology, is described by Thoreau as the "pure mythology" he had called on the poet to produce. And this poetry of pure mythology is "universally true and independent of experience." Naturally poetry must be valued above archaeology. "The ruins of Egypt oppress and stifle us with their dust, foulness preserved in cassia and pitch, and swathed in linen, the death of that which never lived." Greek ruins give us a dead, material, meaningless because mute past. "But the rays of Greek poetry struggle down to us, and mingle with the sunbeams of the recent day." Physical ruins only add to the burden of the past, but poetry, conceived as the "pure mythology" written by the poet, helps us cast off that burden because its effect is to induce the present poet to live his own life and then write his own poem or myth. Thoreau found Homer not a weight but a model.

Thus he could say, "So, too, no doubt, Homer had his Homer, and Orpheus his Orpheus, in the dim antiquity which preceded them."[22]

Thoreau closes the first half of this remarkable excursus into myth by saying that "the mythological system of the ancients" is still "the mythology of the moderns," and characterizing it as "the poem of mankind." Thoreau has tried in "Sunday" to redeem the idea of myth from the common or negative associations it had at the time and to associate myth with true religion as opposed to institutional and sectarian versions, with true history as opposed to chronicle or ruin, and with poetry. He was able to do all this because he conceived of myth as individual as opposed to social in origin, significance, and function. Thoreau's idea of the function of the poet was, we have seen, to "write some pure mythology today without the aid of posterity." The modern writer can learn a great deal about his proper function from other and older mythologies. Thoreau learned most from Greek myth, but he was also strongly influenced by Nordic myth and by Indic myth. Indeed, it is to Indic myth that Thoreau turns in the next section of *A Week*.

2. The Lesson of Indic Myth

The first Eastern book Thoreau takes up in "Monday" is the *Bhagavad-Gita,* in Charles Wilkins's translation.[23] The introduction, contributed by Warren Hastings, describes the book as "a very curious specimen of the literature, the mythology, and Morality of the ancient Hindus," and Wilkins's own preface speaks of his desire to pursue his study of "the theology and mythology of the Hindoos."[24] Thus, while we might prefer to describe the *Bhagavad-Gita* as a theologic book, Thoreau had ample precedent for thinking of it as mythology. At any rate, the *Bhagavad-Gita* seems to have impressed Thoreau as the written record of the kind of vision he himself hoped to receive; witness the rare plaintive lament it wrung from him:

> I would give all the wealth of the world and all the deeds of all the heroes, for one true vision. But how can I communicate with the gods who am a pencil-maker on the earth, and not be insane?[25]

The Indic scriptures appear to have hit Thoreau with the force of a revelation. They showed him a plausible way to advance toward life rather than retreating from it, a whole new way of considering the conduct of life, a kind of pastoral monasticism in which both active and contemplative sides had a part, as they did in no familiar Western scripture. The *Bhagavad-Gita* does not rest its arguments on one's duty to the state, but on one's duty to oneself. Thoreau must have warmed toward this remarkable document's steady assumption of the dignity of the self, as well as the doctrine of the essential unity of all things. Though he does not quote it, it is impossible that Thoreau was not struck by the eloquent pantheism of such passages as the following:

> I am the sacrifice; I am the worship. I am the spices; I am the invocation; I am the ceremony to the manes of the ancestors; I am the provisions; I am the fire, and I am the victim. I am the father and the mother of this world, the grandsire and the preserver. . . . I am the journey of the good; the comforter; the creator; the witness; the resting-place; the asylum, and the friend. I am generation and dissolution; the place where all things are reposited, and the inexhaustible seed of all nature.[26]

(One can also see why Thoreau, when he went to see Walt Whitman in 1856, asked whether Whitman knew the Hindu writings. "No," Whitman had replied, "tell me about them.")

The second Indic book Thoreau mentions in "Monday" is the *Heetopades of Veeshnoo Sarma,* and the basis of his admiration for this volume is, as he says, its "common sense," its "playful wisdom," and the aphoristic style of the short fables or apologues which make up the work. But the other important book treated in "Monday" is *The Laws of Menu,* in Sir William Jones's translation. For this book Thoreau wrote a lovely and extravagant description, so fresh and earnest that one cannot help concluding that the book was a major experience for him. He admired the scope of the *Laws,* universal and eternal in intent, he admired the impersonal style and sincere tone. "It seems to have been uttered from some eastern summit, with a sober morning prescience in the dawn of time." He admired the spare, direct sentences, "clean and dry as fossil truths." He quotes a sentence from Menu's account of creation, "When that power awakes, then has this world its full expansion: but when he slumbers with a tranquil spirit, then the whole system fades away," and from what he then finds to praise in "the very indistinctness of their theogony," it is clear that he welcomes the account as an intelligent alternative to the creation account in Genesis.[27] But it is clearly the tone and style of *The Laws of Menu* that impressed Thoreau above all else. It was, for one thing, a style well adapted to giving an uncolored account of nature:

> Most books belong to the house and street only, and in the fields their leaves feel very thin. They are bare and obvious, and have no halo nor haze about them. Nature lies far and fair behind them all. But this, as it proceeds from, so it addresses what is deepest and most abiding in man. It belongs to the noontide of the day, the midsummer of the year, and after the snows have melted, and the waters evaporated in the spring, still its truth speaks freshly to our experience.[28]

As remarkable as his perception of *The Laws of Menu* as a language of nature is his delighted emphasis on the sense of origins continually suggested to him by the book. "As our domestic fowl are said to have their original in the wild pheasant of India, so our domestic thoughts have their prototypes in the thoughts of her philosophers. We are dabbling in the very elements of our present conventional and actual life."[29] Just as the book's style seemed to Thoreau to interpose almost no filter or screen between nature and the reader, so the bold clarity of thought seemed in its simplicity to reflect the earliest ages of civilized man.

"Monday" now moves to the explicit question of the uses of mythology, and we are to understand that the Eastern stories are now to be included under the general heading of myth.

> If we will admit time into our thoughts at all, the mythologies, those vestiges of ancient poems, wrecks of poems, so to speak, the world's inheritance, still reflecting some of their original splendor, like the fragments of clouds tinted by the rays of the departed sun; reaching into the latest summer day, and allying this hour to the morning of creation . . . these are the materials and hints for a history of the rise and progress of the race.[30]

Turning from the past to the present Thoreau goes on to say that the "morning of the race" described in the old mythologies will be "succeeded by a day of equally progressive splendor; that, in the lapse of the divine periods, other divine agents and godlike men will assist to elevate the race as much above its present conditions. But we do not know much about it."[31]

What Thoreau will not quite come out and say directly is that the writer of a new mythology will himself have some claim to being a divine agent and godlike man. This is the high office of the true poet and mythmaker, the one who deals in origins, and who traces things to their foundations. Indian mythology seems to have sharpened and focused Thoreau's purposes. Far from shrinking before their vast Asiatic distance and antiquity, Thoreau was both challenged and encouraged in his own calling by the Indic sacred books.

3. Nordic Myth and the Idea of the Heroic

Thoreau's knowledge of Nordic myth came mainly from Carlyle.[32] He also knew the Ossianic poems and wrote in very Carlyleian terms about Ossian in the *Week*, defending Ossian's "heathenism" as primitive and perfectly valid religion. Ossian is grouped with poets of the "most refined and rudest eras," with Homer, Pindar, Isaiah, and the American Indian, and is praised for the heroic simplicity of his poems.

Thoreau knew more of Nordic saga and legend than he got from Carlyle.[33] He made entries in one of his fact books from Mallet's *Northern Antiquities,* and he also read Snorri Sturluson's *Heimskringla, or Chronicle of the Kings of Norway.* But for Thoreau's real understanding of the meaning of Norse mythology and legend, and its hero-centeredness, we must turn to Carlyle.

While living at Walden Pond, Thoreau wrote an essay on Carlyle strongly praising both his style and his approach to heroes and the heroic. Thoreau indeed felt that *On Heroes* was the essential Carlyle, remarking that "all his books might well enough be embraced under that title." Thoreau refers repeatedly to the first lecture in Carlyle's book, the one entitled "The Hero as Divinity. Odin. Paganism: Scandinavian Mythology." Thoreau noted that Carlyle "answers your question, What is poetry? by writing a special poem, as that Norse one, for instance, in the Book of Heroes, altogether wild and original." This can only refer to the lecture on Odin; calling it a poem is Thoreau's way of praising the lecture, just as he praises, in the next paragraph, Carlyle's *History of the French Revolution* as a "poem," "an *Iliad* indeed."[34]

Carlyle's lecture on Odin begins with an attack on mere debunking:

> Some speculators have a short way of accounting for the Pagan religion; mere quackery, priestcraft, and dupery, say they; no sane man ever did believe it,—merely contrived to persuade other men, not worthy of the name of sane, to believe it! It will be often our duty to protest against this sort of hypothesis about men's doings and history; and I here, on the very threshold, protest against it in reference to Paganism, and to all other *isms* by which man has ever for a length of time striven to walk in this world. They have all had a truth in them, or men would not have taken them up.[35]

Carlyle rules out any easy superiority or condescension on the part of the modern interpreter, and he insists that one cannot begin to understand the mythology of a people until one is prepared to take it as seriously as it was originally meant.

> We shall begin to have a chance of understanding Paganism, when we first admit that to its followers it was, at one time, earnestly true. Let us consider it very certain that men did believe in Paganism; men with open eyes, sound senses, men made altogether like ourselves; that we, had we been there, should have believed in it.[36]

Having prepared the way for a sympathetic reading of Nordic myth, Carlyle goes on to assert that Scandinavian myth, in common with all pagan mythology, has as its essence the "recognition of the divineness of Nature; sincere communion of man with the mysterious invisible Powers visibly seen at work in the world around him."[37] Paganism is the worship of this nature, these powers, and worship is in turn defined by Carlyle as "transcendent wonder." What particularly distinguishes Scandinavian from other pagan religions is the way it adds Hero worship to Nature worship. Scandinavian myth puts the warrior god Odin at its center and thus puts the highest possible premium on heroic virtues:

> That the man Odin, speaking with a Hero's voice and heart, as with an impressiveness out of Heaven, told his People the infinite importance of Valour, how man thereby became a god; and that his People, feeling a response to it in their own hearts, believed this message of his, and thought it a message out of Heaven, and him a Divinity for telling it them: this seems to me the primary seed-grain of the Norse Religion, from which all manner of mythologies, symbolic practices, speculations, allegories, songs and sagas would naturally grow.[38]

Thoreau must have been impressed by this ringing assertion of one of his favorite ideas, that all things became possible once one had adopted a heroic attitude. Of course, Thoreau understood the concept of heroism in his own personal and even interior terms. But there must have been a little of the Carlyleian blood-rush of excitement in Thoreau's eager embracing of those heroic ages which the morning brought back.

Another of Carlyle's claims chimed in with Thoreau's own hopes and assumptions. Carlyle too believed that while myth may have been revised, expanded, and refined by later generations, and even by whole peoples, any given myth was nevertheless the work of one man in the beginning, a man who stood in a representative relationship to all the others:

> Innumerable men had passed by, across this Universe, with a dumb vague wonder, such as the very animals may feel; or with a painful, fruitlessly inquiring wonder, such as men only feel;—till the great Thinker came, the *original* man, the Seer: whose shaped spoken Thought awakes the slumbering capability of all into Thought. It is ever the way with the Thinker, the Spiritual Hero. What he says, all men were not far from saying, were longing to say.[39]

These are the main themes of the essay lecture on Odin which Thoreau thought so highly of, and if we may trust his own essay review of Carlyle, it was the idea of the hero that impressed him most deeply. Carlyle, he said, served to remind us "that Heroes and Demi-gods, Fates and Furies, still exist." Carlyle himself seemed rather like one of his Scandinavian figures. Thoreau describes him as having the "constitutional vigor of one of his old Norse heroes, struggling in a lurid light, with Jötuns still, striving to throw the old woman and 'she was time,'—striving to lift the big cat, and that was 'the Great World-Serpent, which, tail in mouth, girds and keeps up the whole created world.' "[40]

Thoreau's admiration is tempered, however. He finds that "Carlyle has not the simple Homeric health of Wordsworth," and he is disappointed that "the common man is nothing to him." And speaking about Carlyle's book and Emerson's not yet printed lectures on *Representative Men,* Thoreau notes that there are a few things missing in both performances. There is "nothing of Christ, who yet awaits a just appreciation from literature," there is no "peacefully practical hero" such as Columbus, "but above and after all, the Man of the Age, come to be called Workingman, it is obvious that none yet speaks to his condition, for the speaker is not yet in his condition."[41] Going beyond both men, Thoreau's own democratic idealism comes attractively to the fore. Both he and Whitman will try to make a hero of the common man, Whitman more successfully than Thoreau, neither fully succeeding, but both moved to write myth or the equivalent of myth for their own times.

As Carlyle powerfully presented it, Nordic myth taught the necessity of heroism; but so too did Homer and Greek myth. What Thoreau did was to take what he had learned about the battlefields of Scandinavia and Greece and apply it to the beanfield of Walden Pond. Thoreau's version of heroism was a heroic self-sufficiency. Primitive myth celebrated objective, public heroism; modern myth might well set out to celebrate subjective, private heroism. For Thoreau, as for Whitman, this was not a retreat from the public sphere, but the only workable approach to it.

4. Greek Myth: Prometheus on Ktaadn

Of the mythologies that played a part in forming Thoreau's imagination—and these included Egyptian, Polynesian, and American Indian as well as Indic and Nordic—Greek is without question the most important. From college on, the references to Greek myth in his journals, essays, and books outweigh all other references to myth. Even when he is directly discussing Nordic myth he looks for "Homeric health" or refers, in an offhand manner, to "titanic" and "Promethean" qualities in his effort to describe Carlyle. Greek culture was his customary standard. Menu is measured by Homer. Even Thoreau's half-playful half-rueful identification of himself with Apollo constrained to keeping the flocks of King Admetis shows how easily Greek myth rose to mind and came to hand. The importance of Homer to *Walden* is obvious, and mythology is not the least important aspect of Thoreau's Homer. That Greek myth appealed to Thoreau and that he was widely acquainted with it is clear.[42] What may not be so obvious is that Greek myth was crucial to Thoreau's great writings, in that it provided him with a way to generalize and universalize—indeed mythicize—his own direct encounters with nature. It is not so much that myth gave him metaphors or characters or themes—although this was sometimes the case—but that ancient myth showed him how to make myth of his own experiences. This is a difficult but important process, which can perhaps be clarified by examining the role of myth in Thoreau's account of his ascent of Mt. Ktaadn.

Thoreau's expedition to Ktaadn was an interlude in his residence at Walden Pond. His account of the expedition is a skillful blending of travelogue and natural detail with a personal narrative—written with Melvillian intensity—of how this wilderness adventure affected him. It is one of the best statements in American literature about what happens when one comes face to face with the primeval world of matter and force.

The first view of the mountain is of a "summit veiled in clouds, like a dark isthmus in that quarter, connecting the heavens with the earth."[43] The description is heavy with portent; the mountain stands between two realms of experience. Thoreau does not use an allusion from Greek myth here; it is easy enough to imagine him comparing Ktaadn to Olympus, but he wants to give the reader the sense that Ktaadn is *itself* a sacred mountain, not merely *like* a sacred

mountain. A few pages later, he does let a little playful mythiness
creep into a description. "The summit . . . had a singularly flat
table-land appearance, like a short highway, where a demigod might
be let down to take a turn or two in an afternoon, to settle his
dinner."[44]

But these are just hints; the first time the reader is clearly shown
that we are coming close to a primal world whose natural expression
is via myth is the extraordinary description Thoreau gives of standing on the banks of the Aboljacknagesic River catching the "perfect
shower" of trout being tossed to shore by the rest of the party
standing out in the stream.

> While yet alive, before their tints had faded, they [the trout] glistened
> like the fairest flowers, the product of primitive rivers; and he [Thoreau
> is speaking of himself] could hardly trust his senses, as he stood over
> them, that these jewels should have swum away in that Aboljacknagesic
> water for so long, so many dark ages;—these bright fluviatile flowers,
> seen of Indians only, made beautiful, the Lord only knows why, to swim
> there![45]

So far this is only bright and imaginative nature writing, but
Thoreau goes on immediately to explain this undoubtedly real experience in terms of myth, and while we may find the direction of
his thought odd or unfamiliar, it is important to try to follow him.
The passage continues:

> I could understand better, for this, the truth of mythology, the fables of
> Proteus, and all those beautiful sea-monsters—how all history, indeed,
> put to a terrestrial use, is mere history; but put to a celestial, is mythol-
> ogy always.[46]

By history Thoreau means natural history, that is, the history of
nature, the organic unfolding of things. Thoreau sees change,
growth, and development in nature. What modern thought and
imagination express via the master concept of evolution, everything from the evolving of a single plant from seed to leaf to the
agelong changing of one species into another, was, for Thoreau and
many of his contemporaries, best expressed via the image of trans-

formation or metamorphosis. And in this last era before Darwin's thesis planted evolution as an image in the modern imagination, metamorphosis expressed itself most characteristically in myth. (After Darwin, evolution, expressing itself through science, took the place of metamorphosis as a concept and image.) So when Thoreau looks at the glorious and delicate colors of a wet trout just caught from the stream and sees "brilliant fluviatile flowers," he realizes that his imagination has reacted metamorphically, so to speak, that he has just performed, inadvertently perhaps, and on a small scale, the kind of imaginative transfiguration which on a large scale could be called mythmaking.

That night Thoreau dreams about trout fishing, wakes thinking it was all "a fable," gets up before dawn and goes fishing again, and, like Keats's account of Adam's dream, "I once more cast my line into the stream, and found the dream to be real and the fable true."[47] Whether we take the positive term "myth" or the negative term "fable," the incident proves true. Thoreau now turns the reader toward "the dark side of Ktaadn," a mountain of "distinct and cloudless outline in the moonlight." We are returned to the principal narrative, but with a disquieting sense that we are moving through another, older, more meaning-filled world, a primitive, fresh, and awesome world in which myth still stirs as the primitive and necessary expression of the innermost nature and deepest significance of things.

It is important to keep in mind that Thoreau does not permit the narrative to depend on myth. Myth is at best only a clue to some significance in nature that, but for myth, might remain obscure, and the significance myth uncovers is far more important than the myth itself. The narrative depends, quite properly, on Thoreau's ability to describe the climb up Ktaadn in ordinary narrative prose that rings true for anyone, whether or not he has ever ventured into the woods around Katahdin, as it is now more tamely spelled. These myth references only become effective because they are imbedded, like jewels themselves, in the midst of straightforward description.

When the group stops for the night part way up the mountain, with the summit in view, Thoreau plunges on alone to see what is ahead:

> We were in a deep and narrow ravine, sloping up to the clouds, at an angle of nearly forty-five degrees, and hemmed in by walls of rock, which were at first covered with low trees, then with impenetrable thickets of scraggy birches and spruce-trees, and with moss, but at last bare of all vegetation but lichens, and almost continually draped in clouds. Following up the course of the torrent which occupied this—and I mean to lay some emphasis on this word *up*—pulling myself up by the side of perpendicular falls of twenty or thirty feet, by the roots of firs and birches, and then, perhaps, walking a level rod or two in the thin stream, for it took up the whole road, ascending by huge steps, as it were, a giant's stairway, down which a river flowed.[48]

The reference to the giant's stairway is not the final point of the passage; it is no more than a passing reference, a clue to the scale of the scenery. In the description that follows, there are similar mythical references, but they are too played down and made subservient to the actual landscape.

> . . . I began to work my way, scarcely less arduous than Satan's anciently through Chaos, up the nearest, though not the highest peak. At first scrambling on all fours over the tops of ancient black spruce-trees (*abies Nigra*), old as the flood, from two to ten or twelve feet in height, their tops flat and spreading, and their foliage blue and nipt with cold, as if for centuries they had ceased growing upward against the bleak sky, the solid cold.[49]

The Miltonic allusions enhance the setting by invoking invisible presences. But the dark, hard, rocky, and tangled landscape is kept in front of the reader, while biblical and Miltonic references and statements such as "here the principle of vegetation was hard put to it" obliquely suggest that unseen forces are at work behind the effectively described appearances.

In a journal entry for 1853, as we have seen, Thoreau wrote about a condition in which he would be "overflowing with life," "rich in experience" for which he lacked expression, and about finding that nature would then come to provide that missing language, so that "all nature" would "fable" and "every natural phenomenon" would come to constitute "a myth."[50] It is this process which is at work in the "Ktaadn" essay and which explains the rather queer passage which comes next as Thoreau describes reaching the top of this ravine.

> Having slumped, scrambled, rolled, bounced, and walked, by turns, over this scraggy country, I arrived upon a side-hill, or rather side-mountain, where rocks, gray, silent rocks, were the flocks and herds that pastured, chewing a rocky cud at sunset. They look at me with hard grey eyes, without a bleat or a low. This brought me to the skirt of a cloud, and bounded my walk that night.[51]

It is an extravagant passage, partly intended for humor perhaps, and perhaps not altogether successful, but it is important that we recognize it for what it is, a production of the mythmaking mind, a mind that habitually assumes all nature to be alive, or at least to be the outward expression of inner, perhaps long-departed, forces.

It can be argued that the stony flocks passage is a misstep, detracting from more than advancing the narrative, but it can also be understood as a calculated bit of the bizarre, designed to unsettle the reader by displaying the unsettled animistic imagination of the traveler. The wild, almost fevered tone the narrative now begins to take makes the latter quite plausible.

Thoreau returns now to his companions and they turn in for the night. Their camp site is "a savage and dreary" place, "wildly rough." The descriptions have an air of strangeness. The "trees here seemed so evergreen and sappy that we almost doubted if they would acknowledge the influence of fire; but fire prevailed at last." The spruce boughs cut for bedding are described as feathers "plucked from the live tree." It is an eerie, almost magical forest in which everything is animated, and it is all the more effective because it is not the allegorical forest of "Young Goodman Brown" or the overly magical forest of German romance and fairy story. Here we have just the natural elements, but described so as to seem half sentient. The winds "rushed and roared through the ravine all night, from time to time arousing our fire, and dispersing the embers about. It was as if we lay in the very nest of a young whirlwind." The image of the whirlwind as a young bird is a bold and fine one. For Thoreau, myth begins not so much in metaphor as in the conviction that everything is alive.

With morning, they all strike out for the summit and Thoreau is soon alone in the lead, having outstripped the others. Although it is a clear day, the top is shrouded in mist. Everywhere there are huge rocks, and Thoreau describes his passage in language that reminds one of the descriptions of the thawing clay bank in *Walden,* when he felt himself in the laboratory of the world. "The mountain seemed a vast aggregation of loose rocks, as if sometime it had rained rocks. . . . They were the raw materials of a planet dropped from an unseen quarry, which the vast chemistry of nature would anon work up, or work down. . . . This was an undone extremity of the globe."[52] The language makes clear that we are coming to the core of the experience, to some glimpse of origins, of the beginnings of things. It is equally clear that Thoreau feels surrounded by powerful and alien forces. "I was deep within the hostile ranks of clouds. . . . Occasionally, when the windy columes broke in to me, I caught sight of a dark, damp crag to the right or left; the mist driving ceaselessly between it and me." At this point, Thoreau makes the most extensive mythical allusion of the entire piece. "It reminded me of the creations of the old epic and dramatic poets, of Atlas, Vulcan, the Cyclops, and Prometheus. Such was Caucasus and the rock where Prometheus was bound. Aeschylus had no doubt visited such scenery as this."[53] It sounds casual, and is put as something suggested to him by the scenery. Thoreau had translated Aeschylus' *Prometheus Bound,* starting sometime in the late 1830s, and it had been printed in *The Dial.* The storm scene that closes the play is perhaps the best part of the translation. Prometheus cries:

> Therefore 'gainst me let there be hurled
> Fires' double-pointed curl, and air
> Be provoked with thunder, and a tumult
> Of wild winds;

Hermes and the chorus have an exchange, and then, in the last speech of the play, the called-for natural cataclysm commences. Prometheus speaks again:

> Earth is shaken;
> And a hoarse sound of thunder
> Bellows near; and wreathes of lightning
> Flash out fiercely blazing, and whirlwinds dust
> Whirl up: and leap the blasts
> Of all winds, 'gainst one another
> Blowing in opposite array;
> And air with sea is mingled.[54]

The wild crags of the top of Ktaadn and particularly, we may guess, the "tumult of wild winds" recall to Thoreau the final scene of Aeschylus' play. Nature here not only recalls myth, but for once nature lives up to myth. Unforced and spontaneous as the suggestion of Prometheus seems at this point in the narrative, we may still wish to recall the blowing campfire of the previous night and all the myth and dream references that have gone before. For it is not by accident that we have come to the Aeschylean scale of things and the image of Prometheus, as Thoreau makes quite apparent in what follows. After saying that Aeschylus must have visited similar scenes, Thoreau goes on:

> It was vast, Titanic, and such as man never inhabits. Some part of the beholder, even some vital part, seems to escape through the loose grating of his ribs as he ascends. He is more lone than you can imagine. There is less of substantial thought and fair understanding in him, than in the plains where men inhabit. His reason is dispersed and shadowy, more thin and subtle like the air.[55]

Once the myth of Prometheus has suggested itself to him, he uses it, quite originally and freely. He is not constrained by conventional images of Prometheus as the creator of man, as the fire stealer, or as the well intentioned rebel against the tyranny of Zeus. The figure described in the paragraph above is none of these. It is Thoreau himself, but it is a Thoreau trying to puzzle out his own condition with the help of Aeschylus' great figure of Prometheus.

What is important is that Thoreau uses the image of Prometheus to press on beyond the familiar figure of Promotheus. Actual experience, in this case the ascent of Ktaadn, is heightened into myth; and the two kinds of experience flow together to make a new image, emphasizing loneliness and a sense of being diminished. The figure atop Ktaadn is very much alone, and he conveys very vividly his sense of how that alien high place can diminish a man. Instead of a re-robed Prometheus, we have a fresh perception; instead of Prometheus, we have Thoreau, but the figure of Thoreau has gained depth and subtlety from the image of Prometheus.

Thoreau does not insist on the Prometheus image, and the reader is grateful. The narrative is not sidetracked into Greece, but continues in Maine. Thoreau stands on top of the mountain, feeling diminished, unwanted, out of place. "Vast, Titanic, inhuman Nature has got him at disadvantage, caught him alone, and pilfers him of some of his divine faculty. She does not smile on him as in the plains. She seems to say sternly, 'why came ye here before your time? This ground is not prepared for you.'" Almost as in Holbach or Volney, nature continues to address the traveler, impressing man with nature's indifference to him. "Shouldst thou freeze or starve, or shudder thy life away, here is no shrine, nor altar, nor any access to my ear."[56]

The experience of climbing Ktaadn culminates in Thoreau's coming face to face with the raw forces of nature, personified here half seriously as gods. But the gods or forces here experienced are not those of Trancendentalism. Here is no divine aspect of man, no smiling pantheism, but an archaic experience, undoubtedly religious in nature, of some profoundly *other* force. That other force is Nature, not Emerson's anthropocentric nature, not the cultivated nature of Alcott's garden, but a primeval, wild Nature, in the presence of which man is a little and alien creature able to express his awe only in the language of myth, whether Greek or American Indian.

> The tops of mountains are among the unfinished parts of the globe, whither it is a slight insult to the gods to climb and pry into their secrets, and try their effect on our humanity. Only daring and insolent

men, perchance, go there. Simple races, as savages, do not climb
mountains—their tops are sacred and mysterious tracts never visited by
them. Pomola is always angry with those who climb to the summit of
Ktaadn.[57]

The account of the ascent and the encounter with a bleak, powerful,
and unhuman Nature stops at this point, ending with this smooth,
un-urgent and not quite satisfactory paragraph with its allusion to
the Abnaki Indian guardian goddess of Ktaadn. While the paragraph is evidence that Thoreau does not wish to move the scene—
even in imagery or by allusion—to Greece, such casual passing
reference to the gods of Maine simply does not exert much influence
on our imagination. Perhaps Thoreau felt the inadequacy of this, for
after a few pages of circumstantial detail about the return trip, the
narrative returns rather unexpectedly to the prinicipal event again,
and, for the fourth time in this essay, the attempt to write honestly
and fully about a direct encounter with nature compels Thoreau
toward the language of classic myth. At the critical moment, it is
again a Greek mythological conception that serves as the decisive
image.

Thoreau begins again to try to evoke his full sense of this encounter by saying "perhaps I most fully realized that this was
primeval, untamed, and forever untameable *Nature,* or whatever else
men call it, while coming down this part of the mountain." The
long paragraph emphasizes how "vast, dreary, and inhuman" it was.
"This was that Earth of which we have heard, made out of Chaos and
Old Night. Here was no man's garden, but the unhandselled
globe." Milton's imagery, Greek imagery, and the language of King
Lear prove useful and right. The sentimental language of proverbs
and folklore proves wrong. "It was Matter, vast, terrific,—not his
Mother Earth that we have heard of . . . the home this of Necessity
and Fate." Trying to articulate this experience of the otherness or
alienness of nature, Thoreau is driven again to the language of
religion and myth. "There was there felt the presence of a force not
bound to be kind to man. It was a place for heathenism and
superstitious rites,—to be inhabited by men nearer of kin to the

rocks and to wild animals than we." The perception of primitive force requires primitive expression; archaic men and rites are invoked. The perception of earth as Matter forces Thoreau to follow—in what is admittedly a not fully coherent passage, but a passage of undoubted passion—the idea of the unspiritual nature of things back until it reaches his own body. The passage seems to record a moment when, as Thoreau looked full face into a completely unfamiliar animating force operating in material bodies, he feared the nature and intentions of that force.

> I stand in awe of my body, this matter to which I am bound has become so strange to me. I fear not spirits, ghosts, of which I am one,—*that* my body might,—but I fear bodies, I tremble to meet them. What is this Titan that has possession of me?

One way to read this is to say that Thoreau saw in "bodies" some spirit or force, perhaps akin to what Melville grimly called the lurking demonism in nature. Perhaps also it is not demonic, and as the passage feverishly concludes with a Whitman-like emphasis on the sense of touch and contact, we may wish to think the Titan in possession is some sort of paradoxical spirit of pure matter, materiality, and sense experience.

> Talk of mysteries!—think of our life in nature,—daily to be shown matter, to come in contact with it,—rocks, trees, wind on our cheeks! the *solid* earth! the *actual* world! the *common sense! Contact! Contact! Who* are we? *where* are we?[58]

The experience here recorded, whatever its exact nature, was a powerful one and Thoreau fell back on the Prometheus image even to hint at it. There is, besides the passion, a strong sense of paganism too, an ecstatic reveling in the solidity of that nature so alien to man. And whatever may be unclear about the passage, the ending is not; surely it is a cry from the depths. But all allusion to Prometheus' cry from the rock or Christ's from the cross is kept back. We are not to be impressed with Thoreau's learning but with his own actual experience on the mountain.

Greek myth, especially that of Prometheus, is thus crucial to "Ktaadn," though it is very little in evidence in the finished work. It intervenes in at least four different places, and is instrumental in crystallizing an image of man alone in an indifferent, perhaps hostile, universe. The actual encounter is real enough, and narrated as real, but for getting at the significance of myth in general, Greek myth becomes, momentarily, indispensable.

Greek myth was in fact an inextricable part of Thoreau's imagination—and it shows itself not only in moments of high excitement but in his everyday imagination. Walking out to Fair Haven Bay by moonlight one evening in September 1851, Thoreau was reminded of a lake in the Maine woods, and he looked on the scene with what can only be called a Greek eye.

> What gods are they that require so fair a vase of gleaming water to their prospect in the midst of the wild woods by night? Else why this beauty allotted to night, a gem to sparkle in the zone of night? They are strange gods now out; me thinks their names are not in any mythology. I can fairly trace its zigzag border of sheeny pads even here. If such is then to be seen in remotest wildernesses, does it not suggest its own nymphs and wood gods to enjoy it?

There may be elements of playfulness, nostalgia, and seeing with the eye of faith here, but there is also a heightened sense of the simple loveliness of the moment. Thoreau's mythmaking is not intended to raise altars, but to express the individual's awareness of nature. Thoreau now climbs up Fair Haven Hill and sits down:

> All the earth's surface like a mountain-top, for I see its relation to heaven as simply, and am not imposed upon by a difference of a few feet in elevation. In this faint, hoary light, all fields are like a mossy rock and remote from the cultivated plains of day. All is equally savage, equally solitary and cool-aired, and the slight difference in elevation is felt to be unimportant. It is all one with Caucasus, the slightest hill pasture.[59]

Greek myth enables Thoreau to live common events at an uncommon pitch. Out walking by moonlight he can live as though there were gods in all the streams and trees, he can mythicize and thus universalize any experience, divesting it of its provinciality and giving the daily and familiar things of this world an importance and an interest less fortunate people experience only in rare moments of high excitement.

5. "Walking": The Call for Myth

As the Ktaadn essay shows, myth was indeed crucial to Thoreau's literary expression, but crucial in an unorthodox way. He did not take a mythic figure and update it. No *Prometheus Unbound* for him. Nor does he reach for a mythological theme or plot, an eternal return or an Odyssey of the modern soul. Thoreau's major use of myth is none of these. To say that myth was for Thoreau a mode of the imagination is not quite right either. What Thoreau found most impressive in myth was the *process* of myth, the process by which myth universalizes and generalizes personal or individual experience, giving it general significance and narrative shape. Thoreau learned from myth how to mythicize his own perceptions and experiences.

Above all, myth was important to Thoreau for what it taught him about how to perceive and express nature, the green world and human nature both. Thoreau's essay on walking is his most explicit discussion of this central aspect of myth, while *Walden* is his most sustained and successful attempt to put the theory into practice. "Walking" includes a section that is virtually an essay on myth, together with some examples. In fact, in the finished version of "Walking" (which was at one time two lectures, one on wildness and one on walking), the first substantial bit of myth is a cryptic and playful fable or parable of Thoreau's own contriving.

Nowadays almost all man's improvements, so called, as the building of houses, and the cutting down of the forest and of all large trees, simply deform the landscape, and make it more and more tame and cheap. A people who would begin by burning the fences and let the forest stand! I saw the fences half consumed, their ends lost in the middle of the prairies, and some worldly miser with a surveyor looking after his bounds, while heaven had taken place around him, and he did not see the angels going to and fro, but was looking for an old post-hole in the midst of paradise. I looked again, and saw him standing in the middle of a boggy, stygian fen, surrounded by devils, and he had found his bounds without a doubt, three little stones, where a stake had been driven, and looking nearer, I saw that the Prince of Darkness was his Surveyor.[60]

This is mythological fun, comic demonology, reminiscent perhaps of Bunyan and Hawthorne and seeming a bit out of place in an essay of this sort. The playful quality, so noticeable in *Walden,* may be partly a self-conscious way of admitting that these modern "myths" and fables are a little old-looking and farfetched, and it may be partly due to Thoreau's perception that in fact a good deal of Greek, Roman, and Nordic myth had a fanciful and playful quality. One might also say that Thoreau's tone here is Ovidian and his little fable is a Concord metamorphosis. It would however be a mistake to conclude that because the tone is light the experience is not real. Similar moments of myth happened to Thoreau so frequently that we may suspect he actively courted them. The fable above appeared first in his journal, as did many others, including the following:

It is something to know when you are addressed by Divinity and not by a common traveler. I went down cellar just now to get an armful of wood and, passing the brick piers with my wood and candle, I heard, methought, a commonplace suggestion, but when, as it were by accident, I reverently attended to the hint, I found that it was the voice of a god who had followed me down cellar to speak to me.[61]

It seems clear that here, and elsewhere, Thoreau is mythicizing personal experience as he imagines the Greeks to have done. The results are, at least to a modern reader, more distracting than the direct or heroic tack often taken by Thoreau when he claims that since one age is as good as another, his experience is fit to stand beside any. Two pages after the fable of the Demon Surveyor comes this example of the direct heroic comparison:

I walk out into a Nature such as the old prophets and poets, Menu, Moses, Homer, Chaucer walked in. You may name it America, but it is not America; neither Americus Vespucius, nor Columbus, nor the rest were the discoverers of it. There is a truer account of it in mythology than in any history of America, so called, that I have seen.[62]

It is not clear whether the mythology here referred to is Greek mythology or American mythology, or whether Thoreau means the word to transcend nationalities. At times, as in "Sunday," Thoreau emphasizes the universality of certain Greek myths that still stir the modern imagination. At other times he seems impressed by the idea that each nation had its own peculiar, characteristic, and appropriate mythology. In "Walking" he does not come out for one or the other view in any exclusive sense. Whether or not he knew Friedrich Schlegel's famous "Talk on Mythology," printed in 1800 in *Dialogue on Poetry,* Thoreau was in fact working out Schlegel's position, that any new mythology that might be written in modern times would not be spun out of whole cloth but would include and extend the old. (Bronson Alcott maintained much the same position one evening in conversation with Margaret Fuller.) Schlegel's formulation of the problem clarifies a good deal about Thoreau's use of myth. Schlegel argued that modern poetry "lacks a focal point, such as mythology was for the ancients; and one could summarize all the essentials in which modern poetry is inferior to the ancients in these words: we have no mythology." But he thought that a new mythology was not far off and that it would not supplant but "encompass all the others. . . . To accelerate the genesis of the new mythology, the other mythologies must also be reawakened according to the measure of their profundity, their beauty, and their form."[63] What is most interesting here is Schlegel's insistence that any new mythology must subsume old mythologies. Schlegel is arguing that the new mythology will consist of self-conscious and deliberately "literary" creations, not primitive communal stories. What Schlegel laid out as a program, Thoreau put into practice. It was for reasons similar to Schlegel's that Thoreau puts so much Indic, Nordic, and Greek myth into his own efforts to create or recognize American mythology. For it is finally nothing less than a modern mythology—a modern American mythology—that Thoreau has in mind.

✓   "Walking" next turns to discuss the pull of the West and the idea
of the westward movement. If we now speak of the myths of the
frontier and the westward movement, then Thoreau is one of the
makers or at least first recorders of these myths.

> We go eastward to realize history and study the work of art and litera-
> ture, retracing the steps of the race; we go westward as into the future,
> with a spirit of enterprise and adventure. The Atlantic is a Lethean
> stream, in our passage over which we have had an opportunity to forget
> the Old World and its institutions. If we do not succeed this time, there
> is perhaps one more chance for the race left before it arrives on the banks
> of the Styx; and that is in the Lethe of the Pacific, which is three times as
> wide.[64]

But for all Thoreau's interest in the westward movement, and for all
the dark premonitions and hintings at the world of Moby-Dick in
such a passage as the above, it is the idea of the West, not the West
itself, that compels Thoreau. As Sherman Paul has so properly insisted, significance, for Thoreau, attached itself mainly to inner
exploration. The heroism, exploration and mythmaking that interested Thoreau were individual, not communal. Thus he kept his
eye not so much on myth as on myth-producing experience. "Walking" goes on to emphasize just this point.

> The island of Atlantis, and the islands and gardens of Hesperides, a sort
> of terrestrial paradise, appear to have been the Great West of the an-
> cients, enveloped in mystery and poetry. Who has not seen in imagina-
> tion, when looking into the sunset sky, the gardens of the Hesperides,
> and the foundation of all those fables?[65]

If one is interested in the kind of experience that can lead to myth,
and if one believes that it is the individual not the society that first
creates the myth, and if one further believes that the present age is as
rich as any in possibilities, then it is not surprising to find one
insisting, as Thoreau does now—apropos of seeing a Panorama of the
Rhine followed by a Panorama of the Mississippi—that *this was the
heroic age itself,* though we know it not, for the hero is commonly the
simplest and obscurest of men."[66] Thoreau the observer says that

this age is *as good as* the heroic age, while Thoreau the participant claims that this *is* the heroic age.

"Walking" now jumps to a consideration of "Wildness," but it is not really a break, since wildness is the chief characteristic of the heroic age. Talking about wildness rather than heroism gives Thoreau's essay a fresh quality that Carlyle, for example, forfeits by using the old language of the heroic. Although Thoreau obviously uses that word a good deal too, here, at least, he has found another way to approach the same topic. From wildness comes not only "the preservation of the world," but eminent civilizations and religion. In language that recalls the Christian creed, Thoreau writes "I believe in the forest, and in the meadow, and in the night in which the corn grows."[67] Thoreau extends wildness even to literature, of which he says, "it is only the wild that attracts us. Dullness is but another name for tameness. It is the uncivilized free and wild thinking in 'Hamlet' and the 'Iliad,' in all the Scriptures and Mythologies, not learned in the schools, that delights us."[68] Thoreau then turns to consider more fully whether literature does fully express the wild or whether it merely catches hints of it:

> I do not know of any poetry to quote which adequately expresses this yearning for the Wild. Approached from this side, the best poetry is tame. I do not know where to find in any literature, ancient or modern, any account which contents me of that Nature with which even I am acquainted. You will perceive that I demand something which no Augustan nor Elizabethan age, which no *culture* in short, can give. Mythology comes nearer to it than anything.[69]

Thoreau understood mythology as a form of expression that historically came from poetry. In *Walden* he says of the sand foliage that "it precedes the green and flowery spring, as mythology precedes regular poetry."[70] And when Thoreau goes on to compare mythology with the literature that comes later, one has to keep in mind just how much he knew and cared for English literature to appreciate the compliment he pays to mythology.

> How much more fertile a Nature, at least, has Grecian mythology its root in than English Literature! Mythology is the crop which the Old

World bore before its soil was exhausted, before the fancy and imagination were affected with blight; and which it still bears, wherever its pristine vigor is unabated.[71]

Years later E. M. Forster was to make the same kind of comment about English literature, and his remark helps explain what Thoreau was getting at. In chapter 32 of *Howards End,* written in 1910, Forster asked:

> Why has not England a great mythology? Our folklore has never advanced beyond daintiness, and the greater melodies about our countryside have all issued through the pipes of Greece. Deep and true as the native imagination can be, it seems to have failed here. It has stopped with the witches and fairies. It cannot vivify one fraction of a summer field, or give names to half a dozen stars. England still waits for the supreme moment of her literature—for the great poet who shall voice her, or, better still, for the thousand little poets whose voices shall pass into our common talk.[72]

Forster's understanding of myth is close to that of Thoreau, and I think it is not a bad description of Thoreau to say that he tried very hard to "vivify" the nature he saw around him. Like Forster, too, he assumes that it is still possible. "Walking" concludes its excursion into myth with nothing less than a call for American mythology:

> The West is preparing to add its fables to those of the East. The valleys of the Ganges, the Nile, and the Rhine, having yielded their crop, it remains to be seen what the valleys of the Amazon, the Plate, the Orinoco, the St. Lawrence, and the Mississippi will produce. Perchance, when, in the course of ages, American liberty has become a fiction of the past,—as it is to some extent a fiction of the present,—the poets of the world will be inspired by American mythology.[73]

Thus Thoreau brings the argument to the present, in which new myth will be made which will subsume the old. Thoreau felt himself a part of this great effort, and *Walden* is his major attempt to create a piece of this new American mythology.

6. A Life of Myth

Before turning to *Walden* there is still one more aspect of Thoreau's engagement with myth that needs to be mentioned, for one cannot fully understand Thoreau's characteristic ease with myth unless one recognizes the extent to which he took myth in a very personal way. The impression is sometimes left by criticism—not just of Thoreau—that myth is a literary ingredient which can be taken up, shrewdly used, and set down again. We are reluctant to believe that a modern writer such as Thoreau could have been religiously committed to myth. It is all very well to use it for metaphor, but to take it seriously seems almost past crediting. But the evidence is that Thoreau did in fact find that certain myths moved him to awe and worship. There is, for example, his much discussed apostrophe, some think to the moon and some think to Lydian Emerson:

> My dear, my dewey sister, let thy rain descend on me. I not only love thee, but I love the best of thee; that is to love thee rarely. I do not love thee every day. Commonly I love those who are less than thou. I love thee only on great days. Thy dewy words feed me like the manna of the morning. I am as much thy sister as thy brother. Thou art as much my brother as my sister. It is a portion of thee and a portion of me which are kin. Thou dost not have to woo me. I do not have to woo thee. O my sister! O Diana, thy tracks are on the eastern hills. Thou surely passedst that way. I, the hunger, saw them in the morning dew. My eyes are the hounds that pursue thee. Ah my friend, what if I do not answer thee? I hear thee. Thou canst speak; I cannot. I hear and forget to answer. I am occupied with hearing. I awoke and thought of thee; thou wast present to my mind. How camest thou there? Was I not present to thee likewise?[74]

From the tone, one would say that this is either a strong personal statement or merely a skilled literary representation, perhaps modeled on an Orphic hymn or on the famous passage on Isis in book nine of *The Golden Ass*. It has been connected with an early piece by Thoreau on "The Sister" and with Thoreau's very personal and emotional letter to Lydian Emerson of June 20, 1843. It could also be maintained that its tone is quite consistent with the eloquent longing expressed in Thoreau's essay on "Night and Moonlight," and it should be noted that W. E. Channing and Franklin Sanborn both saw the passage as nothing more than a hymn to the moon.[75] It may be that modern readers cannot easily imagine anyone addressing Diana in so fervent a way and therefore have sought a real person behind the passage. What seems to have happened is that a real person and a vivid apprehension of a natural night fused together over the years and found expression via the literary device of myth. Thoreau's letter to Mrs. Emerson treats her as a goddess, a "lunal influence." He wrote, "the thought of you will constantly elevate my life: it will be something always above the horizon to behold, as when I look up at the evening star."[76] Perhaps the image of Lydian Emerson became identified with that of Diana and the moon. Whatever the precise situation was that is reflected here, the passage at least opens up the possibility that—like Novalis, Hölderlin, and some others—Thoreau actually entertained Greek myth seriously enough to veer into actual belief now and again. He liked, for example, to think of himself worshipping at the altar of Pan. Even more startling is the assumption in the above passage that he is himself one of the gods. He also liked to compare himself to Apollo, and he enjoyed complaining about having to keep the flocks of Admetis. But this self-identification with Apollo was, I think, largely funning. At least there was that side to it. At other times Thoreau's response is quite serious, even moving. When thinking about the gods as the powers of nature, Thoreau was apt to respond by feeling rather small and mortal. In the *Week*, as we have seen, he cried out "But how can I communicate with the gods who am a pencil-maker on the earth, and not be insane?" while in *Walden* he responds, a touch less meekly, to a storm by saying "The gods must be proud . . . with such forked flashes to rout a poor unarmed fisherman."[77] Sometimes he coaxes himself into mythic moments, sometimes he casts himself as a poor mortal, sometimes as one of the immortals. The well-disposed reader patiently follows, looking for the wry humor which will show that it is all fun, but surprised sometimes at the earnestness and above all the frequency of these allusions. In his desire to lead a "life of allegory" or a mythic life, Thoreau may have tried to surround himself with mythic sugges- ✓ tion. That he succeeded in this, even for his contemporaries, there is some evidence.

There is, for example, a vivid description by Sophia Hawthorne of Thoreau, Emerson, and Hawthorne out skating on the Concord River one afternoon. She describes Thoreau leading, "figuring dithyrambic dances and Bacchic leaps on the ice," followed by Hawthorne, "Who wrapped in his cloak, moved like a self-impelled Greek statue, stately and grave," followed by Emerson, "Evidently too weary to hold himself erect, pitching headforemost, half lying on the air."[78] Perhaps this reference to Thoreau is no more than the conventional use of mythology for familiar allusion one finds everywhere in the period. Indeed, after coming in from this very party, Emerson referred to Hawthorne both as satyr and as Ajax while he was resting and talking to Sophia.

But there are other descriptions of Thoreau in mythic terms which fall somewhere between this conventionally lighthearted allusiveness and full seriousness. His friend and walking companion, the poet W. E. Channing, after quoting the "O my sister, O Diana" passage, was moved to continue the apostrophe to the moon, casting Thoreau as Endymion.

> Thou coulds't look down with pity on that mound. Some silver beams faintly raining through the old locust boughs, for thy lover, thy Endymion, is watching there. He was abroad with thee after the midnight mass had tolled, and the consecrated dust of yesterdays each in his narrow cell for ever laid, which he lived to hive in previous vases for immortality,—tales of natural piety, bound each to each. . . . Thus conversant was he with great Nature. Perchance he reached the wildness for which he longed.[79]

This is perhaps the sort of poetic exaggeration that gives so much of Channing's work a note of semisincerity, but it is still significant that Channing is content to leave the episode on the mythic level and does not try to reduce the experience to a metaphor for something else.

Emerson's son is less self-consciously arty in his memoir of Thoreau, whom he saw as a modern "type" of Pan.

> Surely a better mortal to represent what the Greek typified in his sylvan god we might search New England long to find. For years, a wanderer in the outskirts of our village was like to meet this sturdy figure striding silently through tangled wood or wild meadow at any hour of day or night; yet he would vent his happiness in a wild and gay dance, or yet again lie motionless in any weather in a lonely wood, waiting for his friends, the wild creatures, and winning in the match with them of leisure and patience. When at length the forest began to show its little heads, the utterance of a low continuous humming sound, like those of Nature, spoke to their instincts and drew them to him. Like the wood-gods of all peoples, he guarded trees and flowers and springs, showed a brusque hospitality to mortals wandering in the wood, *so they violated not its sanctities;* and in him was the immortal quality of youth and cheerfulness.[80]

Emerson himself referred to Thoreau as Pan, or the young Pan, and sometimes, as in the following, the reference goes well beyond casual imagery, and well beyond the idea of the genial wood-sprite kind of Pan his son saw:

> Henry Thoreau is like the wood-god who solicits the wandering poet, and draws him into "antres vast and desarts idle," and leaves him naked, plaiting vines and with twigs in his hand. Very seductive are the first steps from the town to the woods, but the end is want and madness.[81]

Emerson's comment expresses uneasiness, and even perhaps fright, an uncanny echo of the primitive fear from which our word "panic" is derived. We cannot completely discount all these mythical descriptions of Thoreau. Clearly he was, even to his contemporaries, larger than life, somehow "other," comparable if not akin to the gods, in tune with nature as only a Greek demigod could be. And perhaps that same quality in Thoreau has led modern readers to "mythologize" him as the Man who Went to Walden Pond or the Man who Spent the Night in Jail. But if he is a legend in our time, he seemed more nearly a creature of myth in his own time, and of the two, the latter is more interesting. Thoreau himself knew that in an age of cheap printing and widespread literacy he would never become an entry in a classical dictionary as "Thoreau; son of _____ and _____. Instructed the Americans in the secrets of Nature. Woke his neighbors up, refused to pay his taxes. Said to have been a pencil-maker, by which our ancestors doubtless symbolized the writer who makes his own tools and is therefore self-sufficient." Thoreau did not wish to be remembered only in the folk memory. He tried to live what he once called a "life of allegory," and he recorded the results of that life with endless care and pains in all his writings and best perhaps in *Walden.*

7. Myth in *Walden*

The success of Thoreau's effort to live and write myth must at last be judged by his expression of it in *Walden.* To begin with, the book is crammed with mythological references in the ordinary sense of the word. There are bits of American Indian myth: a Mucclasse ritual of cleansing by fire, an "Indian Ceres," the Indian legend about Walden.[82] There are bits too of Nordic myth: Valhalla is mentioned twice, once as a description of the vast pile of ice, and Thoreau puns with Thor and Thaw.[83] There is little English mythology to use, but Thoreau does get in Robin Goodfellow. Biblical myth plays a small part too; Adam and Eve are mentioned twice and there is a passage which takes off directly from a theme in Ecclesiastes, "Remember now thy creator in the days of thy youth."[84] *Walden* has been read as a work dominated by Christian myths and by images of Adam, the Fall, and so on, but to judge from the conscious and overt use of myth and symbol in the book, one would have to say that Indic and Greek archetypes and myths far outweigh biblical ones. Similarly Thoreau's use of Indic scriptures in *Walden* far outweighs his use of the Bible. He refers to the *Bhagavad-Gita,* the *Harivansa,* the *Vedas,* the *Vishnu Purana,* Pilpay (whose fables form the *Hitopadesa*), and Calidasa. Thoreau annexes India for his own purposes. It is, for example, in the spirit of Indic myth that Thoreau writes the fantastic passage connecting Walden with the Ganges and

Concord with India, and it is in the spirit of India that Thoreau wrote or included the story of the artist of Kouroo. The example of Indian apologue was clearly important to Thoreau's own fable writing.

The only mythology that Thoreau used so extensively in *Walden* that we may conclude that he was relying on it, and in some ways grounding his book on it, is Greek mythology. Here too, it is not necessary to list all the occurrences, but a brief mention of some of the more important ones may be helpful. In the opening pages there is an extended allusion to Hercules and his labors, including the killing of the Hydra; there is also an allusion to the story of Deucalion and Pyrrha. Also mentioned in significant ways in the first chapter are Minerva, Aurora, Memnon, the removal of the Gods of Troy, Arcadia, Apollo keeping the flocks of Admetis, and Phaeton. There is, in addition, a long passage about Momus (that god who continually satirized the gods) included in the first version but cut from the final manuscript. "Where I Lived" makes use of Atlas, describes the Walden hut as a house "fit for a travelling god," and uses Olympus and Aurora in suggestive ways. "Reading" talks about Greek heroes and the emulation of them by reading. "Solitude" ends with an extensive fantasia on Hygeia and Hebe, while "Visitors" takes up Thoreau's woodcutter friend Therien as Homeric man. "The Beanfield" uses as points of reference Hercules, Antaeus, and the Trojan War, and puts Ceres at the center of a discussion of the religious aspects of husbandry. "The Village" uses Orpheus, "Ponds" uses the Golden Age and Icarus. "Baker Farm" ends, as many chapters do, with Greek myth, here a reference to the Irish getting, like Mercury, talaria to their heels. "Higher Laws" has a humorous parody of Alexander Ross's Christian cleverness at mythic interpretation as Thoreau goes glibly from hunters to Nimrod to Christ. This same chapter has a discussion of fauns and satyrs and downward transmigration. "Brute Neighbors" has the familiar battle of the ants, epically augmented by reference to Achilles and the Myrmidons, a good example of the heroic nagging Thoreau was given to. "Housewarming" makes effective use of the Golden Age and contains a sort of homage to Saturn. There is some light god-play with Vulcan and Terminus, and a quite serious passage on sacred groves. "Spring" relies heavily on images from Ovid's account of Creation and the Golden Age in the *Metamorphoses*.

These major incidents, together with a host of passing references I have not tried to list, give *Walden* an extensive undergrowth of traditional mythology, mostly but not exclusively Greek. The larger purpose behind all the mythological reference is the creation of a context for certain efforts of his own. Thoreau uses traditional myth as a context for making religious points, as in the passage on the sacred grove, as a context for his own flights into myth, and to create a climate favorable to heroism.

In his frequent reference to traditional myths, Thoreau hoped to connect each myth with a fact. All these references taken together create for the book an atmosphere of myth in which we will not be surprised to see Thoreau reversing the process and trying to turn his own facts into fable. He does this in three major ways. The first, and perhaps least effective, is his modern "myths" in the antique manner. One example of this is the extended "fable" which tries to impose the image of the iron horse on a locomotive in a literal way. "Or perchance, at evening, I hear him in his stable blowing off the superfluous energy of the day, that he may calm his nerves and cool his liver and brain for a few hours of iron slumber."[85] This is mock-myth, enjoyable for its bravura, interesting as it shows the persistent Thoreauvian effort to literally animate the inanimate, but not intended seriously. Another example of this bravura fable-making is the story of the Hyperboreans in "The Pond in Winter." Here, as in the above examples, we are amused and perhaps a little baffled by Thoreau's cleverness. These passages are extravagant caricatures of one process of mythmaking, helping to keep that process continually in view and effectively disarming us, making it easier to accept any mythmaking that is just a little less artificial or extreme.

The second and more varied group of vignettes or episodes are those which are treated not as modern subjects mock-mythologized in the Greek manner, but as extensions of familiar mythology into modern affairs. When, for example, Thoreau re-mythologizes God or Pan as the "old settler . . . who is reported to have dug Walden

Pond, and stoned it, and fringed it with pine woods," we detect both a mischievous intent to puzzle us together with a more or less serious spiritualizing of Creation.[86] So too when Thoreau refers to an "elderly dame," who "dwells in my neighborhood, invisible to most persons, in whose odorous herb garden I love to stroll sometimes, gathering samples and listening to her fables; for she has a genius of unequaled fertility, and her memory runs back farther than mythology," most readers recognize the familiar mythical abstraction Mother Nature, but given a new name so as to preclude our stock response.[87] Here Thoreau uses myth to penetrate beyond myth, his point being the quite serious one that Nature is more than a collection of disparate natural facts or events. These sly descriptions represent the extention of traditional myth into the living present. The process is analogous to that used by Thoreau to describe Therien. Therien is given Homeric stature, but in a modern and, so to speak, an aboveboard way, with no sly tricks.

> Who should come to my lodge this morning but a true Homeric or Paphlagonian man,—he had so suitable and poetic a name that I am sorry I cannot print it here,—a Canadian, a wood-chopper and post-maker, who can hole fifty posts in a day. . . . He, too, has heard of Homer, and "if it were not for books," would "not know what to do rainy days."[88]

Thoreau reads Homer to Therien, noting his frank appreciative response. Here Thoreau is trying to link Homer and the woodcutter in actual fact, not just by allusion or metaphor.

In a similar way, though again with a vein of humor, Thoreau magnifies the battle of the ants in "Brute Neighbors" by reference to Achilles and the Myrmidons and by solemnly dating the battle. But for all this aggrandizement by association, the battle is vividly described in great detail and we are impressed with it, quite apart from any epic additive. The heroic comparison is, we conclude, not altogether foolish. It is a question of scale, and Thoreau wins the point. The episode in "The Beanfield" is another example of mythological extension into the present, though neither Thoreau nor his readers takes seriously the image of Thoreau-Achilles cutting down an endless series of weedy Hectors. The laugh here is (intentionally) on Thoreau and his Homeric daydreaming. What impresses one, upon reflection, is how Thoreau can use his associative mythicizing in so many kinds of situations, from the ridiculous to the fully serious.

The story of the artist of Kouroo is one of the most successful of these mythical extensions, if, as seems likely, Thoreau made up the story himself. It is a mythical extension, similar to those already treated only in that it is obviously and deliberately rooted in a recognizable tradition, in this case, Indic sacred legend. The story is of the artist who, having decided to carve a staff, stuck faithfully to his task as ages passed and empires fell, only to find that when at last he accomplished his humble aim, the staff expanded before his eyes into a new world, "fairest of all the creations of Brahma." It has been thought to be a story, parable, or myth epitomizing *Walden* itself, and it is indeed one of the most effective images in the book.[89]

But interesting as the story of the artist of Kouroo is, it is at last only an image and wears the trappings of a world far removed from that of Walden Pond. Of course Thoreau used it deliberately and with admirable success to universalize the experience of the book. Those experiences of living at Walden are the indisputable center of the book, and some of them are conveyed by means of a species of modern mythmaking in which Thoreau uses neither the burlesque techniques (the iron horse) nor the subtler extensions of traditional myth into the present ("reviving mythology," as Thoreau himself calls his conversations with the philosopher Alcott). In a handful of the most spectacular of the episodes in *Walden,* Thoreau tries to stand forward and clear of the elaborate mythological backdrop and "write some pure mythology" of his own, making modern myths out of modern subjects in a modern manner.

There is, for example, the famous parable or fable about the sense of loss:

I long ago lost a hound, a bay horse, and a turtle dove, and am still on their trail. Many are the travellers I have spoken concerning them, describing their tracks and what calls they answered to. I have met one or two who had heard the hound, and the tramp of the horse, and even seen the dove disappear behind a cloud, and they seemed as anxious to recover them as if they had lost them themselves.[90]

The success of this not yet fully explained fable is perhaps best estimated by applying it to the standard Thoreau used on some of the old fables, when he wrote that the "hidden significance of these fables which has been detected, . . . is not so remarkable as the readiness with which they may be made to express any truth."[91]

A similar but less celebrated fable closes the chapter "Higher Laws." It begins "John Farmer sat at his door one September evening, after a hard day's work, his mind still running on his labor more or less." It tells of his hearing a flute which teases him out of his habitual reveries and calls him to other things. The notes of the flute

gently did away with the street, and the village, and the state in which he lived. A voice said to him,—Why do you stay here and live this mean moiling life, when a glorious existence is possible for you? Those same stars twinkle over other fields than these.—but how to come out of this condition and actually migrate thither? All that he could think of was to practice some new austerity, to let his mind descend into his body and redeem it, and treat himself with ever increasing respect.[92]

This passage has puzzled critics, but the self-assured narration of another's innermost thoughts and the oriental flavor of the conclusion strongly suggest that this is another of Thoreau's own contriving. It is a Concord fable concerning Everyman, similar both to other incidents described in *Walden* and to such obvious fables as that of the artist of Kouroo. What makes the fable of John Farmer so successful is its very unobtrusiveness. There is no oriental city, no exotic philosophy, no distracting orientalism; it sounds sufficiently actual to send researchers to the town records. Doubtless something factual suggested the fable, but whatever the incident and whoever the person, its chief use was as Thoreau says in that key phrase, "to link my facts to fable."

Less perfect in form, but nevertheless among the great things in *Walden,* is the prose trumpet voluntary on the theme "Morning brings back the heroic ages," in "Where I Lived and What I Lived For." It is an astonishing piece of writing, an "Ode to Joy" creating in the reader the sense of awakening which is indeed its subject. "That man who does not believe that each day contains an earlier, more sacred, and auroral hour than he has yet profaned, has despaired of life and is pursuing a descending and darkening way."[93] This may have roots in the Bible and in the *Laws of Menu,* but again it stands alone, independent of mythic props. "To him whose elastic and vigorous thought keeps pace with the sun, the day is a perpetual morning." The passage closes with a burst of paradox reminiscent of the famous image of light as the shadow of God. "To be awake is to be alive. I have never yet met a man who was quite awake. How could I have looked him in the face."[94] This lacks parable form and can be called modern mythmaking only by stretching a point; but it is a deliberate effort to create an invocation to dawn, as if it really were the dawn that draws the heroism up to the surface in us. By making that invocation heroic and by turning rhapsodic admiration into modern worship, this is indeed an effort to recast daily experience in a mythic mold.

The single most impressive piece of modern mythmaking in *Walden* is the great description in "Spring" of the thawing of the sand and clay bank in the deep cut for the railroad not far from Thoreau's cabin.

> When the frost comes out in the spring, and even in a thawing day in the winter, the sand begins to flow down the slopes like lava, sometimes bursting out through the snow and overflowing it where no sand was to be seen before. Innumerable little streams overlap and interlace one with another, exhibiting a sort of hybrid product, which obeys half way the law of currents and half way that of vegetation. As it flows it takes the forms of sappy leaves or vines, making heaps of pulpy sprays a foot or more in depth. . . .[95]

The whole passage is too long and too well known to quote in full. As it proceeds Thoreau constructs from this unpromising natural phenomenon an astounding image of origins and transformations. The description of the sandbank is the chief and climactic seasonal metamorphosis of the book. The forms produced by the sand foliage lead Thoreau to a consideration of the whole question of creation:

> What makes this sand foliage remarkable is its springing into existence thus suddenly. When I see on the one side the inert bank,—for the sun acts on one side first,—and on the other this luxuriant foliage, the creation of an hour, I am affected as if in a peculiar sense I stood in the laboratory of the Artist who made the world and me,—had come to where he was still at work, sporting on this bank, and with excess of energy strewing his fresh designs about. I feel as if I were nearer to the vitals of the globe.[96]

From this sense of the origins of things, Thoreau goes on to dwell on the processes of growth and change suggested by the sand foliage. The prose becomes almost a catalog of transformations:

> You find thus in the very sands an anticipation of the vegetable leaf. No wonder that the earth expresses itself outwardly in leaves, it so labors with the idea inwardly. . . . The very globe continually transcends and translates itself, and becomes winged in its orbit. Even ice begins with delicate crystal leaves, as if it had flowed into moulds which the fronds of water plants have impressed on the watery mirror. The whole tree itself is but one leaf, and rivers are still vaster leaves whose pulp is intervening earth, and towns and cities are the ova of insects in their axils.[97]

Finally the process of transformation reaches man, and Thoreau describes it with Ovidian concreteness: "What is man but a mass of thawing clay? The ball of the human finger is but a drop congealed. The fingers and toes flow to their extent from the thawing mass of the body. Who knows what the human body would expand and flow out to under a more genial heaven?"[98]

Thoreau now sums up, observing that "this one hillside illustrated the principle of all the operations of Nature." It is an image of origination through change, of processes that would soon be simplified and labeled evolutionary. What Thoreau has described is the metamorphosis of nature itself. This process, we are told, is the real "spring," the springing forth of the earth itself, and it precedes the conventional springtime just as myth precedes regular poetry. The description of the sandbank is now followed by a description of the green and flowery spring—"The first sparrow of spring" passage—and then by an extended description of the return of the Golden Age, for which Thoreau relies heavily on Ovid's *Metamorphoses*. But, just as the springing of the thawing frost preceded the green spring, so Thoreau has preceded the Ovidian account with an actual account of the metamorphoses of nature itself. Or, to put it another way, the sandbank section relies on the concept of metamorphosis put forward by Goethe in his *Versuch, die Metamorphose der Pflanzen zu erklären* (1790), while the passages on the green spring and the Golden Age rely just as heavily on the concept of change and transformation found in Ovid.[99] In Ovid, of course, the Golden Age is gone never to return, having declined into the Silver Age. Thoreau's optimistic enlistment of an organic concept of metamorphosis enables him to reverse Ovid's account and tell about a new golden age to come, and to link that golden age with the annual coming of spring. Best of all, Thoreau's work puts nature itself in the prominent position. Goethean or Ovidian elements are played down and strictly subordinated, so that nature itself can precede, as it ought, all efforts to explain it. The chapter depends finally not on Goethe or Ovid, but on Thoreau's own observation.

As in the incident of the sand foliage, so in the whole book, there is an unceasing effort to tie facts to fables, and conversely to illustrate fables by referring them to natural facts. The process may reasonably be called one of myth-linking, though a more accurate way to describe the process would be to call it a sort of dialectic that proceeds from fact to myth, and thence on to a greater fact. It is a process of mythicizing facts, steadily counterbalanced by Thoreau's reification or "factualizing" of myth. And just as almost every chapter in *Walden* has its central myth (or legend, or fable, or apologue), so the whole book displays Thoreau's self-conscious efforts to mold fact into fable or mythology. Sherman Paul has called *Walden* a "fable of renewal." It could also be called an epic of solitary heroism, or an American myth of individual self-sufficiency. *Walden* could be subtitled "Metamorphoses in Concord," and since it so labors to attain some of the qualities of myth, it seems not only fit but necessary to try to describe the book in terms of myth.

But even if the entire foregoing case is charitably granted, is anything gained, at last, by calling *Walden* "myth"? Scholarly historians of myth are understandably reluctant to add every good or even every great literary work to the canon of world mythology, while those who take *Walden* seriously as a literary work that still speaks to our condition do not always find the book's value enhanced by the addition of the ambiguous term myth. Rather than call *Walden* a myth, it seems more useful, and nearer the mark, to say that it has a number of the characteristics of traditional myth. It gives narrative shape to conceptions that are essentially religious; it is closely connected with ritual; it arises from and treats of an heroic age. It most impressively resembles the greatest myth, I would say, in its imaginative concern with origins and changes, creation and metamorphosis.

Walden is, to a remarkable extent, a book about origins. The particular form this takes in *Walden* is a concern with the rebirth of the year and with the origins of the free individual. Indeed the originality of *Walden* is much more in its concern with the springs and beginnings of things than with the kind of originality that is meant by the word "novelty." In one way, *Walden* can be understood as a modern myth about "the twice-born" experience of a second birth into knowledge and wisdom.

Though *Walden* is also directly concerned with change and metamorphosis like so much of traditional myth, here too, Thoreau's achievement is integrative and original. He has joined images from Ovid with ideas from Goethe and others and has re-experienced and re-expressed the concept of transformation and change of bodily shape as a compelling and still valid literary metaphor for the essential processes of change in Nature. The changes of the seasons are the setting against which people change. The rebirth of the year at the end of the book is the setting for the rebirth of man. The organic unfolding both of man and of the natural world which is a central theme of *Walden* is a continual round of change, development, and evolution. As noted, before Darwin and social Darwinism made evolution a central and commanding image of the natural world, the concept of metamorphosis served Thoreau and his contemporaries as a master image of the workings of nature.

Finally, *Walden* was intended and still stands as proof of the possibility of heroism. As in myth, the possibilities in life are dramatized for us in the adventures of a hero who is in closer contact than we with what is variously called the divine, or the sense of the sacred. This is not to say that Thoreau had in mind any cult of Thoreau. His own dislike of cult was strong, and he was wise enough to put his teaching in fables and parables, in myth rather than in ritual.

Five

Whitman

1. The Insufficiency of Myth

Emerson saw myth differently at different times; his knowledge of it was rooted both in the rationalistic, anti-myth biblical criticism that went back both to Germany and to Anglo-American deism, and in the romantic revival of myth. Thoreau's characteristic endorsement of myth is partly due to the fact that he was less influenced by rationalist or romantic myth critics or scholars than by his own study of myth, especially classical myth. Whitman rejects myth to about the same degree that Thoreau accepts it. The elements in Whitman's view of myth are many: there is the strong influence of skeptical mythographers and rationalist thinkers such as Volney, Paine, and Frances Wright, not to mention the curious prominence of Egypt in Whitman's study of the past. But the real complexity of Whitman's attitude toward myth comes from the fact that while he tended to reject myth, he was also writing a new scripture and creating the basis for a new religion, and he therefore seems to have accepted and practiced mythmaking in ways recognizably those of our century. Whitman's notes on the *Nibelungenlied* and its relation to his own work make it clear that he intended to supplant traditional "objective" epic with modern "subjective" epic.[1] These are Whitman's own terms, and they also describe Whitman's complicated and shifting attitude toward myth. He also wanted to supplant the old "objective" mythological religions with a new "subjective" religion of humanity that was populist, nationalist, and almost the sort of revolutionary religion that Michelet championed in France.[2]

From a modern point of view, it is possible to claim that Whitman simply exchanged old myths for new, but this is to falsify the problem and to ignore the driving force of Whitman's purpose. It was precisely because he was so much in earnest about religion that he could not take seriously to myth, which he regarded as the fossil religion of expired cultures. Like Thoreau, he sought for himself the original conditions of myth more than an historical knowledge of mythology, but where Thoreau thought of himself as looking for the original conditions of *myth,* Whitman thought of himself as searching for the original conditions of *religion.* It follows from this that he thought of the poet as a prophet and his book as scriptural prophecy. Any view that Whitman was engaged in replacing old myth with new ideologies or myths has the difficulty that Whitman himself wished to disavow the terminology of myth. The word had no magic for him as it did for Thoreau, and perhaps we cheapen Whitman's religious faith and avoid the difficult task of assessing him as a religious poet if we permit ourselves to describe his work in language he himself rejected.

As might be expected, Whitman's disavowal of myth was not a simple matter. At times, especially early in his career, he seems to have had a marked personal fondness for myth. When Alcott and Thoreau went to visit Whitman in Brooklyn in 1856, Alcott was struck by the fact that "some characteristic pictures—a Hercules, a Bacchus, and a Satyr—were pasted, unframed, upon the rude walls." Alcott asked about them:

> I said, while looking at the pictures in his study: "Which now of the three, particularly, is the new poet here—this Hercules, the Bacchus, or the Satyr?" On which he begged me not to put my questions too close, meaning to take, as I inferred, the virtues of the three to himself unreservedly. And I think he might fairly, being himself the modern Pantheon—satyr, Silenus, and him of the twelve labours—combined.[3]

Even discounting Alcott's annoyance at Whitman's breezy self assurance, the episode points to something. It is unlikely that Whitman put up the pictures for self-satire. There is another account of a conversation of Whitman's, probably dating from about the same time, in which Whitman is shown using myth as psychological symbol in a way that suggests easy familiarity:

> He [Whitman] once . . . said that there was a wonderful depth of meaning ("at second or third removes" as he called it) in the old tales of mythology. In that of Cupid and Psyche, for instance; it meant to him that the ardent expression in words of affection often tended to destroy affection. It was like the golden fruit which turned to ashes upon being grasped, or even touched. As an illustration, he mentioned the case of a young man he was in the habit of meeting every morning where he went to work. He said there had grown up between them a delightful silent friendship and sympathy. But one morning when he went as usual to the office, the young man came forward, shook him violently by the hand, and expressed in heated language the affection he felt for him. Mr. Whitman said that all the subtle charm of this unspoken friendship was from that time gone. [4]

In a short note which is undated, but probably early (because two lines in it recur in the early poem "Pictures"), Whitman projected a "Poem of Fables," which was to be a "long string one after another, of Poetical Fables, as Dreams, Spiritualisms, Imaginations." The note continues, with some tentative lines for the poem suggesting that the concept of myth here is, if not exactly that of Thoreauvian endorsement, at least not that of blunt rejection:

> Now this is the fable of a beautiful statue;
> A beautiful statue was lost but not destroyed. [5]

This fragment may or may not have any relation to the poem with which Whitman closed the first edition of *Leaves of Grass*, "Great are the Myths." This poem is not, however, a catalog of fables, and despite the fact that Whitman later dropped the poem from his book, the opening lines are a good example of how Whitman saw himself moving from old "myths" to modern "realities."

> Great are the myths—I too delight in them,
> Great are Adam and Eve—I too look back and accept them,

Great the risen and fallen nations, and their poets,
women, sages, inventors, rulers, warriors, and priests.

Great is Liberty! great is Equality! I am their follower,
Helmsmen of nations, choose your craft! where you sail, I sail,
Yours is the muscle of life or death—yours is the
perfect science—in you I have absolute faith.[6]

If Whitman's attitude toward myth in this poem is equivocal, a note of his, dated "early in the fifties" by Richard M. Bucke, is not. Whitman is now advising himself to "take no illustrations whatever from the ancients or classics, nor from the mythology, nor Egypt, Greece or Rome."[7] Whitman never lived up to this admonition, and I cite it only to show how tempting he must have found it to refer to the subjects he so sternly forbids himself, and also that, at least at this time, he consciously wished to break free of the classics, the ancients, and myth altogether. In another place, but in the same spirit, he observed that "Goethe's poems, competitive with the antique, are so because he has studied the antique. They appear to me as great as the antique in all respects except one. That is the antique poems were *growths—they* were never studied from antiques."[8] Here, one can see clearly that Whitman is more interested in the conditions that underlie the great works of the past than he is in the finished works of that past. This same impulse led Thoreau to cultivate a mythmaking mood, but in Whitman it was joined with a deeply felt sense that myth was in some fundamental way opposed to modern reality. In "A Backward Glance O'er Main Travelled Roads," Whitman explains that myth was among the ornamental and conventional elements he felt obliged to abandon.

> For grounds for "Leaves of Grass," as a poem, I abandon'd the conventional themes, which do not appear in it: none of the stock ornamentation, or choice plots of love or war, or high, exceptional personages of Old-World song; nothing, as I may say, for beauty's sake—no legend, or myth, or romance, nor euphemism, nor rhyme.[9]

A few pages later comes an even more explicit rejection of "poems of myth" in favor of "poems of realities." "The Old World has had the poems of myths, fictions, feudalism, conquest, caste, dynastic wars, and splendid exceptional characters and affairs, which have been great; but the New World needs the poems of realities and science and of the democratic average and basic equality, which shall be greater."[10]

This disparagement of myth is typical of the mature Whitman. In "I Was Looking a Long While," he speaks of "those paged fables in the libraries," and in "Of the Terrible Doubt of Appearances," he writes, "That may-be identity beyond the grave is a beautiful fable only."[11] Occasionally he uses the word in a very modern sounding way, as when he speculates that the existence of Ossian is "very likely a myth altogether," or when, in "The Sleepers," he writes "the myth of heaven indicates peace and night."[12] Sometimes he speaks of myth as lovely but useless; in "Song of the Exposition" he lists among the things that have passed away unlamented, the "Embroider'd, dazzling, foreign world, with all its gorgeous legends, myths."[13] Sometimes myths are even listed among the real evils of history: in "Thoughts" he uncompromisingly notes "How many hold despairingly yet to the models departed, caste, myths, obedience, compulsion, and to infidelity."[14] Just how far Whitman is from Thoreau's acceptance of myth can be gauged by putting the following lines from the "Song of the Exposition" beside Thoreau's treatment of his going to Walden as an event equal to the removal of the Gods of Troy. Whitman's emphasis on the modern is no greater than Thoreau's, but in the process Whitman cheerfully puts Thoreau's much loved classics up for rent.

> Come Muse migrate from Greece and Ionia,
> Cross out please those immensely overpaid accounts
> That matter of Troy and Achilles' wrath, and Aenas',
>   Odysseus' wanderings,
> Placard "Removed" and "To Let" on the rocks of your
>   snowy Parnassus.[15]

Whitman's rejection of myth can be understood at least partly as the result of a strong Enlightenment streak in his thought, which shows itself in various ways. He was proud that his father had known

Tom Paine, and Whitman himself refers to Paine's religious as well as his political ideas. Whitman repeatedly acknowledged Frances Wright's *A Few Days in Athens* and Volney's *Ruins* as important influences on his early thought.[16] Aside from using Volney as a source for information on a variety of religions ("Salut au Monde" has long sections that were lifted from Volney), Whitman's reiterated high opinion of the book suggests he not only found it a useful source of information but that he also approved of the book's general hostility to conventional religion and mythology. There is little doubt that it helped shape his own outlook. Frances Wright's little known but interesting book of imaginary philosophical dialogues among Epicurus and his disciples is also dominated by a line of argument that ends with a sweeping rejection of conventional religion and, by implication, of myth as well. The climactic chapter of *A Few Days in Athens* hands down this conclusion:

> The essence of religion is fear, as its source is ignorance. In a certain stage of human knowledge, the human mind must, of necessity, in its ignorance of the properties of matter, and its dark insight into the chain of phenomena arising out of those properties—must of necessity reason falsely on every occurrence and existence in nature; it must of necessity, in the absence of fact, give the rein to fancy, see a miracle in every uncommon event, and imagine unseen agents as producing all that it beholds. In proportion as the range of our observation is enlarged, and as we learn to connect and arrange the phenomena of nature, we curtail our lists of miracles, the number of our super-natural agents. An eclipse is alarming to the vulgar, as denoting the wrath of offended deities; to the man of science it is a simple occurrence, as easily traced to its cause, as any the most familiar to our observation. The knowledge of one generation is the ignorance of the next. Our superstitions decrease as our attainments multiply; and the fervor of our religion declines as we draw nearer to the conclusion which destroys it entirely. The conclusion, based upon accumulated facts, as we have seen, [is] that matter alone is at once the thing acting and the thing acted upon,—eternal in duration, infinitely various and varying in appearance, never diminishing in quantity and always changing in form.[17]

Vernon Parrington has called Whitman the most deeply religious of American writers, and William James discussed him in connection with the religion of healthy-mindedness. But these qualities attain full significance only when seen as movements away from or in spite of the strong skepticism that marks much of Whitman's early work. His affirmation of a modern religion of humanity required a previous rejection of old mythological religions. And once one begins to look for the skeptical strain in Whitman, it becomes apparent everywhere, even in matters of diction. He uses "philosophe" as an accolade in "Song of the Answerer," and in "Pictures" he even speaks of the "crazy enthusiast," using the word as standard Enlightenment disparagement. More importantly, one can see a skeptical line of thought in such passages as the following from "Song of Myself":

> Taking myself the exact dimensions of Jehovah,
> Lithographing Kronos, Zeus his son, and Hercules his grandson,
> Buying drafts of Osiris, Isis, Belus, Brahma, Buddha,
> In my portfolio placing Manito loose, Allah on a leaf, the crucifix engraved,
> With Odin and the hideous-faced Mexitli and every idol and image,
> Taking them all for what they are worth and not a cent more.[18]

The point of this is not so much outright rejection as it is a matter of domesticating the old deities as common human qualities. Any suggestion that the old myths have any special claims on us is, however, dismissed:

> Accepting the rough deific sketches to fill out better in myself, bestowing them freely on each man and woman I see,
> Discovering as much or more in a framer framing a house,
> Putting higher claims for him there with his roll'd-up sleeves driving the mallet and chisel,
> Not objecting to special revelations, considering a curl of smoke or a hair on the back of my hand just as curious as any revelation,
> Lads ahold of fire-engines and hook-and-ladder ropes no less to me than the gods of the antique wars.[19]

This is, it will be recognized, a standard Enlightenment approach. Whitman here turns the idea of the divine upside down, claiming,

as had Paine and other eighteenth-century thinkers, that man is not
set apart from God, man is himself God. In admiring mythology,
one is admiring oneself. This is a constant theme in Whitman, and
it is interesting to note that it is also developed in *A Few Days in
Athens*. After the destruction of the false religion, or supernaturalism, Frances Wright asks the reader to

> Imagine the creature man in the full exercise of all his faculties; not
> shrinking from knowledge, but eager in its pursuit; not bending the
> knee of adulation to visionary beings armed by fear for his destruction,
> but standing erect in calm contemplation of the beautiful face of nature;
> discarding prejudice, and admitting truth without fear of consequences;
> acknowledging no judge but reason, no censor but that in his own
> breast! Thus considered, he is transformed into the god of his present
> idolatry.[20]

Whitman too seems interested not so much in the rejection of the
religious impulse as in the redirection of it. The important thing
about religion is not, for Whitman, God or gods—considered as
beings above and apart from man—but rather the religious nature of
man himself. Whitman is famous for not rejecting things, of course,
but in many places he comes very close to flat rejection of the claims
of myth and of conventional religion. His set of mind and his
rhetorical style lead him to accept and embrace everything, but his
acceptance of myth is usually valedictory. He only eulogizes it by
way of bidding it farewell. A good example of this is the "Song of
the Redwood Tree," written in 1873. The poem celebrates the
growth and development of California. As the forests are cut down
to provide for the people's wants, Whitman sees—and clearly
approves—the passing of the old wood-spirits to make way for the
spirit of progress. The poem opens with a reference to "a chorus of
dryads, fading, departing, or hamadryads departing." Much of the
poem is "spoken" by the "voice of a mighty dying tree in the
redwood forest dense." The old tree's time has come and it yields
gladly:

> We who have grandly fill'd our time;
> With Nature's calm content, with tacit huge delight,

We welcome what we wrought for through the past,
And leave the field for them.

Whitman describes how "the wood-spirits came from their haunts of
a thousand years to join the refrain," and the poem moves to a
"loftier strain"; "As if the heirs, the deities of the West,/Joining
with master-tongue bore part." The great tree speaks again, and it is
somehow both believable and awesome, much as the Anglo-Saxon
"Dream of the Rood," which it strangely resembles. The poem is
now summarized as follows, the poet reverting to his own voice:

> Thus on the northern coast,
> In the echo of teamster's calls and the clinking chains,
>   and the music of choppers' axes,
> The falling trunks and limbs, the crash,
>   the muffled shriek, the groan,
> Such words combined from the redwood-tree,
>   as of voices ecstatic, ancient and rustling,
> The century-lasting, unseen dryads, singing, withdrawing,
> All their recesses of forests and mountains leaving,
> From the Cascade range to the Wahsatch, or Idaho far, or Utah,
> To the deities of the modern henceforth yielding,
> The chorus and indications, the vistas of coming humanity,
>   the settlements, features all,
> In the Mendocino woods I caught.[21]

The "Song of the Redwood Tree" is a perfect example of Whitman's
willingness to let the old myths and whatever they stand for go by
while he rushes to greet the gods of progress. Yet here, as in most of
the poems in which Whitman tries to weaken the hold of the old
myths, there is a curious and also typical counterimpulse at work.
Whitman's poetic animation of the inanimate gives the great tree
the dominant prophetic voice in the poem, and is, in this instance,
an act of mythmaking. The strategy of the poem calls for a
mythologized tree, while the point of the poem is the obsolescence
and gracious self-effacement of the old nature myths. But at bottom

the poem is in fact consistent. The trees, however grand and however eloquent, are never associated with any higher spirits than wood-sprites or dryads. The trees are never called deities; only the "heirs," the "vistas of coming humanity" are associated with deity. What the "Song of the Redwood Tree" celebrates, then, is the passing of the myths of nature and the advent of the religion of humanity.

Essentially the same point is made in "Passage to India," in which lines 18 to 29 were once intended as a separate poem to be called "Fables":

> Not you alone proud truths of the world,
> Nor you alone ye facts of modern science,
> But myths and fables of eld, Asia's, Africa's fables,
> The far-darting beams of the spirit, the unloos'd dreams,
> The deep diving bibles and legends,
> The daring plots of the poets, the elder religions;
> O you temples fairer than lilies pour'd over by the rising sun!
> O you fables spurning the known, eluding the hold of the known,
>   mounting to heaven!
> You dazzling and lofty towers, pinnacled, red as roses, burnish'd with
>   gold!
> Towers of fables immortal fashion'd from mortal dreams!
> You too I welcome and fully the same as the rest!
> You too with joy I sing.[22]

These lines were incorporated into the longer poem and are there preceded by a call to "Eclaircise the myths Asiatic, the primitive fables." Eclaircise means, and meant at the time, to clear up, not simply to clarify. The difference is slight, but indicative of Whitman's essentially patronizing inclusion of myth. The above lines are Whitman's most appreciative of myth, but the undercurrent of the lines still suggests that the proud truths of the world and the facts of modern science and the urgent call of the present will combine to carry man past myth, however fair and too-much-loved.

Similar too is a comment in *Specimen Days and Collect* (1882) on how Darwin has inverted and surpassed the mythological point of view:

Running through prehistoric ages—coming down from them into the daybreak of our records, founding theology, suffusing literature, and so brought onward—(a sort of verteber and marrow to all the antique races and lands, Egypt, India, Greece, Rome, the Chinese, the Jews, &c., and giving cast and complexion to their art, poems, and their politics as well as ecclesiasticism, all of which we more or less inherit), appear those venerable claims to origin from God himself, or from gods and goddesses—ancestry from divine beings of vaster beauty, size, and power than ours. But in current and latest times, the theory of human origin that seems to have most made its mark (curiously reversing the antique), is that we have come on, originated, developt, from monkeys, baboons—a theory more significant perhaps in its indirections, or what it necessitates, than it is even in itself.[23]

Whitman's rejection of myth was never simple, never a matter of flat unbelief or open contempt. Indeed, his rejection of myth was, much like that of the deists, the clearing away of fossil religion to make way for "real" or new religion. In several important ways, Whitman's rejection of myth was accompanied or offset by his advocating something to take the place of the rejected myth, or by his discovery in myth of some saving grace, some useful start. Whitman's work shows myth being displaced by history (together with a Euhemerist reading of myth), by symbol and image, and by prophecy.

2. Myth, History, and Egypt

Whitman seems only to have flirted, and only occasionally, with the Euhemerist explanation of myth. The following is one of the few examples:

Back to ten thousand years before These States, all nations had, and some yet have, and perhaps always will have, tradition of coming men, great benefactors, of divine origin, capable of deeds of might, blessings, poems, enlightenment. From time to time these have arisen, and yet arise and will always arise. Some are called gods and deified—enter into the succeeding religions.[24]

Whitman could have taken this over from Emerson, from Carlyle, from J. G. Wilkinson's *Manners and Customs of the Ancient Egyptians,* or indeed, from a host of sources. Popular handbooks of mythology frequently used or made mention of this theory, as did books on universal history and chronology. This view of myth links the subject—some would say confuses it—with history. What, for example, are we to make of a poetic fragment in which Whitman treats Sesostris as a completely real Egyptian king? or of lists of dates which set "Menu son or grandson of Brahma and first of created beings" side by side with "Milton 1608–1674. Contemporary of Ben Jonson 1574–1637"? or a list which gives, in order, "Abraham's visit to Egypt 2000 B.C. . . . Birth of Hercules 1205 B.C. Alexandrian Library . . . destroyed either by enraged Christians under Theodosius the Great 390 A.C. or by Saracens under Omar 642 A.C. . . ."? or another list which goes, in part: "Sesostris or Remeses 2nd, 1355 B.C. Solomon born 1032 B.C. Solomon's temple (? finished) 600 B.C. Herodotus 430 B.C. Alexander the Great 332 B.C."?[25] These examples, which could be multiplied, reflect the then prevailing state of the study of ancient history, or of universal history, and the still-strong impulse to erect a comprehensive chronological framework. Whether one looks to Archbishop Ussher's work, to Newton's *Chronology of the Ancient Kingdoms Amended* or Volney's anti-Christian chronology in his *New Researches* or the Christian chronologies of the world by Prideaux, Shuckford, and Michael Russell, or at schoolbooks such as the one prepared by Elizabeth Peabody (based on the work of Josef Bem) or volumes in the Peter Parley series, or at the very books on Egypt which Whitman is known to have consulted, books such as C. K. J. Bunsen's *Egypt's place in Universal History* or J. G. Wilkinson's *Manners and Customs of the Ancient Egyptians* or George Glidden's *Ancient Egypt*— one finds the same general condition. The effort to untangle and reconcile the conflicting written accounts, and the drawing up of a chronology, involved, to a greater or lesser extent, taking both the Bible and ancient myth as history. Sesostris is a good example. Now thought to be the name or title of three successive Egyptian kings, he was, in Whitman's time, known through Diodorus and others as a single figure, more legendary than real, who had been a great conqueror, ruler, and lawgiver on the order of Moses, Orpheus, Mohammed, and Manco Capac. Thus the occurrence of many mythical names in Whitman reflects not so much a deliberate Euhemerism on his part as it does the general confusion between legendary and real men and events that prevailed in the study of prehistory, a field then still dominated by classical texts but beginning to be revised by archaeology and the study of inscriptions. Whitman's general view of Sesostris was, for example, not very different from the view of Charles Anthon, the eminent professor of classics at Columbia.

More important than Euhemerism as such to Whitman's own attitude toward myth was the curious prominence of Egypt in Whitman's study of the past.[26] New England writers paid relatively little attention to Egypt; *The Dial,* for example, has very little on the then new and very exciting field of Egyptology. The pervading classicism of most New England writers led them to agree more or less with Goethe's remark that it was all very well to discover and make known the antiquities of India and Egypt, but they "contributed little to our aesthetic or moral education." What New England did know about Egypt was mainly through Herodotus, Plutarch, Diodorus, Apuleius, and other classical writers. Margaret Fuller, for example, could use Isis as a symbol of woman, but her Isis was the Roman one of Apuleius. Whitman may have known Apuleius, though his use of the Cupid and Psyche story could also have come from a handbook, but he seems to have been far more interested in the Egypt revealed by modern travelers and by the research of Champollion and his followers.

Champollion's epoch-making *Précis du Système Hiéroglyphique des anciens Egyptiens* had been published in 1824, and the period's confused but energetic inquiry into ancient Egyptian culture and history was thenceforth launched in an entirely new direction. Champollion's work provided, for the first time since hieroglyphics had fallen into disuse around the third century A.D., a reliable key to the interpretation of the numerous and impressive physical remains of ancient Egypt. Much of the excitement of this development was over the fact that for centuries all knowledge of history prior to the Greek

Olympiads had depended on written texts that were far from full and of doubtful accuracy. The Bible and Herodotus gave an imperfect and relatively recent view of Egypt, while the actual inscriptions in Egypt itself showed, when deciphered, that Egyptian history, recorded on the spot by Egyptians, went back much further than Greek or Hebrew accounts, including the Bible, thought possible. The wonder and excitement of all this new knowledge is very attractively evident in a book by George Glidden (1809–1857), a British-born archaeologist who served for years as United States Vice-Consul for Cairo. Whitman read Glidden's *Ancient Egypt,* and he was also familiar with C. K. J. Bunsen's monumental five-volume *Egypt's Place in Universal History* (1859), the same writer's *Outlines of the Philosophy of Universal History* (1854; translated into English the same year) and J. G. Wilkinson's *Manners and Customs of the Ancient Egyptians* (1837–41). Some time around 1879, Whitman's interest in Egyptology was still keen, for he then read Brugsch-Bey's *History of Egypt under the Pharoahs, Derived entirely from the monuments* (1879) and Renouf's *Lectures on the origin and growth of religion, as illustrated by the religions of ancient Egypt* (1879). Moreover, Whitman was by his own account a frequenter of Murray's Egyptian Museum on Broadway, which he wrote up enthusiastically in a newspaper article.[27] Murray, an English doctor, had lived in Egypt for years and had gathered an extensive collection of Egyptian objects. Coming to America, he had set up his museum in the hopes of making money. His collection, now in the Brooklyn Museum, must have had a great influence on the impressionable Whitman. No comparable experience fired his imagination toward Greece or Rome. The impact this collection made on Whitman can be seen in the article he wrote, in which he went to some lengths to place Egypt exactly in Western history and to describe approvingly Egyptian thought and religion. In addition to this piece, there are numerous references to Egypt scattered through Whitman's poems, prose, and notes, and while he makes sparing use of Egyptian mythology itself, his knowledge of Egypt seems to have colored his attitude toward myth in general.

For one thing, what Whitman learned about the prior antiquity of Egypt seems to have fastened his attention more on Egypt than on Greece as the most venerable of ancient nations. "The definite history of the world cannot go back farther than Egypt, and in the most important particulars the average spirit of man, except in These States, has not gone forward of the spirit of ancient Egypt."[28] This note of admiration for ancient Egypt is in marked contrast to, say, Thoreau's attitude as expressed in his observation that "the Greeks were boys in the sunshine, the Romans were men in the field, the Persians women in the house, the Egyptians old men in the dark."[29] Nonetheless, although Whitman's enthusiasm for Egypt persisted, it did not extend to an enthusiasm for Egyptian myth. Indeed, Whitman's reading on Egypt must have given him further reason to distrust both myth and mythographers. In Glidden's opening chapter, for example, there is a scornful account taken over from Champollion of the great seventeenth-century Jesuit mythographer Athanasius Kircher's misguided efforts to wrest deep mythic import from what turned out, in the nineteenth century, to be straightforward chronicle. The account is worth quoting since it illustrates Whitman's awareness of how the old mystical tradition of mythography was being superseded by archaeology, and by modern linguistic research.

> In the year 1636, a learned Jesuit, the celebrated Father Kircher, published a mighty work, in six ponderous folios, entitled *Oedipus Aegyptiacus,* wherein imagination took the place of common sense, and fantastic conjecture was substituted for fact. Kircher explained every Egyptian Hieroglyph by the application of a sublimity of mysticism, from which to the ridiculous the transition is immediate. Dark and impenetrable as has been the "Isiac Veil," before Kircher directed his gigantic efforts to its removal, we do him but justice in declaring, that he succeeded in enveloping Egyptian studies with an increased density of gloom it has taken nearly two hundred years to dissipate![30]

Kircher and his followers ransacked Egyptian inscriptions using "all the recondite combinations of cabalistic science, and the monstrous reveries of a demonomania the most refined." Glidden gives as an example the interpretation of this cartouche; it occurs on the Pamphilian Obelisk, re-erected in 1651 in the Piazza Navona by Pope Innocent the Tenth. Kircher said the cartouche expressed emblematically that "the author of fecundity and of all vegetation, is Osiris, of which the generative faculty is drawn from heaven into his kingdom, by the Saint Moptha." This solemn specimen of the interpretation of myth as sexual and as associated with fertility ritual turns out, saint and all, to be the merest mythical blather. The actual translation of the cartouche, says Glidden, is simply *Autokrator* or emperor.[31]

Similarly, a bit further on, Champollion's discoveries are represented as sweeping away whole schools of myth interpretation, some of which were still very much in evidence, such as those of Dupuis or Creuzer. Again quotation is worthwhile to show the general skepticism toward myth scholarship that prevailed in the kinds of books Whitman read on Egypt.

> On the one hand, the classical scholars, adhering rigidly to the Hebrew, Greek, and Latin authorities, were not willing to cast aside the errors of their masters; and those, whose schools had nailed their colors to the mast, were not prepared to see Manetho exalted above Herodotus and Diodorus; to find Hermapion confirmed, while Pliny was rejected; to behold in Plato but the translator, or in Pythagoras but the adopter, of Egyptian mythological doctrines: still less to consider what amount of instruction accrued to the Hebrew Lawgiver from his education in Heliopolitan colleges. . . .
>
> On the other hand, the astronomers and mathematicians, the Dupuis, the Bodes and Rhodes, the Goerres and Creuzers, the Fourriers and Biots, who had claimed for the zodiacal planispheres of Dendera and Esnè an antiquity varying from 700 to 17,000 years B.C., were not particularly charmed with a science which demonstrated, by hieroglyphical interpretation . . . that these astrological subjects were the *most modern* productions of Egypto-Roman art, and Egypto-Hellenic science, of the age of Tiberius, Nero, Claudius, Hadrian or Antoninus.[32]

From Glidden's popular account (he lectured in Boston, New York, and Philadelphia, and *Ancient Egypt* went through fifteen editions by 1850) Whitman must have gathered that most Egyptian myth scholarship before Champollion was at worst wrong and at best silly, certainly not worth bothering with. From the eminent J. G. Wilkinson's authoritative book on Egypt Whitman would also have been aware of the new claims that were there presented for Egyptian religion. Wilkinson compared Egyptian religion and mythology with Greek, much to the disadvantage of the latter. Following the early eighteenth-century work of the Abbé Banier very closely, Wilkinson argues that Greek mythology was a degenerate and imperfect recollection of early Greek history. Not only is Greek myth full of absurdities and guilty of demeaning the gods into mere men (Wilkinson is especially scornful of the Greek's bringing down "the character of the creative power, the demiurge who made the world, to the level of a blacksmith," i.e. Vulcan) but it also failed to understand the true nature of Egyptian religion and mythology.[33] Wilkinson explains at length how Egyptian myth is symbolic of a high noble religion. He quickly disposes of the long-standing charge of zoolatry with which it was customary to mock the Egyptians.

> That the images of the Egyptian deities were not supposed to indicate real beings, who had actually existed on earth, is abundantly evident from the forms under which they were represented; and the very fact of a god being figured with a human body and the head of an ibis, might sufficiently prove the allegorical character of Thoth, or Mercury, the emblem of the communicating medium of the divine intellect, and suggest the impossibility of any other than an imaginary or emblematic existence; in the same manner as the sphinx, with a lion's body and human head, indicative of physical and intellectual power, under which the kings of Egypt were figured, could only be looked upon as an emblematic representation of the qualities of the monarch.[34]

Wilkinson's praise of Egyptian myth and religion is elaborate and lengthy. He agrees with the self-estimate of the Egyptians that they were "the nation in whom had originated most of the sacred institutions afterwards common to other people." He claims that unlike Greek myth, Egyptian myth reflects "the existence of an Omnipotent Being, whose various attributes being deified, formed a series of divinities, each worshipped under its own peculiar form,

and supposed to possess its particular office." Wilkinson's tone
is one of unqualified admiration for the nobility of Egyptian religion
and the "idea respecting the manifestation of the Deity on earth,
which the Egyptians entertained in common with the Hindoos."[35]
He goes to great length to show that the idea of the Trinity is
present in Egyptian religion, and among the many "triads" which
he cites, the following, credited to Plutarch, might have interested
Whitman.

Plutarch gives		
Intelligence,	Matter,	*Kosmos*, beauty, order, or the world;
the first being the		
same as Plato's	the second,	and the third,
Idea,	Mother,	Offspring,
Exemplar,	Nurse,	
or Father,	Receptacle of generation,	Production.[36]

Wilkinson goes in extensively for mystic triads and sacred numbers,
and for Pythagorean and Hermetic philosophies. What Whitman
may have made of all this cannot be said for certain, but he could
have found support for his "Square Deific" in Wilkinson's observation that the number "four was particularly connected with Mercury, as the deity who imparted intellectual gifts to man; to Vulcan
it was assimilated as the Demiurgos, whence the *Tetraktys* was the
mystic name of the Creative Power."[37]

Wilkinson had also insisted that Egyptian religion stressed the
concept of immortality, and this is one of the points Whitman makes
in the description of Egyptian religion he included in his account of
Murray's Egyptian Museum. "The theology of Egypt was vast and
profound. It respected the principle of life in all things—even in
animals. It respected truth and justice above all other attributes of
men. It recognized immortality."[38]

In general, Wilkinson may have helped Whitman to formulate
his remarkably high opinion of Egyptian religion. In his notes
Whitman associates Egypt with early natural and unspoiled reli-

gion, though, as Wilkinson and others were careful to point out, it was known fully only to its priests. Whitman once noted:

> Egypt (and probably much of the sentiment of the Assyrian Empire) represents that phase of development, advanced childhood, full of belief, rich and divine enough, standing amazed and awed before the mystery of life—nothing more wonderful than life, even in a hawk—a bull or a cat—the masses of the people reverent of priestly and kingly authority.[39]

From Glidden, Wilkinson, and Bunsen the idea of Egypt that emerges is an attractive one, and all the accounts agreed on the nobility of Egyptian religion and on its mythology as essentially symbolic. Furthermore, the ancient hieroglyphs are, after Champollion, another example of the Egyptian tendency to express things symbolically and pictorially, and it is just possible that Whitman's imagist ideas and his poems that are pictures owe something to his reading in Egyptology. Hieroglyphs had been mysterious for centuries and writers had used the word to suggest whatever was darkly hinted and mysteriously hidden. But in Whitman's reading on Egypt, hieroglyphs were at last revealed as phonetic "signs or representations of *material objects.*" Far from concealing mysteries, hieroglyphics was a mode of writing, of communicating. The hieroglyphs themselves were reduced "into an alphabet composed of 16 distinct articulations, for each of which there was a number more or less great of homophones, *i.e.,* symbols, differing in figure, though identical in *sound,* applicable according to a well defined system, and never solely by graphical caprice." Champollion "proved, that the hieroglyphic mode of writing is a complex system—a system figurative, symbolical and phonetic."[40]

Just as Ezra Pound's poetry was partly shaped by his excited discovery of Chinese ideograms, so it could be argued that Whitman's poetry was influenced by his reading about hieroglyphs, a subject extensively treated with illustrations, tables, and examples in the books Whitman consulted on Egypt. It has been argued that his poem "Scented Herbage of this Breast" owes something to an illustration of wheat sprouting from Osiris' breast that Whitman saw in Rosellini's magnificent work on Egypt, and it could be added that the reference to the grass as a "uniform hieroglyphic" and his reference to Champollion in "Song of Myself" are suggestive. [41] More interesting are the lines in "When Lilacs Last in the Dooryard Bloom'd":

> O what shall I hang on the chamber walls?
> And what shall the pictures be that I hang on the walls,
> To adorn the burial-house of him I love? [42]

It is almost as though his poems and the symbols in his poems are to Lincoln what the hieroglyphs and paintings were to the dead in Egyptian tombs. If Whitman thought at times of his leaves as picture poems, the idea may have been suggested by the hieroglyphs, a kind of writing that was communicative, figurative, and symbolic all at once.

3. From Old Myth to New Religion: Nationalism and Prophecy

Whitman was little inclined to accept the claims of most organized religious groups, but he was constantly willing to put a very high value on religious thought and emotion. In the following note, for example, he goes beyond myth to the religious spirit of antiquity, epitomized this time not by the Egyptians but by the Greeks.

> Probably the great distinction of the Pagan religions, grouped into one and led by the Greek theology, is that they appreciated and expressed the sense of nature, life, beauty, the objective world, and of fate, immutable law, the sense of power and precedence, but also, to a greater or less degree, the mystery and baffling unknownness which meets us at a certain point of our investigation of any and all things. [43]

Whitman has long been recognized as a religious poet, perhaps most often for the expansive pantheism of "Song of Myself." He could write "I hear and behold God in every object," or "In the faces of men and women I see God, and in my own face in the glass." His pantheism and what has been called his panpsychism have been treated at length.[44] What should be emphasized here is that Whitman usually avoided giving his positive and pervasive religious impulses mythological expression. He did not, as did Thoreau or Emerson, find myth a useful form for modern literature. Indeed, a poem such as "Chanting the Square Deific" is much more a theological than a mythological poem. One of its principal points is to open up the traditional triad, so as to insert the principle of evil as part of reality, and it is noticeable that Whitman is more interested in the doctrinal or theological side than in the mythological side of the question.[45] It is not that Whitman always prefers religious doctrines and ideas to the expression of a sense of religious awe or wonder, it is just that traditional myth did not present itself to Whitman as adequate to the needs of modern times. Instead of turning to Greece or to Egypt, Whitman turned to France, to modern democracy, to the idea of the People, and to the idea of the worship of the nation.

For even though he did not treat it in terms of myth, Whitman was indeed receptive to powerful new religious forces that were emerging in his time. Indeed, Whitman's *Leaves* embody, among many other things of course, a reworked form of the republican religion which arose in Revolutionary France and which was transmitted to Whitman mainly through the work of the French historian Jules Michelet. In an excellent article which he later inexplicably ignored in his biography of Whitman, Gay Wilson Allen argued that Michelet's influence on Whitman was crucial. "The fact that Michelet's *The People* contains the fundamental ideas of *Leaves of Grass* is a fact which is of considerable importance in Whitman biography and criticism, for it shows that Walt Whitman was far less the great unique untutored American barbarian than the child of French pre- and post-revolutionary thought."[46] Allen goes further, saying that Michelet's *The People* "contains every major idea of Whitman's philosophy of Democracy, religion, and art." It is hard to say how extensive Whitman's knowledge of Michelet really was, but the similarity between the two is very great, and Whitman clearly was excited by Michelet's leading ideas. Michelet was a man of the people; he had been a printer as a young man, and celebrating the French Revolution became his most important cause. His *History of France,* which Whitman singled out for praise in a short notice of Michelet's work, is a passionate headlong rush of brilliantly narrated enthusiasm for the Revolution as an expression of the popular will.[47] Michelet was deeply anti-Christian, preaching instead the worship of *la patrie,* of France, of the common man, and of the Revolution itself. And where his close friend Edgar Quinet—an early admirer of Emerson—argued that the French Revolution had been the triumph of true Christianity over false, Michelet argued that it represented the triumph of true religion over Christianity. Michelet's work is packed with detail and every page is marked by a Whitman-like sense of identification with the beloved common people who are the real subjects of his history. Edmund Wilson has drawn attention to this aspect of Michelet, quoting for the purpose the following from Michelet's letters:

> I am accomplishing here the extremely rough task of reliving, reconstituting and suffering the Revolution. I have just gone through September and all the terrors of death: massacred at the Abbaye, I am on my way to the revolutionary tribunal, that is to say, to the guillotine, . . . I am about to enter the heart of the convention, I stand at the gates of Terror. At the same time, my wife is on the point of wresting forth a new me from her womb.[48]

Michelet wrote his *History of France* by putting himself into every actor on the stage in turn, much as Whitman, especially in the earliest editions of *Leaves of Grass,* wrote poems about American as though he were a representative of each and every American. In Edmund Wilson's phrase, both men make us feel that they are "the human spirit itself fighting its way through the ages."

It seems likely that Michelet's *The People,* translated into English and published in Philadelphia in 1846, must have hit Whitman with considerable force. At any event, what may be called the Michelet strain appears very strongly in Whitman. The concept of the representative man appears clearly in Michelet; "The people . . . only exist in its truth, and at its highest power, in the man of genius; in him resides the great soul. . . ." (the pauses, indicated by dots, are Michelet's; even his punctuation seems to have been reflected in the earliest editions of *Leaves of Grass*).[49] So too the pose of the cheerful barbarian is quite as explicit in Michelet as in Whitman. Michelet writes: "The rise of the people, the progress, is often, now-a-days compared to the invasion of the Barbarians. I like the word. I accept the term. . . . Barbarians! Yes! that is to say, full of sap, fresh, vigorous, and for ever springing up."[50]

The description of the man of genius as the best exemplar of the People leads immediately to the religious question of the status of such a person: "Is he God or man? To express the instinct of genius, must we seek out mystic names—inspiration? revelation?" The new religion of humanity rejects these and rejects also supernaturalism. Michelet goes on to describe how "gods" originate and thus illustrates how the new faith in man grows out of the radical critique of the mythological view of religion. To the question as to whether we must seek out mystic names, inspiration, or revelation, Michelet replies:

> This is the tendency of the vulgar, which must forge gods for themselves. Instinct? Nature? Fie, they exclaim, "Had it only been instinct, we should not have been led away. . . . it is inspiration from on high, it is God's well-beloved; it is a God, a new Messiah!" Rather than admire a man, than admit the superiority of one's fellow, we make him inspired of God, and, if needs be, God. Each says to himself that nothing less than such a supernatural light could so far have dazzled him. . . . and so we place beyond the pale of nature, of observation and of science, him who was true nature, him whom of all men science must watch; we exclude from humanity him who alone *was man*. . . . Ah! Leave him among us, him who is the giver of life here below. Let him remain man, let him remain people. Separate him not from children, from the poor and simple, where his heart is; exile him not on an altar.[51]

As Michelet goes on describing the genius of humanity come to save and express the People, we begin to see a strong similarity between Michelet's "genius" and Whitman's sense of his own mission:

Let him be surrounded by this crowd of which he is the spirit: let him plunge into full, fecund life, live with us, suffer with us. He will draw out of his participation in our sufferings and weaknesses the strength which God has buried there, and which will be his genius itself.[52]

Traditional myth and religion are rejected, but in their place comes a new religion, both of humanity and of *la patrie*—France for Michelet, These States for Whitman—and the warm endorsement of the new religion leads inevitably to the writer's personifying the new objects of religious worship. Here is Michelet on the religious training of the young: "By a grand, salutary, durable impression, we must found man in the child, create the life of the heart. God, first revealed by the mother, in love and in nature. Next God revealed by the father, in our living country, in its heroic history, in the sentiment of France. God, and the love of God." Michelet now explains in detail how this is to be done.

Let the mother, on St. John's Day, when the earth renews its annual miracle, when every herb is in flower, and you can fancy you can see the plants growing, take him into a garden, embrace him, and say tenderly to him. "You love me, my dear child, you know only me... but listen—I am not all. You have another mother. We have all one common mother,—men, women, children, animals, plants, all that has life, a tender mother, who always feeds us and is invisible, yet present.... Let us love her, dear child, let us embrace her with all our heart." Nothing more for a long time. No metaphysics to stifle the impression.[53]

This is followed by a long account of how the father should later take the child out on an important public holiday and instill love of country by teaching the child to associate the crowds, the parades, and the shouting with the spirit of France itself, and by telling the child "never forget that your mother is France."[54]

As Michelet's religion of patriotism made France an object of worship, so Whitman treated America, and from personification done with religious (as opposed to decorative) intent, it is only a very short step to one form of mythologizing. But Whitman himself, unlike Emerson or Thoreau, never talks about making new myth or the need for new mythologies. Modern readers may wish to describe Whitman's work as mythopoeic, but that was not Whitman's own sense of what he was doing. Whitman's conception of his efforts at religious and literary renewal center instead around his concept of prophecy.

If Thoreau wanted to write some pure mythology, Whitman wanted to found a new religion. "Starting from Paumanok" is only one of the poems that are quite explicit on this point:

> I too, following many and follow'd by many, inaugurate a religion,
> I descend into the arena,
> (It may be I am destin'd to utter the loudest cries there, the winner's pealing shouts,
> Who knows? they may rise from me yet, and soar above every thing.)[55]

Occasionally Whitman was tempted to provide a new ritual or a new theology. "Chanting the Square Deific" leans rather far toward pure theology, and elsewhere a note of his says, "write a new burial service"; but usually he was more sensible, preferring to create a new body of sacred poetry.[56] Another, more typical note reads, "The Great Construction of the New Bible. Not to be diverted from the principal object—the main life work—the three hundred and sixty five—it ought to be ready in 1859 (June '57)."[57] The writer of a new Bible would have to be a poet prophet, the new Bible itself a poem or prophecy.

Whitman's frequent lists of poems and great religious works show that he made no fixed distinction between poetry and prophecy. He makes frequent reference to such things as "the florid, rich, first phases of poetry, and in the oriental poems, in the Bible . . ." or the "very ancient poetry of the Hebrew prophets, of Ossian, of the Hindu singer and ecstatics, of the Greeks, of the American aborigines, the old Persians and Chinese, and Scandinavian Sagas, all resemble each other."[58]

From Herder, from a New York rabbi named Dr. Frederick de Sola Mendes, and from other sources, including probably a Quaker one, Whitman derived a concept of prophecy which deemphasized predicting the future and put its stress on living poetic expression. In the course of commenting on Carlyle, Whitman made his clearest statement of this:

Prophecy

> The word prophecy is much misused; it seems narrow'd to prediction merely. That is not the main sense of the Hebrew word translated "Prophet." It means one whose mind bubbles up and pours forth as a fountain, from inner divine spontaneities, revealing god. Prediction is a very minor part of prophecy. The great matter is to reveal and outpour the God-like suggestions pressing for birth in the soul.[59]

Thoreau thought the deepest and earliest poetry was myth, Whitman thought it was prophecy.

Surveying Whitman's achievement in poetry, one could say, from a modern point of view, that he exchanged new myth for old, faith in science, progress, democracy, and the people, love and comradeship for faith in the old gods of Greece, Egypt, or Christianity. One might also claim that Whitman mythologized himself from plain Walter Whitman into Representative Man and Kosmos Walt Whitman, and later into the Prophet of These States, the Bard, and the Good Gray Poet. There may be something to learn from this point of view, especially if one is interested in what has been made of Whitman. But it is important, and not merely a scholarly quibble, to remember that Whitman himself would have resisted the claim that he was a mythmaking poet. Myth was something negative, something to "eclaircise," to clear up, something to be displaced by new forces and new realities. To call his deeply held belief in the People of "These States" or his religion of Humanity "myths" would be, in Whitman's view, to disparage them and question their validity. For no matter how much or how often Whitman values old myths and religions and the peoples that followed them, myth in Whitman's work inevitably suggests something a little dubious, unclear, and a little fanciful, something not quite consistent with passionate, urgent, realistic conviction.

Yet he cannot avoid recognizing in "Passage to India" and elsewhere the validity of the impulse behind myth. The expression of this primal religious impulse cannot be simply dismissed as a rejection of myth; it is, rather, a deliberate displacement of it by something else. In place of myth Whitman gives us symbols, images of man himself, a new religion of humanity, and prophecy. It is hard to see how any poet could make a greater or more affirmative use of myth than Whitman did by the very process of abandoning it.

Six

Hawthorne

1. Hawthorne, Schlegel, and the Modern Uses of Myth

All of Hawthorne's major uses of myth are efforts to modernize it. His two books of Greek myth for children are a sustained attempt to renovate the myths by removing their "classical" quality and substituting a gothic or romantic tone. Such stories as "Drowne's Wooden Image" and "The Maypole of Merry Mount" show Hawthorne writing New England versions of Ovidian metamorphoses. Myth is also central to Hawthorne's last finished romance, *The Marble Faun,* and his conception of romance itself is remarkably similar to certain nineteenth-century German conceptions of myth.

Indeed, Hawthorne's view of myth had, from the beginning, certain affinities with German romantic mythic thought. It is quite likely that Hawthorne read Friedrich Schlegel's *Lectures on the History of Literature* in 1828, and it can be shown that Hawthorne's understanding of myth is closer to Schlegel's than to any single modern viewpoint.[1] A brief survey of Schlegel's main positions provides an excellent point of departure for assessing Hawthorne's ideas about what was valuable and what reprehensible in Greek myth, his ideas about the nature of medieval Germanic (or as he called it, gothic) versions of myth, and his ideas about the qualities needed by the modern writer of myths.

Schlegel both admired and disparaged classical myth. He admired the scope of Greek myth and found it pretty enough in its way. "The mythology of the Greeks," he wrote, "embraced the whole visible world within the circle of its bold personifications and delightful fables; so that nothing in truth could be imagined which was not connected in some manner with these beautiful fictions, and thus placed within the proper province of ancient poetry."[2] But, says Schlegel, men of sense, starting with ancient Greek philosophers, have objected to the masters of Greek mythology, Hesiod and Homer, condemning them "in the severest terms, for the unworthy, irrational, and immoral representations of the Deity which are contained in their works." Schlegel makes it clear that he agrees with this position. "To us indeed these poetical representations wear no appearance but that of a beautiful play of imagination."[3]

Schlegel much preferred Aeschylus to Homer or Hesiod (a preference that had great implications for the romantic admiration for Aeschylus and the romantic championing of Titanism), because of the way Aeschylus reinterprets myth to serve his own views of man and history. What Schlegel admires in Aeschylus is the example of an artist taking up traditional myth and radically reshaping it; Aeschylus thus becomes the pattern for the romantic poet's efforts to recast myth for his own purposes. Schlegel claims that with Aeschylus

> the whole mythology of the Greeks assumed a new, a peculiar, a characteristic appearance. . . . The subjection of the old gods and Titans—and the history of that lofty race being subdued and enslaved by a meaner and less worthy generation—these are the great points to which almost all his narrations and all his catastrophes may be referred. The original dignity and greatness of nature and man, and the daily declension of both into weakness and worthlessness, is another of his themes. Yet in the midst of the ruins and fragments of a perishing world, he delights to astonish us now and then with a view of that old gigantic strength—the spirit of which seems to be embodied in his Prometheus—ever bold and ever free—chained and tortured, yet invincible within.[4]

This is a *locus classicus* for romantic Titanism, and it has as much relevance to Thoreau and Melville as to Hawthorne. It is cited here because Schlegel's point, that myth is revitalized when a later writer takes it up in his own way, bears an obvious relation to Hawthorne. Also congenial to Hawthorne is the idea that Aeschylean myth is valuable for moral rather than for purely aesthetic or religious reasons. Schlegel felt that Greek myth itself was pretty much dead by the Middle Ages, and that strictly imitative efforts to produce what Emerson called "modern antiques" were pointless. After the time of Theodoric, Schlegel says, "some few indeed still persisted in making a poetical use of the old Pagan mythology; but as all the particulars of that system had already been completely exhausted, and the belief itself was utterly gone, nothing more was attainable than a faint and elaborate imitation of the matchless works of the true Pagans."[5] Hawthorne makes a similar comment on the impossibility of achieving anything through routine imitation of Greek myth. Recalling a conversation with the English sculptor John Gibson, Hawthorne wrote:

> In his own art, he said the aim should be to find out the principles on which the Greek sculptors wrought, and to do the work of this day on those principles and in their spirit: a fair doctrine enough, I should think, but which Mr. Gibson can scarcely be said to practice, giving birth as he has and does to a vast progeny of marble dream-work from the Grecian mythology.[6]

Like Schlegel, Hawthorne did not permit himself to mistake imaginative understanding or aesthetic feeling or the desire to believe for belief itself. Hawthorne's accounts of his trips to churches and museums in Rome, for example, show that he kept the distinction clear. The modern use of myth would have to be different from the Greek in order to succeed. Schlegel's call for new myth or new uses of old myth is not a shallow or destructive reform. It is indeed based on profound respect for Greek myth, and Schlegel reserves his real scorn not for the extravagances of myth but for the rationalists and the sophists who denounced myth only to leave something worse in its place.[7]

What the modern world needs is not more sophistry, but a modern version or equivalent of myth. Schlegel's account of Aeschylus, quoted above, gives one clue to the creative transforming of old myth, but Aeschylus' example is of limited use to later ages and other countries. Schlegel provides a much more modern example in

his lecture on medieval German literature. He is discussing a reference Tacitus makes to the existence of a legend "according to which
Ulysses came in the course of his wanderings to Germany, and there
founded the city of Asciburgum." Schlegel goes on to spell out, with
great clarity, how the writer can find in myth a general or universal
idea which permits any given myth to be changed or extended
without altering its essence.

> Now the ancients were accustomed to consider legends, such as this, in a
> point of view of which we have no notion. They considered nothing in
> such traditions but the universal idea of a deity or a hero. They called the
> god of war, of every nation, by the name of Mars, and every deity
> presiding over science or art by that of Mercury and if they did not
> altogether overlook local differences, they at least attached to them very
> little importance. Ulysses was the common idea of a wandering hero.[8]

It is not my argument that Hawthorne's views on myth were consciously founded on those of Schlegel, it is merely that they were
remarkably similar, and that the views expressed in Schlegel's discussions of myth help to illuminate Hawthorne's fictional and
mythic practice.

2. Greek Myths for Children: From Classic to Gothic

A *Wonder Book* (1852) and *Tanglewood Tales* (1853) are the only
writings of Hawthorne's the sole avowed purpose of which is to retell
Greek myth. A *Wonder Book* includes the myths of Perseus and
Medusa, Midas and the Golden Touch, Pandora's Box, Hercules and
the Golden Apples of the Hesperides, Baucis and Philemon, and
Bellerophon and Pegasus. *Tanglewood Tales* contains versions of
Theseus and the Minotaur, Hercules' battle with Antaeus and the
Pygmies, the Rape of Europa, Cadmus' sowing the Dragon's Teeth,
the story of Circe, the story of Proserpina, and Jason and the Golden
Fleece. Hawthorne's general purpose may be judged from a letter he
wrote to his publisher, James Fields, on May 23, 1851:

As a framework, I shall have a young college student [Eustace Bright] telling these stories to his cousins and brothers and sisters, during his vacation, sometimes at the fireside, sometimes in the woods and dells. Unless I greatly mistake, these old fictions will work up admirably for the purpose; and I aim at substituting a tone in some degree Gothic or Romantic, or any such tone as may best please myself, instead of the classic coldness which is as repellent as the touch of marble.[9]

In the preface to the volume, which was finally called *A Wonder Book for Girls and Boys* (a title which echoes the famous German collection by Arnim and Bretano called *Des Knaben Wunderhorn*), Hawthorne insists that Greek myths are "capable of being rendered into very capital stories for children."[10] He argues that while Greek myths are immortal, it is by their very indestructibility that "they are legitimate subjects for every age to clothe with its own garniture of manners and sentiment, and to imbue with its own morality."[11] Hawthorne goes on to repeat what he had said to Fields about the gothic quality he was evidently quite set on producing. "In the present version, they may have lost much of their classical aspect, (or, at all events, the Author has not been careful to preserve it,) and have perhaps, assumed a Gothic or romantic guise."[12] In general Hawthorne modernized the myths by domesticating them, by setting them in landscapes familiar to New England children, by leaving out, at least in *A Wonder Book,* all mention of Greece, and by giving the stories a homey quality. This is how Hawthorne's version of the story of Baucis and Philemon, retitled "The Miraculous Pitcher," begins: "One evening, in times long ago, old Philemon and his old wife Baucis sat at their cottage-door enjoying the calm beautiful sunset."[13]

What separates Hawthorne's version of the myths from those to be found in innumerable handbooks and schoolbooks of the time is that he has re-imagined the settings, the characters, and even the plots of the old stories for himself. His myth books for children have had a great success. They are still in print in cheap editions meant for children to whom the name Hawthorne means nothing. *A Wonder Book* has had at least a hundred and twenty editions, and at least eighteen different sets of illustrations, including those by Maxfield Parrish and Arthur Rackham. Hawthorne's versions of the Greek myths have had more editions than those other nineteenth-century standbys, Bulfinch's *Age of Fable* and Charles Kingsley's *The Heroes*, though together these three books, perhaps with the addition of John Flaxman's widely known engravings, are pretty much responsible for the popular and genteel view of myth that still persists in this country.

Hawthorne's choice of subjects is suggestive. Stories about heroes (Jason, Hercules, and Theseus) predominate; there are few stories that directly concern the great Olympian deities, the tale of Troy, or the myths of creation. Hawthorne liked stories in which dramatic, magical transformations took place; the ultimate origin of many of his stories is Ovid. Many also come from Apollodorus, only one from Homer. It has been shown in convincing detail that Hawthorne's main source for almost all the tales was Charles Anthon's *Classical Dictionary* (1841), a debt Hawthorne openly recognized in the sketch "Tanglewood Porch," which serves to introduce "The Gorgon's Head."[14]

Anthon's interpretations of Greek myth lean heavily on the work of Friedrich Creuzer, the German scholar who argues for elaborate symbolic readings of myth, and on the work of Thomas Keightley, an Anglo-Irish writer who in the 1830s was the first English-speaking compiler of myth to make significant use of the scholarship of the brothers Grimm, which linked myth with folklore. Hawthorne allows Eustace, who is justly fearful of what a classical scholar would say about his stories, to be very hard on myth-scholars and to mock them as "Old gray-bearded grandsires [who] pore over them [myths], in musty volumes of Greek, and puzzle themselves with trying to find out when, and how, and for what, they were made."[15] It is nevertheless possible that occasional hints from the formidable columns of scholarly comment in Anthon made their way into Hawthorne's work. From Creuzer, via Anthon, Hawthorne might have learned, however, that "Fauns are the rays of the genial spring light personified." It could also be claimed that in his treatment of Circe, Hawthorne follows the interpretation of C. G. Heyne as reported by

Anthon. "Homer merely gave an historical aspect, as it were, to an allegory invented by some earlier poet, and in which the latter wished to show the brutalizing influence of sensual indulgences."

Admitting the central importance of Anthon for Hawthorne's plots, facts, names, occasional treatments and comparisons, and even as a carrier of other scholarship, there remains the distinctive gothic, romantic, or modern tone Hawthorne imparted to these stories—and that tone did not come from Anthon. Indeed, the characteristic style of *A Wonder Book* is closer to some of the children's literature of the time than to any scholarly source. Hawthorne's tales recall at times Charles Lamb's *The Adventures of Ulysses,* Charles Demoustier's *Letters à Émilie sur la Mythologie,* the *Arabian Nights, Gulliver's Travels,* Andersen's *Fairy Tales,* the *Kinder- und Hausmärchen* of the brothers Grimm, and La-Motte-Fouqué's *Undine.*[16] As such a list suggests, the principal tone of Hawthorne's myth stories is closer to fairy tale than to classic mythology. And it is chiefly in matters of style and tone that Hawthorne changes classical myth into gothic or romantic or modern fairy tales. The word used most frequently by Hawthorne to describe the quality he wished to substitute for the classic is "Gothic," and it is evident that the word was of considerable significance to Hawthorne. He has Mr. Pringle take Eustace to task after listening to the story of Hercules, Atlas, and the Golden Apples of the Hesperides:

> Pray let me advise you never more to meddle with a classical myth. Your imagination is altogether Gothic, and will inevitably gothicize everything that you touch. The effect is like bedaubing a marble statue with paint. This giant, now! How can you have ventured to thrust his huge disproportioned mass among the seemly outlines of Grecian fable, the tendency of which is to reduce even the extravagant within limits, by its pervading elegance?[17]

Eustace pertly replies that he has as good a right as ancient poets to remodel the stories at pleasure. But the important point is that "Gothic," as used here, does not refer to the gothic novel. As used here, "gothicize" appears to mean introducing some calculated disproportion, a disregard for classical harmony and symmetry, indeed something anticlassic. "Gothic" can mean "medieval," and "northern"; it has overtones of "Germanic" or "Teutonic" and of "barbarianism." Emerson, for example, used "gothicism" pejoratively to mean "medieval intricacy" in a description of Swedenborg.[18] And Hawthorne himself, in his *Italian Notebooks,* records the slow awakening of an appreciation for classic art in himself as follows:

> I am partly sensible that some unwritten rules of taste are making their way into my mind; that all this Greek beauty has done something toward refining me, who am still, however, a very sturdy Goth.[19]

The word "gothic" also seems to have suggested folklore and fairy-tale qualities to Hawthorne, who makes Eustace undertake to do a story about a "gothic Apollo." This personage appears in "The Miraculous Pitcher" as the more elderly of the two mysterious travelers who stop at the hut of Baucis and Philemon. The gothic Apollo has a deep voice, and a solemn manner, and is first seen inquiring as to whether or not there had once been a lake where the village of unfriendly people now stands.

> He shook his head, too, so that his dark and heavy curls were shaken with the movement. "Since the inhabitants of yonder village have forgotten the affections and sympathies of their nature, it were better that the lake should be rippling over their dwellings again!"
> The traveller looked so stern, that Philemon was really almost frightened; the more so, that, at his frown, the twilight seemed suddenly to grow darker, and that, when he shook his head, there was a roll as of thunder in the air.[20]

Hawthorne's gothic Apollo is partly an angry grandfather, partly a menacing stranger in dark collusion with nature. Altogether, he is more a figure from a North European fairy tale than the shining god of the Greeks.

Finally, there is a passage in Hawthorne's *English Notebooks* that suggests that the gothic is a romantic, ruined inversion of the classic. Hawthorne speaks of a "statue overgrown with moss and lichen, so that its classic beauty was in some sort gothicized."[21] The common link in Hawthorne's use of the words "goth," "gothic," and "gothicize" is that the gothic is clearly opposed to whatever is classical. Gothic for Hawthorne seems to be that element of romanticism or modernity that is not just nonclassical, but anticlassical.

In gothicizing, or declassicizing, the Greek myths, Hawthorne altered them significantly. He meticulously avoids locating any of the stories in *A Wonder Book* in a specific place. Greece is never mentioned, and since the scenery is northern, and certain other details are more fit for New England than for the Mediterranean, a child might be excused for thinking Midas a Berkshire County landowner. Midas' breakfast of "hot cakes, some nice little brook trout, roasted potatoes, fresh boiled eggs, and coffee" is anything but Greek.[22]

In both *A Wonder Book* and *Tanglewood Tales* there is a persistent declassicizing in matters of detail. Circe becomes Dame Circe, her palace is provided with a magic fountain that forms itself into different pictorial shapes as if in a tale by Tieck or Hoffman. Circe's palace is provided with "pinnacles." These and other details change the tone of the Homeric story to that of a medieval tale about an enchantress in a castle. Similarly, in the story of Proserpina, Ceres becomes Mother Ceres, and Pluto is described as a lord of the mines.

Hawthorne did more than change locales and modernize characters. He resorted constantly to unabashed magic to set the tone of most of his stories. The bowl which replenished itself in Ovid's story of Baucis and Philemon becomes the title and focal point in Hawthorne's "The Miraculous Pitcher." Likewise the transformations in the story of Midas, which in Ovid and in Greek myth generally are attended by feelings of awe and mystery, of gods being near, of divine forces just below and occasionally breaking through the smiling surface of things, become in Hawthorne the run-of-the-mill magic of fairy tale. Here, as in his magnifying the role of the invisible helmet in the story of Perseus and the Gorgon's Head, Hawthorne is taking a classical detail and expanding it, while at the same time treating the supernatural elements as profane rather than sacred. Eleusinian mysteries are replaced by parlor magic. Hawthorne's transformations reveal not the power of the gods or nature, but the sleight of hand of sorcerers. It may only be a question of degree and tone, but the effect Hawthorne achieves is a far cry indeed from the effect Ovid or Homer get, and is much closer to that obtained by Grimm or Andersen.

Hawthorne also persistently ruralizes his characters. Baucis and Philemon are, for example, good New England townsfolk, familiar and therefore comfortable. Douglas Bush once remarked on Edmund Spenser's genius for a similar sort of transformation, pointing out that Spenser's portrait of Despair made him seem to be a very realistic Irish peasant living in his poor hovel. Spenser was a childhood favorite of Hawthorne's and it may not be entirely fanciful to see the dragon of Canto One of *The Fairie Queene* in the dragon of Hawthorne's story of Cadmus. Hawthorne's dragon, when stretched out dead, is described as "still wriggling his vast bulk, although there was no longer life enough in him to harm a little child."[23]

Another aspect of Hawthorne's transformation of these tales is his announced intention of cleaning up the stories. In the preface to *Tanglewood Tales,* Hawthorne puts the problem of how to render the Greek myths presentable for children.

> These old legends, so brimming over with everything that is most abhorrent to our Christianized moral-sense, some of them so hideous— others so melancholy and miserable, amid which the Greek Tragedians sought their themes, and moulded them into the sternest forms of grief that ever the world saw;—was such material the stuff that children's playthings should be made of! How were they to be purified? How was the blessed sunshine to be thrown into them?[24]

Although Hawthorne did not try to remove the fighting and violence, he took care to select stories in which most of the fighting was of men against monsters. Much more noticeable is his careful emptying the stories of sex. He leaves no hint, for instance, that Ulysses lived with Circe and had a son by her. Any sexual innuendo in Pluto's carrying off Proserpina is deftly undercut by making her a little girl who is snatched away by Pluto to cheer up his house, somewhat as Phoebe brightens up the house of the seven gables. The rape of Europa by Jupiter in the form of a bull is similarly—and cleverly—made innocuous by turning Europa into a very young girl and the bull into a docile and protective creature rather like a Saint Bernard. Hawthorne turns the dark and bloody myths into gay or sentimental stories, closer in spirit to Louisa May Alcott than to Homer.

A crucial element in Hawthorne's renovation is the careful exclusion of any hint of religion. Gods are demoted to magicians. Miracles become only magic tricks. No reader of Hawthorne's Greek stories would be able to guess that many of these stories had once had religious significance to the Greeks.

Hawthorne frequently solved the problem of how to make the old myths fit for children by changing the persons of the myth into children themselves. In the story of Midas, he invents a little daughter for Midas and makes the story turn on her. In the stories of Europa and Proserpina he makes the main figure a child, and in the story of Pandora's Box he makes both Pandora and Epimetheus children in a nursery. By such means Hawthorne reshaped the Greek myths to fit his youthful audience. He claimed that this was justified, that "the stories (not by any strained effort of the narrator's, but in harmony with their inherent germ) transform themselves, and re-assume the shapes which they might be supposed to possess in the pure childhood of the world." He argues that his method of transforming the stories is necessary because "the inner life of the legends cannot be come at, save by making them entirely one's own property." He thus concludes that the myths once had just such a shape as he is restoring, that they were written in the Golden Age, and that all that now remains of that age is childhood. All the "objectionable characteristics" are merely late "parasitical" growths.[25]

This all sounds a little specious and a little sentimental. Hawthorne is not restoring Greek myth—he does not seriously believe it began as nursery tales, or "baby stories," as he himself more harshly calls them. In the context of his times, Hawthorne's undeniably charming book of Greek myths for children seems simply to have trivialized the subject. Though it is not clear that they succeeded *because* they trivialized myth, it is remarkable that Charles Kingsley's *The Heroes* and Thomas Bulfinch's *The Age of Fable* are, like

Hawthorne's stories, shorn of sex, of religious significance, and of the dark power which marks Homeric or Aeschylean myth. If many Americans grew up thinking of Greek myths only as sunny, proper fairy tales for children, then Hawthorne cannot escape some responsibility in the matter. And while the real impact of his *Wonder Book* and *Tanglewood Tales* has been to help trivialize myth, there are still several other points about these books which significantly modify that harsh judgment.

Despite his unappreciative comments about myth, often part of the elaborate but gentle irony which surrounds the figure of Eustace Bright and often a result simply of museum fatigue, Hawthorne must have had a marked fondness for the subject. His study, as described by his wife, had a painting of Endymion on one wall and a copy of the Apollo Belvedere on a pedestal.[26] Sophia did drawings from Flaxman, and indeed Flaxman's classical drawings seem to have been an important book in the Hawthorne household.[27] Julian Hawthorne has also left a vivid description of his father reading aloud to the children from his own *Wonder Book* in his rich, sure voice.[28] Of a garden Hawthorne saw in Rome and which impressed him favorably, he recorded, in a phrase that recalls Schlegel, that it had "eight marble statues of Apollo, Cupid, nymphs, and other such sunny and beautiful people of classical mythology."[29] Indeed, as we shall see, *The Marble Faun* shows beyond question that Hawthorne could still be captivated by certain things in Greek mythology even then, years after the children's books were done.

Under some circumstances Hawthorne enjoyed and admired Greek myth, but he gives the impression, in several places, that if anything much had been expected from myth in ancient times, one certainly can't expect or get much now, so many ages after the great day of myth. Hawthorne makes Eustace Bright complain that the Greeks, by putting their myths "into shapes of indestructible beauty, indeed, but cold and heartless, have done all subsequent ages an incalculable injury," because the myths by rights belong to all times and nations.[30] Many other examples might be brought forward to show that Hawthorne was thoroughly historicized in his attitude toward myth, as Emerson and Thoreau were not, and he was honest enough not to manufacture religious feeling when he did not feel it. There is a passage in the *Italian Notebooks* (which shows up in a depersonalized form in *The Marble Faun*) which rather movingly shows Hawthorne momentarily experiencing the religious awe he thought one should feel before a Greek divinity.

> I saw the Apollo Belvedere as something ethereal and god-like; only for a flitting moment, however, and as if he had alighted from heaven, or shone suddenly out of the sunlight, and then had withdrawn himself again.[31]

Usually the statues appear lifeless to Hawthorne, but here he shows not only that he knew something of the religious nature of the myths, but also—as he was to argue in *The Marble Faun*—that he was aware that Greek religion could not be revived in its original form.

Not to be overlooked also is his repeated assurance that the myths are immortal, that they belong to everyone. In practical terms, what Hawthorne saved, and may therefore be thought to have value in the myths, were the basic plots or stories, the part which Schlegel too thought was essential. And indeed, it is a perfectly defensible position to argue that he is right, that what is crucial about Greek myth (from Aristotle on) is its core of story, not the trappings and surfaces.

Despite their seeming simplicity, Hawthorne's children's stories also offer a number of suggestions as to the meaning of the stories themselves. Once in a while Hawthorne puts aside the unquestioning and straightforward innocence with which his readers are asked to accept gorgons, flying horses, and armed men springing from dragon's teeth and offers a rationalistic or Euhemerist explanation. Of Chiron the centaur, Hawthorne writes:

> I have sometimes suspected that Master Chiron was not really very different from other people, but that, being a kind-hearted and merry old fellow, he was in the habit of making believe that he was a horse, and scrambling about the schoolroom on all fours, and letting the little boys ride upon his back. And so, when his scholars had grown up, and

grown old, and were trotting their grandchildren on their knees, they told them about the sports of their school days, and these young folks took the idea that their grandfather had been taught their letters by a Centaur, half man and half horse.

This easy debunking is neither convincing nor typical, though it is, in its way, original. More conventional is the idea Hawthorne expresses at times that the gods are symbols of natural forces. Apollo is quite consistently associated with sunlight (not with the power of the sun, but with what Hawthorne repeatedly calls the "genial" sunbeams) and Ceres is associated with the growth of the crops in the fields. One particularly effective use of this explanation is in the story of "The Golden Touch," in which the gift of the golden touch is conferred by a radiant stranger, a sort of fairy godfather who is never named but whom the reader guesses to be Apollo. The gift becomes effective the morning after the stranger's visit, but not until the first rays of the morning sun come through the windows and "gild" the ceiling over Midas as he lies in bed. As the story unfolds, there is a running comparison between the natural gold of sunlight and the metallic gold into which everything is turned by the deadly Midas.

Another brief but revealing comment on the true nature of myth—and upon the ideal conditions for creating it—occurs in the interlude just before the start of "The Golden Touch." Hawthorne says of Eustace's storytelling that

> His mind was in a free and happy state, and took delight in its own activity, and scarcely required any external impulse to set it at work. How different is this spontaneous play of the intellect, from the trained diligence of maturer years, when toil has perhaps grown easy by long habit, and the day's work may have become essential to the day's comfort, although the zest of the matter has bubbled away![32]

The implications of this comment are that myth is a product of fresh, free imagination, something from the world's childhood, now long gone though faintly revived in the imaginative efforts of gifted youth.

More pervasive than these scattered comments and attitudes is the obvious and, for Hawthorne, the characteristic view of myth as a vehicle for moral teaching. Indeed, these stories, taken together, form a sort of pageant of moral qualities—a kind of children's version of the pageant of the seven deadly sins. "The Golden Touch" is about avarice, "Pandora's Box" is about disobedience (the Miltonic and biblical parallels are quite deliberate), "Baucis and Philemon" is about inhospitableness, and "Circe's Palace" is about gluttony.

Just as Hawthorne himself transformed the classic myths into gothic stories, so the *idea* of transformation or metamorphosis runs through all the stories. A great deal could be said about this theme in the stories, but since it also forms an important part of the discussion of *The Marble Faun,* perhaps it will be enough to say here that metamorphosis is a major technique in these stories, as well as a major theme, an image of life, a connection point between the real and the imagined, and the best description of what Hawthorne himself has done to the old Greek myths.

It should also be noted, to Hawthorne's credit, that while so many scholars were treating the subject of myth with an almost forbidding erudition and seriousness, linking mythology to psychology, history, philosophy, and religion, Hawthorne himself decided to emphasize the gaiety, the narrative verve, and the high sense of fun in myth. He may easily be forgiven such liberties as the flat denial that Theseus ever left Ariadne stranded on an island, because of his steady, good humored, and, we must add, successful intention to make the stories come alive in the present.

3. Transformations and Metamorphoses

Hawthorne's modern reworking of myth was not confined to his children's stories. Indeed it can be seen in short stories written long before *A Wonder Book* and in his last finished romance, *The Marble Faun.* In "Drowne's Wooden Image," first published in 1844, Hawthorne took the story of Pygmalion from the tenth book of Ovid's *Metamorphoses* and retold it as a story of Boston in the early 1770s. Drowne is a Yankee wood-carver who produces workmanlike but lifeless figures. One day he is asked by a Captain Hunnewell to carve a figurehead for his ship. Drowne, hiding himself away from public view, produces a wooden carving of a beautiful woman. The carving is far beyond anything he has been able to do before. "It seemed as if the hamadryad of the oak had sheltered herself from the unimaginative world within the heart of her native tree, and that it was only necessary to remove the strange shapelessness that had incrusted her, and reveal the grace and loveliness of a divinity."[33] Hawthorne adds other hints and touches from mythology to the story of Pygmalion. The passage about the hamadryad prepares us for a brilliant explanation of how great sculpture is formed, while the story of the speaking prow of the Argo may have given Hawthorne the original suggestion on how to turn Ovid's story into a modern one. At any rate, it is made painfully clear that until now Drowne has simply not been able to give a single figure of his the spark of life it needed to become a real work of art. But his lovely figurehead-woman is now praised by none other than John Singleton Copley, the historical figure. (Drowne is also an historical figure, best known for his grasshopper weather vane on Faneuil Hall in Boston.) Copley's opinion lends weight to the verdict, and his presence in the story produces an interesting effect, a quite remarkable blending of history and myth.

> "What is here? Who has done this?" he broke out, after contemplating it in speechless astonishment for an instant. "Here is the divine, the life-giving touch. What inspired hand is beckoning this wood to arise and live?"

Drowne's reply, as Edgar Allan Poe noted, echoes a famous reply of Michelangelo's to a similar question. Drowne says: "The figure lies within that block of oak, and it is my business to find it."[34] This remark shows how well Hawthorne really understood sculpture, a point not always conceded. The important point is, however, the one brought out by Copley, who perceives that it is the power of love, acting in Drowne, that has enabled him to work the miracle of art. Copley looks "earnestly at Drowne, and again saw that expression of human love which, in a spiritual sense, as the artist could not help imagining, was the secret of the life that had been breathed into

this block of wood."[35] The statue has a startling effect on all who see
it. First they think it an actual young woman, "then came a sensa-
tion of fear; as if, not being actually human, yet so like humanity,
she must therefore be something preternatural."[36] An old Puritan
impulse stirs some of the townsfolk to mutter, but Hawthorne does
not permit the dark hint of witchcraft to be taken seriously. The
statue presently "comes to life" and is seen walking in the street
with Captain Hunnewell.

The rational explanation for all this is that Drowne fell in love
with the Captain's lady while he was carving her portrait, and his
love for her inspired his first and only work of real art, for he
afterwards subsides into his usual stolid work. But the story as told
suppresses any mention of the model and we are encouraged to
entertain the idea that the statue comes alive from the love lavished
on its making. The story ends on a rational grace note, however. As
the lady sweeps by on Captain Hunnewell's arm, she somehow
breaks her fan, then disappears into Drowne's waterfront studio. We
enter the studio, only to hear Captain Hunnewell in the distance
ordering his men to make room for the lady in the boat. In the
studio stands the figurehead, as lovely as ever, but the figurehead's
fan is also broken. We cannot apply Yvor Winter's famous formula
of alternative possibilities here, since the detail of the fan is there
only to amuse the reader, not to confound him. Though we may
balk at the coincidence, we smile and accept it, and the rational
explanation of the story along with it.

Ovid's story of Pygmalion is a very sensual one, which can easily
be read as a story of awakening sexuality (among English versions,
Dryden's makes this quite clear). Hawthorne's story is not so much
Ovid as Ovid Bostonized, or Boston-plated. We are left not with the
wedding of sculptor and statue, but with a statement about the
power of love to compel an artist to make his work come to life. This
kind of metamorphosis can fit comfortably into New England history and is also a very successful symbol of the transforming process
characteristic of the highest art.

Just as "Drowne's Wooden Image" uses the image and process of
metamorphosis to dramatize a story about myth and the artist, so

"The Maypole of Merry Mount" (published in 1835) is a story about the constancy of love in a world of changes or metamorphoses involving youth and age, paganism and Puritanism, Old England and New. The metamorphosis in Drowne's art is wonderful and blessed, though not without its twinge of fear; the metamorphoses around the Maypole are for the most part deceitful, wicked, or just heavily ominous. The story begins with a wild pagan festival at Merry Mount, in the midst of which a young couple, of far greater natural dignity than those around them, are about to be married. A band of grim Puritans, led by the iron man Endicott, breaks up the festivity, cuts down the Maypole, and takes away the revelers. Endicott's heart is softened by the selflessness of the young couple, each wishing to bear the other's punishment. In the end, the Lord and Lady of the May stand forth as plain Edith and Edgar. Their "wild mirth" behind them, they face the world with all its "moral gloom" and they face it bravely, "supporting each other along the difficult path which it was their lot to tread, and never wasted one regretful thought on the vanities of Merry Mount."[37]

"The Maypole" is one of Hawthorne's best stories, and it reveals a subtle and complex structure when once we can refrain from the mistaken assumption that it is a simple anti-Puritan piece. The opening scene around the gayly decked Maypole describes a "Golden Age." All is sunshine and laughter, Merry Mount is a paradise of flowers in a green and carefree world:

But what was the wild throng that stood hand in hand about the Maypole? It could not be that the fauns and nymphs, when driven from their classic groves and homes of ancient fable, had sought refuge, as all the persecuted did, in the fresh woods of the West. These were Gothic monsters, though perhaps of Grecian ancestry. On the shoulders of a comely youth uprose the head and branching antlers of a stag; a second, human in all other points, had the grim visage of a wolf; a third, still with the trunk and limbs of a mortal man, showed the beard and horns of a venerable he-goat. There was the likeness of a bear erect, brute in all but his hind legs, which were adorned with pink silk stockings. And here again, almost as wondrous, stood a real bear of the dark forest, lending each of his fore paws to the grasp of a human hand, and as ready for the dance as any in that circle. His inferior nature rose half way, to meet his companions as they stooped. Other faces wore the similitude of man or woman, but distorted or extravagant, with red noses pendulous before their mouths, which seemed of awful depth, and stretched from ear to ear in an eternal fit of laughter. Here might be seen the Salvage Man, well known in heraldry, hairy as a baboon and girdled with green leaves. . . .[38]

This remarkable pageant, coming as it does at the opening of the story, and immediately after a short but glowing description of the Maypole itself and the Golden Age over which it presided, sets the stage for all the changes that now follow in quick succession. The passage is a richly textured description, reminding one pointedly of the Circe episode in the *Odyssey,* the Bower of Bliss in *The Faerie Queene,* and Milton's *Comus.* The idea of a gothic version of certain classic themes and figures is already present here, fifteen years before the children's stories; and it is important here, too, since it suggests a way to set up a pagan versus Christian opposition by using not Greece but Merrie England, with its rural pagan survivals, as a foil to Christian Puritanism. Around the Maypole are seen humans changed outwardly into beasts, a beast partly altered toward human form, and humans distorted but not yet transformed. As in Milton, these outward shapes are indicative of animal states. But it is more complex than that, since the truth about this wild throng depends on one's point of view. To the Merry Mount people, full of "glee-some spirits," it is a "wild revelry." On the other hand, the Puritans, "who watched the scene, invisible themselves, compared the masques to those devils and ruined souls with whom their superstition peopled the black wilderness." By way of contrast with these viewpoints we are told that to a "wanderer, bewildered in the melancholy forest," had any such been present, the dancers might have appeared to be "the crew of Comus, some already transformed to brutes, some midway between man and beast, and the others rioting in the flow of tipsy jollity that foreran the change."[39] This appears to be a neutral or objective view. It tallies with the narrator's previous description, and it recalls Milton's *Comus* explicitly, the theme of which is, like this story, the "unassailable security of the virtuous mind amid every circumstance of violence and wrong."[40]

Against this lavish setting, the wedding of Edith and Edgar, Lord and Lady of the May, takes place; but as soon as their hearts glow "with real passion," as opposed to the "continual carnival" of "jest and delusion, trick and fantasy" of their surroundings, they change into real people with real cares in a real world, and the tipsy insubstantiality of Merry Mount vanishes for them. From here on through the story, Edith and Edgar remain firm against the vaguely menacing changes that surround them. The Puritans breaking in on the scene are described, for example, as "black shadows" who "have rushed forth in human shape." Endicott stands like a "dread magician" in the center of a circle of "evil spirits." The Maypole is cut down and nature itself is darkened. "As it sank, tradition says, the evening sky grew darker, and the woods threw forth a more sombre shadow."[41] The revelers are all changed back into men, and made into recreants, and the final change which ends the story is the unsuspected but welcome one of Endicott's change of heart toward Edith and Edgar.

The metamorphoses of Merry Mount are indeed sombre. No Ovidian lightness, but a deep New England gloom hangs over the story. Hawthorne uses metamorphoses as outward signs of inward conditions, as a way to dramatize different points of view, or, in other words, as a way to give concrete form to the conflict between pagan and Christian views of life. As "Drowne's Wooden Image" uses metamorphic myth both as a theme and as a structuring principle to dramatize the vital action of love upon the artist, so "The Maypole of Merry Mount" uses metamorphoses to dramatize the stability of love caught between conflicting visions of life, one raucously pagan, the other militantly Puritan.

Metamorphosis or transformation is simultaneously a major theme and a major structuring principle in Hawthorne's fiction. With roots in classical, mainly Ovidian myth, it is used in many different ways in many different novels and tales, but nowhere is it so central as in *The Marble Faun*. Indeed, this romance—the last one Hawthorne finished—depends heavily on myth in quite a number of ways. From the innumerable transformations which take place in the story, to the use of myth to represent an early stage in human history, to the employment of mythic themes, figures, and methods to work out the enormously complex web of pagan, Hebrew, and Christian threads in the story, myth—especially metamorphic myth—is central to *The Marble Faun.* The book is also, let us admit it, maddeningly vague, not so much about whether Donatello has pointed faun's ears or not, a detail no more important than the broken fan in "Drowne's Wooden Image," but about the main lines of the plot. No doubt Hawthorne intended the book to be open to various interpretations, since he takes pains throughout to show his interest in the sympathetic theory of art, in which the spectator completes any work of art by his own response to it.

The importance of myth to the book is evident from the opening chapters, in which three friends in Rome (an American sculptor named Kenyon, an American copyist named Hilda, and a vaguely Jewish artist of uncertain background and very certain beauty named Miriam) are struck by the uncanny resemblance between the Faun of Praxiteles and their new friend, an Italian nobleman named Donatello. The likeness, we are assured, is very close indeed, and the description of the Faun serves also to characterize Donatello:

The Faun is the marble image of a young man, leaning his right arm on the trunk or stump of a tree; one hand hangs carelessly by his side; in the other, he holds the fragment of a pipe, or some such sylvan instrument of music. His only garment—a lion's skin, with the claw upon his shoulder—falls half-way down his back, leaving the limbs and entire front of the figure nude. The form, thus displayed, is marvellously graceful, but has a fuller and more rounded outline, more flesh, and less of heroic muscle, than the old sculptors were wont to assign to their types of masculine beauty. The character of the face corresponds with the figure; it is most agreeable in outline and feature, but rounded, and somewhat voluptuously developed, especially about the throat and chin; the nose is almost straight, but very slightly curves inward, thereby acquiring an indescribable charm of geniality and humour. The mouth, with its full, yet delicate lips, seems so nearly to smile outright, that it calls forth a responsive smile. The whole statue—unlike anything else that ever was wrought in that severe material of marble—conveys the idea of an amiable and sensual creature, easy, mirthful, apt for jollity, yet not incapable of being touched by pathos. It is impossible to gaze long at this stone image without conceiving a kindly sentiment toward it, as if its substance were warm to the touch, and imbued with actual life.[42]

Insofar as *The Marble Faun* is the story of Donatello, it is the story of the Birth of Morals. The Faun, "endowed with no principle of virtue," at the beginning of the story undergoes a series of humanizing changes—much as Undine does (a resemblance that a contemporary review of *The Marble Faun* noted[43])—and indeed, from one point of view, the romance describes the evolution of the human soul or spirit. Hawthorne's starting point is the Faun, who is not yet a man, but no longer a creature of nature, all animal gladness. Donatello is the link between the two. "Neither man nor animal, and yet no monster, but a being in whom both races meet, on friendly ground!" The Faun also stands for the Golden Arcadian Age. This too is as explicit as possible.

> . . . if the spectator broods long over the statue, he will be conscious of its spell; all the pleasantness of sylvan life, all the genial and happy characteristics of creatures that dwell in woods and fields, will seem to be mingled and kneaded into one substance, along with the kindred qualities in the human soul. Trees, grass, flowers, woodland streamlets, cattle, deer, and unsophisticated man! The essence of all these was compressed long ago, and still exists, within that discoloured marble surface of the Faun of Praxiteles.[44]

Hawthorne adds a bit more. He suggests that the idea of the statue, and of Donatello, is "a poet's reminiscence of a period when man's affinity with Nature was more strict, and his fellowship with every living thing more intimate and clear."[45] Myth thus preserves that earliest and best era when man was closest to nature. Hawthorne pointedly insists that nothing supernatural is involved. "Nature needed, and still needs, this beautiful creature, standing betwixt man and animal, sympathizing with each, comprehending the speech of either race, and interpreting the whole existence of one to the other."[46] There is one other trait in Donatello, and it is significant that Miriam, who shares it, is the first to see in Donatello "a trait of savageness hardly to be expected in such a gentle creature as he usually is."[47]

This, then, is Hawthorne's starting point for a story which was admirably summarized by James Russell Lowell:

> Nothing could be more original or imaginative than the conception of the character of Donatello in Mr. Hawthorne's new romance. His likeness to the lovely statue of Praxiteles, his happy animal temperament, and the dim legend of his pedigree are combined with wonderful art to reconcile us to the notion of a Greek myth embodied in an Italian of the nineteenth century; and when at length a soul is created in this primeval pagan, this child of earth, this creature of mere instinct, awakened through sin to a conception of the necessity of atonement, we feel that, while we looked to be entertained with the airiest of fictions, we were dealing with the most august truths of psychology, with the most pregnant facts of modern history, and studying a profound parable of the development of the Christian Idea.[48]

The ease with which Lowell perceives the central issue suggests that this sort of Christian Hegelianism or concept of history as the unfolding in time of the Idea of God (idea here used in the sense of final and determining reality) was not strange to the era. Indeed *The Marble Faun* is very much a book of its time. The theme of paganism versus Christianity, viewed as an historical struggle, marked much fiction from Mme. de Staël's *Corinne* to William Ware's novels, especially *Zenobia* and *Aurelian,* to the various accounts of the fall of Pompeii and to much of Melville's work. The literary use of sculpture as an integral part of the plot also goes back at least to *Corinne,* while the idea of the statue being endowed with life, going back of course to Pygmalion, was also used by Prosper Merimee in *The Venus of Ille,* by Eichendorff in *The Marble Statue,* and appears in one of Henry James's early stories, *The Last of the Valerii.*[49] Hawthorne's choice of Praxiteles' Faun is not surprising either. Not only was he strongly and repeatedly moved by the statue itself, as his *Italian Notebooks* show, but the statue figures prominently in the various guidebooks he used, and is treated in several different ways—including a line drawing of the whole statue and a page of line drawings of fauns' ears, both hidden and not hidden—in the Lodge translation of Winckelmann's *History of Ancient Art,* which Hawthorne probably had read in 1850.[50] Winckelmann (1717–1768) was also quoted endlessly in the guidebooks, and if Hawthorne's views on sculpture are basically those of Winckelmann, it may be because the eminent German had still no serious rival.

The art of sculpture as understood in the nineteenth century was closely related to the Hegelian view of history in which ideas were progressively revealed in matter. Hawthorne's description of Kenyon's studio is quite explicit on this point. After a brief introduction, Hawthorne guides our attention to

> some hastily scrawled sketches of nude figures on the white-wash of the wall. These . . . are probably the sculptor's earliest glimpses of ideas that may hereafter be solidified into imperishable stone, or perhaps may remain as impalpable as a dream. Next there are a few very roughly modelled little figures in clay or plaister, exhibiting the second stage of the Idea as it advances towards a marble immortality; and then is seen the exquisitely designed shape of clay, more interesting than even the final marble, as being the intimate production of the sculptor himself, moulded throughout with his loving hands, and nearest to his imagination and heart. In the plaister-cast, from his clay-model, the beauty of the statue strangely disappears, to shine forth again, with pure, white radiance, in the precious marble of Carrara.[51]

Elsewhere Hawthorne quotes a saying of Thorwaldsen's which he had heard at a party in Rome. "The reader is probably acquainted with Thorwaldsen's threefold analogy;—the Clay-model, the Life; the Plaister-cast, the Death; and the sculptured Marble, the Resurrection."[52] Indeed, all through the book the creation of sculpture is a kind of running metaphor for the process at work in the characters, the Idea of Christianity working itself out in history.

Thus the novel dramatizes what the nineteenth century thought of as the idea of the progress or growth of the human spirit. We might today call it the guiding "myth" of *The Marble Faun,* but Hawthorne was quite clear that it was an "idea" and he distinguished it from myth, which he saw as a working out of the inner idea of paganism. Both Christianity and paganism have their "ideas," in a Hegelian sense, but paganism calls its idea "myth" and Christianity in the mid-nineteenth century did not.

Miriam's model, and former accomplice in some exasperatingly undisclosed past crime, now emerges from the catacombs—described by Hawthorne as a "dark realm under the earth"—to haunt her. He is described as a satyr and is associated with a kind of wicked paganism quite different from that associated with Donatello. Indeed, the model comes quickly to be identified with a devil.[53]

Miriam is carefully associated with Jewish history and tradition. Many of her paintings are described and we are encouraged to associate her with the heroines in her paintings of Jael and Sisera, Judith and Holofernes, and the daughter of Herodias and the head of John the Baptist. "Over and over again," Hawthorne tells us, "there was the idea of woman, acting the part of a revengeful mischief towards man."[54] As Praxiteles' Faun is the clue to Donatello, so Miriam's work is the clue to her. Art imitates life, and if it does so faithfully, its reward is that life will one day imitate it.

Hilda, the New England girl who eventually marries Kenyon, is associated with the idea of Christian womanhood. Hawthorne makes Hilda represent the one great feminine aspect of Christianity. Hilda tends a shrine to the Virgin, but is herself no Catholic. It pleases her to "pay honor to the idea of Divine Womanhood."[55] We cannot substitute "myth" for "idea" here, even if we maintain a sympathetic or positive meaning of the word "myth." For this would obscure one of Hawthorne's important points, that the "idea," the dynamic spirit or principle of paganism became dead when it was embalmed in mythology, while the corresponding "idea" of Christianity became dead when it became embalmed in the Church. Mythology may once have been the embodiment of a living paganism, but it is now only the husk, a kind of fossilized survival. Similarly, the Christian spirit has died out of the Church, leaving only an empty shell. Only in an individual can either the Golden Age or Christianity ever come alive again.

The novel's pivotal transformation comes as Donatello, now desperately in love with Miriam, hurls the sinister model to his death from the Tarpeian rock. This terrible event both crushes Donatello and begins to humanize him. One can regard the event as the end of the era of Arcadian innocence or the beginning of the Christian era of seeking redemption from sin. But however one puts it, the Golden Age is now past, devastated by sin and evil. The divinity has ebbed away from the classical forms. In the Rome of Donatello's murder of the model, the ruined temple of Minerva now serves as a mere bakery, and the vast heaps of stone and rubbish only increase the burden of the grim past.

Even the myths of the Golden Age become a part of this burden now. Donatello leaves Rome for his ancestral home at Monte Beni, and Kenyon follows him. Two more chapters are now devoted explicitly to the problem of the significance of myth. Donatello's family traces itself back into prehistory and myth. The Monte Beni family were Pelasgians,

> the same noble breed of men, of Asiatic birth, that settled in Greece; the same happy and poetic kindred who dwelt in Arcadia, and—whether they ever lived such life or not—enriched the world with dreams, at least, and fables, lovely, if unsubstantial, of a Golden Age. In those delicious times, when deities and demi-gods appeared familiarly on earth, mingling with its inhabitants as friend with friend; when nymphs, satyrs, and the whole train of classic faith or fable, hardly took pains to hide themselves in the primeval woods;—at that auspicious period, the lineage of Monte Beni had its rise.[56]

The family began when "a sylvan creature, native among the woods, had loved a mortal maiden," and the lives of the ensuing family "were rendered blissful by an unsought harmony with nature."[57] Hawthorne now goes on to explain that once in every century a member of the family emerges bearing a strong resemblance to the original wild creature. "Beautiful, strong, brave, kindly, sincere, of honest impulses, and endowed with simple tastes, and the love of homely pleasures, he was believed to possess gifts by which he could associate himself with the wild things of the forests, and with the fowls of the air, and could feel a sympathy even with the trees, among which it was his joy to dwell."[58] Donatello himself is one of these rare creatures, of course. Hawthorne is using myth to give significance to what seems at first to be only the reemergence of certain family traits. Hawthorne does this quite deliberately, commenting that for "a great many years past, no sober credence had been yielded to the mythical portion of the pedigree. It might, however, be considered as typifying some such assemblage of qualities, (in this case, chiefly remarkable for their simplicity and naturalness) as, when they reappear in successive generations, constitute what we call family character."[59] Mythology, like typology, brings out the pattern in history.

Against this background Donatello tells Kenyon another of the family myths, about one of the descendants of the original Faun, a knight, who falls in love with a water nymph in a fountain. All goes smilingly until one day the knight comes and tries to wash off a bloodstain. He has, it appears, committed a great crime, which serves effectively to break off the natural intimacy of the knight and the water spirit. Kenyon sets himself to interpret the story, which is much more Germanic than Greek or Roman, resembling the Undine story much more than anything in Homer, Hesiod, or Ovid.

> Whether so intended, or not, he understood it as an apologue, typifying the soothing and genial effects of an habitual intercourse with Nature, in all ordinary cares and griefs; while, on the other hand, her mild influences fall short in their effect upon the ruder passions, and are altogether powerless in the dread fever-fit or deadly chill of guilt.[60]

Kenyon's interpretation is rather limited. A fuller explanation is that the mythic events of Donatello's family past are being reenacted in him, first the classic myth of the Faun and the mortal, then the gothic myth of the knight and the water sprite. Like his ancestor the Faun, Donatello fell in love with a mortal, in this case Miriam. Like his ancestor the knight, he fell in love with a water sprite, again Miriam, only this time as nymph in the grounds of the Villa Borghese and at the Fountain of Trevi. He has committed a great sin now which separates him from her, and the loss of intimacy between the knight and the nymph is reenacted as Donatello tries to show

Kenyon how he used to call the animals to him (this trait of Donatello's reminded Moncure Conway of Henry Thoreau) and succeeds in demonstrating that he no longer can speak with the wild things. Hawthorne's whole conception of the reenactment of old myth in the present lives of his characters reminds one of Thomas Mann's use of myth in the Joseph novels. Myth seems the clue to the way history really works; circling and recircling, the old lives, patterns, and myths are repeated, reenacted in each generation.

Kenyon leads Donatello down to Perugia to meet and be reconciled with Miriam under the bronze benediction of the statue of Pope Julius the Third. The scene serves to counter an earlier scene in which the friends stood under the bronze imperiousness of the equestrian statue of Marcus Aurelius. The change, the implied moral progress in going from Roman Paganism to Papal Christianity, is dwelt on by Kenyon, who is given a long and loving description of the Gothic architecture of Perugia, culminating in his turning to the statue and making an explicit comparison between Gothic and Classic:

> Those sculptors of the Middle-Age have fitter lessons for the professors of my art than we can find in the Grecian master-pieces. They belong to our Christian civilization; and, being earnest works, they always express something which we do not get from the antique.[61]

One aspect of *The Marble Faun* is the triumph of the Gothic imagination over the Classic, of an ideal Christianity over ideal Paganism. The point is a religious one in the sense that what is at issue is the question of what shall we believe. But Hawthorne is insistent that art rather than theology or prophecy is at last the best interpreter of faith. Hawthorne closes a long, almost rapt description of Sodoma's fresco of Christ bound to a pillar by insisting that this

> hallowed work of genius shows what pictorial art, devoutly exercised might effect in behalf of religious truth; involving, as it does, deeper mysteries of Revelation, and bringing them closer to man's heart, and making him tenderer to be impressed by them, than the most eloquent words of preacher or prophet.[62]

In harmony with this view, the numerous works of art in the romance are used to comment on a series of problems that are essentially religious. And insofar as the story of Donatello is central, the central religious theme is the loss of Arcadia, the waning of the Golden Age, and the triumph of a Gothic Era in whose works the Idea of Christianity is expressed. In a classic or an heroic age, even in the age of the Old Testament, Donatello's action in killing the model would have been accounted a hero's act, and Donatello would have been a Theseus, a Hercules, or a David, ridding the world of a nuisance. But in Christian Rome the act itself loses the very world that gave it meaning.

There is, I think, no fortunate fall here. The idea is repudiated by the novel's characters and, indeed, Donatello's act is fortunate for no one. All are worse off after it than they were before. The doctrine of the fortunate fall shocks Kenyon when Miriam brings it up and shocks Hilda when Kenyon brings it up in his turn. Hilda points out, quite rightly, that to believe the fall was fortunate is to lose the ability to tell good from evil, and to accept a god who ruins us for our own good. Furthermore, unless one simply ignores all the myth material Hawthorne has put into the story, it is hard to maintain that the chief image in the reader's mind of the main events of the novel is the Fall of Man at all. Hawthorne is at great pains to show that the passing of the Golden Age is a loss not of Eden but of Arcadia.

The Marble Faun is too long and too complex and too deeply enmeshed in myth to permit detailed treatment here, but the foregoing, sketchy and suggestive as it is, may suggest how Hawthorne's fictional use of myth works together with his understanding of how the Gothic and Christian Middle Ages superseded Classic and Pagan antiquity to produce a novel that may fairly be called, in Lowell's phrase, "a history of the Christian Idea."

Because Hawthorne scrupulously distinguishes "myth" from an analogous term like "idea," it has seemed to me necessary to avoid the modern habit of describing this writer's pervasive theme as his "myth." Yet there is one aspect of Hawthorne's art which does lend itself to a sweepingly general concept of myth, even though Hawthorne himself never uses the language of myth to describe it. It is remarkable that the description of the background, context, and setting for his romances is very close to several contemporaneous German descriptions of the proper realm of myth. First in the prefatory sketch to *The Scarlet Letter,* and then in the preface of each succeeding full-length work, Hawthorne argued that the *romance,* as he conceived it, needs "a neutral territory, somewhere between the real world and fairy-land, where the Actual and the Imaginary may meet, and each imbue itself with the nature of the other."[63] With great consistency Hawthorne argues for a "poetic or fairy precinct" or an "available foothold between fiction and reality."[64]

Hawthorne's repeated descriptions of the conditions necessary for romance are uncannily close to K. O. Müller's description of myth as that in which "the real and the Ideal were most intimately combined, and in which their authors themselves placed entire faith."[65] And Hawthorne's desire to create a place where "the Actual and the Imaginary may meet" is very close to a description of the realm of myth as described in a treatise on mythology by K. P. Moritz in which Goethe is supposed to have had a hand. The introduction of the treatise concludes:

> Here then [in myth] it is where the region of imagination borders the nearest to that of reality, and where it is of importance to consider the language of fancy, or mythological fiction, merely as such, and to guard against all premature historical interpretation.[66]

I am not suggesting that Hawthorne's theory of romance can be traced to Goethe, Moritz, or K. O. Müller, and it is always easy to magnify evidence to suit one's theme, but the above resemblance could indeed be carried further. If one were to seek a concept of myth broad enough to cover all of Hawthorne's work, at least one starting point might be the fact that his conception of romance itself is in some important respects quite close to then current German conceptions of myth.

Seven

Melville

Herman Melville was better informed about and more deeply interested in problems of myth than any other American writer of his time, and the more he knew the more pronounced became the oscillation in his work between the extremes of Enlightenment skepticism and romantic acceptance. In such skeptical books as *Mardi* and *The Confidence Man,* he treats myth as an insidious and powerful means for almost unlimited deception, both of others and of self. In other books, such as *Moby-Dick* or *Billy Budd,* Melville recognized in myth the most profound truths and, moreover, in mythic form the only possible literary expression for such truths. *Mardi* is to a great extent a book about myth and—more importantly—about mythmaking. Melville's treatment of Yillah, for example, is not so much a fictionalized as a consciously mythicized account of how certain kinds of myth arise and evolve. *Mardi* is also an account of how symbols follow and grow out of myth. Indeed, it may be said that both *Mardi* and *Moby-Dick* demonstrate that myth precedes symbol; this is obviously an important perception and one that runs counter to the then prevailing Creuzerian view. In *Moby-Dick* Melville also achieves what has come to seem a modern myth, an accomplishment which depends heavily on his having shown the processes by which such myths originate. If Thoreau succeeds in making the reader accept the results of the mythmaking process as intellectually valid, Melville succeeds—at least in *Moby-Dick*—in making those results fictionally believable. What is unusual about both *Mardi* and *Moby-Dick* is that these books try both to create myth and simultaneously to expose to view the processes by which myths are created and gain credence. The full ambitiousness of this achievement is

195

grasped only when one has a fairly comprehensive understanding of just how thoroughly Melville was acquainted with contemporaneous theories about myth.

1. Melville's Reading in Myth

Melville had some knowledge of Greek, Egyptian, Indic, Nordic, Persian, Mohammedan, Peruvian, Polynesian, Gnostic, and biblical mythology.[1] He was also familiar with at least sixteen different theories of myth apart from at least a dozen eighteenth- and nineteenth-century examples of the use of myth in modern literature. The idea that myths arose in conjunction with the constellations of the zodiac, the purpose of which was calendrical, crops up all through *Mardi* and even in *Moby-Dick*. Melville could have gotten it from the notes to R. G. Latham's edition of *Frithiof, a Norwegian Story*. Drawing on Dupuis, the general authority for nineteenth-century zodiacal interpretations of myth, Latham supplied the poem with such notes as the following:

> Those who look at the Northern mythology, beyond its surface, see in the attributes and the actions of its Deities, either simple though wonderful accounts of dead men deified, or allegorical representations of physical (especially astronomical) phenomena. . . . In the following description, Frithiof's bracelet exhibits, not merely the mansions of Odin and Balder, and Frey, but also the course of the sun; in other words, it is a Scandinavian Zodiac.[2]

The Euhemerist view also glanced at here ("dead men deified") was familiar to Melville from a wide variety of other sources, including Bayle and Carlyle.

Melville also knew about Sabeism—the view that myth derives from star worship—from Layard's *Nineveh,* and references in *Mardi* suggest there was another or other sources. Layard's account is, however, particularly clear and free of skeptical scorn.

The origin of the Chaldean theology has ever been a favorite theme of the poet and philosopher. The Assyrian plains, uninterrupted by a single eminence, and rarely shadowed by a passing cloud, were looked upon as a fit place for the birth of a system which recognized the heavenly bodies as types of the supreme power, and invested them with supernatural influences. . . . If the attributes of the Deity were to be typified—if the limited intellect of man required palpable symbols to convey ideas which he could not understand in the abstract, more appropriate objects could not have been chosen than those bright luminaries whose motions and influences were enveloped in mystery, although they themselves were constantly present.[3]

The idea that myths were allegories containing ancient wisdom was familiar to Melville through Francis Bacon's *De Sapientia Veterum*. Bacon's interpretations of myth were predominantly, but not exclusively, as political allegories. The elaborate introduction of Memnon in *Pierre* seems to spring in part from Bacon's version of Memnon as "a Youth too forward," which Bacon explained as a result "of the fatal precipitancy of youth."[4]

K. O. Müller's view that myth was the principal key to prehistory is treated at great length and very persuasively in George Grote's *History of Greece* and will be taken up later. Melville might also have been struck by a simpler expression of the same idea, applied specifically to America in Alexander Bradford's *American Antiquities,* a book which has been connected with Melville. In his preface, Bradford wrote:

It is known that the mythological systems of the ancients were but the expression of certain religious ideas, sometimes interwoven with cosmogonical philosophy, or were descriptive of real events transformed into theological fables. In these, and in tradition, whereof some are as old as the deluge, should we search for the relics of the history of knowledge and civilization.[5]

This is an argument for studying myth as a clue to what was best and finest in a people, whether Greek or American Indian, and it agrees with the Herderian view that a given mythology expresses a given people's conception of nature, a view that permeates *Moby-Dick*.

There is no doubt that Melville was familiar with certain kinds of comparative mythology. Sir William Jones is mentioned in *Typee* and in *Moby-Dick,* but as a linguist rather than a mythographer, though H. Bruce Franklin has argued that Jones's ideas about myth as expressed in "The Gods of Greece, Italy, and India" provide the basic structure of *Mardi.* [6] Howard Vincent has argued persuasively that Melville knew Thomas Maurice's *Indian Antiquities,* a book which tries persistently to undercut the claims of Indic religion. Maurice is a Christian—his book discovers trinities everywhere— and he is, even more than Jones, a Christian comparative mythologist. [7] Indeed, most of the writers who could be called comparative in their approach to myth and with whom Melville was familiar defended Christianity. The "Inquiry into the religious tenets and philosophy of the Bramins," presumably by Julius Mickle, and printed as part of the apparatus to his translation of *The Lusiad,* is openly hostile to Indic religion, treating it as "a boundless chaos of confusion and contradictions." Melville also knew the rather similar *Polynesian Researches* of William Ellis. Although he used such books for matters of detail, and for the names and functions of the specific deities, he could not have relied on them for ideas; they would all have come to the same thing. Ellis, Mickle, Maurice, and, to a lesser extent, Jones all took up non-Christian mythologies only in order to vindicate Christianity. The common method here was to "harmonize" or assimilate pagan or savage myth with Christianity. Insofar as *Mardi* tends to subsume all myth and religion with Oro (God) and Alma (Christ), it is a fictional fantasia on Christian comparative mythology.

Hawthorne could make a distinction between Christian truth and pagan myth, but for Melville the problem was quite different. He included biblical with pagan myth, and the conflict was thus not between biblical and pagan but between myth itself, both pagan and biblical, as something high, wondrous, and significant, and the countervailing view of all myth, both pagan and Christian, as fraud and error. On the latter point, Melville's skepticism was reinforced by wide reading.

To begin with, there is Melville's often noted fondness for Sir

Thomas Browne and Pierre Bayle. One cannot of course call Browne a skeptic, but he does discuss such problems as whether or not Adam and Eve had navels, or just what sort of fruit it was that Adam and Eve ate—apples not being grown in that part of the world. Browne's conclusions are inevitably the proper Christian ones (no, Adam and Eve did not have navels, "yet was not his posterity without the same; for the seminality of his fabrick contained the power thereof," and whatever was the fruit Eve ate we should be "rather troubled that it was tasted, than troubling ourselves in its decision"), and he often leaves the well-disposed and educated Christian wishing that the matter had never come up at all.[8]

Bayle is different; the reader constantly suspects him of being a thorough skeptic who is obliged to conceal it. Perhaps he really was a good Christian, but his long, salacious, gossipy, scandalmongering treatments of religious figures present the antireligious argument so effectively that we are converted rather to skepticism than to belief. Bayle treats David and Jupiter exactly alike, for example, and his manner with both is that of an examining magistrate with a felon. The great cosmogonic myths of the Greeks became for Bayle a string of criminal offenses. His article on Jupiter begins, typically, "Jupiter, the greatest of all the *Heathen* Gods, was the Son of *Saturn* and *Cybele*. There was no crime, but what he was defiled with; for besides that he Dethroned his own Father, that he castrated him, and bound him in Chains in the deepest Hell, he committed Incest with his Sisters, Daughters, and Nurses, and attempted to ravish his mother...."[9] The opportunities for burlesque and satire in Bayle's essentially historical approach to myth were not lost on Melville, whose work often shows a Bayleian sense of high fun and irony in the construction of mock myth. The characteristically humorless tone of the later deists is not so evident in Melville, though he must have known the work of Volney and Paine and perhaps that of Ethan Allen and Thomas Young. Paine's *The Age of Reason* is warmly and accurately described in *Clarel*. Volney is also mentioned as a "pilgrim deist" to the Holy Land in *Clarel,* and there is a strongly sympathetic portrait of Ethan Allen in *Israel Potter.*[10]

If Browne and Bayle seem to have been congenial to Melville, the skeptical and historical work of D. F. Strauss and B. G. Niebuhr seems to have had a devastating effect on him.[11] What Strauss did for the New Testament Niebuhr did decisively for ancient Roman history. The result, for Melville, was a world stripped not only of belief but of believable myth, a world of fact, artifact, bones, and stones. Finally, Melville knew the chief geological arguments against myth, as well as the growing evolutionist position. All of these approaches made it increasingly hard to take myth as true in any important way.[12]

One reason perhaps why Melville could come so close to the tone of authentic myth in his own writings was his respect for myth as more than a symbolic or cryptic version of something else. Melville's respect for myth as irreducible and important in its own right would have been reinforced by an acquaintance with George Grote's long sympathetic account of myth in the first volume of his *History of Greece*. From Grote, Melville could have had this simple but important definition of myth as a word which "in its original meaning, signified simply a statement or current narrative, without any connotative implication either of truth or falsehood."[13] More specifically, the nature of this narrative is such that "the mythe both presupposes, and springs out of a settled basis and a strong expansive force of religious, social, and patriotic feeling, operating upon a past which is little better than a blank as to positive knowledge." Grote goes on to say that myth "resembles history, in so far as it is occasionally illustrative; but in its essence and substance, in the mental tendencies by which it is created as well as in those by which it is judged and upheld, it is a popularized expression of the divine and heroic faith of the people."[14] Grote defines myth as something important and irreducible, a category in itself. His summary recapitulation insists on this. "The Grecian Mythes," he writes, "are a special product of the imagination and feelings, radically distinct both from history and philosophy: they cannot be broken down and decomposed into the one nor allegorized into the other."[15] Some of Melville's best writing is the result of his accepting this approach to myth as an autonomous form in which the highest, rarest sort of truth is expressed. It is a view of myth as valuable in itself and as an expressive medium of perfect integrity, not reducible to allegory, symbolism, fiction, or idea. As Pound thought of an epic as a poem that "included history," perhaps we may say that in Melville's hands the romance is a novel that includes myth.

Melville was thus not content merely to refer to ancient myth, however often. He was also alive to the possibilities for modern myth, and his reading of modern authors who tried in one way or another to incorporate myth or to create new myth in their writings was extensive. Melville was a careful reader, as his marginalia show, and we may therefore be sure that he learned something about myth in modern writing from his reading of Goethe, E. T. A. Hoffman, Fénelon's *Télémaque,* Ossian, the poems of Akenside, the mythic-philosophical romances of Jean-Paul Richter, Mary Shelley's *Frankenstein,* Tegner's *Frithiof's Saga,* Carlyle's *German Romance,* Thoreau's *A Week on the Concord and Merrimack Rivers,* Emerson, Hawthorne, and Friedrich Schlegel, to pick a few of the obvious names.

Given Melville's extensive and many-sided acquaintance with various mythologies, theories of myth, and modern uses of myth in literature, we should be prepared, to some extent, for *Mardi,* which is not just a book filled with mythic references, nor indeed merely a catalog of myths and myth theories—though it is both of these things—but a self-conscious attempt to piece together for himself a coherent view of myth from the conflicting tangle of myth material with which he was familiar.

2. Psyche in Polynesia

Mardi is Melville's book of myths, a fact quite evident to some readers from the start. A British parody published in May of 1849 makes this point delightfully:

And so the grey eyed dawn, pale daughter of Night, broke upon the coral island, and the sea, and the temple of the god Jumbo. Indeed the rustle of his godship's wings came pealing down the breeze of the morn, and the light of his eye sparkled in the surf which gemmed the green shores of Mardi.[16]

Mardi is more than mythic flummery, though. As James Baird remarked, *Mardi* "is the most important of all American experimental literary works documenting the development of the symbolistic imagination."[17]

Mythic elements in *Mardi* have been defended and cataloged, notably by Merrell Davis and H. Bruce Franklin, and their accounts serve in different ways as starting points, alerting us to look for myth and mythmaking at every turn.[18] One no longer needs to prove that a principal subject of the book is the role of myth in man's efforts to understand the world, nor that this subject is taken up from many points of view. *Mardi* is not unusual in this. Neither its form nor its myth-centered subject would have seemed strange to readers of Thomas Moore's *Loves of the Angels* and *Lalla Rookh* or Shelley's *Queen Mab* in England, of Novalis's *Henry of Ofterdingen* and *The Novices of Sais* or Jean-Paul Richter's *Flower Fruit and Thorn Pieces* and *The Titan* in Germany, of Edgar Quinet's *Ahasuerus* in France, or of Poe's angelic colloquies in America.

The sheer number of varieties of myth and mythmaking in *Mardi* is intimidating and confusing. Melville deploys directly or indirectly more than a dozen theories of myth and gives many different examples of how myths arise. Most of these have been or can be identified.[19] But clear, fixed identifications of *Mardi*'s main characters with one or another specific concept of myth have not been very convincing, and there is a good reason for this.[20] *Mardi* is not a catalog of mythic ideas and practices, but more a symbolic—at times allegorical—narrative about the *evolution* of mythic ways of thinking and perceiving. Or, put differently, *Mardi* is not a survey of myths, but a fictionalizing of the development and history of myth. Most of the major characters in the book embody an attitude toward myth. King Media, for example, is a cynical, self-deifying monarch—a fictionalized embodiment of the process of politically motivated Euhemerism. Media, and the other main characters, change and develop as the book proceeds, not according to ordinary ideas of character development, but according to Melville's conception of how the various kinds of myth personified in his "characters" grew and evolved. An excellent example is Yillah. As many readers have found, Yillah appears to stand for different things at different points in the story. This is not inconsistency on Melville's part. In fact, the story of Yillah (and similar cases can be made for Taji, Media, and others) is a very carefully worked out account—in fictional terms—of the rise, development, evolution, and eventual demise of a whole class of myths. The story of Yillah is Melville's effort to account for myths of idealization, which, as he shows, are accomplished in different ways, for different reasons, at different stages of social development.

Yillah is the object of the search that unifies the book. Her story begins when the narrator (not named at this point, but clearly a mortal) meets a strange craft designed and decorated like a floating temple, commanded by a decidedly Egyptified old priest, Aleema, who is guarding a tent-like enclosure, a sort of Ark of the Covenant, in the midst of this craft. Aleema's crew point at the enclosure "as if it contained their Eleusinian mysteries." The old priest informs the narrator "that it would be profanation to enter it." The narrator now learns that in "that mysterious tent was concealed a beautiful maiden. And in the pursuance of a barbarous custom, by Aleema the priest, she was being borne an offering from the island of Amma to the gods of Tedaidee."[21] Since it is a beautiful girl at stake here, we are not much surprised to find the narrator's conscience leading him to intervene forcibly in the barbarous errand. After a fight in which he kills the priest, the narrator advances to the tent and rends the veil. "In front, a deep-dyed rug of osiers, covering the entrance way, was intricately laced to the standing part of the tent. As I divided this lacing with my cutlass, there arose an outburst of voices from the Islanders. And they covered their faces, as the interior was revealed to my gaze." The veil is rent, the ark opened, the mystery penetrated. Inside there is not a book, scroll, or collection of sacred objects, though, but a beautiful girl who, "like a saint from a shrine, . . . looked sadly out from her long, fair hair. A low wail issued from her lips, and she trembled like a sound."[22]

The story of Yillah thus begins *in medias res,* with the dramatic unveiling of the mystery and the revelation that the closely guarded, divinely prohibited religious mystery is only a captive girl. The

narrative now doubles back, and we learn how this priestly deception began. It is a complex story and it takes a while to come out.
Yillah has been so long a captive of Aleema that she herself does not
know who she really is. The first story she tells the narrator is at once
recognized, by narrator and reader alike, as a "myth," a pretty but
transparent falsehood. The narrator is, however, under no illusions.
He sees that the girl is, in reality, simply a "luckless maiden,"
possibly a "beautiful maniac," and it is clear that the reader is
supposed to share the narrator's skepticism about the pretty tale she
tells, the "myth" of her origin. "She declared herself more than
mortal, a maiden from Oroolia, the Island of Delights, somewhere
in the paradisiacal archipelago of the Polynesians." The story has not
yet reached the allegorical world of Mardi, it is still in the ordinary
world. The Yillah myth is in fact the entrance to the whole myth
world of Mardi. The myth continues:

> To this isle, while yet an infant, by some mystical power, she had been
> spirited from Amma, the place of her nativity. Her name was Yillah.
> And hardly had the waters of Oroolia washed white her olive skin, and
> tinged her hair with gold, when one day strolling in the woodlands, she
> was snared in the tendrils of a vine. Drawing her into its bowers, it
> gently transformed her into one of its blossoms, leaving her conscious
> soul folded up in the transparent petals.
>
> Here hung Yillah in a trance, the world without all tinged with the
> rosy hue of her prison. At length when her spirit was about to burst
> forth in the opening flower, the blossom was snapped from its stem and
> borne by a soft wind to the sea; where it fell into the opening valve of a
> shell; which in good time was cast upon the beach of the Island of
> Amma.
>
> In a dream, these events were revealed to Aleema the priest; who by a
> spell unlocking its pearly casket, took forth the bud, which now showed
> signs of opening in the reviving air, and bore faint shadowy revealings,
> as of the dawn behind crimson clouds. Suddenly expanding, the blossom
> exhaled away in perfumes; floating a rosy mist in the air. Condensing at
> last, there emerged from this mist the same radiant young Yillah as
> before; her locks all moist, and a rose-colored pearl on her bosom.
> Enshrined as a goddess, the wonderful child now tarried in the sacred
> temple of Apo, buried in a dell; never beheld of mortal eyes save
> Aleema's.

The story ends with Yillah's account of Aleema's dream that she is to go to Tedaidee and descend into the whirlpool there, "at last to well up in an inland fountain of Oroolia."[23]

The myth Melville has Yillah tell of herself is cobbled together from several mythic traditions (the birth of Venus, dryads, genii from bottles, the *peri* as opposed to the *houri,* Undine, etc.), but this is not the important point here. The point is that the reader and the narrator see the myth as a tissue of pretty but deadly lies, spun out, probably, by Aleema. It is also important to note that Yillah, who has never known any world but that of Aleema, wholly believes the tale she tells. Melville next moves to show how and why the myth was fabricated in the first place.

The narrator's first reaction, even without knowing any of the facts, is essentially accurate. "Mystical as the tale most assuredly was, my knowledge of the strange arts of the island priesthood, and the rapt fancies indulged in by many of their victims, deprived it in good part of the effect it otherwise would have produced." The narrator explains that Yillah's self-deception is that of a classic victim of "priestcraft"; "For ulterior purposes connected with their sacerdotal supremacy, the priests of these climes oftentimes secrete mere infants in their temples; and jealously secluding them from all intercourse with the world, craftily delude them, as they grow up, into the wildest conceits." Melville's narrator is concerned with priestly duplicity, and how the victim can be brought to believe such mythic deceptions. In his concern for the psychology of the process, Melville differs from most skeptics who propound the priestcraft theory of myth when he suggests that the victims themselves contribute a certain dreamy self-indulgence to the process. "Thus wrought upon," says Melville, the priest's pupils "almost lose their humanity in the constant indulgence of seraphic imaginings."[24] Progress toward mythical status is thus, by definition, progress away from the human.

In the light of what follows, it is significant that the narrator is almost sorry he can see through the fairy tale. "Would that all this had been hidden from me at the time. For Yillah was lovely enough to be really divine." The narrator now, from motives we cannot be

altogether sure of, tries to induce Yillah to take him for "some
gentle demi-god." Whether from love or mere desire, the narrator
now indulges in exactly the same thing he has just exposed. Love
takes the place of priestcraft as the motive for myth, and he makes
up a myth about his own "divine origin in the blessed isle of
Oroolia."[25] Electing to fight myth with myth, the narrator un-
abashedly concocts a story in which he and Yillah grew up together
in Oroolia, before she was spirited away and came under the influence of Aleema. By means of this obviously invented "myth" the
narrator succeeds in supplanting Aleema in Yillah's regard. The
narrator's "myth" drives out or supersedes Aleema's. Yillah is as
helpless before the one as before the other. Having been rescued
from one mythic imposition, Yillah is now romanticized into a new
mythic role.

At the same time, the narrator pushes farther into the past for the
real explanation of the story of Yillah. The priest, it is suggested,
must have thought Yillah was an albino of a sort that die early,
whence the superstition that the class of beings to which Yillah
belongs "pertain to some distant sphere." Melville is trying here to
account psychologically for the rise of the conception of a pre-earthly
existence. It is in his best prose, reminding us of the passage in
Moby-Dick in which he suggests how rumor invests the white whale
with terror unborrowed from any natural object.

> But these conceits of a state of being anterior to an earthly existence may
> have originated in one of those celestial visions seen transparently steal-
> ing over the face of a slumbering child. And craftily drawn forth and
> re-echoed by another, and at times repeated over to her with many
> additions, these imaginings must at length have assumed in her mind a
> hue of reality, heightened into conviction by the dreamy seclusion of her
> life.[26]

The next chapter has Yillah tell us what she *remembers*, not what she
was *told*. Merrell Davis has shown how the actual events behind
Yillah's strange myths can be pieced together from things she inno-
cently drops in this chapter. It becomes apparent that Yillah was a
white child, sequestered and raised by the priest, who gave her

"mythical" explanations for everything he did. When he shot a youth who appeared one day in the valley, the priest told Yillah that the youth was a "bad spirit come to molest her" and he attributed the youth's death to the god Apo.[27]

Up to this point the story of Yillah has been told in such a way that the reader participates in the narrator's process of piercing the mythic veil that surrounds her. As time passes, however, and as the intimacy between Yillah and the narrator grows, Yillah's self-image as a mythical creature begins to weaken; as the narrator puts it, "these fancies seemed to be losing their hold." As Yillah keeps questioning the narrator about his own made-up past, he resorts to saying that "whatever I had said of that clime, had been revealed to me in dreams." These petty deceptions now begin to increase. Soon the same narrator who could so coolly debunk Yillah's myth stories begins himself to invest Yillah with a new sort of mythic significance. "For oh, Yillah; were you not the earthly semblance of that sweet vision, that haunted my earliest thought?" In short, he is in love with her and he makes her over into the embodiment of all his previous love-longings. He himself now dwarfs "down to a mortal," with some regrets, while he rejoices (without regret) to see "the extinguishment in her heart of the notion of her own spirituality." This chapter marks the fulfillment of their love, a love which is sufficiently real to drive out myth. The narrator is for the moment only a man, Yillah only a woman. "We lived and we loved; life and love were united; in gladness glided our days."[28]

At this point the narrative takes a turn, leaving the familiar realistic world and entering a symbolic—at times even allegorical—realm henceforward to be called Mardi, and the quiet nonmythic moment passes. The narrator and Yillah find it convenient to let on, in Huck Finn's phrase, to be certain white deities long foretold; we meet Media, a king who has divinized himself for purposes of safeguarding his monarchical position, and we are off on another cycle of mythmaking. The story of Media is in fact a complex and interesting study of the techniques of politically motivated mythmaking. In King Media, Melville dramatizes the evolution of myth in a later historical era than that represented by Yillah. First comes the priestly invention of myth, then its romantic-idealism phase, then political mythmaking. We are soon introduced to the grim conditions of Media's rule, the ignorance and bondage on which his state rests. Yillah, meanwhile, is evolving into a different sort of myth herself. As the tough political realities of Media's land come into view, the narrator falls under Media's influence and becomes himself *convinced* that he actually is Taji, a demigod, in much the same way that he so clearly saw had once happened to Yillah. Himself deceived, the narrator first loses sight of the real girl or woman in Yillah, and he next loses sight of her mythic status. Thus, by a process of progressive abstraction, Yillah becomes, for Taji and for the reader, a symbol. Yillah now is seen as an incarnation of the dawn, then she changes, almost before our eyes, into an emblematic figure of Soul or Psyche.

Long waited for, the dawn now comes.

First, breaking along the waking face; peeping out from the languid lids; then shining forth in longer glances; till, like the sun, up comes the soul, and sheds its rays abroad.

When thus my Yillah did daily dawn, how she lit up my world: tinging more rosily the roseate clouds, that her summer cheek played to and fro, like clouds in Italian air.[29]

The process is now virtually complete: Yillah has gone from girl to myth to symbol. The symbolic narrative of *Mardi* now accelerates. Religions, philosophies, and political arrangements pass by in a dizzying parade. On the realistic level, Yillah now disappears, never to be seen again, except perhaps at the bottom of the whirlpool at the end of the book. Yet Yillah's name continues to be invoked and much of the rest of *Mardi* is unified by Taji's fruitless search for the happiness she now symbolizes. The Yillah that Taji now seeks is not just a girl, she is a symbolic abstraction evolved out of myth and capable of lapsing back into it at times. She stands for lost love, lost innocence, lost harmony, and as such, she resembles the figure of Harmony in "Klingsohr's Fairy Tale" in Novalis's *Henry of Ofterdingen*.[30] But Harmony triumphs at the end of Novalis's modern fable, while Melville's Yillah does not. At the end of *Mardi*, after a long stretch of time during which politics becomes more and more dominant, the narrative abruptly returns to the mythic level while maintaining the symbolic. Yillah, standing now for Psyche or Soul, clashes with sensuality, as personified in the figure of Hautia, and Yillah is defeated.

The ending of *Mardi*, thought somewhat puzzling, can usefully be compared with another American work of slightly later date. The ending of Paul Hamilton Hayne's "The Temptation of Venus" in *Poems* (1855) is very much the same as the ending of *Mardi*. Venus in Hayne's poem is analogous to Hautia in *Mardi*. Here is Hayne's own account of what he sought to show.

> Venus, establishing her abode in the heart of beautiful and solitary locations, waylaid Christian pilgrims and travellers, and having seduced them to her enchanted Palace, completed their ruin by the employment of every art of voluptuous fascination. When her triumph was perfected, she abandoned disguises, and revealing her true character of a devil, the tragedy ended of course in a brimstone conflagration. Having no fancy for a melodramatic termination like this, I have endeavored to give to the legend a deeper moral significance, to enforce the truth that the apotheosis of Sense is the funeral of the Soul, and that in the maelstrom of the passions, virtue and happiness are sure to go down together.[31]

There are, of course, many problems about the ending of *Mardi*, not least of which is the flower symbolism of the final section (the obscurity of which is not helped by the fact that there are some inadvertent transpositions in the key to the flower language as given in the standard article on the subject).[32] Yet, insofar as Yillah is the object of the search or quest that forms the main action of *Mardi*, the ending is clear enough. The story of Yillah is a story about the rise and development of a whole class of myths, myths of the Good, the True, the Beautiful. These myths involve idealization, but the motives vary from the religious to the romantic, and may be narrow, sordid, and self-seeking as well as high or noble. Yillah begins as a sacred maiden, a product of priestly duplicity mingled with self-delusion. She next becomes the core of a new set of delusory idealizations, this time springing from Taji's love for her. Finally, when Taji himself becomes deluded into thinking himself a divinity, Yillah ceases to have *any* real existence for him. The idealization replaces the original object, and she becomes a symbolic abstraction, with no human admixture left (or none that is perceptible). The quest for Yillah becomes a symbolic quest for lost happiness, innocence, and harmony.

The reason the narrative of *Mardi* returns to the mythic level at the end is to drive home the point that the book *Mardi* is itself a myth, having for a large part of its subject the evolution of myth. Throughout the latter part of the book, the narrator pursues the ideal of the happiness and love he has lost. Succumbing or nearly succumbing to the snaky enchantress Hautia, a figure of sensuality, the narrator gets one last glimpse of Yillah, drowned in a whirlpool beneath Hautia's island. At the book's end, he has lost not only the happiness of the past, and the myth of that happiness, but now also and finally the symbol of it. With the final disappearance of the myth-derived symbol of Yillah, life becomes a frenzied but meaningless quest, the questor himself only a spiritless, soulless phantom. Far from being a story of the triumph of Psyche or the Soul, the Yillah story in *Mardi* is a tragic story of the death of the myth of the Soul.

3. Mythic Investiture in *Moby-Dick*

In *Moby-Dick* Melville returned to the question of how myths arise: the figures of the great white whale and Captain Ahab are the result of his most successful and concentrated effort to create believable figures of mythic proportions and to show at the same time the actual processes by which such figures arise and command belief. There are interesting similarities between *Mardi* and *Moby-Dick,* but it is the differences which are most instructive. *Mardi* begins with a realistic setting, but it dissolves into symbol and allegory just at the point where we are becoming aware that the story of Yillah is a story about the growth of a myth. The result is that all the subsequent mythmaking in *Mardi* seems as contrived as the rest of the obviously allegorical narrative line. The reader is never asked to believe or to suspend disbelief in the mythicized Yillah or the mythicized King Media. Melville's overtly allegorical technique gives the book the forced and unreal quality of an allegorical fable.

In *Moby-Dick* we find the same interest in how myth originates, but the story never abandons the realistic level—at least not in the way *Mardi* does. Instead of our being given an abstract and mythical allegory, we are shown, by means of the thoroughly real figures of Ahab and the white whale, not only how myths arise but how they come to be believed by ordinary people like us. In the figure of Moby Dick, Melville shows how a real creature becomes a legend, a symbol, a scapegoat, and finally a visible symbol of the god-like in nature. In the figure of Ahab, Melville traces and makes us accept the evolution of a plain old whale-hunter into an heroic quest-figure of Promethean proportions. In both cases, Melville not only provides a reasonable explanation of how this change happens, but he compels us ourselves to believe in these grand creations of the mythic imagination.

It is, I think, misleading to think of the white whale as a modern version of the Egyptian Typhon or the Hindu Vishnu in his fish avatar, or indeed as a modern version of any single mythological figure. For one thing, there are simply too many mythological strands in *Moby-Dick* for any single one to be an adequate key.[33] The very fact that Egyptian, Hindu, Persian, Gnostic, Greek, and Christian myths are *all* called upon for the book suggests that the book is not formed around a single mythic center, as is Joyce's *Ulysses,* for example. What Melville has done is to take the story of Ahab's hunt for the whale, and, instead of working it out as a modern version of old myth, he has tried to invest his own modern story with the attributes of myth. It is too easy to say flatly that Melville has created a new myth, though the extent to which the story of Ahab and the white whale has become a part of the folk or popular imagination may lead us to think that this is to some degree so. Rather, I should prefer to say that Melville has tried to show us, in the figures of Ahab and the white whale, not only how myths are generated but how it is that such figures and stories can gain such a powerful hold on the imagination. Insofar as we accept Ahab and the white whale as real (in the same way in which we may be said to accept Hamlet or

Lear as real), *Moby-Dick* is a powerful demonstration of the plausibility of myth. In the end I think Melville is suggesting that there are certain men, certain ideas and truths that can be fully understood or adequately expressed only by myth. Underlying and informing *Moby-Dick* is nothing less than a conception of myth as a necessary category of the imagination.

In the case of the great white whale itself, Melville is trying to create a believable sequence of events and appearances able to convince the reader that it is "natural" for something very grand in nature to be taken for a god, invested with divinity. It was, of course, a common rationalist assumption that this is how gods evolved in the past. Melville's originality consists in his fictional demonstration that this process can still take place among modern and supposedly reasonable people. The main principle is not hard to set down—carrying it out is a different matter—and Melville could have found what he needed in Hawthorne's conception of romance or in the German idea of myth as a meeting place between the actual and the imaginary. The principle is to imbue the visible with the invisible, to endow the tangible with intangible qualities. A contemporaneous statement of this, which Melville may well have read, puts it this way:

> The powerful influence exercised by natural objects in giving shape and life to those forms in which the Imagination embodies the ideas of superhuman power, is finely illustrated by Wordsworth in one of the noblest passages of *The Excursion:* where he casts a glance over the workings of this principle in the mythologies of the Persians, the Babylonians, the Chaldeans, and the Greeks; shewing with what plastic power the imaginative love of Nature wedded and harmonized the dim conceptions of the mysteries which lie behind the curtain of the senses, with the objects by which it happened to be surrounded, incarnating the invisible in the visible, and impregnating the visible with the invisible.[34]

We are familiar with the idea of incarnating the invisible in the visible as a religious conception, but it can also be thought of as a literary process, a fictional technique, which I call mythic investiture and which can be seen at work in Melville's handling of the

white whale. Although we never lose sight of the fact that Moby
Dick is simply a large albino sperm whale, it is, from the start, the
idea of the great white whale that compels us as it compels Ishmael.
In the opening chapter of the book, Ishmael tells us that chief
among his motives for going whaling was "the overwhelming idea of
the great whale itself." From the very beginning, we associate the
whale with "wild and distant seas" and shudder before "the undeliv-
erable, nameless perils of the whale." The book, like the voyage,
commences with "the great flood-gates of the wonder-world swung
open," and we glimpse, in a kind of dim premonition, "one grand
hooded phantom, like a snow hill in the air."[35] From the start,
then, it is more the idea of the whale than the whale itself that holds
our attention and excites our anticipation. We see the whale through
a veil of rumor, scholarship, legend, and myth; by imperceptible
degrees we come to acquiesce in the appropriateness of such things,
and we eventually find ourselves regarding the whale as something
more than a whale.

Early on, the whale is linked to Jonah's whale, to Vishnu's Matse
avatar, to the monster killed by Perseus. During the scene on the
quarterdeck in which Ahab welds the crew into a personal weapon
for his own vengeance, the object of the unholy ceremony of communion is the whale. Starbuck sees what Ahab has done to the crew,
and he perceives that to the crew "the white whale is their demigor-
gon," or as Ishmael puts it, "the gliding great demon of the seas of
life."[36] It is the chapter "Moby Dick," however, where the most
concentrated and sustained mythical investiture of the whale takes
place. Melville describes the process by which the encounter between Ahab and the whale combines with other sightings and incidents to form a growing cloud of dread, rumor, doubt, and pre-
sumption. What Melville evokes in these few pages is the same sort
of meeting ground between the actual and the imaginary that
Hawthorne talked about; here, however, it is a grim and not a genial
confluence.

Nor did wild rumors of all sorts fail to exaggerate, and still the more
horrify the true histories of these deadly encounters. For not only do

fabulous rumors naturally grow out of the very body of all surprising terrible events—as the smitten tree gives birth to its fungi; but in maritime life, far more than in that of terra firma, wild rumors abound, wherever there is any adequate reality for them to cling to.[37]

Melville persuasively creates such a climate of superstition— always with a solid base in fact—that when he tells us that "the whaleman is wrapped by influences all tending to make his fancy pregnant with many a mighty birth," we are more than half prepared to believe that Moby Dick is half a real whale and half a product of the whalemen's collective imagination. The paragraph that follows describes the actual process by which a single fearful monster is produced from such origins.

No wonder then, that ever gathering volume from the mere transit over the widest watery spaces, the outblown rumors of the White Whale did in the end incorporate with themselves all manner of morbid hints, and half-formed foetal suggestions of supernatural agencies, which eventually invested Moby Dick with new terrors unborrowed from anything that visibly appears. So that in many cases such a panic did he finally strike, that few who by those rumors, at least, had heard of the White Whale, few of those hunters were willing to encounter the perils of his jaw.[38]

Wrapped in such suggestiveness, Moby Dick becomes something more than just another whale, and the supernatural aspects with which the whale has by now been invested are carefully maintained all through the book. The chapter on the whiteness of the whale makes extensive comparison between Moby Dick and various white gods. In subsequent chapters, through the suggestion of the spirit spout, whales in constellations, and the hieroglyphical bower in the Arsacides, Melville keeps piling deific attributes on the whale. His very choice of words warps the whale godwards. "But in the great Sperm Whale, this high and mighty god-like dignity inherent in the brow is so immensely amplified, that gazing on it, in the full front view, you feel the Deity and the dread powers more forcibly than in beholding any other object in living nature."

In "The Symphony" chapter Melville's mythological investiture and magnification take an unexpected and spectacular turn. He carefully mythicizes the air, the sea, and the sun, personifying and animating all visible nature, the setting from which the white whale will soon make its first appearance. The passage, a clear example of self-conscious mythmaking, is intended to provide the necessary context for the long anticipated appearance of the whale, for that myth-invested creature can only properly appear in a mythicized world.

[margin note: Pers.]

[margin note: The realist and the personified]

It was a clear steel-blue day. The firmaments of air and sea were hardly separable in that all-pervading azure; only, the pensive air was transparently pure and soft, with a woman's look, and the robust and man-like sea heaved with long, strong, lingering swells, as Samson's chest in his sleep.

Hither, and thither, on high, glided the snow-white wings of small, unspeckled birds; these were the gentle thoughts of the feminine air; but to and fro in the deeps, far down in the bottomless blue, rushed mighty leviathans, sword-fish and sharks; and these were the strong, troubled, murderous thinkings of the masculine sea. . . .

Aloft, like a royal czar and king, the sun seemed giving this gentle air to this bold and rolling sea, even as bride to groom. . . .[39]

Into this magical world the white whale now enters, grandly, and Melville turns to another of his mythic similes to do justice to our first actual glimpse of Moby Dick.

A gentle joyousness—a mighty mildness of repose in swiftness, invested the gliding whale. Not the white bull Jupiter swimming away with ravished Europa clinging to his graceful horns; his lovely, leering eyes sideways intent upon the maid, with smooth bewitching fleetness, rippling straight for the nuptial bower in Crete; not Jove, not that great majesty Supreme! did surpass the glorified White Whale as he so divinely swam.[40]

Goethe had once shown how to understand the statues of the Greek gods as nature itself finding expression. "Statues of gods in themselves have no meaning outside themselves, but are really what they represent." Or, put otherwise, this view means that "a statue of Jupiter thus expresses the 'idea' of majestic power, but not allegorically; the statue is, rather, the form majestic power would itself take could it become plastic."[41] Melville has done something similar here, but has gone one step further, making us see how a story such as that of Jupiter (Zeus) and Europa could have gained credence. And all this is merely by the way, since it is Moby Dick, not Jupiter, that we are intent upon. Melville's real point here is to make us feel how a powerful and lovely animal can be thought to partake of the divine so strongly that the divine comes to seem his chief attribute.

Moby Dick is now, after "The Symphony," fully invested with everything that can be borrowed from myth in order to bring out the wonderousness of the creature, and we are not now surprised when Melville drops metaphor and describes the whale in simple divine language. "The grand god revealed himself, sounded, and went out of sight."[42] From his first appearance as a premonitory phantom in Ishmael's mind to his final victorious fight with Ahab and his crew, the whale has been carefully invested with grand mythic attributes, becoming at last, for the reader as for Ahab, a revelation of the divine in nature.

If Melville's skillful presentation of the whale shows how the human conception of deity arises from mighty occurrences in nature, the treatment of Ahab shows how heroes arise from mighty human beings. Just as Moby Dick is at first just a whale, so Ahab at first is only a poor old Nantucket whale-hunter. The whale is mythologically invested with divine qualities; Ahab is mythologically invested with the qualities of a great hero. It is important to note that Ahab is not worked up into a god of any sort. If there is a suggestion of Euhemerism here (a man becoming a hero in the second generation and a god in the third), Melville has the good sense not to push Ahab all the way to divinity, as he had, for example, with King Media in *Mardi*.

Ahab remains a hero, but not one whose greatness rests merely on traditional or inherited qualities. Melville writes of Ahab: "This august dignity I treat of, is not the dignity of kings and robes, but that abounding dignity which has no robed investiture. Thou shalt see it shining in the arm that wields a pick or drives a spike; that democratic dignity which, on all hands, radiates without end from God."[43] Ahab's heroism, then, is achieved by mythical investiture rather than "robed investiture." It is a device used frequently by Melville. In *Israel Potter* he says of Ethan Allen that "Allen seems to have been a curious combination of a Hercules, a Joe Miller, a Bayard, and a Tom Hyer; had a person like the Belgian giant, mountain music in him like a Swiss; a heart plump as Coeur de Lion's." And in one place in *Moby-Dick* Melville reverses the process, democratically investing Hercules by calling him "that antique Crockett and Kit Carson."[44] Melville's best statement of how he understands the process of democratic mythmaking occurs at the close of chapter twenty-six. It is a process which applies not only to Ahab but to all the characters in the book.

> If then, to meanest mariners, and renegades and castaways, I shall hereafter ascribe high qualities, though dark; weave round them tragic graces; if even the most mournful, perchance the most abased, among them all, shall at times lift himself to the exalted mounts; if I shall touch that workman's arm with some ethereal light; if I shall spread a rainbow over his disastrous set of sun; then against all mortal critics bear me out in it, thou just Spirit of Equality, which has spread one royal mantle of humanity over all my kind![45]

These processes of weaving, touching, and spreading are in fact processes of mythic comparison and mythic heightening. By such means, any man great of soul can come to have the dignity of a king.

> Bear me out in it, thou great democratic God! who didst not refuse to the swart convict Bunyan, the pale, poetic pearl; Thou who didst clothe with doubly hammered leaves of finest gold, the stumped and paupered arm of old Cervantes; Thou who didst pick up Andrew Jackson from the pebbles; who didst hurl him upon a war-horse; who didst thunder him higher than a throne! Thou who, in all Thy mighty, earthly marchings, ever cullest thy selectest champions from the kingly commons; bear me out in it, O God![46]

It is in the name of the Spirit of Equality, the god of democracy, that Melville invests these common men—including, especially,

Ahab—with heroic stature. The result is the fashioning of heroes from the ordinary ranks of men. This is what Thoreau found lacking in both Carlyle's and Emerson's treatment of heroes, it is what Thoreau tried to do in *Walden,* and Whitman in *Leaves of Grass.* *Moby-Dick* is a serious effort to make great heroes from plain men. The description applies to Starbuck, to Queequeg, to Daggoo, Tashtego, and Pip, but most of all to Ahab. Ahab is no democrat himself, but his heroic stature is the result of the mythic investiture possible in a democracy, rather than the "robed investiture" typical of an aristocratic society.

If the emphasis on democratic conditions for heroism is peculiarly Melville's, some of the techniques for fashioning such a hero, techniques for raising a man to heroic stature, may be found in Carlyle. Much of what Carlyle says about Odin, for example, is applicable to Ahab, and some of the phrasing is so close as to suggest that Melville actually had Carlyle in mind.

Melville's Nantucketers are like Carlyle's Scandinavian sea-kings. Melville himself makes the comparison, calling Ahab a sea-king, and it is easy to see Ahab in Carlyle's description. "In the old Sea-Kings, too, what an indomitable rugged energy! Silent, with closed lips, as I fancy them, unconscious that they were specially brave: defying the wild ocean with its monsters, and all men and things."[47] And in both the idea and the prose of the following, one can see why the Carlyleian conception of Scandinavian hero worship becomes a useful point of comparison for Melville's conception of Ahab. "This poor Scandinavian Hero-worship, that whole Norse way of looking at the Universe, and adjusting oneself there, has an indestructible merit for us. A rude childish way of recognizing the divineness of Nature, the divineness of Man; most rude, yet heartfelt, robust, giantlike."[48] And Carlyle's description of how time works to spread an aura of myth sounds very close to Melville's description of how rumor and apprehension work, darkly, to similar ends. Assuming that Odin was originally just a man, Carlyle asks "how the man Odin came to be considered a *god.*" After considering "what if this man Odin—since a great deep soul, with the afflatus and mysterious tide of vision and impulse rushing on him he knows not whence, is ever an enigma, a kind of terror and wonder to himself—should have felt that perhaps *he* was divine," Carlyle goes on to suggest what the passage of time can do to such a man's memory.

> And then consider what mere Time will do in such cases; how if a man was great while living he becomes tenfold greater when dead. What an enormous *camera-obscura* magnifier is Tradition! How a thing grows in the human Memory, in the human Imagination, when love, worship, and all that lies in the human Heart, is there to encourage it. . . . Why, in thirty or forty years, were there no books, any great man would grow *mythic,* the contemporaries who had seen him being once all dead.[49]

The passages just quoted from Carlyle seem particularly appropriate to Ahab, because Carlyle, like Melville, insists that there must be a genuinely great human being as the indispensable kernel for any hero. So too, in a passage which is of great importance for *Moby-Dick,* Carlyle insists that one does not start with myth. Belief must precede myth. Talking about allegorical theories of myth, Carlyle makes the excellent point that an allegory is the result of some conception, not the conception itself.

> The *Pilgrim's Progress* is an Allegory, and a beautiful, just and serious one: but consider whether Bunyan's Allegory could have *preceded* the Faith it symbolizes! The Faith had to be already there, standing believed by everybody;—of which the allegory could *then* become a shadow.[50]

If, in a religious sense, the faith must precede the allegory, then, in a work of fiction, the story, the events, and the characters must precede myth. Therefore Ahab—in this view—is not Prometheus, Faust, Osiris, or Lucifer, but only Ahab. And it will be belief in Ahab's own natural greatness that permits Ishmael and Melville to weave around him tragic graces and mythic qualities. Ahab's greatness is thus warranted by mythic magnification and mythic investiture, carefully managed by Melville. But Ahab himself is valorous and powerful enough, and the tumultuous reality of his quest is seldom far behind the mythic front. Reality keeps outrunning myth in *Moby-Dick,* even in the final chase.

Ahab is an heroic figure, and appears larger than life right from the start. Just as Melville first gave us the awesome idea of the white whale and then gradually let the actual whale fill in the outline thus created, so now he first creates a theoretical hero—a pattern for a hero—and then gradually realizes the pattern in Ahab. Speaking of the fighting Quakers of Nantucket, before we have seen Ahab at all, Melville observes:

> So that there are instances among them of men, who, named with Scripture names—a singularly common fashion on the island—and in childhood naturally imbibing the stately dramatic thee and thou of the Quaker idiom; still, from the audacious, daring, and boundless adventure of their subsequent lives, strangely blend with these unoutgrown peculiarities, a thousand bold dashes of character, not unworthy a Scandinavian sea-king, or a poetical Pagan Roman. And when these things unite in a man of greatly superior natural force, with a globular brain and a ponderous heart; who has also by the stillness and seclusion of many long night-watches in the remotest waters, and beneath constellations never seen here at the north, been led to think untraditionally and independently; receiving all nature's sweet or savage impressions fresh from her own virgin voluntary and confiding breast, and thereby chiefly, but with some help from accidental advantages, to learn a bold and nervous lofty language—that man makes one in a whole nation's census—a mighty pageant creature—formed for noble tragedies.[51]

This is a generalized figure to be sure, but it is also a portrait of Ahab in advance, for Ahab will come to incarnate this heroic outline as the story unfolds.

A few pages later, Captain Peleg throws out a larger hint about Ahab when he says, "He's a grand, ungodly god-like man, Captain Ahab."[52] Anticipation, once set running, is further encouraged in the succeeding chapters; we are awed by Elijah's prophecy and by Bulkington's brief, cryptic apotheosis. In chapter twenty-six, when Melville begins to describe the ship's officers, occurs the passage about the "just Spirit of Equality" that provides the peculiarly democratic basis for hero-making. Ahab himself finally appears in chapter twenty-eight. "Reality outran apprehension; Captain Ahab stood upon his quarter-deck." But even that reality is at once heightened, hammered out and wrought up into something heroic. "His whole high, broad form, seemed made of solid bronze, and shaped in an unalterable mould, like Cellini's cast Perseus."[53] Ahab's is no common woe, there is "a crucifixion in his face." Nothing about him is ordinary. Even when discussing a little ivory stool Ahab sits on, Melville manages to work it up into something grand. "In old Norse times, the thrones of the sea-loving Danish kings were fabricated, saith tradition, of the tusks of the narwhale. How could one look at Ahab then, seated on that tripod of bones, without bethinking him of the royalty it symbolized. For a Khan of the plank, and a king of the sea, and a great lord of Leviathans was Ahab."[54] This is an excellent example of the mythic investiture that works to ennoble and enlarge Ahab. (There is the constant danger of mere inflation or puffing, which arises when there is not enough substance, but Melville keeps the real and very substantial Ahab always in view, and in a passage like this, the slight rhetorical swelling is nicely offset by a touch of whimsy. "A Khan of the plank," indeed.)

After the cetology chapter, which works to magnify the whale, Melville turns, in "The Specksynder," to a discussion of the position of captain on a whaler, and concludes the chapter with the most explicit statement in the book of *how* Ahab is to be made a mighty figure.

> But Ahab, my Captain, still moves before me in all his Nantucket grimness and shagginess; and in this episode touching Emperors and Kings, I must not conceal that I have only to do with a poor old whale-hunter like him; and, therefore, all outward majestical trappings and housings are denied me. Oh, Ahab! what shall be grand in thee, it must needs be plucked at from the skies, and dived for in the deep, and featured in the unbodied air.[55]

What Melville thus plucked at, dived for, and featured forth was myth.

The first part of *Moby-Dick,* through chapter thirty-three, carefully and insistently mythicizes Ahab by comparing him to mythic and heroic figures. With this pattern established, the book now begins to explore Ahab himself. Chapters thirty-six to forty-one are central to Ahab, and they consist largely of a brilliant study, convincing in both detail and outline, of the psychopathology of fanaticism. At first glance it would seem that Melville's elaborate psychological portrayal of Ahab is intended to anchor the mythmaking in undeniable realities of mind. We have been accustomed, after all, since Freud, to finding myth reduced to psychology or explained in terms of psychology. It is one of Melville's great achievements to have done just the opposite. If we follow the portrayal of Ahab with sufficient care, we will find that Melville has enlarged psychology into myth. Melville validates psychology by myth, rather than the other way round. As ways of getting at Ahab, Melville takes up such things as prophecy, demonic possession, and a species of enthusiasm soured into fanaticism; he explores each of these for what it shows about the human mind, and eventually he pushes back each of these strange and fearful subjects until we find ourselves in the world of myth and dark power.

Chapter thirty-six uses the language, then fashionable, of mesmerism and animal magnetism to show Ahab the enthusiast. "'Good!' cried Ahab, with a wild approval in his tones; observing the hearty animation into which his unexpected question had so magnetically thrown them."[56] Ahab's own enthusiasm and that with which he infects the crew are of a special kind. Enthusiasm by Melville's time was generally not the scornful term of religious self-delusion it had been for, say, Swift. Enthusiasm had become a noble and exalted state of the soul. Here, for example, is the beginning of Mme. de Staël's admiring treatment of enthusiasm:

> Many people are prejudiced against enthusiasm; they confound it with fanaticism, which is a great mistake. Fanaticism is an exclusive passion, the object of which is an opinion; enthusiasm is connected with the harmony of the universe; it is the love of the beautiful, elevation of soul, enjoyment of devotion, all united in one single feeling which combines grandeur and repose. The sense of this word amongst the Greeks affords the noblest definition of it; enthusiasm signified *God in us*.[57]

Ahab however is an *inverted* enthusiast; he is, as he himself recognizes, "demoniac." If there is a good principle and an evil in Melville's personal Gnostic theology, Ahab is an example—a fearful one—of enthusiasm as the *evil god in us*. And in Ahab's case the maleficent enthusiasm is indeed, as Mme. de Staël suggests, the opposite of enthusiasm: fanaticism itself. These central chapters are a study in a pathological fanaticism so powerful that it not only possesses Ahab completely, but through Ahab is extended to the entire crew. Starbuck is the last to succumb. Ahab storms at him, and Starbuck at last falls silent. Ahab gloats: "Something shot from my dilated nostrils, he has inhaled it in his lungs. Starbuck now is mine."[58]

Ahab is himself possessed or intoxicated. Not god-intoxicated, as Carlyle called Novalis, but demon-intoxicated, and this demon-intoxication or possession is, I think, the single most impressive achievement of Melville's mythic investiture. For Melville shrewdly rests the case for Ahab's demonism not on theological grounds, but places it firmly and repeatedly on psychological grounds. In turn, the psychological explanation leads on inexorably into myth. In the chapter "Moby Dick," Melville describes how Ahab's peculiar state came about. After describing how the whale had become "invested . . . with natural terror" for most whalemen, and how Moby Dick had "reaped away Ahab's leg," Melville described how

> ever since that almost fatal encounter, Ahab had cherished a wild vindictiveness against the whale, all the more fell for that in his frantic morbidness he at last came to identify with him, not only all his bodily woes, but all his intellectual and spiritual exasperations. The White Whale swam before him as the monomaniac incarnation of all those malicious agencies which some deep men feel eating in them, till they are left living on with half a heart and half a lung.[59]

Ahab's peculiar wound, his monomania, and the full force of his tightly focused fanaticism lead him—and the reluctant reader—not into falsehood and error but into a true if unwelcome apprehension of how things really are.

> That intangible malignity which has been from the beginning; to whose dominion even the modern Christians ascribe one-half of the world; which the ancient Ophites of the east reverenced in the statue devil;—

Ahab did not fall down and worship it like them; but deliriously trans-
ferring its idea to the abhorred white whale, he pitted himself, all
mutilated, against it. All that most maddens and torments; all that stirs
up the lees of things; all truth with malice in it; all that cracks the
sinews and cakes the brain; all the subtle demonisms of life and thought;
all evil, to crazy Ahab, were visibly personified and made practically
assailable in Moby Dick.[60]

Ahab's peculiar nature, his illness, his quest, and his very craziness
all converge to uncover what Melville regards as a general truth.
Psychology, mythology, and religion all bear it witness. Melville
goes on to describe the rise of Ahab's monomania, when, after the
fight, lying in his hammock and rocked by the storms of the
Patagonian Cape, "his torn body and gashed soul bled into one
another; and so interfusing, made him mad." This remarkable chapter, which is constructed like a maelstrom which goes faster and
faster and ever downward, goes on to describe how Ahab's madness
deepeningly sped and finally gained full control of his broad natural
intellect without in the least damaging its great power. "If such a
furious trope may stand, his special lunacy stormed his general
sanity, and carried it, and turned all its concentrated cannon upon
its own mad mark; so that far from having lost his strength, Ahab,
to that one end, did now possess a thousand fold more potency than
ever he had sanely brought to bear upon any one reasonable object."[61] So far, Melville has given us a remarkable account of how a
physical wound unites with mental anguish in a craziness that comes
to possess and redirect the mind upon a single, insane object. Ordinary madness scatters and confuses the mind; Ahab's madness con-
centrates his. The effects of this will be, we understand, terrible, yet
Melville insists, here and elsewhere, that in some fearful way crazy
Ahab, because of that selfsame craziness, sees things as they truly
are, but as we cannot bear to have them.

The passage in which Melville works this out is central to the
book, following immediately after the "furious trope" above, and it
insists that at last we must move from psychology to myth (and
myth here leads us back to the oldest and darkest religions of mankind) for an adequate expression of those truths.

This is much; yet Ahab's larger, darker, deeper part remains unhinted. But vain to popularize profundities, and all truth is profound. Winding far down from within the very heart of this spiked Hotel de Cluny where we here stand—however grand and wonderful, now quit it;—and take your way, ye nobler, sadder souls, to those vast Roman halls of Thermes; where far beneath the fantastic towers of man's upper earth his root of grandeur, his whole awful essence sits in bearded state; an antique buried beneath antiquities, and throned on torsoes! So with a broken throne, the great gods mock that captive king; so like a Caryatid, he patient sits, upholding on his frozen brow the piled entablatures of ages. Wind ye down there, ye prouder, sadder souls! question that proud, sad king! A family likeness! aye, he did beget ye, ye young exiled royalties; and from your grim sire only will the old State-secret come.[62]

Ahab is only as explicable as that ancient captive king, enthroned but buried, like Enceladus, and mocked by the great gods. It was daring of Melville to draw his image from this little-known and little-visited place in Paris, but its point would probably not be clearer (and might well be almost banal) had he used a more familiar image such as that of the pyramids. The point is that only by confronting the mythic figures of ancient religion can the problem of evil be fully taken in. The ancient religions recognized and made room for the principles of evil, darkness, blood ties, and revenge as well as the more smiling aspects of things, and Melville insists that more recent, more hopeful religions such as Unitarianism and its Transcendental offshoots have, in this respect, failed us. The ancient kings and gods still in their place in those old halls which lie beneath the modern halls of Cluny give us our best hints as to the basis in nature for such a man as Ahab.

This pattern of description occurs again, later in the book, in the chapter called "Ahab's Leg," where we hear of Ahab's second wound, resulting from a fall in Nantucket, which splintered his ivory leg and "all but pierced his groin." The account of this injury too is followed by an account of its psychological effect, and that account, not reaching bottom, gives way once more to the mythic level. "To trail the genealogies of these high mortal miseries, carries us at last among the sourceless primogenitures of the gods; so that, in the face of all the glad, hay-making suns, and soft-cymballing, round, harvest-moons, we must needs give in to this; that the gods themselves are not for ever glad. The ineffaceable, sad birthmark in the brow of man, is but the stamp of sorrow in the signer." Thus Ahab's "mishap," which he does not himself account for, "invested itself with terrors, not entirely underived from the land of spirits and wails," from the dark past where the myths began.[63]

In *Moby-Dick,* Melville was no longer debunking myth, as he had been doing in *Mardi;* he was out now to show the nature and the consequences of our susceptibility to myth. *Moby-Dick* shows that myth cannot simply be reasoned away. Indeed, our very susceptibility to it argues that it is, in an important sense, true. In Ahab and the white whale Melville has created mythic figures before the reader's eyes and with the reader's willing complicity. Not only has Melville succeeded in making the reader accept the naturalness of the process, he has also made us accept its results.

Epilogue: Melville after *Moby-Dick*

Melville was serious in his effort to suggest the divine power in nature when he compared the white whale to Jupiter as the white bull making off with Europa; and when he treated Ahab as a Scandinavian sea-king, it was with full confidence that the old myths and legends had not lost their hold upon our imaginations and that Ahab will grow in our eyes by being invested with mythic and heroic qualities. Thus Melville affirmed, at the same time, myth as truth and myth as a form for the modern writer. As importantly perhaps, he showed that the very process by which myths are formed was itself amenable to fictional representation.

These hard-won convictions about myth, very different from the playful mythiness in *Mardi,* mark much of Melville's writing in the early and middle 1850s. *Pierre* contains extended and effective mythic analogues for the hero in the figures of Enceladus and Memnon. "Bartleby the Scrivener" is another example; Bartleby is an original conception, and Henry Murray has well said that we can henceforth speak of the Bartleby Complex and be understood.

Another creation of Melville's mythic investiture, Bartleby comes in the end to be a modern martyr living out his lonely passion in stony Wall Street, a modern Petra, and coming to his end in the green heart of a prison pyramid. *The Confidence Man,* "The Tartarus of Maids," even *Israel Potter* retain some of Melville's conviction that myth will tell us the truth, and that the modern artist can, if he will, mythicize his fictional characters without betraying reality, indeed, that he *must* reach the level of myth if he is to deal with those deeper, more profound and often hidden truths of the human condition.

Sometime in the late 1850s, however, this double conviction waned for Melville. First from his journal and later from *Clarel,* it appears that Melville came to feel that modern thought was systematically stripping the world of myth. From Barthold Niebuhr and D. F. Strauss, principally, Melville seems to have caught, and almost choked on, a new view of history and religion, a revised skepticism which argued persuasively, with elaborate and seemingly unanswerable demonstrations, that the mythical was simply the false.

In his journal for February 5, 1857, during his trip to the Mediterranean, Melville made the following comment as his ship passed through the Greek Isles:

> Patmos is pretty high, & peculiarly barren looking. No inhabitants.—Was here again afflicted with the great curse of modern travel—skepticism. Could no more realize that St. John had ever had revelations here, than when off Juan Fernandez, could believe in Robinson Crusoe according to De Foe. When my eye rested on arid height, spirit partook of the barrenness.—Heartily wish Niebuhr & Strauss to the dogs. The deuce take their penetration and acumen. They have robbed us of the bloom. If they have undeceived anyone—no thanks to them.[64]

Later, in *Clarel,* Melville was again to complain that "Zion, like Rome, is Niebuhrized," and it is clear from the following lines that Melville understood "Niebuhrizing" as the process of destroying myth.

Yes, doubt attends. Doubt's heavy hand
Is set against us; and his brand
Still warreth for his natural lord—
King Common-Place—whose rule abhorred
Yearly extends in vulgar sway,
Absorbs Atlantis and Cathay;
Aye, reaches towards Diana's moon,
Affirming it a clinkered blot.[65]

Darwin was not the only major thinker whose work undercut a religious view of the world. Indeed, in some ways Niebuhr and Strauss—in different fields but both employing modern critical historical methods—were far more damaging than Darwin, whose major ideas could at least be made to confirm ideas of progress and evolution. But Niebuhr factualized Roman history, and scholars in his wake did the same for all history, while Strauss stripped the New Testament of myth and his method was subsequently applied to all other religious texts. Niebuhr's great book is his *Roman History,* first published in 1813–14 and revised and extended until his death in 1831. It was translated in the 1840s by J. C. Hare (whose *Guesses at Truth* Melville probably knew) and Connop Thirlwall, when the reputation of the book was already immense. Niebuhr was, according to an authoritative modern estimate, "the first commanding figure in modern historiography, the scholar who raised history from a subordinate place to the dignity of an independent science, the noble personality in whom the greatest historians of the succeeding generation found their model or their inspiration."[66] Central to his work is the mythological viewpoint. He believed that the earliest era of Roman history was, as reported to us, all mythical and poetical (Niebuhr's synonyms for "false by definition"). There follows a period half mythical and half historical; the third period is the purely historical. Niebuhr is without question a great historian, but even today his work has a rigid and exclusive passion for fact, almost that of a Thomas Gradgrind, which prevents him from seeing any value, even historical, in myth and which sets him apart from such historians as K. O. Müller. Here, for example, is Niebuhr on Aeneas.

If the object of an investigation concerning the Trojan colony in Latium were to decide with historical probability, by means of direct and circumstantial evidence, whether such a colony actually settled on that coast, a prudent inquirer would decline it. He would deem it absurd to expect any testimonies with regard to an event five hundred years antecedent to the time when all is still fabulous and poetical in the history of Rome. What traces too could have been preserved, to supply the place of evidence, which obviously cannot possibly exist?[67]

Niebuhr's only interest in Aeneas is to chart the rise of the legend. "The real object of this investigation is, to make out whether the Trojan legend was ancient and homesprung, or whether the Latins adopted it from the Greeks; and whether its origin can be explained."[68] This sounds fair enough, but it is Niebuhr's manner which chills. For after reviewing the evidence, he concludes:

By this combination of evidence, I think I have established the correctness of the view, that the Trojan legend was not imported into Latium by Greek literature, but must be considered as homesprung. When I have added, that in spite of this it has not the least historical truth,—any more than the descent of the Goths from the Getes, or that of the Franks and Saxons from the Macedonians, all which are related with full faith by native writers,—nor even the slightest historical importance, I should wish to quit the subject.[69]

So much for Virgil. The result of this sort of investigation, it need hardly be said, was to found the new school of positivist history by creating an unbridgeable chasm between poetry, legend, myth, and religion on one side, and history, regarded as fact and approached "scientifically," on the other.

D. F. Strauss, whose *Life of Jesus* has been discussed in an earlier chapter, worked with the same historical critical method and treated the New Testament as Niebuhr treated the *Aeneid*. The effect of their works (taken together with that of their very numerous predecessors, colleagues, and followers) was to separate, with rigorous method and impeccable scholarship, the mythical from the historical. Both history and religion, they thought, were better off without any taint of myth. In stripping Rome of the legendary heroes who had inspired men for centuries, and Christianity of everything but an unimportant "historical" residue, it might well have seemed, to Melville and to others, that these men had made a needless division of the past, and, worse yet, had then thrown away the more valuable part. Melville's revulsion—it must be called that since he was in no position to refute either Niebuhr or Strauss—is evident in his speaking of Zion as "Niebuhrized," and he must at times have felt, in George Eliot's phrase, "Strauss-sick."[70]

Melville's journal of his trip to Jerusalem, Greece, and Rome is filled with passages that reflect the impact of this viewpoint on him. The hearty skepticism which had for years lent vigor and sinew to his thought deepened into angry and depressed disbelief. Passing Delos, the most famous of the Cyclades and birthplace of Apollo, Melville grumpily noted that it was "of a most barren aspect, however flowery in fable."[71] This journal too contains Melville's most intransigent denunciations of Christian monotheism, which he took to have its origins in Egypt. In a now famous passage, he wrote "I shudder at idea of ancient Egyptians. It was in these pyramids that was conceived the idea of Jehovah. Terrible mixture of the cunning and awful. Moses learned in all the lore of the Egyptians."[72] And a few pages later he again broke out on the subject, this time with something approaching loathing. Noting that neither man nor Nature had much to do with the pyramids, Melville continues, in his terse, cryptic, journal notes,

> it was that supernatural creature, the priest. [One is reminded of how Aleema the priest invented the idea of Yillah.] They must needs have been terrible inventors, those Egyptian wise men. And one seems to see that as out of the crude forms of the natural earth they could evoke by art the transcendent mass & symetry & . . . of the pyramid so out of the rude elements of the insignificant thoughts that are in all men, they could rear the transcendent conception of a God. But for no holy purpose was the pyramid founded.[73]

Melville's vehemence here is unusual, and his account of the origins of religion in fear is worthy of a Holbach or a Paine. The old *philosophe* tone runs through the journal: in one place, Melville echoes Volney as he asks "is the desolation of the land the result of the fatal embrace of the Deity? Hapless are the favorites of Heaven."[74] Passing by Cyprus, Melville found he could imagine neither Venus nor Christ rising. "Coming near long reach of whitish & yellowish coast with lofty mountains inland. From these waters rose Venus from the foam. Found it as hard to realize such a thing as to realize on Mt. Olivet that from there Christ rose."[75]

At this point, both Greek and Christian myth had failed Melville. And one is tempted to generalize his experience and say that by the late 1850s, myth, considered either as a form for religious narrative or as a form for modern art, was indeed dead, having lost its ability to stir either the religious or the literary imagination. There is some truth in this conclusion, for indeed the latter part of the nineteenth century is not a time when younger writers turned to myth with anything like the confidence of either the writers we have been considering or those of the early twentieth-century revival of interest in myth. Rationalist condescension to myth as mere ideology or as primitive thought carried the day. In America, the skeptical tradition traceable to Paine seems to have marked what little new interest in myth arose—outside theosophy and other mythy new religions.[76] Apart from the writers we have been looking at, no American writer of the late nineteenth century makes a significant use of myth, in the senses in which I have been using the term, which are after all the terms in which the nineteenth century itself saw myth.

But if generally true for the latter nineteenth century, Melville's journal comments do not mark the end of his own fascination with myth. Shortly after returning home from his trip to Rome and the Holy Land, he turned to platform lecturing, and his first lecture, "Statues in Rome," shows that however hard he had been hit by skepticism he was still fully capable of an imaginative response to great works of art. His description of the Apollo Belvedere represents, for example, almost the exact opposite of his journal notes on similar themes.

It is not a mere work of art that one gazes on, for there is a kind of divinity in it that lifts the imagination of the beholder above "things rank and gross in nature" and makes ordinary criticism impossible. If one were to try to convey some adequate notion, other than artistic, of a statue which so signally lifts the imagination of men, he might hint that it gives a kind of visible response to that class of human aspirations of beauty and perfection that, according to Faith, cannot be truly gratified except in another world.[77]

This is not mere tourists' praise but a convincing and finely tempered description of what is still called the sense of the divine. Nor is it an idiosyncratic or private response. Melville had an uncannily accurate conception of Greek art, as Vincent Scully has so admirably shown.[78] A comment such as the following—also from "Statues in Rome"—is only possible upon the basis of such an understanding, suggesting that, at this point in Melville's life, Greek and Roman mythic conceptions again seemed adequate to his sense of what is great and wonderful in nature.

> Remarkable, however, among all are the sculptured horses of Monte Cavallo, riderless and rearing, seeming like those of Elijah to soar to heaven. . . . The equestrian group of Castor and Pollux illustrates the expression of untamed docility, rather than conquered obedience, which ancient artists have given the horse. From this can be deduced the enlarged humanity of that older day, when man gave himself none of the upstart airs of superiority over the brute creation which he now assumes. The horse was idealized by the ancient artists as majestic next to man, and they longed to sculpture them as they did heroes and gods. To the Greeks nature had no brute. Everything was a being with a soul, and the horse idealized the second order of animals just as man did the first. This ideal and magnificent conception of the horse, which had raised that animal into a sort of divinity, is unrivaled in its sublime loftiness of attitude and force of execution.[79]

In this description of the horses of Monte Cavallo, the same sense of divinity with which the White Whale has been invested breaks out anew. Once more it is only myth that can give an adequate account of nature.

To the end of his life, Melville would continue to veer back and forth between the all-consuming doubt of the mythless world of modern scholarship and an imaginative and artistic reassertion of myth. *Clarel* is Melville's most extensive survey of a world without myth, but in his late poems, classicism and paganism again join—as they did in the lecture on "Statues in Rome"—to revive the claim for myth. In "After the Pleasure Party" it is Eros which Melville shows reasserting myth's ancient strength. And in *Billy Budd*, Melville once more took a theme of Aeschylean proportions—the question of justice—and by his old device of mythic investiture, gave us one last example of the power of myth, when properly handled, to stir even the modern imagination. After Melville's achievement, no one can doubt the powerful hold of myth on the American imagination, and no one has yet gone further than Melville in showing that its power is exerted as often for evil as for good.

Appendix

Psyche an Evangele; in Four Books
A. B. Alcott

Psyche. Book I. Innocence

I.

Stealthily doth the Soul dawn on the vision of the Ages. Century after century glides by while this divine nature beams ever serenely in the face of man. Yet tardy is he to apprehend its significance or appropriate its proffered gifts. Observation shuts her eyes, or scarce wags her lazy lids, oppressed by the leaden slumbers of the senses. Reflection reposes sluggishly on the face of things and suffers their shapes and shows to pass devoid of meaning or name. Genius sleeps. Creation stands a puzzle. Providence is a mystery; Revelation a fable: man a thing: God a phantom.

Wisdom, as must needs be, thus neglected and condemned, doth pine in solitary reclusion. She doth not frequent the thoroughfares of life, lest her sacred and venerable form receive insult. Shall she cast her pearls before swine to be trampled under foot, and herself rent in twain? Not so. For she hath a fair sister, by whom she maketh her appeal to the human race. Poesy taketh their infirmities at heart, and appeareth among them dispenser of song. And now interuptions [*sic*] no more, they flock around her transfigured face, charmed by the serene presence of wisdom when thus appearing in guise of beauty.

But seldom does this charming visitant vouchsafe to appear, incarnate and real, among men. The sweet singer is the child of the century. Centuries call her from her retreat. Centuries ripen her genius. And knowing her lineage, she goes gloriously forth, in her time, to animate the age, and quicken it with her own divine life. She transfers her titles through the genius of the ages assured that she shall abide in her works. And these she leaves for the good of the ages.

Long hath she now been silent, her harp hanging on the willows, while Humanity hath been pleading for a song. And all the while false and strange notes have been piped in the ear of the ages. The Human Race hath had no song. The lyre of genius hath wakened no harmonies in the ear of Messiah, as he visits the families of the earth, wherein, forlorn, bereft of sympathy and care he hath bemoaned his state.

Hath Harmony then left the earth? O no! Yet doth she linger, and visit the dwelling of men, although her presence is oft unheeded and her harp tuneless. Ashamed of the garb of Adult man, she appears in the guise of a child. For thus does Wisdom transfigure the Babe and in saintly wise, appeal to the human father, if, perchance, she shall quicken the sleeping instincts, and reassure the soul of the spiritual might that slumbers in its faculties.

Even thus doth the Divine Psyche seek the renewal of Humanity, and its instauration in Holiness. From the blessed moment of vision, doth she descend, a simple minstrel, into the vales of terrestrial life, and entering the household of men, in the guise of a Babe, would harmonize the discord and attune the souls of adults.

Childhood is a bard inspired and divine. Listen, ye Parents, and catch the heavenly strains; sit reverently before the lyre, and, while the bard sweeps its chords, attune your own beings!

The above is from a manuscript in the Harvard University Library, *59M 30G (9) dated 1838.

Notes

Introduction

1. The reductionist concept of myth in Smith's *Virgin Land* has given rise to the only serious reservations about that valuable book. See Smith's "Preface to the Twentieth Anniversary Printing" (Cambridge: Harvard University Press, 1970), as well as the excellent critique by Bruce Kuklick, "Myth and Symbol in American Studies," *American Quarterly,* vol. 24 (Oct. 1972), 435–450, which argues that the myth and symbol approach exemplified by *Virgin Land* may have value "for determining the significance *to us* of certain texts," but that "it does not tell us what the authors meant, what they intended to say about the world." Kuklick argues that "if myth-symbol generalizations have any substance, they must be subject to falsification [or corroboration, no doubt] by the conclusions of 'lower level' historical research."

2. Michael J. Colacurcio, "The Symbolic and the Symptomatic: D. H. Lawrence In Recent American Criticism," *American Quarterly,* vol. 27 (Oct. 1975), 486–501.

3. Peter Gay, *A Loss of Mastery: Puritan Historians in Colonial America* (Berkeley and Los Angeles: University of California Press, 1966), p. 121. See David Levin's excellent critique of Gay in *History and Theory,* vol. 7 (1968), 385–393.

4. Joseph Campbell, "Myths from West to East," in *Myths,* Alexander Eliot et al. (New York: McGraw Hill, 1976), p. 37.

Chapter 1

1. See Cotton Mather, *Magnalia Christi Americana* (1702; repr. Hartford, 1855), book three, part two, chapters one and twenty-three for Mather's accounts of Janus as a name for Noah and Cadmus as a Gibeonite. Many of Mather's observations about these and other mythical figures can be found in standard seventeenth-century works on myth such as Samuel Bochart's *Geographia Sacra,* and were kept in circulation all through the eighteenth century in Tooke's *Pantheon.*

2. Timothy Dwight, "On Revelation," Sermon one, on the text Job 28: 20, 21, in *Sermons* (New Haven: N. Howe and Durrie, 1828), p. 47.

3. Fuller accounts of eighteenth-century mythography, both deist and Christian, may be found in Frank Manuel, *The Eighteenth Century Confronts the Gods* (Cambridge: Harvard University Press, 1959), and B. Feldman and R. Richardson, *The Rise of Modern Mythology* (Bloomington: Indiana University Press, 1972).

4. *The Rise of Modern Mythology*, pp. 7–18.

5. See David Lundberg and Henry F. May, "The Enlightened Reader in America," *American Quarterly*, vol. 28, no. 2 (Summer 1976).

6. "Ancient Faith and Fable," in *The Writings of Voltaire*, Vol. 4 (New York: W. H. Wise & Company, 1931), p. 59.

7. Abbé Noël Pluche, *Histoire du Ciel* (Paris, 1739–41), translated as *The History of the Heavens* (London: J. Osborn, 1741); Charles F. Dupuis, *l'Origine de tous les cultes ou la Religion universelle* (Paris, 1795), abridged by Dupuis in 1798, translated as *The Origin of all Religious Worship* (New Orleans, 1872).

8. John Adams's interest in myth theory, especially Dupuis's, has been discussed by Frank Manuel, *The Eighteenth Century Confronts the Gods*, ch. 4, sec. 4, "John Adams and the Gods."

9. Banier's principal work is *La Mythologie et les fables expliquées par l'histoire*, 3 vols. (Paris: Briasson, 1738–40). It was translated at once as *The Mythology and Fables of the Ancients, explain'd from History*, 4 vols. (London: A. Millar, 1739–40), and it served as the basis for many subsequent influential accounts of myth, such as the articles on mythology in Diderot's *Encyclopédie* (1751–65) and the first edition of the *Encyclopaedia Britannica* (1771). Even in the nineteenth century, Banier's work formed the basis for handbooks such as Robert Mayo's *A New System of Mythology* (Philadelphia: T. S. Manning, 1815–19), and for such widely respected work as Sir J. G. Wilkinson's *Manners and Customs of the Ancient Egyptians* (London, 1837–41).

10. Paul Henri Thiery, Baron d'Holbach, *Système de la nature, ou des loix du monde physique et du monde moral* (Amsterdam, 1770) was issued as though by M. Mirabaud and as though at London. A translation by H. D. Robinson was issued in New York in 1835.

11. Thomas Paine, *The Age of Reason*, pt. 1, ch. 4.

12. *The Age of Reason*, pt. 1, ch. 2.

13. Thomas Paine, *Works*, ed. Moncure Conway (New York, 1894–96), vol. 4, pp. 293, 423, 262.

14. Henry F. May, *The Enlightenment in America* (New York: Oxford University Press, 1976), p. 226.

15. The idea that Franklin suggested the subject of *The Ruins* to Volney seems to stem from V. Jeanvrot's "Volney, sa vie et ses oeuvres," *Revolution Francaise*, Sept. 1898, pp. 278–286, and Oct. 1898, pp. 348–377. See esp. p. 355. Jefferson's translation of the first twenty chapters of *The Ruins* was a discovery of Gilbert Chinard. Until Chinard carefully assembled a

series of references that leave no doubt that Jefferson did the translation and that he wished it concealed, it was commonly thought that Joel Barlow had translated the whole. In fact, though, Jefferson's version has been in circulation for years, but under Barlow's name. See Gilbert Chinard, *Volney et l'Amerique* (Baltimore: The Johns Hopkins Press, 1923), ch. 4. There are at least three early English translations of *The Ruins,* and since they are often anonymous it may help to give here the opening sentences of Jefferson's translation of the Invocation. "Hail solitary ruins! holy sepulchres and silent walls! you I invoke; to you I address my prayer." This edition first appeared as *A New Translation of Volney's Ruins or Meditations on the Revolutions of Empires,* made under the inspection of the author. Printed for Levrault, Quai Malaquais, Paris, 1802.

16. See *The Adams-Jefferson Letters,* ed. Lester J. Cappon (Chapel Hill: University of North Carolina Press, 1959), vol. 2, p. 608; Joseph Priestley, *Letters to Mr. Volney occasioned by a Work of his entitled Ruins, and by his letter to the author,* in vol. 17 of his *The Theological and Miscellaneous Works,* ed. J. T. Rutt (London: Hackney, 1817–31); Book nine of Barlow's *Columbiad* clearly shows the influence of Volney.

17. Lawrence Willson, "Thoreau, Student of Anthropology," *American Anthropology,* vol. 61, no. 2 (Apr. 1959), 284; Poe's review of Stephens's *Arabia Petraea;* M. L. Houser, *Lincoln's Education* (New York: Bookman Associates, 1957). Whitman's remark is quoted in Horace Traubel, *With Walt Whitman in Camden,* vol. 2 (New York: D. Appleton and Co.) p. 445. See also David Goodale, "Some of Walt Whitman's Borrowings," *American Literature* 10 (1938), 202–203 (concerns Volney and Frances Wright); Melville, *Clarel,* bk. II, canto xvi, line 31.

18. C. F. Volney, *The Ruins, or, Meditations on the Revolutions of Empires . . .* (New York: The Truth Seeker Co. 1913), p. 7.

19. *Ruins,* p. 112.

20. *Ruins,* pp. 146–147.

21. *Ruins,* pp. 161–162.

22. See *The Jefferson Bible,* ed. O. I. A. Roche (New York: Clarkson N. Potter, Inc., 1964), pp. 329, 339, 379.

23. See Barlow's notebook dated c. 1796–97, bMS Am 1448 (13) in the Harvard College Library.

24. Barlow's translation (of an unlocated French original) "Genealogy of the Tree of Liberty" is also at Harvard, bMS Am 1448 (13); his unfinished poem "The Canal" is transcribed and discussed by K. R. Ball, "Social and Political Thought of Joel Barlow," diss., University of Wisconsin, 1967.

25. The best account of the development of the mythological point of view in biblical studies is Christian Hartlich and Walter Sachs, *Der Ursprung des Mythosbegriffes in der Modernen Bibelwissenschaft* (Tübingen, 1952). Useful accounts in English include D. F. Strauss, *The Life of Jesus*

Critically Examined, tr. George Eliot, ed. Peter Hodgson (Philadelphia: Fortress Press, 1972) (Strauss's famous *Life* opens with a section on the development of the mythological point of view); Theodore Parker's review "Strauss' Life of Jesus," in *Critical and Miscellaneous Writings* (Boston: Little, Brown and Company, 1856); and Albert Schweitzer, *The Quest of the Historical Jesus,* originally published in 1906 as *Von Reimarus zu Wrede: Eine Geschichte der Leben-Jesu-Forschung.*

26. The indispensable work on typology is Erich Auerbach's essay "Figura," in *Scenes from the Drama of European Literature* (New York: Meridian Books, Inc., 1959). The persistence of typological habits of mind in nineteenth-century American thought and literature has been demonstrated convincingly by Ursula Brumm in *American Thought and Religious Typology* (New Brunswick, N.J.: Rutgers University Press, 1970), and by Sacvan Bercovitch in *The Puritan Origins of the American Self* (New Haven and London: Yale University Press, 1975). At the same time, it must be recognized that there were anti-typological forces at work even in biblical criticism itself. See, for example, Hans Frei, *The Eclipse of Biblical Narrative* (New Haven and London: Yale University Press, 1974), esp. pp. 6–9 for the argument that the entire critical-historical movement was antitypological. For a reflection of this point of view in American biblical studies see Jerry W. Brown, *The Rise of Biblical Criticism in America* (Middletown, Conn.: Wesleyan University Press, 1969), esp. p. 135.

27. Quoted in Henry F. May, *The Enlightenment in America,* p. 242.

28. *The Journals and Miscellaneous Notebooks of Ralph Waldo Emerson,* ed. Gilman et al., vol. 2 (Cambridge: Harvard University Press, 1961), p. 193.

29. Quotations from Blackwell in this paragraph are taken from Feldman and Richardson, *The Rise of Modern Mythology,* pp. 99–111. For a general account of Blackwell, see Donald Foerster, *Homer in English Criticism* (New Haven: Yale University Press, 1947).

30. Quotations from Lowth in this paragraph are also from *The Rise of Modern Mythology,* pp. 144–150. For Lowth's importance to the evolution of Romanticism, see Murray Roston, *Prophet and Poet: The Bible and the Growth of Romanticism* (Evanston: Northwestern University Press, 1965). For an excellent account of the various editions of Lowth, including Calvin Stowe's American edition, see the introduction by Vincent Freimarck to Robert Lowth, *Lectures on the Sacred Poetry of the Hebrews* (Hildesheim: Georg Olms Verlag, 1969).

31. *Thomas Taylor the Platonist,* ed. Kathleen Raine and George Mills Harper (Princeton: Princeton University Press, 1969), p. 46.

32. On the Nordic Renaissance see Anton Blanck, *Den Nordiska Renässanses i Sjuttonhundratalets Litteratur* (Stockholm: Albert Bonniers Förlag, 1911). Most eighteenth-century knowledge of Norse myth comes from P.

H. Mallet, *Monumens de la mythologie et de la poésie des Celtes, et particulièrement des anciens Scandinaves,* which is volume two of his *Introduction a l'Histoire du Danemarc* (Copenhagen, 1755–56). See also P. Van Tieghem, "La mythologie et la poésie Scandinaves" and "Ossian et l'ossianisme," both in his *Le Préromantisme* (Paris, 1924). For Ossian in America, see F. I. Carpenter, "The Vogue of Ossian in America: A Study in Taste," *American Literature,* vol. 11 (1931), and G. Chinard's "Jefferson and Ossian," *Modern Language Notes,* vol. 38 (April 1923).

33. Edward Gibbon, *Decline and Fall of the Roman Empire,* ed. Milman (Philadelphia, 1845), ch. 10, vol. 1, p. 303, and ch. 71, vol. 5, p. 548.

34. There is little written on Alsop. See K. P. Harrington, *Richard Alsop, a Hartford Wit* (Middletown, Conn.: Wesleyan University Press, 1939), and A. B. Benson, "Scandinavian Influences on the Works of William Dunlap and Richard Alsop," *Scandinavian Studies,* vol. 9 (Nov. 1927), pp. 239–257.

35. See Chinard, "Jefferson and Ossian," *Modern Language Notes* (Apr. 1923).

36. J. B. Linn, *The Death of Washington* (Philadelphia, 1800), p. 6.

37. See *The Early Lectures of Ralph Waldo Emerson,* ed. S. E. Whicher and R. E. Spiller (Cambridge: Harvard University Press, 1959), vol. 1, p. 302, and *Journals of Ralph Waldo Emerson,* ed. E. W. Emerson and W. E. Forbes (Boston and New York, 1909–14), vol. 8, p. 361; *The Complete Writings of Walt Whitman,* Camden edition (New York: Putnam, 1902), vol. 9, pp. 94–95; H. Thoreau, *A Week on the Concord and Merrimack Rivers,* Walden edition (Boston and New York: Houghton Mifflin Company, 1906), p. 367.

38. See Raymond Schwab, *La Renaissance orientale* (Paris, 1950), for the best general account of eighteenth-century Europe's discovery of ancient Indic culture.

Chapter 2

1. The persistence into the nineteenth century of the conservative Christian point of view toward myth can be seen, tellingly, in most of the mythological handbooks of the period, including William Sheldon's *History of the Heathen Gods* (Boston: Isaiah Thomas, Jr., 1809); Christopher Irving's *Catechism of Mythology* (New York: F. and R. Lockwood, 1822); and Robert Mayo's *A New System of Mythology* (Philadelphia, 1815–19). The last of these was lifted primarily and without acknowledgment from Banier's *Mythology and Fables of the Ancients, Explain'd from History* (London: A. Millar, 1739).

The persistence of a thoroughgoing, Enlightenment-like skepticism toward myth may be traced through nineteenth-century deism and freethinking, in such representative books as George B. English's *The Grounds of Christianity Examined* (Boston, 1813); Abner Kneeland's *National Hymns for those who are Slave to no Sect* (Boston, 1832); H. D. Robinson's translation of Holbach's *The System of Nature* (New York: G. W. & A. J. Matsell, 1835); Frances Wright D'Arusmont's *A Few Days in Athens* (Boston: J. P. Mendum, 1850); Samuel Ludvigh's *Reden, Vorlesungen und Prosaische Aufsaetze, im Gebiete der Religion, Philosophie und Geschichte* (Baltimore: Verlag des Verfassers, 1850); and Robert Ingersoll's celebrated lecture on the Gods, published in *The Gods and other Lectures* (Peoria, 1874). The Enlightenment attack on myth has continued to our own times, through such books as Andrew D. White's *A History of the Warfare of Science with Theology* (New York: D. Appleton & Company, 1896), esp. ch. 18; H. L. Mencken's *Treatise on the Gods* (New York: A. A. Knopf, 1930) and Peter Gay's *The Enlightenment* (New York: Knopf, 1966–69) esp. book one, ch. 2, sec. 1, and his *A Loss of Mastery* (Berkeley and Los Angeles: University of California Press, 1966), esp. the opening of the bibliographical essay.

2. For the origin of the concept of myth characteristic of the higher criticism, see C. Hartlich and W. Sachs, *Der Ursprung des Mythosbegriffes in der Modernen Bibelwissenschaft* (Tübingen, 1952). E. S. Shaffer's *Kubla Khan and the Fall of Jerusalem; The Mythological School in Biblical Criticism and Secular Literature, 1770-1880* (Cambridge: Cambridge University Press, 1975) assesses the influence of the higher criticism on the work of Coleridge, Browning, and George Eliot.

3. There is no adequate history of the higher criticism in English. Albert Schweitzer's *The Quest of the Historical Jesus* (1906; English translation, 1910; repr. Macmillan, 1961) ignores French, English, and American contributions. It nonetheless serves to show how the critical study of the Bible undermined instead of shoring up the faith of many of its exponents. This seems to have been the fate, for example, of Edward Everett and George Bancroft, the first Americans who were sent to Göttingen to study under Eichhorn.

4. See the introduction and chapter one of Shaffer's *Kubla Khan and the Fall of Jerusalem.*

5. Jerry Wayne Brown, *The Rise of Biblical Criticism in America 1800–1870* (Middletown, Conn.: Wesleyan University Press, 1969). Brown claims, in this important book, that "the tradition of biblical study that flourished in New England before the Civil War has been almost entirely forgotten."

6. R. W. Emerson, "Historical Notes of Life and Letters in New England," in *Lectures and Biographical Sketches,* vol. 10 in the Riverside Edition of *Emerson's Works.*

7. Quoted in Brown, *The Rise of Biblical Criticism in America,* p. 43.

8. Perry Miller, *The Transcendentalists* (Cambridge: Harvard University Press, 1950), p. 226.

9. *The Dial,* vol. 1, no. 3 (Jan. 1841) 322; reprinted 1961.

10. *Theodore Parker's Experience as a Minister* (Boston: R. Leighton, Jr., 1859), p. 42.

11. Ibid., pp. 42–43.

12. Ibid., pp. 63–64.

13. Parker's translation appeared in *The Scriptural Interpreter,* vol. 6 (1836), pp. 218–226; vol. 7 (1837), pp. 23–31, 80–94.

14. John Weiss, *Life and Correspondence of Theodore Parker* (New York: D. Appleton & Company, 1864), vol. 1, p. 258.

15. *A Critical and Historical Introduction to the Canonical Scriptures of the Old Testament,* from the German of W. M. L. De Wette, tr. and enlarged by Theodore Parker (Boston: Little, Brown and Co., 1843; repr. 1858), vol. 1, sec. 4, p. 3.

16. De Wette, vol. 1, sec. 100, p. 377.

17. Ibid., vol. 1, sec. 12a, pp. 21–22.

18. Ibid., vol. 2, sec. 136a, pp. 22–23.

19. Ibid., vol. 2, sec. 146, pp. 38–39.

20. Strauss was dismissed from his tutorship at Tübingen in 1835. His name became anathema in German universities; no professorship was open to him. When he finally was given an appointment at Zurich, the outcry was so great that a public referendum was held. The overwhelming vote against Strauss (39,225 to 1,048) forced the government to revoke the offer. Two excellent accounts of Strauss's life are the editor's introduction to D. F. Strauss, *The Life of Jesus Critically Examined* (Philadelphia: Fortress Press, 1972), ed. Peter G. Hodgson, and ch. vii of Albert Schweitzer, *The Quest of the Historical Jesus* (1906; English translation, 1910; repr. Macmillan, 1961).

21. Theodore Parker, "Strauss's Life of Jesus," in *The Critical and Miscellaneous Writings of Theodore Parker* (Boston: Little, Brown and Company, second edition 1856, first published in *The Christian Examiner* for April 1840), p. 288.

22. Parker, "Strauss's Life of Jesus," pp. 291–292.

23. Ibid., p. 327. Parker is quoting Strauss.

24. Ibid., pp. 331–334.

25. For the dating of Parker's review and for his admission that "I could not say all I would say," see the quotation from Parker's Journal for April 1, 1839 in O. B. Frothingham's *Theodore Parker* (New York: Putnam, 1886), p. 121. The letter to Francis is dated March 22, 1839 and is in the same volume, pp. 117–118.

26. Theodore Parker, "The Previous Question. . . ," in *The Transcendentalists*, p. 229.

27. The contents of his library, even as partially recorded in the ms. catalog in the Boston Public Library, also shows the astonishing range of myth-related scholarship Parker knew. He owned Creuzer's *Symbolik* in German and in French, three titles by Bruno Bauer, fifteen by F. C. Baur, Bayle's *Dictionaire* and his *Oeuvres Diverses,* Lowth, Bochart, Chateaubriand's *Genius of Christianity,* H. T. Colebrook's *Essays,* thirteen volumes by Constant, the *Kalevala,* nineteen titles by De Wette, Diderot's *Encyclopédie,* five titles by Eichhorn, nine by Strauss, nineteen by the Grimms, twelve by Hammer Purgstall, Herder's *Complete Works,* five titles by Klaproth, eight by F. Korn, Lobeck's *Aglaophamus,* Mallet, three titles by K. O. Müller, including the 1825 *Prolegomena,* Paine's *Age of Reason,* Priestley's *A Comparison of the Institutes of Moses with those of the Hindoos,* the complete works of William Schlegel, De Brosses's *Du culte des dieux fétiches,* and a great many more.

28. *The Transcendentalists,* p. 275. Parker's title is evidently derived from an 1838 piece by Strauss called "Vergängliches und Bleibendes in Christenthum."

29. *The Transcendentalists,* p. 267.

30. E. S. Shaffer, *Kubla Khan and the Fall of Jerusalem,* pp. 53–54.

31. Creuzer's great work is his *Symbolik und Mythologie der alten Völker, besonders der Griechen,* 4 vols. (Leipzig/Darmstadt, 1810–12). The French translation is J. D. Guignaut, *Religions de l'antiquité considerées principalement dans leurs formes symboliques et mythologiques,* 4 vols. (Paris, 1825–51). For Creuzer's impact on modern myth study, see Feldman and Richardson, *The Rise of Modern Mythology,* and Jan de Vries, *The Study of Religion,* tr. Kees W. Bolle (New York; Harcourt Brace Jovanovich, 1967).

32. Emerson discusses Everett in "Life and Letters in New England," *Works,* vol. 10, p. 312. Everett's use of Creuzer may be seen in Edward Everett's *Synopsis of a course of Lectures on the History of Greek Literature* (n.d.) in the Harvard College Library. Emerson's use of Joseph Marie de Gérando's *Histoire Comparée* is discussed by F. I. Carpenter in *Emerson's Asia* (Cambridge: Harvard University Press, 1930), pp. 10–11. J. G. E. Oegger's *The True Messiah,* tr. and pub. by E. P. Peabody (Boston, 1842), is discussed in K. W. Cameron, *Emerson the Essayist* (Raleigh, N.C., 1945), vol. 1, and reprinted in vol. 2.

33. Karl Otfried Müller's *Prolegomena zu einer wissenschaftlichen Mythologie . . .* (Göttingen, 1825) was not translated into English until 1844, but his two-volume work on *The Dorians* was available in English from 1830, and his influence in Europe and America was very great by the time his *History of the Literature of Ancient Greece* appeared in English in

1840. For a general estimate of Müller, see Feldman and Richardson, *The Rise of Modern Mythology,* and G. P. Gooch, *History and Historians in the Nineteenth Century* (London: Longmans & Co., 1913).

34. The influence of K. O. Müller on Elizabeth Peabody may be traced from her *Key to History, Part III, the Greeks* (Boston: Marsh, Capen & Lyon, 1833) through her conversations as discussed by G. W. Cooke, *Historical and Biographical Introduction to Accompany The Dial* (1855; repr. New York: Russell & Russell, 1961), to her essay on "The Dorian Measure," in *Aesthetic Papers* (Boston, 1849; repr. Gainesville, Fla.: Scholar's Facsimiles & Reprints, 1957), and her "Introduction to Bem's History," in her *Universal History* (1859; rev. ed., 1875).

35. E. Peabody, *Key to History, Part III, The Greeks,* p. 8. By 1859, in her *Universal History,* this remarkable and too little studied woman could confidently say, ". . . the time is past for supposing mythology to be the *fictions* of vanity or superstition. It was an inevitable expression of truth whose keys we have lost, and which only can be restored by the imagination, cultivated by research into facts" (p. xxvi).

36. A. B. Alcott, *Tablets* (Boston: Roberts Brothers, 1868), p. 7.

37. Ibid., p. 10.

38. *The Journals of Bronson Alcott,* sel. and ed. Odell Shepard (Boston: Little, Brown and Company, 1938), p. 350.

39. *Journals of Bronson Alcott,* pp. 350–351.

40. Harold C. Goddard, *Studies in New England Transcendentalism* (New York: Hillary House, 1960), p. 189.

41. Ibid., p. 186.

42. George Mills Harper, "Thomas Taylor in America," in *Thomas Taylor, the Platonist,* ed. K. Raine and G. M. Harper (Princeton: Princeton University Press, 1969), p. 51. This volume has an excellent and extensive bibliography.

43. See also G. M. Harper, "Towards the Holy Land, Platonism in the Middle West," *South Atlantic Bulletin,* 32 (1967), pp. 1–6.

44. Thomas Taylor, "A Dissertation on the life and theology of Orpheus," in *Thomas Taylor, the Platonist,* p. 171. See also Kathleen Raine's excellent account, "Thomas Taylor in England," in the same volume.

45. *Thomas Taylor, the Platonist,* p. 173.

46. Ibid., p. 175.

47. Ibid., p. 179.

48. This and subsequent quotations from Alcott's "Orphic Sayings" are taken from *The Dial.* Numbers one through fifty appeared in the issue for July 1840, numbers fifty-one through one hundred in that for January 1841.

49. See, for example, the section "Satyr" in Hugo's *La Légende des Siècles.*

50. Odell Shepard, *Pedlar's Progress* (Boston: Little, Brown and Company, 1937), p. 155.

51. See *Pedlar's Progress,* pp. 139–145.

52. K. W. Cameron, *Emerson the Essayist* (Raleigh, N.C.: The Thistle Press, 1945), vol. II, p. 108. Cameron has printed, from *Psyche or the Breath of Childhood,* "chiefly those passages which Emerson said were worthy of being saved." It is well known that Emerson read, edited, and advised against the publication of *Psyche.*

53. *Emerson the Essayist,* vol. II, p. 120.

54. Richard L. Herrnstadt, *The Letters of A. Bronson Alcott* (Ames: Iowa State University Press, 1969), p. 28.

55. A. B. Alcott, *Tablets,* p. 176.

56. Noah Porter, "Transcendentalism," in the *American Biblical Repository,* 2d series, VIII, 1842, p. 198.

Chapter 3

1. *The Journals and Miscellaneous Notebooks of Ralph Waldo Emerson,* ed. W. H. Gilman, A. R. Ferguson, et al. (Cambridge: Harvard University Press, 1960—), vol. 4, p. 374, vol. 5, p. 7. Emerson's lively participation in Margaret Fuller's Conversations is recorded in Caroline W. Healy Dall, *Margaret and her Friends, or Ten Conversations with Margaret Fuller upon the Mythology of the Greeks* (Boston: Roberts Brothers, 1895), esp. p. 45.

2. Emerson's reading in mythology and myth scholarship and criticism was prodigious. His library included John Lempriere, *A Classical Dictionary* (London, 1788; 6th ed., 1806), and Alexander Adam, *Roman Antiquities* (Glasgow, 6th ed, 1835). According to Walter Harding (*Emerson's Library,* Charlottesville, Va.: Published for the Bibliographical Society of the University of Virginia by the University Press of Virginia, 1967), Emerson knew the second of these as early as 1821. He had ten editions of Homer in various languages, including two of Pope's Homer and one with Flaxman's drawings. He had three versions of Aeschylus and three of Ovid. For Emerson's knowledge of Indic myth, see Kenneth Cameron's exhaustive annotation in his edition of Emerson's poem *Indian Superstition* (Hanover, N.H.: Friends of the Dartmouth Library, 1954). Cameron's book lists an enormous number of works that touched on India and were available in and around Emerson's Harvard; indeed, there are many more things listed than Emerson's poems and journals show him to have known. The collection of books on the Orient, which Cholmondely gave Thoreau, and Thoreau in turn gave Emerson, is conveniently listed in Carpenter's

Emerson and Asia. Emerson's acquaintance with the life and work of Sir William Jones goes back to his senior year at Harvard when he read Teignmouth's *Life of Sir William Jones* (London: J. Hatchard, 1804). The volumes on Nordic myth in Emerson's library include Amos Cottle's *Icelandic Poetry* (Bristol, 1797), G. W. Dasent's *The Prose or Younger Edda* (London, 1842), and P. H. Mallet's *Northern Antiquities* (London, 1847). Carlyle's opening lecture on Odin in *Heroes and Hero Worship,* published in 1841, is important for Emerson's attitude toward Nordic myth. Emerson's copy of Ossian is a Boston edition of 1857. From the piece on "Stonehenge" in *English Traits,* it is clear that Emerson had some knowledge of William Stukeley's *Stonehenge, a Temple restor'd to the British Druids* (London, 1740) and Edward Davies, *The Mythology and Rites of the British Druids* (London: J. Booth, 1809).

Emerson owned Ralph Cudworth's *The True Intellectual System of the Universe* (a seventeenth-century work) in an edition edited by Thomas Birsh, 4 vols. (London, 1820). For his knowledge of Bayle, see John Clendinning, "Emerson and Bayle," *Philological Quarterly* 43 (January 1964), pp. 79–86. Emerson withdrew Volney's *Ruins* from the Harvard College Library in 1828. References to John Gillies, *The History of Ancient Greece . . .* 4 vols. (London, 1786) occur all through his early journals. He withdrew William Mitford's *History of Greece* from the Boston Library Society in 1822. Emerson owned an edition of George Bancroft's translation of Arnold Heeren's general history of Greece somewhat oddly titled *Reflections of the Politics of Ancient Greece* (Boston: Cummings, Hilliard & Co., 1824), which insists that Greek myth and religion constitute the starting point for Greek culture. Emerson's acquaintance with K. O. Müller's *The Dorians* dates from 1831, when he took it out of the Boston Athenaeum. *Selected Writings of Thomas Taylor,* edited by Kathleen Raine and George Mills Harper, contains an excellent essay on Taylor's influence on Alcott and Emerson. Emerson owned Taylor's five-volume *Works of Plato* (London, 1804), Taylor's *Select Works of Plotinus* (London, 1817), Taylor's five-volume edition of Plutarch's *Morals,* Taylor's *Iamblichus on the Mysteries of the Egyptians, Chaldeans, and Assyrians* (Chiswick, 1821), and Taylor's two-volume *Commentaries of Proclus on the Timaeus of Plato* (London, 1820), as well as various other editions of books of these writers. Emerson owned August Schlegel's *Lectures on Dramatic Art and Literature,* translated by John Black and published in Philadelphia in 1833, as well as Friedrich Schlegel's *The Philosophy of History,* tr. J. B. Robertson (London, 1835). He also owned Novalis's *Henry of Ofterdingen,* tr. J. Owen (Cambridge, Mass., 1842). Emerson withdrew Herder's *Outlines of a Philosophy of the History of Man* from the Harvard Library in 1829 and later from the Boston Athenaeum in 1831. Emerson owned the *Deutsches Wörterbuch,* published in 1854 by Jacob and Wilhelm Grimm, and had withdrawn the famous *Kinder- und Hausmärchen* from the Athenaeum in 1836. For Emerson's anecdote about Strauss see *The Journals of Ralph Waldo Emerson*, ed. E. W. Emerson and W. E. Forbes (Boston, 1912), vol. 7, p. 396, and his correspondence with Parker in spring and summer of 1842. Emerson's knowledge of Creuzer's ideas comes mainly from two books explicitly indebted to Creuzer: Joseph Marie de Gérando, *Histoire comparée des systèmes de philosophie* (2d ed., Paris, 1822–23), 4 vols., and J. G. E. Oegger, *The True Messiah*, tr. and pub. E. P. Peabody (Boston, 1842).

Thomas Blackwell's *An Enquiry into the Life and Writings of Homer* (1735) and Robert Lowth's *The Sacred Poetry of the Hebrews* (1753; Eng. tr., 1787) both appear in Emerson's "Catalogue of Books Read" between 1819 and 1824, printed in *Journals and Misc. Notebooks*, vol. 1, p. 396.

Emerson owned a copy of Newton's *The Chronology of the Ancient Kingdoms Amended* (London and Dublin, 1728). Emerson's knowledge of Humphrey Prideaux's *The Old and New Testaments connected* (London, 1716–18) is attested by entries in his journal in 1824. See *Journals and Misc. Notebooks*, vol. 2, pp. 307, 402. Emerson's knowledge of Hegel and Schelling is discussed by Prof. Wellek in his "Emerson and German Philosophy," *New England Quarterly*, vol. 16 (March 1943), 41–62. Emerson owned George Eliot's translation of L. A. Feuerbach's *The Essence of Christianity* (New York: C. Blanchard, 1855). Emerson was withdrawing books by F. Max Müller starting in 1861. He took out Müller's *History of ancient Sanskrit Literature* (London, 1859) in 1861, and at least part of the famous *Chips from a German Workshop* (London: 1867–75), in 1868. He also owned copies of the book Müller dedicated to him, the *Introduction to the Science of Religion* (London, 1873).

F. O. Matthiessen's *American Renaissance* (London and New York: Oxford University Press, 1941) contains a brilliant and suggestive discussion of Emerson's awareness of the possibilities of myth. I am greatly indebted to this book. J. Russell Reaver's *Emerson as Mythmaker* (Gainesville: University of Florida Press, 1954) approaches Emerson from the vantage of modern ideas about myth, particularly those of depth psychology. Some of Reaver's findings are sound, but he neglects almost entirely Emerson's own thoughts and comments on myth and mythmaking: Reaver's later article, "Mythology in Emerson's Poems," *Emerson Society Quarterly*, no. 39 (1965), pt. 2, pp. 56–63, is much more satisfactory in this respect. John S. Harrison's *The Teachers of Emerson* (New York: Sturgis & Walton Company, 1910) has an excellent chapter on Emerson's mythology and its debt to Plato. Sherman Paul's brilliant *Emerson's Angle of Vision* (Cambridge: Harvard University Press, 1952) also takes up Emerson's mythology. Among recent studies must be singled out Sacvan Bercovitch's *The Puritan Origins of the American Self* (New Haven: Yale University Press, 1975), which ends with an excellent section on how Emerson "expressed himself by expressing the myth of America" in essentially Puritan terms, and Harold Bloom's *Figures of Capable Imagination* (New York: Seabury Press, 1976), which contains a brightly suggestive treatment of what Bloom calls Emerson's American Orphism.

3. *Journals and Misc. Notebooks,* vol. 1, p. 98.

4. Ibid., vol. 1, pp. 138, 174.

5. Ibid., vol. 1, p. 200.

6. Ibid., vol. 1, p. 327; vol. 2, p. 63.

7. Ibid., vol. 5, p. 13.

8. Ibid., vol. 5, p. 155.

9. Ibid., vol. 5, pp. 496–497.

10. Ibid., vol. 1, p. 76; vol. 8, pp. 389–390. See also Emerson's essay "Experience."

11. *Journals and Misc. Notebooks,* vol. 8, p. 401.

12. Ibid., vol. 1, p. 314; vol. 3, p. 17.

13. Ibid., vol. 3, p. 148.

14. Ibid., vol. 5, p. 322; vol. 7, pp. 167–168.

15. Ibid., vol. 5, p. 468; vol. 7, pp. 403, 194; vol. 8, p. 196.

16. *Journals,* vol. 7, pp. 233, 317–318, 383.

17. Alfred North Whitehead, *The Aims of Education* (1929; repr. New York: Macmillan, 1967), p. 4, and "Historical Changes," in *Science and Philosophy* (New York: Philosophical Library, 1948), p. 213.

18. *Journals,* vol. 7, p. 434; *Journals and Misc. Notebooks,* vol. 3, p. 26; vol. 5, p. 443.

19. *Journals and Misc. Notebooks,* vol. 7, p. 280. See also "Self Reliance."

20. *Journals and Misc. Notebooks,* vol. 4, p. 282; vol. 7, pp. 506–507.

21. Ibid., vol. 7, p. 111; vol. 5, p. 371.

22. Ibid., vol. 5, pp. 198–199; "History," in *Essays* (1841).

23. "History," in *Essays* (1841), p. 25; Introductory lecture on "Philosophy of History," in S. E. Whicher, R. E. Spiller, and W. E. Williams, *The Early Lectures of Ralph Waldo Emerson,* vol. 2 (Cambridge: Harvard University Press, 1964), p. 8; *Journals and Misc. Notebooks,* vol. 5, p. 262.

24. "History," in *Essays* (1841), pp. 1–2, 25–26.

25. *Journals and Misc. Notebooks,* vol. 1, p. 71.

26. Ibid., vol. 7, p. 144.

27. *Journals,* vol. 10, p. 27; *Journals and Misc. Notebooks,* vol. 4, p. 375. For a general discussion see Daniel B. Shea's excellent "Emerson and the American Metamorphosis," in *Emerson: Prophecy, Metamorphosis, and Influence* (New York: Columbia University Press, 1975).

28. *Journals and Misc. Notebooks,* vol. 8, p. 411; vol. 3, pp. 167–168;

vol. 4, p. 323; vol. 7, p. 385; vol. 5, pp. 417, 175; "The Poet," in *Essays: Second Series* (1844), p. 66.

29. *Journals,* vol. 7, pp. 120–121; vol. 6, p. 477; *Journals and Misc. Notebooks,* vol. 7, pp. 524, 539; "The Poet," in *Essays: Second Series* (1844), p. 24; *Journals,* vol. 7, p. 177.

30. "History," in *Essays* (1841), p. 11.

31. *Journals and Misc. Notebooks,* vol. 8, pp. 221, 223, 23; *Journals,* vol. 7, pp. 313–314.

32. R. W. Emerson, *Representative Men* (Boston and New York: Houghton Mifflin Company, Centenary edition, 1903–4); "Goethe," p. 275.

33. *Representative Men,* "Goethe," p. 284; *Journals and Misc. Notebooks,* vol. 5, p. 417.

34. *Representative Men,* "Napoleon," p. 241; *Journals and Misc. Notebooks,* vol. 2, p. 70; vol. 5, pp. 249, 354; vol. 7, p. 24; *Journals,* vol. 6, p. 472; *Journals and Misc. Notebooks,* vol. 7, pp. 45, 217.

35. *Journals and Misc. Notebooks,* vol. 7, p. 519; *Representative Men,* pp. 9–11, 260, 35, 267–269, 271–272.

36. *Journals and Misc. Notebooks,* vol. 5, pp. 179, 295; vol. 7, p. 277.

37. *Journals and Misc. Notebooks,* vol. 7, pp. 438–439; *Journals,* vol. 7, p. 552; *Journals and Misc. Notebooks,* vol. 8, p. 26; vol. 5, p. 223.

Chapter 4

1. Sherman Paul, *The Shores of America* (Urbana: University of Illinois Press, 1958), p. 190. Other work of interest for Thoreau's knowledge and use of myth includes Ethel Seybold, *Thoreau: The Quest and the Classics* (New Haven: Yale University Press, 1951); Jonathan Bishop, "The Experience of the Sacred in Thoreau's *Week,*" *English Literary History,* vol. 33, no. 1 (March 1966), 66–91; Richard Fleck's "Henry David Thoreau's Interest in Myth, Fable and Legend," Ph.D. dissertation, University of New Mexico (1970), and his "Thoreau as Mythologist," *Research Studies,* vol. 40 (September 1972), 195–206.

2. *The Journals of Henry D. Thoreau,* ed. Bradford Torrey and Francis H. Allen (Boston: Houghton Mifflin Company, 1906; repr. New York: Dover Publications, 1962), vol. 1, p. 244.

3. *Journals,* vol. 5, p. 135.

4. Ibid., vol. 3, p. 99.

5. Henry D. Thoreau, *Walden,* ed. J. Lyndon Shanley (Princeton, N.J.: Princeton University Press, 1971), p. 184.

6. *Journals,* vol. 2, pp. 82, 87.

7. Ibid., vol. 2, p. 169.

8. Henry D. Thoreau, *A Week on the Concord and Merrimack Rivers* (Boston and New York: Houghton Mifflin Company, 1906, Walden edition), p. 57.

9. *Week,* pp. 57–58.

10. Ibid., p. 58.

11. Ibid.

12. Ibid., p. 59.

13. Ibid., pp. 60–61.

14. Ibid., p. 60.

15. Ibid., p. 61. A version of the passage occurs in vol. 1 of the Journals, p. 342, amongst notes taken from Alexander Ross's *Mystagogus Poeticus.*

16. *Week,* p. 61.

17. Ibid., p. 65.

18. Ibid., p. 67.

19. Ibid., p. 69.

20. Ibid., pp. 77–78.

21. Ibid., pp. 93–94.

22. Ibid., pp. 95, 97.

23. Sources for studying the extent of Thoreau's acquaintance with Indic myth include Arthur Christy's *The Orient in American Transcendentalism* (New York: Columbia University Press, 1932) and his edition of Thoreau's *The Transmigration of the Seven Brahmans* (New York: W. E. Rudge, 1932); William B. Stein, "A Bibliography of Hindu and Buddhist Literature Available to Thoreau through 1854," *Emerson Society Quarterly,* no. 47 (1967), 52–56; Ernest E. Leisy, "Sources of Thoreau's Borrowings in *A Week,*" *American Literature,* vol. 18 (1946), 37-44, and K. W. Cameron, *Emerson and Thoreau as Readers* (Hartford, Conn.: Transcendental Books 1958). There are convenient reprints of the *Hitopadesa* (Gainesville, Florida: Scholars' Facsimiles & Reprints, 1968) of Rammohun Roy's *The Veds* and William Ward's *A View of the History, Literature and Mythology of the Hindoos* (London, 1785; repr. Gainesville, Fla.: Scholars' Facsimiles & Reprints, 1967) and of *The Bhagavat-Geeta,* tr. by Charles Wilkins (Gainesville, Fla.: Scholars' Facsimiles & Reprints, 1959). Recent studies include Sreekrishna Sarma, "A Short Study of Oriental influence upon H. D. Thoreau,"*Jahrbuch für Amerikastudien* 1 (1956), pp. 76–92; William B. Stein, "Thoreau's *Walden* and the *Bhagavad Gita,*" *Topic,* no. 6 (Fall 1963), 38–55, and his "Thoreau's First Book, a Spoor of Yoga. The Orient in *A Week,*" *Emerson Society Quarterly,* no. 41 (1965), 3–25.

24. *The Bhagavat-Geeta,* pp. 5, 25.

25. *Week,* pp. 145–146.

26. *The Bhagavat-Geeta,* Lecture nine, p. 80.

27. *Week,* pp. 155, 159.

28. Ibid., pp. 156–157.

29. Ibid., p. 156.

30. Ibid., pp. 164–165.

31. Ibid., p. 165.

32. See A. B. Benson, "Scandinavian Influences in the Writings of Thoreau," *Scandinavian Studies,* vol. 16 (May, August 1941), 201–211, 241–256, and Ernest E. Leisy, "Thoreau and Ossian," *New England Quarterly,* vol. 18 (March 1945), 96–98. For his interest in British Druids see his *Journals,* vol. 1, pp. 18–19. He owned a copy of Macpherson's Ossian and he also used Patrick MacGregor's *The Genuine Remains of Ossian* (London, 1841).

33. Walter Harding. *The Days of Henry Thoreau* (New York: Knopf, 1965), p. 323, tells about Thoreau telling the Hosmer children Norse myths. He appears to have used the Bohn library edition of Mallet's *Northern Antiquities* (London, 1847). See *Thoreau Fact Book,* ed. K. W. Cameron (Hartford, Conn.: Transcendental Books, 1966), vol. 1.

34. Henry D. Thoreau, "Thomas Carlyle and his Works," in vol. 4 of the Walden edition of *The Writings of Henry David Thoreau,* pp. 341–342.

35. Thomas Carlyle, *On Heroes, Hero-Worship and the Heroic in History* (1841; repr. London: Chapman & Hall, 1870), p. 6.

36. Ibid., pp. 7–8.

37. Ibid., p. 35.

38. Ibid., p. 39.

39. Ibid., pp. 25–26.

40. "Thomas Carlyle and his Works," p. 248.

41. Ibid.

42. The indispensable book for studying the importance of classical antiquity for Thoreau is Ethel Seybold, *Thoreau: The Quest and the Classics* (New Haven, Conn.: Yale University Press, 1951; repr. Anchor Books, 1969). See also F. E. Eddleman, "Use of Lempriere's *Classical Dictionary* in *Walden,*" *Emerson Society Quarterly,* no. 43 (1966), 62–65; Kenneth Cameron, "Ralph Cudworth and Thoreau's Translations of an Orphic Hymn," *Emerson Society Quarterly,* no. 8 (1957), 31–35; Reginald L. Cook, "Ancient Rites at Walden," *Emerson Society Quarterly,* no. 39 (1965), 52–56. For Thoreau's earliest interest in Greek myth see Carl Bode, "A New College Manuscript of Thoreau's," *American Literature,* vol. 21 (November 1949), 315.

43. Henry D. Thoreau, *The Maine Woods,* ed. J. J. Moldenhauer (Princeton, N.J.: Princeton University Press, 1972), p. 33.

44. Ibid., p. 45.
45. Ibid., p. 54.
46. Ibid.
47. Ibid., p. 55.
48. Ibid., p. 60.
49. Ibid., p. 61.
50. *Journals,* vol. 5, p. 155.
51. *The Maine Woods,* pp. 61–62.
52. Ibid., p. 63.
53. Ibid., p. 64.
54. Henry D. Thoreau, "Prometheus Bound," in *The Dial,* vol. 3, no. 3 (January 1843), p. 386.
55. *The Maine Woods,* p. 64.
56. Ibid.
57. Ibid., p. 65.
58. Ibid., pp. 69–71.
59. *Journals,* vol. 2, pp. 476–478.
60. Henry D. Thoreau, "Walking," in *Excursions* (Boston, 1863; repr. New York: Corinth Books, 1962), pp. 169–170.
61. *Journals,* vol. 2, p. 143.
62. *Excursions,* p. 72.
63. Feldman and Richardson, *The Rise of Modern Mythology,* pp. 309–310, 312. Alcott's comments about a new mythology made out of old can be found in Conversation number 5 in Carolyn Healey Dall's *Margaret and her Friends* (Boston, 1895).
64. *Excursions,* p. 177. For a full account of Thoreau's attitudes toward the West, see Edwin Fussell, *Frontier: American Literature and the American West* (Princeton: Princeton University Press, 1965).
65. *Excursions,* p. 179.
66. Ibid., p. 185.
67. Ibid.
68. Ibid., p. 193.
69. Ibid., p. 195.
70. *Walden;* p. 308.
71. *Excursions,* p. 195.
72. E. M. Forster, *Howards End* (New York: Alfred A. Knopf) ch. 33.
73. *Excursions,* pp. 195–196.
74. *Journals,* vol. 2, p. 78.
75. See Ethel Seybold, *Thoreau: The Quest and the Classics,* p. 67; W. E. Channing, *Thoreau: The Poet-Naturalist* (Boston: Roberts Brothers, 1873), pp. 70–71; F. B. Sanborn, *Henry D. Thoreau* (Boston and New York: Houghton, Mifflin and Company, 1882), pp. 259–260; and H. S. Canby, *Thoreau* (Boston: Houghton, Mifflin Company, 1939).

76. *The Correspondence of Henry David Thoreau*, ed. W. Harding and C. Bode (New York: New York University Press, 1958), p. 119.

77. *Week*, p. 170; *Walden*, p. 203.

78. Rose Hawthorne Lathrop, *Memories of Hawthorne* (Boston and New York: Houghton, Mifflin and Company, 1897), p. 53.

79. Channing, *Thoreau*, p. 53.

80. Edward Waldo Emerson, *Henry Thoreau as Remembered by a Young Friend* (Boston and New York: Houghton Mifflin Company, 1917; repr. 1968), pp. 85–86.

81. Ibid., p. 106.

82. *Walden*, pp. 68, 229, 182.

83. Ibid., pp. 201, 296, 309.

84. Ibid., pp. 29, 179, 207.

85. Ibid., p. 117.

86. Ibid., pp. 137, 152.

87. Ibid., p. 137.

88. Ibid., p. 144.

89. Ibid., pp. 326–327. See Sherman Paul's provocative treatment in *The Shores of America*, pp. 351–353.

90. *Walden*, p. 17.

91. *Journals*, vol. 1, p. 392.

92. *Walden*, pp. 221–222.

93. Ibid., p. 89.

94. Ibid., pp. 89–90.

95. Ibid., p. 305.

96. Ibid., p. 306.

97. Ibid., pp. 306–307.

98. Ibid., p. 307.

99. Emerson's essays "Goethe" and "Life and Letters in New England" show that he understood the larger implications of Goethe's theory of plant morphology. Thoreau probably took the hint from Emerson. The only contemporaneous English translation of Goethe's *Metamorphosen* is the very inadequate one in *The Gardener's Chronicle*, vol. 4, 1844, pp. 117, 133. See Agnes Arber, "Goethe's Botany," *Chronica Botanica*, vol. 10, no. 2 (1946).

Chapter 5

1. See William A. Little, "Walt Whitman and the *Nibelungenlied*," *PMLA*, vol. 80, no. 5 (December 1965), 562–570.

2. The opening section of Michelet's *Historical View of the French Revolution*, tr. by C. Cocks (London: H. G. Bohn, 1848), and his *The People* (New

York: D. Appleton & Company, 1846), which is discussed below, are good sources for Michelet's civic religion and for seeing how it differed from that of Robespierre.

3. Odell Shepard, *The Journals of Bronson Alcott* (Boston: Little, Brown and Company, 1938), p. 290.

4. Quoted in Gay Wilson Allen, *The Solitary Singer* (New York: Macmillan, 1955; rev. ed. 1967), p. 200.

5. *The Complete Writings of Walt Whitman,* Camden edition (New York and London: G. P. Putnam's Sons, 1902), vol. 10, p. 30.

6. Walt Whitman, *Leaves of Grass,* Comprehensive Reader's edition (New York: New York University Press, 1965), p. 585.

7. *Complete Writings,* vol. 9, p. 35.

8. Ibid., p. 112.

9. *Leaves of Grass,* p. 564.

10. Ibid., p. 568.

11. Ibid., pp. 387, 120.

12. *Complete Writings,* vol. 9, p. 94; *Leaves of Grass,* p. 431.

13. *Leaves of Grass,* p. 198.

14. Ibid., p. 492.

15. Ibid., p. 196.

16. For Whitman's admiration for Fanny Wright (Frances Wright D'Arusmont) see H. Traubel, *With Walt Whitman in Camden,* vol. 2, p. 445. For his opinion of Volney see the same passage, and also Whitman's letter to Bucke of June 30, 1890, quoted in David Goodale, "Some of Walt Whitman's borrowings," *American Literature,* vol. 10 (March 1938–January 1939), 202–213. The most valuable single work for assessing literary influences on Whitman is Floyd Stovall, *The Foreground of Leaves of Grass* (Charlottesville: University Press of Virginia, 1974).

17. Frances Wright D'Arusmont, *A Few Days in Athens* (Boston: J. P. Mendum, 1850; repr. New York: Arno Press, 1972), pp. 203–204.

18. *Leaves of Grass,* p. 75.

19. Ibid.

20. *A Few Days in Athens,* p. 205.

21. *Leaves of Grass,* pp. 206–210. Gabriel Sarrazin has commented on the Anglo-Saxon quality in Whitman. See *A Century of Whitman Criticism,* ed. E. H. Miller (Bloomington: Indiana University Press, 1969), p. 94.

22. *Leaves of Grass,* p. 412.

23. Walt Whitman, *Prose Works 1892,* ed. Floyd Stovall (New York: New York University Press, 1963–64), vol. 2, p. 523.

24. *Complete Writings,* vol. 9, pp. 104–105.

25. *Leaves of Grass,* p. 687; *Complete Writings,* vol. 10, pp. 8–9.

26. Sources for studying Whitman's reading in Egyptology include

Walt Whitman, *New York Dissected* (New York: R. R. Wilson, Inc., 1936), ed. E. Holloway and R. Adimari, pp. 27–40, and Floyd Stovall, "Notes on Whitman's Reading," *American Literature* 26, no. 3 (November 1954), 337–362. The excellent article by John T. Irwin, "The Symbol of the Hieroglyphics in the American Renaissance," *American Quarterly* 26, no. 2 (May 1974), 103–126, gives valuable background but does not discuss Whitman.

27. See *New York Dissected*.

28. *Complete Writings,* vol. 9, p. 103.

29. Thoreau, *Journals,* vol. 1, p. 165.

30. George Glidden, *Ancient Egypt* (Baltimore, 1845), p. 2.

31. Ibid., pp. 2–3.

32. Ibid., p. 7.

33. John Gardner Wilkinson, *Manners and Customs of the Ancient Egyptians* (London, 1837–1841), vol. 2, ch. 12, p. 478.

34. Ibid., p. 475.

35. Ibid., pp. 454, 499–500, 475.

36. Ibid., p. 488.

37. Ibid., p. 492.

38. *New York Dissected,* p. 38.

39. *Complete Writings,* vol. 9, p. 103.

40. Glidden, *Ancient Egypt,* p. 6.

41. See Esther Shepard, "Possible Sources of Some of Whitman's Ideas and Symbols in *Hermes Mercurias Trismegistus* and Other Works," *Modern Language Quarterly* 14 (March 1953), 60–81. See also Ippolito Rosellini, *I Monumenti dell' Egitto e della Nubia . . .* (Pisa, 1832–44).

42. *Leaves of Grass,* p. 332.

43. *Complete Writings,* vol. 9, pp. 173–174.

44. *Leaves of Grass,* pp. 86–87. See the excellent account of Whitman's panpsychism in G. W. Allen's *Walt Whitman Handbook* (Chicago: Packard and Company, 1946).

45. See George L. Sixbey ("'Chanting the Square Deific'—A Study in Whitman's Religion," *American Literature,* vol. 9, no. 2 (May 1937), 171–195.

46. Gay Wilson Allen, "Walt Whitman and Jules Michelet," *Etudes Angelaises,* vol. 1 (May 1937) 237. See also Adeline Knapp, "Walt Whitman and Jules Michelet, Identical Passages," *Critic,* vol. 44, pp. 467–468.

47. See Jules Michelet, *The People* (New York: D. Appleton and Co., 1846). Whitman's notice of Michelet is in the *Brooklyn Daily Eagle* for April 22, 1847. Whitman singled out, among his other works, Michelet's *History of France.* This must be the one-volume edition that was translated and published in 1845–47, since Michelet's great multi-volume *History of*

France and the *Historical View of the French Revolution* had not then appeared in English.

48. Edmund Wilson, *To the Finland Station* (New York: Harcourt, Brace, and Company, 1940), p. 25.

49. *The People,* p. 135.

50. Ibid., p. 24.

51. Ibid., pp. 135–136.

52. Ibid., p. 136.

53. Ibid., p. 179.

54. Ibid., p. 180.

55. *Leaves of Grass,* p. 20.

56. *Complete Writings,* vol. 9, p. 4.

57. Ibid., p. 6.

58. Ibid., p. 96.

59. *Prose Works 1892* (New York, 1963), vol. 1, p. 250. See also Whitman's essay on "The Bible as Poetry," in *Prose Works 1892* (New York, 1964), vol. 2, pp. 545–549.

Chapter 6

1. See Marion L. Kesselring, *Hawthorne's Reading, 1828-1850* (New York: New York Public Library, 1949). The version of Schlegel listed here is that translated by Christopher North.

2. F. Schlegel, *Lectures on the History of Literature, Ancient and Modern* (Edinburgh, 1818), vol. 1, p. 103.

3. Ibid., p. 64.

4. Ibid., pp. 43–44.

5. Ibid., p. 251.

6. Norman H. Pearson, "Nathaniel Hawthorne's French and Italian Notebooks," diss., Yale, 1941, p. 162.

7. Schlegel, *Lectures,* vol. 1, p. 76.

8. Ibid., p. 259.

9. Quoted in R. H. Pearce's "Introduction to Hawthorne's Children's Books," in N. Hawthorne, *True Stories* (Columbus: Ohio State University Press, 1972).

10. N. Hawthorne, *A Wonder Book and Tanglewood Tales* (Columbus: Ohio State University Press, 1972), p. 3. Hawthorne's myths for children have been admirably treated by Calvin E. Schorer, "The Juvenile Literature of Nathaniel Hawthorne," diss., University of Chicago, 1949. See also Daniel Hoffman's excellent essay "Myth, Romance, and the Childhood of Man," in *Hawthorne Centenary Essays,* ed. R. H. Pearce (Columbus: Ohio State University Press, 1964). See also the fine introduction by Robert

Lowell in Nathaniel Hawthorne, *Pegasus, the winged horse; a Greek myth retold.* ... (New York: MacMillan, 1963).

11. *A Wonder Book and Tanglewood Tales,* p. 3.

12. Ibid., pp. 3–4.

13. Ibid., p. 118.

14. Hawthorne's use of Anthon has been treated in length in Hugo McPherson, *Hawthorne as Myth-maker* (Toronto: University of Toronto Press, 1969). Also useful is Roger Cuff, "A Study of the Classical Mythology in Hawthorne's Writings," diss., Geo. Peabody College for Teachers, 1936. In his *Hawthorne Reading* (Cleveland: The Rowfant Club, 1902) Julian Hawthorne tells an anecdote that shows Hawthorne's knowledge of Lempriere. Hawthorne "once asked Mr. Henry Bright in England, whether a certain Mr. Lempriere Hammond whom he was to meet, was a descendant of Lempriere's Classical Dictionary? or perchance a mythical personage?" pp. 108–109.

15. *A Wonder Book and Tanglewood Tales,* p. 9.

16. Charles Demoustier's *Lettres à Émilie, sur la Mythologie* (Paris, 1822) was charged out to Hawthorne from the Salem Athenaeum on July 15, 1831. The book had quite a vogue in France and had already been translated into English and published serially in a Boston monthly, *The Polyanthos,* in 1812–14. *The Arabian Nights* was a childhood favorite of Hawthorne's. In the story of "The Three Golden Apples," Hawthorne calls Nereus The Old Man of the Sea—a figure from the fifth voyage of Sinbad the Sailor. The influence of *Gulliver's Travels* may be seen in "The Pygmies." The Swiftian tone may have been suggested by a remark in Anthon, but the story shows Hawthorne's loving familiarity with *Gulliver's Travels* itself. Hans Christian Andersen's *Fairy Tales* had just been translated into English in 1846. Andersen was in vogue at the time, and there was a copy in the Hawthorne household. Also in the Hawthorne home was the work of the brothers Grimm. Hawthorne's *American Notebooks,* ed. Claude M. Simpson (Columbus: Ohio State University Press, 1972), pp. 414, 652, record his reading to the children from Eliza Follen's *Gammer Grethel,* a book drawn mainly from Grimm and published in Boston in 1840. It is possible that the countryside quality of *A Wonder Book* in general and the troll-like description of Medusa in "The Gorgon's Head" in particular are directly traceable to the Grimms. There is a marked Undine theme in much of Hawthorne's writing. He must have known La Motte-Fouqué's story, as it was one of the three or four most frequently translated German stories, and one of the early translations had been brought out in Boston by Sophia's sister, Elizabeth Peabody, as *The Water-Spirit* (2d ed., 1833). The Undine theme can be seen in Hawthorne's story of Circe, where the fountain makes itself into prophetic shapes, in "The Snow Image," in Pearl in *The Scarlet Letter,* and in the myth about the water nymph who loved the knight in *The Marble Faun.*

17. *A Wonder Book and Tanglewood Tales*, p. 112.

18. R. W. Emerson, *Representative Men* (Boston and New York, 1903), p. 127.

19. Pearson, *French and Italian Notebooks*, p. 191.

20. *A Wonderbook and Tanglewood Tales*, p. 124.

21. Cited in the O.E.D.

22. *A Wonder Book and Tanglewood Tales*, p. 48.

23. Ibid., p. 258.

24. Ibid., pp. 178–179. It was, of course, commonly accepted at this time that Greek myth needed to be expurgated, and not only for children. See, for example, *The North American Review* for October 1835, p. 332, or *The Knickerbocker's* reference to the "Needful work of expurgation" in the issue for May 1841, pp. 432–433.

25. *A Wonder Book and Tanglewood Tales*, pp. 179–180.

26. See Rose Hawthorne Lathrop, *Memories of Hawthorne* (Boston and New York: Houghton, Mifflin and Company, 1897), p. 192 and *American Notebooks*, p. 310.

27. See *American Notebooks*, p. 416; *English Notebooks* (New York: Russell & Russell, Inc., 1962), p. 609.

28. Julian Hawthorne, *Hawthorne Reading*, pp. 123–124.

29. *French and Italian Notebooks*, p. 118.

30. *A Wonder Book and Tanglewood Tales*, pp. 112–113.

31. *French and Italian Notebooks*, p. 154.

32. *A Wonder Book and Tanglewood Tales*, p. 39.

33. N. Hawthorne, *Mosses from an Old Manse* (Boston and New York: Houghton, Mifflin and Company, 1882), p. 351.

34. Ibid., p. 353. See *The Complete Works of E. A. Poe*, ed. James A. Harrison (New York: A.M.S. Press, 1902), vol. 16, p. 43.

35. *Mosses*, p. 355.

36. Ibid., p. 356.

37. N. Hawthorne, *Twice Told Tales* (Boston and New York, 1882), p. 84.

38. Ibid., pp. 71–72.

39. Ibid., p. 72.

40. James Holly Hanford, *A Milton Handbook*, 4th ed. (New York: F. S. Crofts & Co., 1946), p. 159.

41. *Twice Told Tales*, p. 80.

42. N. Hawthorne, *The Marble Faun* (Columbus: Ohio State University Press, 1968), pp. 8–9.

43. See the anonymous review in *The Times* (April 7, 1860), p. 5, reprinted in *Hawthorne: the Critical Heritage*, ed. J. Donald Crowley (New York: Barnes & Noble, 1970), p. 328.

44. *The Marble Faun,* p. 10.

45. Ibid., pp. 10–11.

46. Ibid., p. 13.

47. Ibid., p. 18.

48. Reprinted in *Hawthorne: the Critical Heritage,* p. 322.

49. A recent treatment of this motif is Patricia Merivale's "The Raven and the Bust of Pallas; Classical Artifacts and the Gothic Tale," *PMLA,* vol. 89, no. 5 (1974), 960–966.

50. For Winckelmann see Kesselring, *Hawthorne's Reading,* and the description of Praxiteles' Faun in John Murray's *A Handbook of Rome and its environs* (London, 1858) and in Charlotte A. Eaton's *Rome in the Nineteenth Century* (Edinburgh, 1820).

51. *The Marble Faun,* pp. 114–115.

52. Ibid., p. 380.

53. See especially chapter 4, "The Spectre of the Catacomb."

54. *The Marble Faun,* p. 44.

55. See chapter 6, "The Virgin's Shrine."

56. *The Marble Faun,* p. 233.

57. Ibid., pp. 233–234.

58. Ibid., p. 235.

59. Ibid., pp. 235–236.

60. Ibid., p. 246.

61. Ibid., p. 313.

62. Ibid., p. 346.

63. N. Hawthorne, *The Scarlet Letter* (Columbus: Ohio State University Press, 1962), p. 36.

64. See respectively the prefaces to *The Marble Faun* and *The Blithedale Romance.*

65. K. O. Müller, *Introduction to a Scientific System of Mythology,* tr. John Leitch (London, 1844), p. 110. See also A. W. Schlegel *Lectures on Dramatic Art and Literature* (London, 1846), lec. 5, p. 66.

66. Charles [Karl] Philip Moritz, *Mythological Fictions of the Greeks and Romans,* trans. C.F.W.J. (New York: G.&.C.&.H. Carvill, 1830), p. 12. For another perspective on the question of myth and romance, see the brilliant essay by Q. D. Leavis, "Hawthorne as Poet, part 2," *Sewanee Review,* vol. 59 (Spring-Summer 1951), 426–458.

Chapter 7

1. Melville's knowledge of Greek and Roman myth, most impressively seen in the Memnon and Enceladus sections of *Pierre,* and in the lecture

"Statues in Rome," was drawn from Homer, from Bayle, from Winckelmann, and from George Grote's *History of Greece*. See the listings in the invaluable *Melville's Readings* (Madison: University of Wisconsin Press, 1966) by Merton M. Sealts, Jr. A recent and helpful study is G. M. Sweeney, *Melville's Use of Classical Mythology* (Amsterdam; Rodopi, 1975). Almost the entire first volume of Grote's great history is devoted to a lengthly discussion of the role of myth in early Greek history and to the significance of myth both to the Greeks and to any modern understanding of the Greek mind.

Melville's knowledge of Egyptian mythology shows up in *Mardi,* in *Moby-Dick,* and in *Clarel;* his sources of information about Egyptian myth included Thomas Moore, Sir Thomas Browne, Bayle again, and such modern travelers as Arthur Stanley and William Henry Bartlett. Curiously, there is nothing to suggest that Melville read any of the better informed post-Champollion works available on Egyptian myth.

Concerning Melville's acquaintance with Indic myth, there is the testimony of Maunsell Field, who left the following account of an evening with Melville and Oliver Wendell Holmes: "At length, somehow, the conversation drifted to East India religions and mythologies, and soon there arose a discussion between Holmes and Melville, which was conducted with the most amazing skill and brilliancy on both sides. It lasted for hours and Darley and I had nothing to do but listen." (Maunsell B. Field, *Memories of Many Men and of Some Women* [New York: Harper & Brothers, 1874], pp. 201–202.) Indic myth plays a part in *Moby-Dick* and in *Clarel;* Melville knew something of Friedrich Schlegel's view on Indic myth, he probably knew the *Indian Antiquities* of Thomas Maurice (see Howard Vincent, *The Trying-Out of Moby-Dick* [1949; repr. Carbondale and Edwardsville: Southern Illinois University Press, 1965], pp. 278–280.), and he may have known Sir William Jones's famous essay "On the Gods of Greece, Italy and India." The importance of Sir William Jones for *Mardi* has been argued by H. Bruce Franklin in *The Wake of the Gods: Melville's Mythology* (Stanford, Calif.: Stanford University Press, 1963). Melville also knew the long and hostile "Inquiry into the religious tenets and philosophy of the Brahmins" attached to Mickle's translation of Camoen's *Lusiads* (see Vincent, *Trying-Out,* p. 278), and he appears to have read the *Ramayana* (see Hemant Balvantrao, *Moby-Dick: a Hindu Avatar* [Logan: Utah State University Press, 1970]).

Nordic myth is evident in Melville's treatment of Jarl in *Mardi,* and the Scandinavian sagas may have had some influence on *Moby-Dick.* Melville knew Nordic myth through Carlyle's lecture on Odin in *Heroes, Hero-Worship and the Heroic in History* and through Esaias Tegner's *Frithiof's Saga.* Melville's knowledge of Mohammedan mythology probably derives from

Moore's *Loves of the Angels* and *Lalla Rookh*. There is no lengthy treatment of Peruvian myth in Melville, but Manco Capac occupies a curiously prominent place as Manko in the Mardian trilogy of Gods, "Brami, Manko, and Alma" and in the portentous opening sentence of *The Confidence Man*. Melville's familiarity with the story could have come from Joel Barlow, from Prescott's *Conquest of Peru* (1847), or from William Robertson's *History of America* (1777). The Polynesian mythology throughout *Mardi* came mainly from William Ellis's *Polynesian Researches* and has been carefully discussed by Merrill R. Davis, *Melville's Mardi: A Chartless Voyage* (New Haven, Conn.: Yale University Press, 1952; repr. Archon Books, 1967).

Melville's knowledge of Gnosticism has been plausibly traced to his reading in Gibbon, Bayle, John Kitto's *A Cyclopedia of Biblical Literature,* and Andrews Norton's *Evidences of the Genuineness of the Gospels* (Boston: J. B. Russell, 1837–1844) by Thomas Vargish, "Gnostic *Mythos* in *Moby-Dick,*" *PMLA,* vol. 81 (1960), 272–277. On Melville's use of Kitto, see Vincent, *Trying-Out,* pp. 271–272. For Melville's knowledge of Persian myth, which he equated with Assyrian, Chaldean, Zoroastrian, and Babylonian mythology, the principal source seems to have been Austin Layard's *Nineveh and its Remains* (New York, 1849). See also D. M. Finkelstein, *Melville's Orienda* (New Haven: Yale University Press, 1961). In his chapter on the religion of the Assyrians, Layard observed that the "identity of the Assyrian and Persian systems appears also to be pointed out by the uncertainty which exists as to the birthplace and epoch of Zoroaster. According to the best authorities, he was a Chaldean, who introduced his doctrines into Persia and central Asia" (*Nineveh,* p. 335). Melville followed Layard in considering all these names to refer to one mythology, which plays a large part in *Moby-Dick.*

Nathalia Wright in *Melville's Use of the Bible* (New York: Octagon Books, 1969) has shown admirably how the Bible became for Melville "mythology in the most profound sense," and how in his reading, "he arrived almost inevitably at what was for him the true religious significance of the *Bible;* its mythology, or its allegorical representation of metaphysical truth" (pp. 16–17). Among the encyclopedias and handbooks from which Melville mined information on most of the above mythologies, the most important were Bayle's *Dictionary,* Chambers's *Cyclopedia,* and Kitto's *Handbook.* Isaac D'Israeli's *Curiosities of Literature* and Sir Thomas Browne's *Enquiries into Vulgar and Common Errors* also contain material on myth among their riches.

2. *Frithiof, A Norwegian Story,* from the Swedish of Esaias Tegner by R. G. Latham (London: T. Hookham, 1838), notes. Melville borrowed either this or an earlier translation from Duyckinck.

3. Layard, *Nineveh,* p. 336.

4. In his comparison of Pierre to Memnon, Melville quotes from Bacon's *De Sapientia Veterum*. The phrase "the flower of virtue cropped" on p. 135 of the Northwestern Newberry edition of *Pierre* is from Bacon's account of Memnon.

5. Alexander Bradford, *American Antiquities* (New York: Dayton and Saxton, and Boston: Saxton and Pierce, 1841), pp. 10–11. See Elizabeth Hanson, "Melville and the Polynesian-Indian," in *Extracts,* an occasional newsletter of the Melville Society, no. 17, pp. 13–14.

6. This is only one of a number of ideas put forward in Franklin's extremely interesting and groundbreaking study *The Wake of the Gods: Melville's Mythology* (Stanford, Calif.: Stanford University Press, 1963).

7. It cannot be maintained, however, that Maurice's work was "the last major Christian defense against psychological theories of mythology" as Franklin claims (*Wake of the Gods,* p. 8). Maurice is not even a contender for this honor, which might better go to Herder, Coleridge, Chateaubriand, Schelling, or Max Müller.

8. Thomas Browne, *Vulgar Errors,* in *Works,* ed. G. Keynes (London: Faber & Gwyer, 1928–31), vol. 3.

9. Pierre Bayle, *An Historical and Critical Dictionary* (London: C. Harper, etc., 1710).

10. On Paine, see *Clarel,* I, xvii; on Volney, see *Clarel,* II, xvi.

11. On Strauss, see *Clarel,* I, xli, and *Journal up the Straits,* ed. R. Weaver (New York: The Colophon, 935), p. 107. On Niebuhr, see *Journal,* p. 107, and *Clarel,* I, xxxiv.

12. See *Mardi,* ch. 132, and Tyrus Hillway, "Melville's Geological Knowledge," *American Literature,* vol. 21 (May 1949), 232–237.

13. George Grote, *A History of Greece* (London, 1846–56), vol. 1, part 1, ch. xvi, p. 321.

14. *History of Greece,* vol. 1, pp. 396–397.

15. Ibid., pp. 401–402.

16. See Theodore R. Ellis III, "Another Broadside into *Mardi,*" *American Literature,* vol. 61, no. 3 (November 1969), 419–422.

17. James Baird, *Ishmael: A Study of the Symbolic Mode in Primitivism* (Baltimore: Johns Hopkins Press, 1956; repr. New York: Harper & Brothers, 1960), p. 192.

18. See Merrell R. Davis, *Melville's Mardi: A Chartless Voyage,* and H. Bruce Franklin, *The Wake of the Gods: Melville's Mythology.* There is a good deal more myth in *Mardi* than Davis accounts for, but his discussion of Yillah is exemplary for its approach, needing only to be further pursued. Franklin's work is valuable for its awareness of the extent and range of myth in *Mardi,* but he is too schematic in his approach. He tries to make *Mardi* fit into Sir William Jones's neat enumeration of the four main causes of

myth. The trouble with this is that it distorts the proportions of *Mardi*. There are more varieties of mythmaking in *Mardi* than Sir William Jones mentions; and some of the ones Jones mentions as important are almost neglected in *Mardi*—such as philosophic or scientific myth. One might, with as much reason, look in *Mardi* for the sixteen kinds of myth mentioned by Banier, or to the kinds of myth touched on by Bayle, or in the *Encyclopédie*. Furthermore the Jonesian scheme only comes into play with chapter 65 of *Mardi*, *after* the most concentrated single mythic episode of the book—that dealing with Yillah.

    19. Celestial explanations (myths are efforts to account for natural, often astronomical, events) are first put forward in chapter 3. Starting with chapter 44, the theory that myth arises from priestly duplicity is presented. Euhemerism is introduced in chapter 55, while the link between politics and myth comes up in chapters 59 and 60. Chapter 69 provides an example of etiological myth, chapter 72 an example of popular superstition producing myth. Even indigestion as the mother of mythic devils comes up, in chapter 86. Chapter 89 shows the role of the philosopher in rejecting myth: he doesn't provide myths of early science or primitive philosophy, as we might expect. Instead, he suggests that time and study will eventually sift the true from the false in myth. Ironically enough, this is the very process which Strauss and Niebuhr undertook and which Melville was later to find so chilling. Monotheistic myth is taken up in chapters 105 and 106. Polytheistic myth in chapters 57 and 115. Saviour or intercessor gods first appear in chapter 105, false prophets in chapter 110. Chapter 119 is a minor masterpiece, complete in itself, showing how dreams give rise to myth. Chapter 120 reaches for some sort of balance, rejecting what Melville calls "a brutality of indiscriminate skepticism," just as fully as he rejects credulous or superstitious myth-mongering. Chapter 132 takes up the arguments against myth from geology and biology, while chapter 133 is a parody of the Socratic daemon or familiar. Myth and politics come up again in chapter 161, where we see how the revolutions of 1848 are working against myth and undoing the demigod kings.

    20. See for example Franklin's treatment of Yillah in *The Wake of the Gods*, pp. 45–46.

    21. *Mardi; and a Voyage Thither* (Evanston and Chicago: Northwestern University Press and The Newberry Library, 1970), ch. 41, p. 131.

    22. Ibid., ch. 43, p. 136.

    23. Ibid., pp. 137–138.

    24. Ibid., ch. 44, p. 139; ch. 120, p. 370.

    25. Ibid., ch. 44, pp. 139–140; ch. 45, p. 142.

    26. Ibid., ch. 49, p. 153.

    27. Ibid., ch. 50, p. 156; see Davis, *Melville's Mardi*, pp. 128–133.

28. *Mardi*, ch. 51, pp. 158–159.

29. Ibid., ch. 58, p. 174.

30. Novalis's *Henry of Ofterdingen* was translated by J. Owen and published in Cambridge, Mass. in 1842. There is no proof that Melville ever read it.

31. Paul Hamilton Hayne, *Poems* (Boston: Ticknor and Fields, 1855), pp. v–vi.

32. See Merrell R. Davis, "The Flower Symbolism in *Mardi*," *MLQ*, vol. 2 (December 1941), pp. 625–638. In the appendix to this article Davis gives a "Floral Dictionary" for *Mardi*, based on Frances S. Osgood's *Poetry of Flowers and Flowers of Poetry* (New York: J. C. Riker, 1841). This list of flowers and their corresponding "sentiments" or meanings is indispensable to deciphering the meaning of the flower symbolism in *Mardi*. It should therefore be noted that four of the flower entries beginning with the letter p in Davis's list have the wrong sentiment attached. A glance at Mrs. Osgood's book will show that pansy stands for "think of me," pink for "lovely and pure affection," poppy for "consolation of sleep," and privet for "prohibition." These changes will help a little in the reading of chapters 136 and 192

33. See for examples of reading *Moby-Dick* in terms of a single myth, H. B. Kulkarni, *Moby-Dick; a Hindu Avatar* (Logan: Utah State University Press, 1970); H. B. Franklin, *The Wake of the Gods*, ch. 3; Thomas Woodson, "Ahab's Greatness: Prometheus as Narcissus," *ELH*, vol. 33 (Sept. 1966), pp. 351–369; M. A. Isani, "The Naming of Fedallah in *Moby-Dick*," *American Literature*, vol. 40, pp. 280–285; C. C. Walcutt, "The Fire Symbolism in *Moby Dick*," *MLN*, vol. 59 (May 1944), 304–310; Thomas Vargish, "Gnostic Mythos in *Moby-Dick*," *PMLA*, vol. 81, pp. 272–277.

34. Julius Charles and Augustus William Hare, *Guesses at Truth* (3d ed., London, 1847), pp. 52–53. This book was charged to Lemuel Shaw (Melville's father-in-law) by the Boston Atheneaum in late June and early July of 1852, well after *Moby-Dick* was written. Whether or not Melville saw the book before this time, if he saw it at all, is not so much the issue as the correspondence between the ideas expressed in this passage and Melville's fictional practice.

35. *Moby-Dick*, ed. L. S. Mansfield and H. P. Vincent (New York: Hendricks House, 1962), ch. 1, p. 6.

36. Ibid., pp. 167–184.

37. Ibid., p. 176.

38. Ibid., p. 177.

39. Ibid., pp. 344–345, 533.

40. Ibid., p. 539.

41. *The Rise of Modern Mythology,* p. 262.

42. *Moby-Dick,* p. 540.

43. Ibid., p. 114.

44. *Israel Potter* (Constable ed. repr., New York: Russell and Russell, 1963), p. 148; *Moby-Dick,* p. 361.

45. *Moby-Dick,* p. 114.

46. Ibid.

47. Thomas Carlyle, *On Heroes, Hero-Worship and the Heroic in History* (Chapman and Hall Limited, 1904; repr., Lincoln: University of Nebraska Press, 1966), p. 32.

48. Ibid., p. 29.

49. Ibid., pp. 26–27.

50. Ibid., p. 6.

51. *Moby-Dick,* p. 73.

52. Ibid., p. 79.

53. Ibid., p. 120.

54. Ibid., p. 126.

55. Ibid., p. 145.

56. Ibid., p. 159.

57. Mme. de Staël, *Germany* (London, 1813), vol. 2, pt. 4, ch. 10, p. 388.

58. *Moby-Dick,* p. 162.

59. Ibid., p. 181.

60. Ibid.

61. Ibid., pp. 182–183.

62. Ibid., p. 183.

63. Ibid., pp. 460–461.

64. Herman Melville, *Journal up the Straits* (New York: The Colophon, 1935), pp. 107–108.

65. Herman Melville, *Clarel,* ed. W. E. Bezanson (New York, 1960), Part 1, canto 34, lines 20–27, p. 112.

66. G. P. Gooch, *History and Historians in the Nineteenth Century* (Longmans, Green and Company, 1913; new ed., Boston: Beacon Press, 1959, third printing, 1965), p. 14.

67. B. G. Niebuhr, *The History of Rome* (Cambridge and London, 1828–42) tr. by J. C. Hare and C. Thirlwall, vol. 1, p. 179.

68. Ibid., p. 180.

69. Ibid., pp. 189–190.

70. Quoted in Marghanita Laski, *George Eliot and Her World* (London: Thames and Hudson, 1973), p. 30.

71. *Journal up the Straits,* p. 48.

72. Ibid., p. 58.

73. Ibid., p. 64.

74. Ibid., p. 92; cf. Volney's *Ruins,* ch. 2.

75. Ibid., p. 104.

76. Skeptical rationalist interest in myth in post Civil War America can be seen in Robert Ingersoll's works, especially a lecture on "The Gods" in *The Gods and other Lectures* (Peoria, Ill., 1874). Dupuis's *Origin of all Religious Worship* was printed in American in 1872, as was Volney's *New Researches* in Boston in 1874. Mark Twain's contempt for myth echoes his reading in Ingersoll, Voltaire, and in Andrew D. White's *The Warfare of Science with Theology* (New York: George Braziller, 1955).

77. Merton M. Sealts, Jr., *Melville as Lecturer* (Cambridge; Harvard University Press, 1957), pp. 136–137.

78. See Vincent Scully, *The Earth, the Temple, and the Gods: Greek Sacred Architecture* (rev. ed., New York: Praeger, 1969), pp. 6–7.

79. *Melville as Lecturer,* pp. 145–146.

Selected Bibliography of Works Pertaining to Myth and Literature in America Between 1760 and 1860

The following can only be considered a highly selective listing of work bearing on the subject. Modern scholarship has been excluded, because it would have doubled or tripled the length. Modern work upon which I have relied heavily is listed in the notes, and authors' names for both notes and bibliographic entries will be found in the index. Only a few main works relating to myth by the major authors treated in the text have been listed, and much American writing on myth not discussed in the text has been included to expand the usefulness of the bibliography. English and European work important to the period or known to have been influential in America has been included, though here, too, I have been selective.

A much larger list could easily be assembled by extracting every myth-related work to be found in such useful compilations as Marion L. Kesselring, *Hawthorne's Reading, 1828-1850* (New York: The New York Public Library, 1949); Merton M. Sealts, Jr., *Melville's Reading* (Madison, Milwaukee, and London: The University of Wisconsin Press, 1966); Kenneth W. Cameron, *Ralph Waldo Emerson's Reading* (New York: Haskell House, 1966); Walter Harding, *Emerson's Library* (Charlottesville: The University Press of Virginia, 1967); K. W. Cameron, *Emerson and Thoreau as Readers* (Hartford: Transcendental Books, 1958); K. W. Cameron, *Transcendental Reading Patterns; Library charging lists for the Alcotts, James Freeman Clarke, Frederick Henry Hedge, Theodore Parker, George Ripley, Samuel Ripley of Waltham, Jones Very, and Charles Stearns Wheeler* (Hartford: Transcendental Books, 1970); the manuscript catalogue in the Boston Public Library of Theodore Parker's library (incomplete); the *Catalogue of the Library of the Late Joseph Priestley . . .* for sale by Thomas Dobson (Philadelphia, 1816); the "Catalogue of the Original Fruitlands Library," in Clara E. Sears, *Bronson Alcott's Fruitlands* (Boston and New York, 1915); David Lundberg and Henry F. May, "The Enlightened Reader in America," in *American Quarterly*, vol. 28, no. 2 (Summer 1976), 262–293; Lucille King, "Notes on Poe's Sources," in *Texas Studies in English*, no. 10 (1930), 128–134; E. L. Griggs, "Five Sources of Edgar Allan Poe's 'Pinakidia,'" in *American Literature*, vol. 1, no. 2 (May 1929), 196–199. See also the excellent bibliographies in Arthur Christy, *The Orient in American Transcendentalism* (New York: Columbia University Press, 1932, rpr. New York: Octagon

Books, 1963); Kathleen Raine and George Mills Harper, *Thomas Taylor the Platonist* (Princeton, New Jersey: Princeton University Press, 1969) and K. W. Cameron's edition of Emerson's *Indian Superstition* (Hanover, New Hampshire, 1954).

Adam, Alexander. *Roman Antiquities* [orig., 1742]. 6th ed. Glasgow: Blackie, 1835. In Emerson's library.

Adams, Hannah. *An Alphabetical Compendium of the Various Sects which have Appeared in the World from the Beginning of the Christian Era. . . .* Boston: B. Edes and Sons, 1784. A handbook on modern religions which gradually was enlarged to include ancient ones. Joseph Priestley had a copy of 3rd ed.

Adams, John, and Jefferson, Thomas. *The Adams-Jefferson Letters.* Ed. Lester J. Cappon. Chapel Hill: University of North Carolina Press, 1959. Numerous references to Volney, Dupuis, Court de Gebelin, et al.

Akenside, Mark. *The Pleasures of Imagination.* London: 1743. Discusses myth and Orphism in notes. Paradigm for Richard Alsop's *Charms of Fancy.*

Alcott, Amos Bronson. *Conversations with Children on the Gospels.* 2 vols. Boston: J. Munroe, 1836–37. Alcott's sympathy with myth.

Alcott, Amos Bronson. *The Journals of Bronson Alcott.* Ed. Odell Shepard. Boston: Little, Brown and Co., 1938.

Alcott, Amos Bronson. *The Letters of A. Bronson Alcott.* Ed. Richard L. Herrnstadt. Ames: Iowa State University Press, 1969.

Alcott, Amos Bronson. *New Connecticut.* Ed. F. B. Sanborn. Boston: Roberts Bros., 1887. Uses Bunyan's Pilgrim as model.

Alcott, Amos Bronson. "Orphic Sayings." *The Dial,* vol. 1, no. 1 (July 1840), and vol. 1, no. 3 (January 1841).

Alcott, Amos Bronson. "Pictures of thought, comprising Fables, Emblems, Parables and Allegories." Philadelphia 1834. Unpub. ms. in Houghton Library.

Alcott, Amos Bronson. "Psyche or the Breath of Childhood." Boston 1835–36. Unpub. ms. in Houghton Library.

Alcott, Amos Bronson. "Psyche an Evangele: in Four Books." Boston 1838. Unpub. ms. in Houghton Library.

Alcott, Amos Bronson. *Sonnets and Canzonets.* Boston: Roberts Bros., 1882.

Alcott, Amos Bronson. *Tablets.* Boston: Roberts Bros., 1868.

Alcott, Louisa May. *Psyche's Art.* Boston: Loring, 1868. Fiction.

Allen, Ethan [and Thomas Young]. *Reason, the Only Oracle of Man.* Bennington, Vermont: Haswell & Russell, 1784.

Allen, Paul. *Noah, a poem.* Baltimore: Cushing and Jewett, 1821.

Alsop, Richard. *The Charms of Fancy.* Ed. Theodore Dwight. New York:

Appleton, 1856. Written before 1788. Early example of American interest in Oriental myth.

Andersen, Hans Christian. *Eventyr, fortalte for Børn.* Copenhagen: 1835–44. The famous fairy-tale book.

Annet, Peter. *Examen critique de la vie . . . de St-Paul. Avec une dissertation sur St. Pierre, par feu M. Boulanger.* London [Amsterdam: M. M. Rey]: 1770. Known to Barlow, Paine.

Annet, Peter. *History of the Man after God's own heart* [orig., 1761]. Rpt. serially in *The Temple of Reason,* ed. by E. Palmer, New York: D. Driscol, 1800–03.

Anon. *Antediluvian Antiquities. Fragments of the age of Methuselah . . . Tr. by an American traveller in the East.* Boston: Munroe and Francis, 1829.

Anon. *The Decree of the Sun, or France Regenerated.* Boston: 1793. Solar myth and French Revolution.

Anon. *Elements of Mythology.* Philadelphia: Moss and Co., 1830. Handbook. At least 35 editions.

Anon. "Hymn of the Fire-Worshippers." In *The Democratic Review* (January 1838). On Persian religion.

Anon. *Instruction sur l'histoire Romaine et abregé de l'histoire poétique ou des divinités Payennes.* New York: Office Economique, 1811. Textbook.

Anon. "The Zodiac of Denderah." In *The North American Review,* vol. 8 (1823), 233–242. Mentions Dupuis prominently.

Anquetil-Duperron, A. H. *Recherches historiques et chronologiques sir l'Inde.* Paris: 1786. Volume two contains first translation of (four) authentic Upanishads.

Anquetil-Duperron, A. H. *Zend-Avesta, ouvrage de Zoroastre.* Paris: 1771. First translation.

Anthon, Charles. *A Classical Dictionary.* New York: Harper Bros., 1841. A standard work, derived from Lempriere.

Anthon, Charles. *A Manual of Grecian Antiquities.* New York: Harper and Brothers, 1852. Example of textbook treatment of myth.

Anthon, Charles. *A Manual of Greek Literature.* New York: Harper and Brothers, 1853.

Archaeologia Americana: Transactions and Collections of the American Antiquarian Society. Worcester, Mass: 1820–.

Arnim, L. A. von, and Brentano, C. *Des Knaben Wunderhorn.* Heidelberg and Frankfurt: 1806–08. Most important German romantic literary folksong collection.

Asiatick Researches. Calcutta: 1784–1839. 20 vols. Pioneer journal giving scholarly translations, history, etc. of India and East.

Ast, F. *Ideen zu einer allgemeinen Mythologie der alten Welt.* 1808. In Parker's library.

Astruc, Jean. *Conjectures upon the Original Memoires which Moses Made Use of to Compose the Book of Genesis* [orig., 1753]. Tr. by Theodore Parker in *The Scriptural Interpreter*. Vol. 6 (1836), pp. 218–226; vol. 7 (1837), pp. 23–31, 80–94. Early example of historico-textual biblical criticism.

Atlee, Samuel York. *The Religion of the Sun: A Posthumous poem of Thomas Paine*. Philadelphia: Published for the book-sellers, 1826. Parody of the deistic position, not by Paine.

Atwater, Caleb. *Descriptions of the Antiquities Discovered in the State of Ohio and other Western States*. Circleville, Ohio: 1820. Mound-builder hypothesis.

Austin, David. *The Dawn of Day, introductory to the Rising Sun, whose rays shall gild the clouds, and open to a benighted world the glowing effulgence of that Dominion, that is to be given to the people of the Saints of the Most High*. New Haven, Conn.: Read and Morse, 1800. Prophecy.

Austin, David. *The Downfall of Mystical Babylon; or, A key to the Providence of God, in the Political operations of 1793-4*. In *The Millenium, or the Thousand Years of prosperity promised to the Church of God*. Elizabeth, N.J.: Shepard Kollack, 1794. Interp. of Book of Revelation.

Austin, David. *Masonry in its Glory; or, Solomon's Temple illuminated: discerned through the flashes of prophetic light*. East Windsor, Conn.: Luther Pratt, 1799. Connects Freemasonry with myth.

Bacon, Francis. *The Wisdom of the Ancients* [orig. Latin 1609]. London: 1617. Myth as political allegory. Used by Melville.

Balfour, Walter. *An Inquiry into the Scriptural Import of the Words sheol, hades, tartarus, and gehenna: all translated hell, in the common English version*. Charlestown, Mass.: Geo. Davidson, 1824.

Ball, Benjamin West. *Elfin Land: and other Poems*. Boston and Cambridge: J. Munroe, 1851. Title poem takes up both Greek and Eastern myths.

Banier, Antoine. *The Mythology and Fables of the Ancients, Explain'd from History* [orig. 1738-40]. 4 vols. London: A. Millar, 1739-40. Advances sixteen theories for origin of myth, but emphasizes Euhemerist. Very influential.

Banier, Antoine. *Ovid's Metamorphoses in Latin and English . . . with Historical Explications of the Fables Written in French by the Abbot Banier. . . .* Amsterdam: 1732. Garth's translation.

Barlow, Joel. "The Canal: A Poem on the Application of Physical Science to Political Economy." Unfinished ms. poem circa 1802 pr. in K. R. Ball. *Social and Political Thought of Joel Barlow*. Diss. University of Wisconsin: 1967. Myth as primitive science.

Barlow, Joel. *The Vision of Columbus*. Hartford: Hudson and Goodwin, 1787. Includes "a dissertation on the genius and institutions of Manco Capec."

Bauer, Bruno. *Das Entdeckte Christentum.* Zurich and Winterthur: 1843. Post-Hegelian "atheist" attack on religion as myth.

Bauer, G. L. *Hebräische Mythologie des Alten und Neuen Testaments, mit Parallelen aus der Mythologie anderer Völker, vornehmlich der Griechen and Römer.* Leipzig: 1802. Biblical criticism.

Baur, F. C. *Die christliche Gnosis.* Tübingen: 1835.

Bayle, Pierre. *Dictionaire historique et critique.* 4 vols. Rotterdam: 1697. A major source of later skeptical attitudes toward myth and religion.

Beecher, Lyman. *Lectures on scepticism, delivered in Park Street Church, Boston, and in the Second Presbyterian Church, Cincinnati.* Cincinnati: Corey and Fairbank, 1835.

Belzoni, Giovanni. *Narrative of . . . discoveries within the pyramids. . . .* London: John Murray, 1820.

The Bhagvat-Geeta. Tr. by Charles Wilkins. London: C. Nourse, 1785; rpt. Gainesville, Fla.: Scholars' Facsimiles and Reprints, 1959.

Bible. *The Hieroglyphic Bible: or select passages in the Old and New Testaments, represented with Emblematical Figures, for the amusement of youth. . . .* Hartford: Andrus, 1825.

Bible. *The Book of Jasher; Referred to in Joshua and Second Samuel.* Tr. by Mordecai M. Noah. New York: M. M. Noah and A. S. Gould, 1840.

Bible. *A Curious Hieroglyphick Bible . . . for . . . youth.* Worcester, Mass.: Isaiah Thomas, 1788. Pictures substituted for key words.

Bible. *Das Evangelium Nicodemus. . . .* Ed. Johann G. Hohman. Reading, Pa.: Bruckman, 1819. Magic-book for Pennsylvania Germans.

Bidpai. *The Instructive and entertaining fables of Pilpay, an ancient Indian philosopher.* Newport, Rhode Island: n.p., 1784. Early interest in India; based on J. Harris's 1699 translation.

Bielfield, Jacob Friedrick. *The Elements of Universal Erudition. . . .* tr. by W. Hooper. 3 vols. London: G. Scott, 1770. Used by Poe. Vol. 3, ch. 2 is "Of Mythology."

Blackwell, Thomas. *An Enquiry into the Life and Writings of Homer.* 1735. First influential treatment of Homer in historical context; precursor of romantic views.

Blackwell, Thomas. *Letters concerning Mythology.* London: 1748. Derives Homer's mythology from Egypt and allegoric tradition. Used by Joel Barlow.

Bochart, Samuel. *Geographiae Sacrae. . . .* Cadomi: 1646. Standard work. Pagan "gods" are linguistic corruptions of biblical figures.

Bochart, Samuel. *Sacred Zoology. . . .* Vol. 1 only. Richmond: J. Martin, 1828.

Bode, Georg Heinrich. *Orpheus, poetarum Graecorum antiquissimus. . . .* Göttingen: Dieterich, 1824. Thoreau read it "partially." Orphic history and tradition.

Bode, Georg Heinrich. *Scriptores rerum mythicarum latini tres Romae nuper reperti*. Cellis: 1834. Reviewed in *The North American Review* in 1835. Bode began to teach at Harvard in 1835.

Boker, George Henry. "The Vision of the Goblet" in *The Podesta's Daughter, a dramatic sketch*. Philadelphia: A. Hart, 1852. On Bacchus.

Bos, Lambert. *Antiquities of Greece*. London: T. Davies, 1772.

Boulanger, Nicholas A. *L'antiquité dévoilée par ses usages, où Examen critique des principales opinions, cérémonies et institutions religieuses et politiques des differens peuples de la Terre*. Amsterdam: 1766. Derives all myth from traditions after the Flood.

Boulanger, Nicolas-Antoine [Holbach, Paul Henri?]. *Christianity Unveiled; being an examination of the principles and effects of the Christian religion*. Tr. by W. M. Johnson. New York: The Columbia Press, 1795. Rpt. serially in *The Temple of Reason*, ed. Elihu Palmer. New York: D. Driscoll, 1800–1803. Disc. in J. H. Payne, "William Martin Johnson," *Democratic Review*, vol. 2 (1838).

Boulanger, Nicolas Antoine. See Annet, Peter.

Brackenridge, H. H. "On the population and tumuli of the aborigines of North America." In *Transactions of the American Philosophical Society* (1818). Mound-builder hypothesis.

Bradford, Alexander W. *American Antiquities and researches into the origin of the red race*. New York: Dayton and Saxton, 1841. Used by Melville.

Brand, John. *Observations on Popular antiquities of Great Britain*. . . . [orig. 1777]. 3 vols. 3rd edition, arranged, revised and greatly enlarged by Sir H. Ellis . . . with further additions by J. O. Halliwell. London: Bohn, 1848–1855. Early folklore compendium. Used by Thoreau.

Broughton, Thomas. *An Historical Dictionary of All Religions*. London: 1742. Handbook. Used by Hannah Adams.

Browne, Thomas. *Pseudodoxia epidemica; or Enquiries into very many received tenents*. . . . London: 1646. Sometimes titled *Vulgar Errors*.

Bruce, James. *An interesting narrative of . . . the travels . . . into Abyssinia*. . . . London: 1790. Rpt. Boston, 1798.

Brugsch, Heinrich. *A History of Egypt under the Pharoaohs Derived entirely from the monuments*. . . . [orig., 1857]. Tr. and ed. by Philip Smith. London: John Murray, 1879. Used by Whitman.

Bryant, Jacob. *A New System, or an Analysis of ancient mythology: wherein an attempt is made to divest tradition of fable, and to reduce the truth to its original purity*. . . . 3 vols. London: 1774. Traces myth to descendants of Ham. See Wm. Holwell. Influential for Webster, Poe, and many others.

Bryant, William Cullen. *Lectures on Mythology*, 1827–1831 In Silber, Robert Bernard, *William Cullen Bryant's "Lectures on Mythology."* Diss. State University of Iowa, 1962.

Bulfinch, Thomas. *The Age of Fable.* Boston: 1855. Influential Victorian handbook.

Bulfinch, Thomas. *Hebrew Lyrical History; or Select Psalms.* . . . Boston: Crosby Nichols, and Co., 1853. Influenced by Lowth.

Bunsen, Christian K. J. *Outlines of the Philosophy of Universal History, applied to language and religion.* 2 vols. London: Longman, Brown, 1854. Used by Whitman.

Bunsen, Christian K. J. *Egypt's Place in Universal History* . . . [orig., 1845–57]. 5 vols. London: Longmans, Brown, 1848–67. Used by Whitman.

Buttman, Philip. *Greek Grammar . . . for the Use of Schools.* Tr. by Edward Everett, ed. by George Bancroft and George H. Bode. Boston: Everett, 1822.

Carlyle, Thomas. *The French Revolution; a history* [orig., 1837]. Rpt. Boston: 1838.

Carlyle, Thomas. *On Heroes and Hero-Worship and the Heroic in History.* London: Chapman, 1840. Opening lecture is on Odin. Important for Emerson, Thoreau and Whitman.

Chambaud, Louis. *Fables Choisis, a l'usage des enfans* [orig., 1765]. Rpt. Philadelphia: Charles Cist, 1784. Aesopian. Many editions.

Chambers, Ephraim. *Cyclopedia, or Universal Dictionary of Arts and Sciences.* London: 1728. Treats myth extensively as "fable," literary plot, etc.

Chambers, Robert. *Vestiges of the Natural History of Creation* [orig., 1844]. Rpt. New York: 1845. Science vs. myth.

Champollion, J. F. *Précis du Système Hiéroglyphique des anciens Egyptiens.* 2 vols. Paris: 1824. Key work on landmark decipherment. Parker read Champollion in 1836.

Channing, E. T. *Lectures Read to the Seniors in Harvard College.* Ed. by Dorothy I. Anderson and Waldo W. Braden. Carbondale: Southern Illinois University Press, 1969.

Channing, William Ellery (1817–1901). *Conversations in Rome; between an Artist, a Catholic, and a Critic.* Boston: W. Crosby and H. P. Nichols, 1847. Includes treatment of symbolic nature of ancient Roman religion.

Channing, W. H. *Ernest the Seeker.* Ch. 1, *The Dial*, vol. 1, no. 1, (July 1840), ch. 2, vol. 1, no. 2 (October 1840). Only two chapters written. Discusses ancient myth and religion.

Chardin, Sr. John. *The Travels of Sir John Chardin into Persia and the East Indies.* London: M. Pitt, 1686. Early source for Persian religion. Used by Paine.

Chateaubriand, René de. *Le Génie du Christianisme.* Paris: 1802. Romantic Christianity. In Parker's library.

Child, Mrs. Lydia Maria Francis. *The Progress of Religious Ideas, Through Successive Ages.* New York: C. S. Francis and Co., 1855. Comparative myth and religion.

Chivers, Thomas Holley. *Virginalia; or, Songs of my Summer Nights.* Philadelphia: Lippincott, Grambo and Co., 1853. Norse, Greek myths, Orphics.

Colden, Cadwallader. *The History of the Five Indian Nations. . . .* New York: W. Bradford, 1727. Iroquois.

Colebrook, H. T. "On the Philosophy of the Hindus." In *Transactions of the Royal Asiatic Society.* 1823–27. His essays collected in *Misc. Essays* 1873.

Colebrook, H. T. "On the Religious Ceremonies of the Hindous and Brahmans especially." In *Asiatick Researches.* Vol. 5, 1799. Important early studies of Vedas.

Coleridge, Hartley. "On Poetical Use of Heathen Mythology." Written 1822. Pub. in *Essays and Marginalia.* Ed. D. Coleridge. London: 1851.

Coleridge, Henry Nelson. *Introductions to the Study of the Greek Classic Poets.* London: J. Murray, 1830. Read by Thoreau, Poe.

Coleridge, Samuel Taylor. *Aids to Reflection,* with a preliminary essay by James Marsh. Burlington, Vermont: 1840. Important book for American Transcendentalists.

Constant, Benjamin. *De la religion considérée dans sa source, ses formes et ses développements.* 5 vols. Paris: 1824–31. French eclectic school. Extracts ("The Progressive development of Religious Ideas," etc.) in George Ripley, *Specimens of Foreign Standard Literature,* vol. 2. Boston: Hilliard, Gray and Co., 1838.

Constant, Benjamin. *Du Polythéisme romain considéré dans ses rapports avec la philosophie grecque et la religion chrétienne.* 2 vols. Paris: 1833. French eclectic school.

Copway, G. *The Traditional History and Characteristic Sketches of the Ojibway Nation.* Boston: Benjamin B. Mussey & Co., 1851. Chapter 13 concerns myth and religion. Copway was a chief of the Ojibway nation.

Cottle, Amos. *Icelandic Poetry, or the Edda of Saemund,* tr. into English verse. . . . Bristol: N. Biggs, 1797. Early Nordic interest.

Court de Gebelin, Antoine. *Monde primitif analysé et comparé avec le monde moderne.* Paris: 1773. Read by John Adams, Parker.

Creuzer, F. *Symbolik und Mythologie der alten Völker. . . .* Heidelberg: 1810. German romantic *cause célèbre;* India as source of Greek myth and mystery religions. The French translation used by Parker and Fuller is J. D. Guigniaut, *Religions de l'antiquité considérées principalement dans leurs formes symboliques et mythologiques.* 4 vols. Paris: Trenttel et Wurtz, 1825–51.

Cudworth, Ralph. *The True Intellectual System of the Universe* [orig., 1678]. Rpt. London: R. Priestley, 1820. In Emerson's library.

Darlington, William. *A Catechism of Mythology.* . . . Baltimore: W. Lucas, 1832. Handbook.

D'Arusmont, Frances Wright. *Course of Popular Lectures.* . . . New York: Office of the Free Enquirer, 1829. Radical rationalism.

D'Arusmont, Frances Wright. *A Few Days in Athens.* . . . [orig., 1822]. Rpt. Boston: J. P. Mendum, 1850. Conversations on Epicurean philosophy. Important for Whitman.

Dasent, George W. *The Prose or Younger Edda.* . . . London: Pickering, 1842. In Emerson's library.

Davies, Edward. *Celtic Researches.* London: 1804. Celts descended from Patriarchs.

Davies, Edward. *The Mythology and Rites of the British Druids.* . . . London: J. Booth, 1809. Used by Emerson.

Davis, Andrew Jackson. *Arabula; or the Divine Guest, containing a new collection of Gospels.* Boston: W. White, 1867. Contains Gospels according to St. Ralph, St. Margaret, and St. Theodore, et al.

David, Andrew Jackson. *The Principles of Nature, Her Divine Revelations, and a voice to mankind.* New York: S. S. Lyon and W. Fishbough, 1847.

De Brosses, Charles. *Du culte des dieux fétiches, ou Parallèle de l'ancienne religion de l'Egypte avec la religion actuelle de Nigritie.* 1760. First claim for fetishism as first stage in all religions. In Parker's library.

Demoustier, Charles A. *Lettres à Emilee, sur la mythologie.* Paris: 1790–99. Tr. and pub. serially in *The Polyanthos,* Boston, 1812–14. Children's handbook. Seen by Hawthorne?

Dermott, Laurence. *Ahiman Rezon* . . . [orig., 1756]. Rpt. New York: Southwick and Hardcastle, 1805. Freemasonry.

De Wette, Wilhelm M. L. *A Critical and Historical Introduction to the Canonical Scriptures of the Old Testament* [orig., 1806–7]. 2 vols. Tr. Theodore Parker. Boston: Little, Brown, 1843.

D'Israeli, Isaac. *Curiosities of Literature.* . . . London, Philadelphia: Gibbons, 1791. Myth anecdotes. Read by Melville.

Drummond, Sir William. *The Oedipus Judaicus.* London: 1811. Old Testament as astronomical allegory. Read by Parker, 1834.

Dulaure, J. A. *Des cultes qui ont précédé et amené l'idolatrie où l'adoration des figures humaines.* Paris: 1805. Fertility interpretation of myth and religion.

Dupuis, Charles. *The Origin of all Religious Worship* [orig., 1795]. New Orleans: 1872. Rationalist derivation of myth from zodiac and sun worship. Influential in America from Paine and Barlow on.

Dwight, Mary Ann. *Grecian and Roman Mythology, with an introductory notice by . . . T. Lewis . . .* New York: 1849. Handbook.

Dwight, Timothy. *A dissertation on the History, Eloquence, and Poetry of the Bible.* New Haven: Thomas and Samuel Green, 1772. Rpt. in *The Major Poems of Timothy Dwight.* Ed. McTaggart and Bottorff. Gainesville, Fla.: Scholars' Facsimiles and Reprints, 1969. Argument parallels Lowth's.

Dwight, Timothy. *The Duty of Americans, at the Present Crisis. . . .* New Haven: Thomas and Samuel Green, 1798. Strongly anti-Deist.

Dwight, Timothy. *Greenfield Hill: a poem. . . .* New York: Childs, Swaine, 1794. Mentions Lowth.

Dwight, Timothy. *The Nature, and Dangers, of Infidel Philosophy. . . .* New Haven: Bunce, 1798. Comments on rationalist mythography.

Eaton, Charlotte A. *Rome, in the Nineteenth Century. . . .* Edinburgh: Constable, 1820. Guidebook. Used by Hawthorne.

Eichhorn, J. G. *Einleitung in das Alte Testament.* 1780–82. Seminal work in "Higher" biblical criticism.

Eichhorn, J. G. *Einleitung in das Neue Testament.* 5 vols. Leipzig: 1804–27. "Higher" biblical criticism.

Eichhorn, J. G. *J. G. E.'s Urgeschichte.* Ed. J. P. Gabler. Altdorf and Nürnberg: 1790–93. Important early work in "Higher" biblical criticism, written in 1775.

Ellis, William. *Polynesian Researches. . . .* 2 vols. London: 1829. Early standard work. Used by Thoreau and Melville.

Emerson, Ralph Waldo. *Early Lectures.* Vol. I. Ed. by S. E. Whicher and R. E. Spiller. Cambridge, Mass.: Harvard University Press, 1959.

Emerson, Ralph Waldo. *Indian Superstition.* Ed. Kenneth Cameron, with a dissertation on Emerson's Orientalism at Harvard. Hanover, N.H.: Friends of Dartmouth Library, 1954.

Emerson, Ralph Waldo. *The Journals and Miscellaneous Notebooks.* Ed. by William H. Gilman, Alfred R. Ferguson, et al. Cambridge, Mass.: Harvard University Press, 1960.

Emerson, Ralph Waldo. *Journals of Ralph Waldo Emerson.* Ed. Edward Waldo Emerson and Waldo Emerson Forbes. 10 vols. Boston and New York: Houghton Mifflin, 1909–14.

Emerson, Ralph Waldo. *Letters from Ralph Waldo Emerson to a Friend, 1838–1853.* Ed. Charles Eliot Norton. Boston: Houghton Mifflin, 1899.

Emerson, Ralph Waldo. *Representative Men.* Boston: Phillips, Sampson, 1850.

English, George B. *The Grounds of Christianity Examined. . . .* Boston: 1813. Extreme rationalist. Knows Michaelis, etc.

Everett, Edward. *Synopsis of a course of lectures, on the history of Greek Literature.* N.p.: 18——. Shows Everett's knowledge of Eichhorn, Creuzer, Jones, Wolf, Blackwell, Heyne, Wood, et al.

Faber, G. S. *A General . . . View of the Prophecies, relative to the Conversion, Restoration, Union, and Future Glory of the Houses of Judah and Israel.* Boston: Wm. Andrews, 1809.

Faber, G. S. *A Dissertation on the Mysteries of the Cabiri; or, the Great Gods of Phenicia, Samothrace, Egypt, Troas, Greece, Italy, and Crete. . . .* Oxford: 1803. Traces all myth back to Noah and ark. Used by Noah Webster, Albert Pike.

Faber, G. S. *A Dissertation on the Prophecies. . . .* Boston: Andrews and Cummings, 1808.

Faber, G. S. *The Origin of Pagan Idolatry. . . .* 3 vols. London: 1816. Myth as debased types of Noah and ark.

Fairbairn, Patrick. *The Typology of Scripture.* Edinburgh: 1845. Revival of Christian "type" interpretation.

Fairfield, Sumner Lincoln. *The Last Night of Pompeii.* New York: Elliot and Palmer, 1832. Verse romance. Deals with pagan religion.

Farmer, Hugh. *An Essay on the Demoniacs of the New Testament.* London: G. Robinson, 1775. Fell-Farmer dispute over demoniac possession. Known to John Adams, Parker.

Felton, C. C. "Classic Mythology." In *North American Review,* no. 89 (October 1835), 327–348. Sympathetic essay on ancient myth as religion.

Felton, C. C. "Orphic Poetry." In *North American Review.* Vol. XXI, New Series, vol. XII (1825), 388–397. Review of a book by G. H. Bode.

Fénelon, Francois de Salignac de L. Mothe. *Télémaque* [orig., 1699]. Rpt. in French in Philadelphia: 1784. Romance about the son of Odysseus. An unpub. Eng. translation was done in America by Elizabeth Graeme in the eighteenth century.

Feuerbach, Ludwig Andreas. *The Essence of Christianity* [orig., 1841]. Tr. by George Eliot. New York: C. Blanchard, 1855. Post-Hegelian materialist transforming of theology into anthropology. Myth as nature worship. In Emerson's library.

Flaxman, John. *Illustrations of Homer's Iliad, engraved from the Compositions of John Flaxman. . . .* Boston: Hilliard, Gray and Co., 1833.

Follen, Eliza. *Gammer Grethel. . . .* Boston: Munroe, 1840. From Grimm's fairy tales. Used by Hawthorne.

Fontenelle, Bernard de. *De l'origine des Fables.* 1724. Brief, sophisticated, many-sided rationalist overview of myth.

Fourmont, Étienne. *Réflexions critiques sur les histoires des anciens peuples,*

Chaldéens, Hébreux, Phénicians, Egyptiens, Grec, etc. . . . Paris: 1735. Gods as debased Patriarchs, etymological method.

Fuller, Margaret. "Goethe." In *The Dial,* vol. 2, no. 1 (July 1841). Contains her trans. of his poem "The God-Like."

Fuller, Margaret. *Margaret and her Friends, or Ten Conversations with Margaret Fuller upon the Mythology of the Greeks.* . . . reported by Caroline W. Healy Dall. Boston: Roberts Bros., 1895. Conversations held in 1841.

Fuller, Margaret. *Memoirs of Margaret Fuller Ossoli.* 2 vols. Ed. James Freeman Clarke, Ralph Waldo Emerson, et al. Boston: Phillips, Sampson, 1851.

Fuller, Margaret. *Woman in the Nineteenth Century.* New York: Greeley, 1845.

Fuller, Margaret. *Works.* 5 vols. MS, Houghton Library.

Fuller, Margaret. *The Writings of Margaret Fuller.* Ed. and sel. by Mason Wade. New York: Viking, 1941.

Gallaher, James. *The Pilgrimage of Adam and David, with Sketches of their Heavenly Employment.* Cincinnati: Derby, Bradley and Co., 1846. Bunyanesque-Miltonic Christian allegory.

Gannett, Ezra, ed. *The Scriptural Interpreter,* vol. 1, 1831 periodical. Work by Theodore Parker, et al. "Higher" criticism in America.

Garcilaso de la Vega (the Inca). *The Royal Commentaries of Peru.* Tr. by Sir Paul Rycaut. London: S. Heyrick, 1688. Main source for Peruvian mythology.

Gérando, Joseph Marie de. *Histoire comparée des systèmes de philosophie.* Paris: 1804. New edition 1822 shows strong influence of Creuzer; influenced Emerson.

Gérando, Joseph Marie de. *Self Education; or, the Means and Art of Moral Progress.* Tr. by Elizabeth P. Peabody. Boston: Carter and Hendee, 1832.

Gessner, Salomon. *The Death of Abel* [orig., 1758]. Tr. by Mrs. Collyer. Philadelphia: Robert Johnson, 1806. Widely read Miltonic poem.

Gibbon, Edward. *Essai sur l'étude de la litérature.* London: 1761. Includes rationalist account of mythic origins.

Gillies, John. *The History of Ancient Greece* [orig., 1786]. Rpt. in 4 vols. Philadelphia: J. V. Humphreys, 1882. Important book for Emerson.

Gliddon, George. *Ancient Egypt.* New York: J. Winchester, 1844. Clear popular account of impact of Champollion on ideas about Egyptian myth. Read by Poe, Whitman.

Gobineau, Joseph Arthur, comte de. *The Moral and Intellectual Diversity of Races.* . . . [orig., 1853–55]. Tr. by H. Hotz. Philadelphia: J. B.

Lippincott, 1856. Argument for racism partly based on theories of primal "blood" and nation.

Godwin, William. *Baldwin's Fables.* New Haven: J. Babcock and Son, 1819. Copy in Melville's home.

Goethe, Johann Wolfgang von. *The Metamorphosis of Plants.* Partially tr. in *The Gardener's Chronicle,* vol. 4, 1844, 117, 113. Original, in German, important for Emerson, Thoreau.

Goodrich, S. G. *A Book of Mythology, for Youth.* Boston: Richardson, Lord and Holbrook, 1832. Handbook.

Goodrich, S. G. *Fairy Land and other Sketches for Youth.* Boston: J. Munroe and Co., 1844.

Görres, Johann von. *Mythengeschichte der asiatischen Welt.* 2 vols. Heidelberg: Mohr, 1810.

Gray, Thomas (1803-1849). *The Vestal: or, A Tale of Pompeii.* Boston: Gray and Bowen, 1830. Christianity compared to pagan religion, Isis etc.

Greene, G. W. "Visit to the Dead in the Catacombs of Rome." In *Harper's Magazine,* vol. 10, no. 59 (April 1855). Contrasts paganism and Christianity.

Greenough, Horatio. *The Travels, Observations and Experience of a Yankee Stonecutter, Part I.* New York: G. P. Putnam, 1852. Includes comments on ancient gods.

Greppo, J. G. H. *Essay on the hieroglyphic system of M. Champollion Jun. and on the advantages which it offers to Sacred Criticism.* Tr. by Isaac Stuart. Boston: Perkins and Marvin, 1830. Has preface by Moses Stuart and appendix on Egyptian mythology.

Grimm, J. *Deutsche Mythologie.* Göttingen: 1835. Folklore as key to "Germanic," i.e., non-Nordic, myth. In Parker's library.

Grimm, W. and J. *Kinder—und Hausmärchen.* Berlin: 1812–15.

Grote, George. *A History of Greece.* 12 vols. London: 1846–56. See esp. Vol. I, "Grecian mythical vein compared with . . . modern Europe." Standard work; views on myth influenced by Lobeck. Read by Melville.

Hall, Robert. *Modern Infidelity considered with respect to its influence on Society . . .* [orig., 1800]. Rpt. Charlestown, Mass.: Etheridge, 1801.

Hammer-Purgstall, Joseph. *Ancient Alphabets and Hieroglyphic Characters Explained.* London: Bulmer, 1806. Pre-Champollion.

Hare, Julius Charles. *Guesses at Truth. . . .* London: J. Taylor, 1827. 3rd ed. Among Melville's books.

Hart, J. W. *The New Pantheon.* 1809. Handbook.

Haven, Samuel F. *Archaeology of the United States, or, Sketches Historical and*

Bibliographical, of the progress of Information and opinion respecting vestiges of Antiquity in the United States. Washington, D.C.: Smithsonian Contributions to Knowledge, 1855. Useful contemporaneous assessments of Ethan Smith, Samuel Mitchell, C. S. Rafinesque, Josiah Priest, etc.

Hawthorne, Nathaniel. "Drowne's Wooden Image." In *Mosses from an Old Manse.* New York: Wiley & Putnam, 1846. Boston-plated Ovid.

Hawthorne, Nathaniel. "The Maypole of Merry Mount." In *Twice Told Tales.* Boston: American Stationers, 1837. Metamorphosis-myth.

Hawthorne, Nathaniel. *The Marble Faun.* Columbus: Ohio State University Press, 1968. The myths of paganism and the ideas of Christianity.

Hawthorne, Nathaniel. *A Wonder Book and Tanglewood Tales.* Columbus: Ohio State University Press, 1972. Greek myths retold as fairy stories for children.

Hayne, Paul Hamilton. "The Temptation of Venus." In *Poems.* Boston: Ticknor and Fields, 1855. Version of Tannhäuser legend. Analogue to Melville's *Mardi.*

Hayne, Paul Hamilton. "Ancient Fables." In *Sonnets, and other Poems.* Charleston: Harper, Calvo, 1857. On decline of pagan myths.

Heeren, Arnold H. *Reflections on the politics of ancient Greece* [orig., 1804–5]. Tr. by George Bancroft. Boston: Cummings, Hilliard, 1824. Harvard textbook. 1st ed. in Emerson's library.

Hegel, G. W. F. "Introduction to the Philosophy of History." In F. Hedge, *Prose Writers of Germany.* Philadelphia: Carey and Hart, 1848.

Hennell, Charles C. *An Inquiry Concerning the Origins of Christianity.* London: 1838. "Higher" biblical criticism. Reviewed by Parker in *The Dial,* vol. 4, no. 2 (October 1843).

Herder, J. G. *The Spirit of Hebrew Poetry* [orig., 1782–83]. Tr. by James Marsh. Burlington, Vermont: E. Smith, 1833. Important preromantic document: Bible as "sublime" poetry, myth and poetry as "symbols" of truth. Important for Emerson.

Herder, J. G. *Outlines of a Philosophy of the History of Man* [orig., 1784–91]. Tr. by T. Churchill. London: J. Johnson, 1800. Seminal work; mankind's cultural-spiritual development from beginnings. Used by Emerson.

Herder, J. G. "Metempsychosis." In F. Hedge, *Prose Writers of Germany.* Philadelphia: Carey and Hart, 1848.

Herma, John. *The Spirits of Odin, or the Father's Curse.* New York: Collins and Hannay, 1826. Rationalist romance.

Hermann, Gottfried. *Uber das Wesen und die Behandlung der Mythologie. Ein Brief an Herrn Hofrath Creuzer.* Leipzig: 1819. In Parker's library.

Heyne, C. G. "Sermonis mythici sive symbolici interpretatio ad causas et rationes ductasque inde regulas revocate." In *Comm. Soc. Reg. Gott.,* vol. XVI, 1807. Primitive philosophy and history proceed from myth.

"Hieroglyphics." In *The North American Review*. Vol. 32 (1831), 95–126. Learned review essay on Greppo.

"Hieroglyphs." In *Encyclopaedia Americana*. 1836. Has section on Egyptian mythology.

Higginson, Thomas W. *The Sympathy of Religions*. Boston: 1871. Written 1855. Comparative religion.

Hillard, George S. "Thomas Crawford: A Eulogy." *Atlantic Monthly* (July 1809). Has letter from Crawford to sister on his "Orpheus."

Hirst, Henry B. *The Coming of the Mammoth, The funeral of time. . . .* Boston: Phillips and Sampson, 1845. Mound-builder hypothesis. Also has poem "Astarte," known to Poe.

Holbach, Paul Henri, Baron d'. *La Contagion sacrée, où Histoire naturelle de la superstition, ouvrage traduit de l'Anglois*. London: 1768. Terror as origin of religious superstition.

Holbach, Paul Henri, Baron d'. *The System of Nature . . .* [orig., 1770]. Tr. by H. D. Robinson. New York: Matsell, 1835. Rationalist-pantheist nature mythology.

Holwell, William. *A mythological . . . Dictionary; extracted from the Analysis of Ancient Mythology*. London: C. Dilly, 1793. A popular version of Jacob Bryant's work.

Humboldt, Alexander von. *Researches, concerning the Institutions and Monuments of the ancient inhabitants of America. . . .* [orig., 1810]. 2 vols. Tr. by H. M. Williams. London: 1814.

Hunt,Gaillard. *The Seal of the United States: how it was developed and adopted*. Washington: Department of State, 1892. Symbolic intentions of designers of U. S. Seal.

Ingersoll, Robert. *The Gods and other Lectures*. Peoria, Ill.: 1874. Rationalist.

Irving, Christopher. *A Catechism of Mythology, being a compendious history of the heathen gods, goddesses and heroes. Designed chiefly as an introduction to the study of the ancient classics*. New York: F. and R. Lockwood, 1822.

Irving, Washington. *Mahomet and his Successors*. 2 vols. New York: G. P. Putnam's Sons, 1949–50.

Jablonski, Paul. *Pantheon Aegyptiorum*. Frankfurt: 1750–52. In Fruitlands library.

James, Henry, Sr. *The Nature of Evil*. New York: D. Appleton and Co., 1855. Swedenborgian, Fourierist.

Jarves, James Jackson. *The Art Idea*. New York: Hurd and Houghton, 1864. Has a chapter on myth.

Jarves, James Jackson. *History of the Hawaiian or Sandwich islands, embracing their antiquities, mythology, legends, . . .* Boston: Tappan and Dennet, 1843.

Jarves, James Jackson. *Kiana; a tradition of Hawaii.* Boston and Cambridge: J. Munroe and Co., 1857.

Jarvis, Samuel Farmar. *A discourse on the religion of the Indian tribes of North America.* New York: C. Wiley & Co., 1820.

Jefferson, Thomas. *The Jefferson Bible; The Life and morals of Jesus of Nazareth.* Ed. O. I. A. Roche. New York: Clarkson N. Potter, 1964.

Jones, Sir William. *Dissertations on Asia.* Dublin: 1793. Widely read in America.

Jones, Sir William. *Institutes of Hindu Law: or the Ordinances of Menu.* Calcutta: Printed by the order of government, 1794. Important book for Thoreau. MS synopsis by Francis Lieber in Huntington Library.

Jones, Sir William. "On the Gods of Greece, Italy and India." Written 1785, pub. in *Asiatick Researches,* vol. 1 (1799). Excerpts pub. by Noah Webster in *The Christian Disciple,* orig. series, vol. II (1814), 343–344.

Jones, Sir William. *The Works of Sir William Jones.* London: G. G. and J. Robinson, 1799.

Judd, Sylvester. *Margaret, a Tale of the Real and the Ideal.* Boston: Phillips, Sampson, and Co., 1851. Orphic, idealist romance.

Kalevala. Tr. by Anton Schiefner. St. Petersburg: 1849.

Kalidasa. *Sacontalá.* Tr. by Sir William Jones [orig., 1789]. Rpt. in *The Monthly Anthology.* Boston: 1803–05.

Keightley, Thomas. *The Fairy Mythology.* London: W. H. Ainsworth, 1828. Grimm's folklore theories applied to fairy tales.

Keightley, Thomas. *The Mythology of Ancient Greece and Italy. . . .* London: Whitaker, Treacher, 1831. Standard history modelled on methods of German historical mythic school, K. O. Müller, et al. Many American editions.

Keith, Alexander. *Evidence of the Truth of the Christian Religion.* 3rd ed., 1828. Rpt. New York: J. and J. Harper, 1832. Prophecy. Influenced Poe.

Kingsley, Charles. *The Heroes; or Greek Fairy Tales for my Children.* London: Ward, Loch, 1855. Popular, influential.

Kircher, Athanasius. *Oedipus Aegiptiacus. Hoc est, Universalis hieroglyphicae veterum doctrinae temporum iniuria obolitae instauratio.* Rome: 1652-54. Famous thesis about Egyptian origins for Greek myth. Discussed in Gliddon.

Kitto, John, ed. *A Cyclopaedia of Biblical Literature.* 2 vols. Edinburgh: A & C Block, 1845. Used by Melville.

Klaproth, J. H. *Grammaire générale. Théorie des signes; apercu de l'origine des diverses écritures de l'ancien monde.* [Paris: 1823?]. Parker read Klaproth.

Kneeland, Abner. *The Columbian Miscellany.* Keene, New Hampshire: 1804. Free thought.

Kneeland, Abner. *National Hymns . . . for the use of those who are "Slaves to no Sect."* Boston: Office of the Investigator, 1832. Mythologizing Reason and Nature.

Kneeland, Abner. *A Review of the Evidence of Christianity,* 1829. 3rd ed. Boston: Office of the Investigator, 1831. Rationalist.

Koran. *The Koran, commonly called the Alcoran of Mahomet.* Springfield: Isaiah Thomas, Jr., 1806. Andre DuRyer's translation.

Lafitau, Joseph. *Moeurs des Sauvages Ameriquains comparées aux moeurs des premiers temps.* 2 vols. Paris: 1724. Influential comparison of Iroquois to ancient pagans. Known to Jefferson, Thoreau, Parkman.

Lamb, Charles. *The Adventures of Ulysses.* London: T. Davison, 1808. Myths for children.

La Motte-Fouqué, Friedrich. *Undine* [orig., 1811]. Tr. by Elizabeth Peabody as *The Water Spirit.* 2nd ed. Boston: Stimpson and Clapp, 1833. Popular romance, influenced Hawthorne.

Layard, Sir Austin H. *Nineveh and its Remains.* New York: Putnam's, 1849. Layard's work at Nineveh was widely noticed from 1847 on in *The Knickerbocker, The North American Review, The Literary World,* etc.

Lempriere, John. *Bibliotheca Classica; or, a Classical Dictionary. . . .* Reading, England: 1788. Most popular scholarly handbook. Used by Emerson, Thoreau. Basis of Anthon's *Classical Dictionary.*

Lieber, Francis. *Reminiscences of an intercourse with Mr. Niebuhr, The Historian of Rome. . . .* Philadelphia: Carey, Lea, 1835. Lieber (edited *Encyclopaedia Americana*) an American exponent of Niebuhr.

Linn, John Blair. *The Death of Washington. . . .* Philadelphia: Ormod, 1800.

Lobeck, C. A. *Aglaophamus: sive, de theologiae mysticae Graecorum causis. . . .* 1829. Massive rebuttal of Creuzer's *Symbolik;* unsympathetic to romantic mythology. In Parker's library.

Locke, John. *The Reasonableness of Christianity, as delivered in the Scriptures.* London: 1695. Influential Deist tract.

Longfellow, Henry W. *The Song of Hiawatha.* Boston: Ticknor and Fields, 1855. American Indian Mythology from Schoolcraft, Kalevala meter.

Longfellow, Henry W. *Hyperion; a romance.* New York: Colman, 1839. Mythico-idealist romance.

Lönnrot, Elias. *Kalevala.* Helsinki: 1835. Finnish mythology. In Parker's library.

Lord, Henry. *A Display of two forraigne sects in the East Indies viz: the sect of the Banians . . . and the Sect of the Persees. . . .* London: 1630. Early source for near-Eastern religion. Used by Paine.

Lowth, Robert. *The Sacred Poetry of the Hebrews* [orig., 1753]. Tr. by G. Gregory and ed. by Calvin E. Stowe. Boston: Crocker and Brewster, 1829. Landmark treatment of Scripture as poetry. Read by Emerson, Parker.

Ludvigh, Samuel. *Reden, Vorlesungen und Prosaische Aufsaetze, im Gebiete der Religion, Philosophie und Geschichte.* Baltimore: Verlag des Verfassers, 1850. Radical rationalism.

Macpherson, James. *The Genuine Remains of Ossian.* Ed. Patrick MacGregor. London: Smith, Elder and Co., 1841. Edition used by Thoreau.

Macpherson, James. *Fingal: an Ancient Epic Poem in Six books . . . composed by Ossian the son of Fingal.* London: T. Becket and P. A. De Hondt, 1762.

Macpherson, James. *Fragments of Antient Poetry collected in the Highlands of Scotland and translated from the Gaelic or Erse Language.* Edinburgh: G. Hamilton and J. Balfour, 1760. Dubious mythic Celtic epic.

Macpherson, James. *Temora, an Ancient Epic Poem.* London: T. Becket and P. A. De Hondt, 1763.

Mallet, Paul Henri. *Northern Antiquities* [orig., 1755–56]. Tr. by Thomas Percy. London: 1770. Frequently reprinted standard source for Nordic myth. Used by Bulfinch.

Marx, Karl. *Die Deutsche Ideologie.* 1845–46. Co-author, F. Engels. Posthumous publication; myth subsumed into ideology.

Mather, Cotton. *Magnalia Christi Americana.* London: T. Parkhurst, 1702. Promulgates Bochartian view of myth.

Mather, Samuel (1626–1671). *The Figures or Types of the Old Testament* [orig., 1683]. Rpt. Philadelphia: A. Tower, 1834. Revival of typological interpretation.

Mathews, Cornelius. *Behemoth: A Legend of the Mound Builders.* Boston: Weeks, Jordan and Co., 1839.

Maurice, Thomas. *Indian antiquities. . . .* 7 vols. London: 1793–1800. Reduced Indic myth to Christian Trinity.

Mayo, R. *A New System of Mythology.* 3 vols. Philadelphia: T. S. Manning, 1815–19. Handbook. Plagiarism of Banier.

Melville, Herman. *Clarel* [orig., 1876]. Ed. by Walter E. Bezanson. Rpt. New York: Hendricks House, Inc., 1960.

Melville, Herman. *The Confidence-Man: His Masquerade* [orig., 1857]. Ed.

Elizabeth S. Foster. Rpt. New York: Hendricks House, Inc., 1954.

Melville, Herman. *Israel Potter, His Fifty Years of Exile* [orig., 1854]. Rpt. New York: Russell and Russell, 1963.

Melville, Herman. *Journal Up the Straits.* Ed. by Raymond Weaver. New York: The Colophon, 1935.

Melville, Herman. *Mardi, and A Voyage Thither* [orig., 1849]. Rpt. Evanston and Chicago: Northwestern University Press and The Newberry Library, 1970.

Melville, Herman. *Moby-Dick or, The Whale* [orig., 1851]. Ed. by Luther S. Mansfield and Howard P. Vincent. Rpt. New York: Hendricks House, 1962.

Melville, Herman. *Pierre, or The Ambiguities* [orig., 1852]. Rpt. Evanston and Chicago: Northwestern University Press and The Newberry Library, 1971.

Merimee, Prosper. "The Venus of Ille." Tr. John Hunter in *The Knickerbocker* (December 1843), 537-558. Metamorphosis.

Michelet, Jules. *The People.* New York: D. Appleton, 1846. Religion and mythology of *la patrie.* Important book for Whitman.

Michelet, Jules. *History of France.* Tr. by G. H. Smith. New York: D. Appleton, 1847. Known to Whitman.

Michelet, Jules. *Historical View of the French Revolution.* Tr. C. Cocks. London: H. G. Bohn, 1848. Whitman reviewed Michelet.

Mickle, W. J. "Inquiry into the religious tenets and philosophy of the Brahmins." In his tr. of Camoens' *The Lusiad . . .* 1776. Influential popular treatment.

Middleton, Conyers. *A Letter from Rome.* London: W. Innys, 1729. Famous comparison between Roman Catholicism and Roman paganism.

Middleton, J. I. *Grecian remains in Italy.* London: J. J. Middleton, 1812.

Mill, William Hodge. *Observations on the attempted application of Pantheistic principles to the Theory and Historic Criticism of the Gospel.* London: Rivington, 1840. Noted by T. Parker in his review of Strauss's *Life of Jesus.*

Milman, Henry Hart. *Samor, Lord of the Bright City.* New York: C. Wiley and Co., 1818.

Mitford, William. *History of Greece.* 5 vols. London: J. Murray and J. Robson, 1784-1818. Among Emerson's books.

Molina, Juan Ignacio. *The Geographical, Natural and Civil history of Chili.* 2 vols. Tr. by Richard Alsop. Middletown, Conn.: I. Riley, 1808. South American myth.

Moore, Thomas. "The Loves of the Angels," and "Lalla Rookh." In *The Poetical Works.* New York: E. and J. B. Young, 1800. Mohammedan mythology. Influenced Poe, Melville.

Morgan, Lewis Henry. *League of the Ho-dé-no-sau-nee, or Iroquois.* Rochester: Sage and Brothers, 1851. Famous early anthropologist. Kinship theory. Read by Thoreau.

Moritz, K. P. *Mythological Fictions of the Greeks and Romans* [orig., 1792]. Tr. by C. F. W. J. New York: Carrill, 1830. Gods as aesthetic symbolic expressions of nature; possibly co-authored by Goethe.

Mounier, Jean-Joseph. *De l'influence attribuée aux Philosophes, aux Francs-Macons et aux illuminés sur la Révolution de France.* Tübingen: J. G. Cotta, 1801. Skepticism and Freemasonry.

Mouradgea D' Ohsson, Ignatius. *Oriental Antiquities, and General view of the Othoman customs, laws, and ceremonies.* Philadelphia: 1788. Early Mohammedan interest.

Müller, F. Max. *Chips from a German Workshop.* London: Longmans, Green, 1867–75.

Müller, F. Max. *Comparative Mythology.* London: 1856. Epochal argument for "nature" mythology, "disease of language" theory and comparative philologic method.

Müller, F. Max. *A History of Ancient Sanskrit Literature so far as it Illustrates the primitive Religion of the Brahmans.* London: Williams and Norgate, 1860.

Müller, F. Max. *Introduction to the Science of Religion.* London: Longmans, Green, and Co., 1873. Dedicated by Müller to Emerson.

Müller, Karl Otfried [or C. O.]. *The History and Antiquities of the Doric Race.* Oxford: J. Murray, 1830. Often cited as *Dorians.* Emerson read in 1831. Influenced Elizabeth Peabody.

Müller, Karl Otfried. *A History of the Literature of Ancient Greece.* London: 1840. Influential standard work, myth as tool for study of early Greek history.

Müller, Karl Otfried. *Introduction to a Scientific System of Mythology* [orig., 1825]. Tr. by John Leitch. London: 1844. Key figure in classical historical school; stresses mutual integrity and origins of Greek myth. German ed. in Parker's library.

Munday, William. *An Examination of the Bible; or an impartial investigation of supernatural and natural Theology.* Baltimore: 1808. Rationalism.

Murray, John, publisher. *A Handbook of Rome and its environs.* London: 1858. Guidebook. Used by Hawthorne.

"Mythology." In *Encyclopaedia Americana.* Ed. Francis Lieber. Philadelphia: Carey, Lea and Carey, 1829–. Emphasizes German scholarship.

"Mythology." In *Encyclopaedia Britannica.* 1st ed., vol. III. Edinburgh: 1771.

"Mythology." In *Encyclopaedia Britannica.* 3rd ed., vol. XII, 1797. Substantially different from first edition.

"Mythologie." In *Encyclopédie, où Dictionaire raisonné des sciences, des arts et des métiers.* Paris: 1751–65. Fréret's work, adapted by Jaucourt, myth as key to Greek mind.

Newton, Isaac. *The Chronology of the Ancient Kingdoms Amended* . . . . London: 1728. Christian Euhemerist chronology. In Emerson's library. Read by Parker 1835.

Niebuhr, Barthold G. *The History of Rome* [orig., 1811–12]. Tr. by Julius C. Hare and C. Thirlwall. 3 vols. Cambridge: Taylor, 1828–42. Polarizes history and myth.

Niebuhr, Barthold G. *Stories of the Gods and Heroes of Greece told by B. Niebuhr to his son* [orig., 1842]. Tr. by S. Austin. London: Nutt, 1843.

Nork, F. [F. Korn]. *Biblische Mythologie des Alten und Neuen Testaments.* . . . Stuttgart, 1842. Popularizer of neo-Christian comparative mythology. In Parker's library.

Norton, Andrews. *The Evidences of the Genuineness of the Gospels.* 3 vols. Boston: Russell, 1837–44. Refutation of historical-critical interpretation.

Novalis [Georg Friedrich von Hardenberg]. *Henry of Ofterdingen* [orig., 1802]. Tr. by J. Owen. Cambridge, Mass.: Owen, 1842. Used by Margaret Fuller.

Novalis [Georg Friedrich von Hardenberg]. "Die Christenheit oder Europa." 1799. Essay urging new Christian mythology.

Novalis [Georg Friedrich von Hardenberg]. *The Novices of Saïs* [orig., 1798]. Read by American romantics.

Oegger, Guillaume. *The True Messiah . . .* [orig., 1829]. Tr. by Elizabeth Peabody. Boston: E. Peabody, 1842. Swedenborgian; Christianity has replaced myth as language of nature. Important also for Emerson. Mentions Creuzer, Dupuis.

Orsini, Abbé Mathieu. *Life of the Blessed Virgin Mary . . .* [1837]. Tr. by Mrs. J. Sadlier. New York: D. & J. Sadlier, 1861. Compares Mary to goddesses in other mythologies.

Osgood, Frances S., ed. *The Poetry of Flowers and Flowers of Poetry.* . . . New York: J. C. Riker, 1841. "Symbolic" language of flowers. Used by Melville.

Ovid. *Ovid's Art of Love etc.* New York: 1827. Translations by Dryden, Tate, Hopkins, etc. Example of American interest in Ovid.

Paine, Thomas. *The Age of Reason: Being an investigation of the True and of the Fabulous Theology.* . . . New York: 1794 (Part I); 1796 (Part II).

Paine, Thomas. *The Theological Works of Thomas Paine* [orig., 1818]. Rpt.

New York: W. Carver, 1830. Extreme rationalist view. Influenced by Dupuis.

Palmer, Elihu. *Principles of Nature. . . .* New York: 1801. Extreme deistic position.

Parker, Theodore. *A Discourse of the Transient and Permanent in Christianity.* Boston: 1841.

Parker, Theodore. "German Literature." *The Dial,* vol. 1, no. 3 (1841).

Parker, Theodore. *Life and Correspondences of Theodore Parker. . . .* Ed. John Weiss. New York: Appleton, 1864.

Parker, Theodore. "The Previous Questions between Mr. Andrews and his alumni." In *The Transcendentalists.* Ed. Perry Miller. Cambridge, Mass.: Harvard University Press, 1950.

Parker, Theodore. "Strauss's Life of Jesus." In *The Critical and Miscellaneous Writings of Theodore Parker.* Boston: Munroe, 1843. First publication in *The Christian Examiner* (April, 1840).

Parker, Theodore. *Theodore Parker's Experience as a Minister. . . .* Boston: Leighton, 1859.

Payne, J. H. "Our Neglected Poets.—No. I: William Martin Johnson." *Democratic Review,* vol. 1 (March, 1838), 466–468. Johnson translated Boulanger.

Payson, Seth. *Proofs of the Real Existence, and Dangerous Tendency of Illuminism.* Charlestown, Mass.: Etheridge, 1802.

Peabody, Elizabeth Palmer, ed. "The Dorian Measure." In *Aesthetic Papers.* Boston: The Editor, 1849. Champions Apollonian spirit.

Peabody, Elizabeth Palmer. *First Steps to the Study of History. . . .* Boston: Hilliard, Gray, 1832.

Peabody, Elizabeth Palmer. "Introduction to Bem's History." In *Universal History. . . .* New York: Sheldon, 1859. Textbook. Stresses ancient myth as religion.

Peabody, Elizabeth Palmer. *Key to History. Part III. The Greeks. . . .* Boston: Marsh, Capen & Lyon, 1833. Treats myth as admirable Greek religion.

Peabody, Elizabeth Palmer. *Last Evening with Allston, and other Papers.* Boston: D. Lothrop and Co., 1886. Contains essays on primitive man, language, "Dorian Measure."

Percival, James Gates. *The Poetical Works of James Gates Percival.* 2 vols. Boston: Tickner and Fields, 1859. Poem "Ruins" influenced by Volney. Also includes "The Mythology of Greece" and a long poem— "Prometheus."

Percy, Thomas, tr. *Five Pieces of Runic Poetry from the Islandic Language.* London: 1763. Translation influenced by Lowth and Mallet.

Percy, Thomas. *Reliques of Ancient English Poetry.* London: 1765. Most popular collection of ballads and early English poetry.

Pidgeon, William. *Traditions of De-coo-dah.* . . . New York: Thayer, 1852. American Indian myth.

Pike, Albert. *Ancient Faith and Worship of the Aryans, as Embodied in the Vedic Hymns.* MS, vol. 2 and supplement vol. 3, Library of the Supreme Council at Washington, Ancient, Accepted Scottish Rite of Freemasonry, 1872–73.

Pike, Albert. *Essays of Albert Pike.* MS, Library of the Supreme Council at Washington, Ancient, Accepted Scottish Rite of Freemasonry. c. 1880. Includes "Of symbols decaying into idols."

Pike, Albert. "Hymns to the Gods." In *Blackwood's Magazine,* vol. 45 (1839), 819–830. Rpt. *Hymns to the Gods.* Philadelphia: privately printed, 1854.

Pike, Albert. *Morals and Dogma of the Ancient and Accepted Scottish Rite of Freemasonry.* . . . Charleston, S.C.: n.p., 1871. Extensively used by Freemasons. Draws on Dupuis, Bryant, etc.

Pike, Albert. *Indo-Aryan deities and worship as contained in the Rig-Veda.* Louisville: The Standard Printing Co., 1872.

Pluche, Abbé Noël. *The History of the Heavens.* 2 vols. 1738–39. Tr. by J. de Freval. London: 1740. Derives myth from astronomy and agricultural calendar.

Poe, E. A. "Al Aaraaf" and "Israfel." In *Poems,* vol. 1 of *Collected Works of Edgar Allan Poe.* Ed. T. O. Mabbott. Cambridge, Mass.: Harvard University Press, 1969–. Eastern myth a la Moore.

Poe, Edgar Allan. *The Complete Works.* . . . [Virginia edition]. New York: Crowell, 1902. See "The Conversation of Eiros and Charmion," "The Colloquy of Monos and Una," and "The Power of Words," for modern myths; *Eureka* for mythicizing current scientific ideas; "Lionizing," for satire on myth scholarship; "Pinakidia," for myth scraps from Bryant et al.; "Siope," later retitled "Silence a Fable," for burlesque of Eastern mythic exoticism; "Some Words with a Mummy," for satire on George Gliddon.

Pomey, Francois A. *Pantheum Mythicum; seu fabulosa Deorum historia.* 1697. This and its English version, Tooke's *Pantheon,* most popular handbook until Lempriere.

Potter, John. *Archaelogica Graeca; or the Antiquities of Greece* [orig., 1697]. 2 vols. New York: Collins, 1825. Standard reference work.

Powell, Benjamin F. *Bible of Reason.* . . . 2 vols. New York: Wright & Owen, 1831. Skeptical, rationalist.

Prescott, William H. *The Conquest of Peru.* 2 vols. New York: Harper, 1847. Myth of Manco Capek.

Prideaux, Humphrey. *The Old and New Testaments connected in the history of the Jews and neighboring nations.* . . . 2 vols. London: 1716–18. Conventional chronology; collapses pagan history into biblical.

Priest, Josiah. *American Antiquities, and discoveries in the West.* Albany: 1833. American Christian antiquarianism; ark built in Ohio, etc. Read by Thoreau?

Priest, Josiah. *The Anti-Universalist, or History of the Fallen Angels of the Scriptures; Proofs of the Being of Satan and of Evil Spirits; intended as a refutation of the three main points of Universalism namely that there is no Hell after death, no devil or Satan as a being, and no future day of judgement.* 2 vols. Albany: J. Munsell, 1837.

Priest, Josiah. *The Wonders of Nature and Providence Displayed.* . . . Albany: J. Priest, 1825. One section, "The Deist Confuted," is aimed against Volney.

Priestley, Joseph. *A Comparison of the Institutions of Moses with those of the Hindoos and other ancient nations: with remarks on Mr. Dupuis's Origin of all Religions.* . . . Northumberland, Penn.: 1799. Unitarian defense of Old Testament, but sympathetic to Indic scripture. In Parker's library.

Priestley, Joseph. *The Doctrine of Heathen philosophy compared with those of Revelation.* Northumberland, Penn.: Binns, 1804.

Priestley, Joseph. *A General History of the Christian Church, to the Fall of the western Empire.* Birmingham, Eng.: Johnson, 1790 (vols. I and II), 1802–3 (vols. III and IV). Rationalist, Unitarian view.

Priestley, Joseph. *An History of the corruptions of Christianity.* . . . 2 vols. Birmingham, Eng.: Piercy, Jones, 1782.

Priestley, Joseph. *Institutes of Natural and Revealed Religion.* . . . 3 vols. London: J. Johnson, 1772–74.

Priestley, Joseph. *Letters to Mr. Volney, occasioned by a Work of his entitled Ruins, and by his letter to the author.* Philadelphia: Dobson, 1797.

Priestley, Joseph. *Letters to the Philosophers and Politicians of France on the subject of religion.* Boston: Hall, 1793.

Priestley, Joseph. *The Theological and Miscellaneous Works of Joseph Priestley.* . . . Ed. J. T. Rutt. 25 vols. London: Smallfield, 1817–32.

Priestley, Joseph. *Observations on the increase of infidelity. The third edition, in which are added animadversions on the writings of several modern unbelievers, and especially the Ruins of Mr. Volney.* Philadelphia: Dobson, 1797.

Prospect; or View of the Moral World. New York: Palmer, 1803–05. Deist periodical.

Quinet, Edgar. *Ahasuérus.* Paris: A Guyot, 1834. Romantic myth poem.

Quinet, Edgar. *Du Génie des Religions.* Paris: Charpentier, 1842. Inspired by Creuzer. Admired Emerson.

Rafinesque, Constantine Samuel. *Ancient History, or Annals of Kentucky: with a Survey of the Ancient Monuments of North America.* Frankfort, Kentucky: 1824.

Rafinesque, Constantine Samuel. *The Ancient Monuments of North and South America.* 2nd ed. Philadelphia: 1838. Pre-Columbian colonization from Europe.

Rafinesque, Constantine Samuel. *Genius and Spirit of the Hebrew Bible.* Philadelphia: Printed for the Eleutherium of Knowledge and Central University of Illinois, 1838. Idiosyncratic philology.

Ramsay, Andrew M. *The Travels of Cyrus . . . To which is annex'd, a discourse upon the theology and mythology of the ancients.* London: 1727. All myth and religions share three-stage cycle.

Renan, Ernest. "Les religions de l'antiquité." (Originally published May 1853 in *Revue des Deux Mondes.*) Rpt. in *Etudes l'histoire religieuse.* 2nd ed. Paris: 1857. Review-essay of Creuzer, rationalist critique of modern mythology.

Renan, Ernest. *The Life of Jesus.* London: Trübner and Co., 1864.

Renouf, Sir Peter Le Page. *Lectures on the Origin and growth of religion, as illustrated by the religion of ancient Egypt.* London and Edinburgh: Williams and Norgate, 1880. Read by Whitman.

Richter, Jean-Paul *Titan; a Romance.* Tr. Charles J. Brooks. Boston: Ticknor and Fields, 1862. Influential mythic novel.

Ripley, George, ed. *Specimens of Foreign Standard Literature.* Boston: Hilliard, 1838–1845. Included writings by Cousin, Jouffrey, Constant, Goethe, Schiller, Eckermann, Menzel, De Wette.

Rivero, M. E., and Tschudi, J. J. von. *Peruvian Antiquities.* New York: George P. Putnam & Co., 1853. Includes skeptical account of Manco Capek myth. In Thoreau's library.

Robbins, Eliza. *Elements of Mythology.* Philadelphia: 1830. Popular handbook.

Robbins, Thomas. *A View of All Religions: and the Religious Ceremonies of all Nations at the present day.* 2nd ed. Hartford: O. D. Cooke and Sons, 1824. Contains abridgement of William Ward's work on Hindu religion.

Robertson, William. *History of America.* London: W. Strahan, et al., 1777. Rpt. in *The Massachusetts Spy,* 1784–5. Full account of Peruvian myth.

Robertson, William. *An Historical Disquisition concerning the knowledge which the Ancients had of India. . . .* Rpt. Philadelphia: 1792. Crucial for spread of enthusiasm for India.

Rosellini, Ippolito. *I Monumenti dell'Egitto e della Nubia.* Pisa: N. Capurro, 1832–44. Read by Whitman.

Ross, Alexander. *Mystagogus Poeticus.* London: Thomas Whitaker, 1648. Used by Thoreau.

Rowe, Elizabeth. *The History of Joseph.* London: T. Worrall, 1736. Rpt. B. Franklin. Pagan gods are devils.

Russell, Martha. *Leaves from the Tree Igdrasyl.* Boston: J. P. Jewett, 1854. Fiction.

Russell, Michael. *A Connection of Sacred and Profane History from the Death of Joshua to the Decline of the Kingdoms of Israel and Judah.* 2 vols. London: Tegg, 1827. Completes work of Prideaux and Shuckford.

Sale, George. *The Koran . . . Tr. into English . . . with explanatory notes. . . .* London: 1734. Extensive historical introduction.

Schelling, F. W. J. *Philosophie der Mythologie.* Stuttgart: 1856. Most important philosophic exposition of idealist view of myth. Schelling's Berlin Lectures reported in *The Dial.*

Schelling, F. W. J. *System des transcendentalen Idealismus.* Tübingen: 1880. Reinterprets myth in terms of German Idealist philosophy.

Schelling, F. W. J. *Uber Mythen, historische Sagen und Philosopheme der altesten Welt.* 1793. Influenced by Heyne: myth as primitive history and philosophy.

Schiller, J. C. F. von. "Der Götter Griechenlands." 1788. Controversial poem contrasting paganism favorably to Christianity.

Schlegel, August. *A course of Lectures on Dramatic Art and Literature* [orig., 1809–11]. Tr. by John Black. Philadelphia: Hogan, 1833. Myth's role in tragedy.

Schlegel, A. W. *Vorlesungen über schöne Literatur und Kunst.* 1801–04. Incorporates German romantic myth and views into literary and artistic criticism.

Schlegel, Friedrich. *Dialogue on Poetry and Literary Aphorisms.* Ed. and tr. by Ernst Behler and Roman Struc. University Park: Pennsylvania State University Press, 1968.

Schlegel, Friedrich. *Lectures on the History of Literature, Ancient and Modern.* 2 vols. Edinburgh: William Blackwood, 1818. Hawthorne read 1828.

Schlegel, Friedrich. *The Philosophy of History.* Tr. James B. Robertson. London: Saunders & Otley, 1835.

Schlegel, F. "Rede über Mythologie." In *Athenäum.* Berlin: 1800. Calls for modern mythopoesis.

Schlegel, F. *Über die Sprache und Weisheit der Indier.* Heidelberg: 1808. First extensive German interpretation of Indian religion based on philologic competence; influential—finally unsympathetic.

Schoolcraft, H. R. *Algic Researches, comprising inquiries respecting the mental characteristics of the North American Indians. First Series. Indian Tales and legends.* New York: 1839. Includes sections on American Indian myth. Revued in *Gentleman's Magazine* 1839, by Poe?

Schoolcraft, Henry Rowe. *Information respecting the history, condition and prospects of the Indian tribes of the United States. . . .* 6 vols. Philadelphia: Lippincott, 1851–57. His major work. Thoreau used vol. 1.

Schoolcraft, H. R. *The Indian Fairy Book.* New York: Mason, 1856.

Schoolcraft, H. R. *The Myth of Hiawatha, and other oral legends, mythologic and allegoric, of the North American Indians.* Philadelphia: Lippincott, 1856.

Schopenhauer, Arthur. *Die Welt als Wille und Vorstellung. . . .* 1st ed. Leipzig: 1819. Second expanded edition, 1844; crucial interpretation of myth and Western philosophy in Indic terms, stressing Hinduism first, then Buddhism in 1844. Melville had 1888 ed.

[Shannon, Robert H.]. *Vestiges of Civilization: or, the Aetiology of History. . . .* New York: Bailliere, 1851. Large section on Aetiology of History, the first part of which is the "Mythological Cycle." Skeptical analysis of religion.

Sheldon, William. *History of the Heathen Gods, and Heroes of Antiquity.* Boston: Sturtevant, 1809. Handbook.

Shelley, Percy Bysshe. *Queen Mab; with notes.* New York: Wright & Owen, 1831. Focuses attention on the radical Shelley, anti-Christian.

Shuckford, Samuel. *The Sacred and Profane History of the World connected. . . .* [orig., 1728–30]. Rpt. 2 vols. Philadelphia: Woodward, 1824. Continuation of Prideaux 1716 Christian chronology.

Simon, Richard,. *A Critical History of the Old Testament. . . .* London: 1682. Seminal work on historical criticism. In Priestley's library.

Simpson, David. *An Essay on the Authenticity of the New Testament, designed as an answer to Evanson's Dissonance and Volney's Ruins.* Macclesfield: 1793.

Smith, Elihu. *American Poems* [orig., 1793]. Rpt. Gainesville, Fla.: Scholars' Facsimiles and Reprints, 1966. Contains Nordic poems by R. Alsop.

Smith, Ethan. *View of the Hebrews. . . .* Poultney, Vermont: Smith and Shute, 1825. Pre-Columbian Jewish migration to America.

Smith, Joseph. *The Book of Mormon.* Palmyra, New York: 1830. Pre-Columbian migration from Old World to America.

Smith, William. *Memoir of J. G. Fichte. . . .* Boston: Munroe, 1846. Contains Fichte's "On the Nature of the Scholar."

Smith, William. *Consolations from Homar, an hermit of the East.* Newport: 1789. Odd early version of Omar Khayam.

Smith, Sir William, ed. *A Dictionary of Greek and Roman Antiquities.* New

York: Harper, 1843. Standard work. American edition by Charles Anthon, reviewed by Poe.

Southey, Robert. *Madoc*. Boston: Munroe, Francis, 1806. Mound-builder story.

Spaulding, Solomon. *The Manuscript Found*. Lamoni, Iowa: The Reorganized Church of Jesus Christ of Latter Day Saints, 1885. Fictional account of ancient American Indian migrations. Related to *Book of Mormon* (?) and mound-builder controversy.

Spence, Joseph. *Polymetis; or, An Enquiry concerning the Agreement between the Works of the Roman Poets and the Remains of the Ancient Artists*. London: 1747. Chiefly on Roman mythology.

Spencer, John. *De Legibus Hebraeorum*. . . . 2 vols. Cambridge, Eng.: 1727.

Squier, Ephraim G. *The Serpent Symbol, and the Worship of the Reciprocal Principles of Nature in America*. New York: Putnam, 1851.

Squier, Ephraim G., and Davis, E. H. *Ancient Monuments of the Mississippi Valley*. Washington: Smithsonian Contributions to Knowledge, vol. 1, 1848. Read by Thoreau.

de Staël, Mme. *Corinne; ou l'Italie*. Paris: 1820. Influential novel. Paganism contrasted with Christianity.

de Staël, Mme. *Germany*. 1813; tr. London: Murray, 1813. Influential early account of German romanticism and myth.

Stedman, E. D. "Apollo." In *Poems, Lyrical and Idyllic*. New York: Scribner, 1860.

Stephens, John Lloyd. *Incidents of Travel in Egypt, Arabia Petraea, and the Holy Land*. 2 vols. 3rd ed. New York: Harper, 1838. Read by Melville, reviewed by Poe.

Stewart, John. *The moral state of nations*. . . . London: Ridgway, 1791(?) Later editions subtitled "The Apocalypse of Nature."

Stewart, John. *Opus Maximum*. . . . London: 1803.

Stewart, John. *The Scripture of Reason and Nature*. . . . London: Egerton, 1813.

Stiles, Ezra. "Account of a stone bust, supposed to hve been an Indian God." In *Memoirs of the American Academy of Arts and Sciences*, vol. III, pt. 1, 1809, pp. 192–94. Written 1790.

Story, William W. *Poems*. Boston: Little, Brown, 1847; 1856. Poems on Artemis, Prometheus, etc.

Strauss, D. F. *Das Leben Jesu*. Tübingen: 1835. Landmark of "Higher" biblical criticism. Tr. George Eliot. Reviewed by T. Parker.

Strutt, Joseph. *The Sports and Pastimes of the People of England . . . including rural and domestic recreations, May games, mummeries*. . . . London: Tegg, 1831. Used by Hawthorne.

Stukeley, William. *Stonehenge, A temple restor'd to the British Druids*. London:

1740. Druidism as primitive, undefiled Christianity. Used by Emerson.

Sturluson, Snorri. *Heimskringla, or Chronicle of the Kings of Norway.* . . . [orig., 1777–1826]. Tr. by S. Laing. 3 vols. London: Longman, 1844. Used by Thoreau.

Swedenborg, Emanuel. *The Animal Kingdom.* . . . [orig., 1744]. Tr. by J. Wilkinson. 2 vols. Boston: Clapp, 1843–44. Important for Emerson.

Swedenborg, Emanuel. *Arcana Caelestia* [orig., 1749–56]. Tr. in 14 vols. London: Newbery, 1819–48.

Taylor, Bayard. *The American Legend.* Cambridge: Bartlett, 1850. Contains Greek and Norse refs. Claims America born from Greek origins.

Taylor, Bayard. *Poems of the Orient.* Boston: Ticknor and Fields, 1855. Poem discusses two kinds of poetry, one presided over by Apollo, one by Pan.

Taylor, Isaac. *The Spirit of the Hebrew Poetry.* New York: Rudd and Carleton, 1862. Christian.

Taylor, Isaac. *The Natural History of Enthusiasm.* London: 1829.

Taylor, Thomas, tr. *Select Works of Plotinus.* London: 1817. In Fruitlands library.

Taylor, Thomas, tr. *The Works of Plato.* 5 vols. London: 1804. In Fruitlands library.

Taylor, Thomas, tr. *The Mystical Initiations; or, Hymns of Orpheus with a Preliminary Dissertation on the life and Theology of Orpheus.* London: 1787. Rpt. *Thomas Taylor the Platonist: Selected Writings,* ed. by Kathleen Raine and George Mills Harper (Princeton, N. J.: Princeton University Press, 1969).

Taylor, Thomas, tr. *Commentaries of Proclus on the Timaeus of Plato* [orig., 1810]. 2nd ed. London: 1820. In Fruitlands library.

Taylor, Thomas, tr. *Jamblichus on the Mysteries of the Egyptians.* Chiswick: 1821. Neoplatonic and Orphic viewpoint. In Fruitlands library.

Taylor, Thomas, tr. *Select Works of Porphyry* . . . *tr. from the Greek by T. Taylor with an appendix explaining the allegory of the Wanderings of Ulysses, by the translator.* London: 1823. Neoplatonic and Orphic viewpoint. In Fruitlands library.

Taylor, Thomas. *A Dissertation on the Eleusinian and Bacchic Mysteries.* London: 1790. Neoplatonic, Orphic viewpoint. Important for Alcott.

Tegner, Esaias. *Frithiof's Saga.* Tr. by W. E. Frye. London: Bailey, 1835. Norse myth.

Teignmouth, John. *Memoirs of* . . . *Sir William Jones.* London: Brettell, 1804.

The Temple of Reason [periodical]. Ed. Elihu Palmer. New York: Driscol,

1802–03. Deist, radical, skeptical view of myth. Rpts. Volney, Boulanger, etc.

Thoreau, Henry D. *Collected Poems of Henry Thoreau*. Ed. Carl Bode. Baltimore: Johns Hopkins, 1964.

Thoreau, Henry D. *Consciousness in Concord*. The Text of Thoreau's Hitherto "Lost Journal" (1840–41). Ed. by Perry Miller. Boston: Houghton Mifflin, 1958.

Thoreau, Henry D. *The Correspondence of Henry David Thoreau*. Ed. by W. Harding and Carl Bode. New York: New York University Press, 1955.

Thoreau, Henry D. *The Journals of Henry D. Thoreau*. Ed. by Bradford Torrey and Francis H. Allen. 14 vols. Boston: Houghton Mifflin, 1906. Rpt. New York: Dover, 1962.

Thoreau, Henry D. *The Maine Woods*. Ed. by J. J. Moldenhauer. Princeton, N.J.: Princeton University Press, 1972.

Thoreau, Henry D., tr. "Prometheus Bound." In *The Dial*, vol. 3, no. 3 (January 1843).

Thoreau, Henry D. "Thomas Carlyle and His Works." In *The Writings of Henry David Thoreau*. Boston and New York: Houghton Mifflin (Walden edition), 1906.

Thoreau, Henry D. *Thoreau Fact Book*. Ed. by Kenneth W. Cameron. 2 vols. Hartford, Conn.: Transcendental Books, 1966.

Thoreau, Henry D. *The Transmigration of the Seven Brahmans*. Ed. by Arthur Christy. New York: 1932.

Thoreau, Henry D. *Walden*. Ed. J. Lyndon Shanley. Princeton, N.J.: Princeton University Press, 1971.

Thoreau, Henry D. "Walking." In *Excursions*. Boston: Ticknor & Fields, 1863.

Thoreau, Henry D. *A Week on the Concord and Merrimack Rivers*. Boston and Cambridge: James Munroe, 1849.

Ticknor, George. *Notes taken at a course of Lectures on the Exegesis of Matthew, Mark, Luke and the four Concluding chapters of John, by J. G. Eichhorn, Göttingen, Germany, Oct. 27, 1815–March 27, 1816*. MS notes in Harvard Library. Early interest in German biblical criticism.

Tocqueville, Alexis de. "On some sources of poetic inspiration in Democracies." In *Democracy in America*. 4 vols. London: Saunders, 1835–40. Sociological explanation of movement from myth and religion to nature.

Toland, John. *Letters to Serena. . . .* London: 1704. Myth originates in worship of dead; Letter III concerns origins of myth. Read by Parker, 1838.

Tooke, Andrew. *The Pantheon: representing the fabulous histories of the heathen Gods*. London: 1698. Translation of Pomey. Popular handbook.

Trenchard, John. *The Natural History of Superstition.* London: 1709. Thomas Hollis owned a copy.

Trumbull, John. *M'Fingal.* Philadelphia: Bradford, 1775. Ossianic-Hudibrastic satire on American Revolution.

Turner, Sharon. *The Sacred History of the World, as displayed in the creation and subsequent events to the deluge.* 3 vols. New York: Harper, 1832–38. Affirms biblical account.

Tyler, Robert. *Ahasuerus.* A Poem. By a Virginian. New York: Harper, 1842.

Ussher, James. *Annales Veteris et Novi Testamenti.* 1650–54. Influential chronology.

Vico, Giambattista. *Principi di una Scienza Nuova.* Naples: 1725. Seminal, indispensable revaluation; third edition, 1744, must also be consulted. Parker withdrew this from the Harvard Library in 1836.

Volney, Comte de. *A New Translation of Volney's Ruins* [orig., 1791]. Tr. by Thomas Jefferson and Joel Barlow. Paris: Levrault, 1802. Rpt. New York: Calvin Blanchard, n.d.; and New York: The Truth Seeker, 1913. Rationalist derivation of myth from astronomy. Read by Emerson, Whitman.

Volney, Comte de. *New Researches on Ancient History* [orig., 1814]. Tr. by Colonel Corbet, under superintendence of author. London: W. Lewis. Rpt. Boston: Mendum, 1874. Non-Christian chronology. Read by John Adams.

Volney, Comte de. *The Law of Nature.* . . . Philadelphia: Stephens, 1796. Rpt. in *The Temple of Reason* [periodical]. New York: Driscol, 1800–03.

Volney, Comte de. *Travels through Egypt and Syria in the Years 1783, 1784, 1785* . . . [orig., 1787]. 2 vols. New York: Tiebout, 1798. Probably known to Melville.

Voltaire, Francois Marie Arouet de. *A Philosophical Dictionary* [orig., 1764]. 2 vols. New York: Duyckinck, 1796. Skeptical, rationalist. Widely read in America. An edition was annotated by Abner Kneeland and pub. in Boston in 1836.

Wagner, Richard. *Die Kunst und die Revolution.* Leipzig: 1849. Myth as revolutionary artistic and social force.

Waleys, Thomas [Thomas, de Walleis]. *Metamorphosis Ovidiana moraliter.* Paris: 1509. Emerson read about this in Rabelais.

Wallace, William. "The Gods of Old." In *The American Review,* vol. 2 (1845), 27–29. Poem about survival of gods "as poetical creations."

Ward, William. *Account of the writings religion and manners of the Hindoos. . . .* 4 vols. Serampore: 1811. Missionary point of view.

Ward, William. *A View of the History, Literature, and Mythology of the Hindoos.* London: Kingsbury, Parbury and Allen, 1822. Rpt. Gainesville, Fla.: Scholars' Facsimiles and Reprints, 1967. Hindu philosophical texts, important for Emerson and Thoreau.

Ware, William. *Zenobia, or the Fall of Palmyra.* Boston: J. H. Francis, 1837. Novel which weighs relative claims of pagan, Jewish and Christian systems of belief. Trans. into German by W. A. Lindau, Leipzig: Kollman, 1839.

Watkins, Tobias. *Tales of the Tripod; or, A Delphian Evening.* Baltimore: F. Lucas Jr., 1821.

Watson, Richard. *An Apology for the Bible, in a series of letters, addressed to Thomas Paine. . . .* 1796. Widely read refutation of *Age of Reason.*

Webster, Noah. "The Origin of Mythology." In *Memoirs of the Connecticut Academy of Arts and Sciences.* Vol. I, pp. 175–216. New Haven: 1810. Reduces all myth to Celtic place names. Webster knows Bryant, Faber, Gebelin, Lempriere, Wilford, Jones, Mallet, etc.

Webster, Noah. "Revolution in America." In *A Collection of Papers on Political, Literary, and Moral Subjects.* New York: Webster and Clark, 1843. Discusses French Revolutionary religions.

Wheatley, Phillis. *Poems.* Ed. Julian D. Mason, Jr. Chapel Hill: University of North Carolina Press, 1966. "Niobe in Distress for her Children slain by Apollo, from Ovid's Metamorphoses Book VI, and from a view of the Painting of Mr. Richard Wilson."

Wheeler, Charles Stearns. "The Mythology of the Greeks." Mentioned in Eidson, J. O. *Charles Stearns Wheeler, Friend of Emerson.* Athens: University of Georgia, 1951. Lecture before Concord Lyceum, March 18, 1840.

Whitman, Walt. *The Complete Writings of Walt Whitman.* Camden edition. New York and London: G. P. Putnam's Sons, 1902. 10 vols.

Whitman, Walt. *Leaves of Grass.* Comprehensive Reader's edition. Ed. by Harold W. Blodgett and Sculley Bradley. New York: New York University Press, 1965.

Whitman, Walt. *New York Dissected.* Ed. by Emory Holloway and Ralph Adimari. New York: R. R. Wilson, Inc., 1936.

Whitman, Walt. *Prose Works 1892.* Ed. by Floyd Stovall. 2 vols. New York: New York University Press, 1963–64.

Wickens, Stephen B. *Fulfillment of Scripture Prophecy. . . .* New York: Lane and Scott, 1841.

Wilkins, Charles, tr. *Bhagvat-Geeta. . . .* London: 1785. First direct complete translation of a major Sanskrit text. Important for Emerson and Thoreau.

Wilkins, Charles, tr. *The Heetopades.* . . . 1787. First translation. Rpt. Gainesville, Fla.: Scholars' Facsimiles and Reprints, 1968. Used by Thoreau.

Wilkinson, Sir J. G. *Manners and Customs of the ancient Egyptians.* 2nd series. 3 vols. London: Murray, 1837–41. Read by Whitman.

Willis, Nathaniel P. "Psyche before the tribunal of Venus." In *The Poems.* . . . New York: Clark and Austin, 1848. Routine, soul over body.

Winckelmann, J. J. *Geschichte der Kunst des Alterthums.* Dresden: 1764. "Apollonian" qualities of Greek art. Hawthorne familiar with Lodge translation.

Winthrop, James. *An Attempt to translate the Prophetic part of the Apocalypse of Saint John into familiar language.* Boston: Belknap and Hall, 1794. Early demythologizing; draws on Jacob Bryant.

Wolf, F. A. *Prolegomena ad Homerum.* . . . Halle: 1795. Standard work on "Homeric" problem, explains Homer as folk-oral epic.

Wood, (Mrs.) Sally S. B. K. *Julia and the Illuminated Baron.* Portsmouth, New Hampshire: Pierce, 1800.

Wright, Frances. *A Few Days in Athens.* Boston: J. P. Mendum, 1850. Rpt. New York: Arno Press, 1972. Important for Whitman.

Index